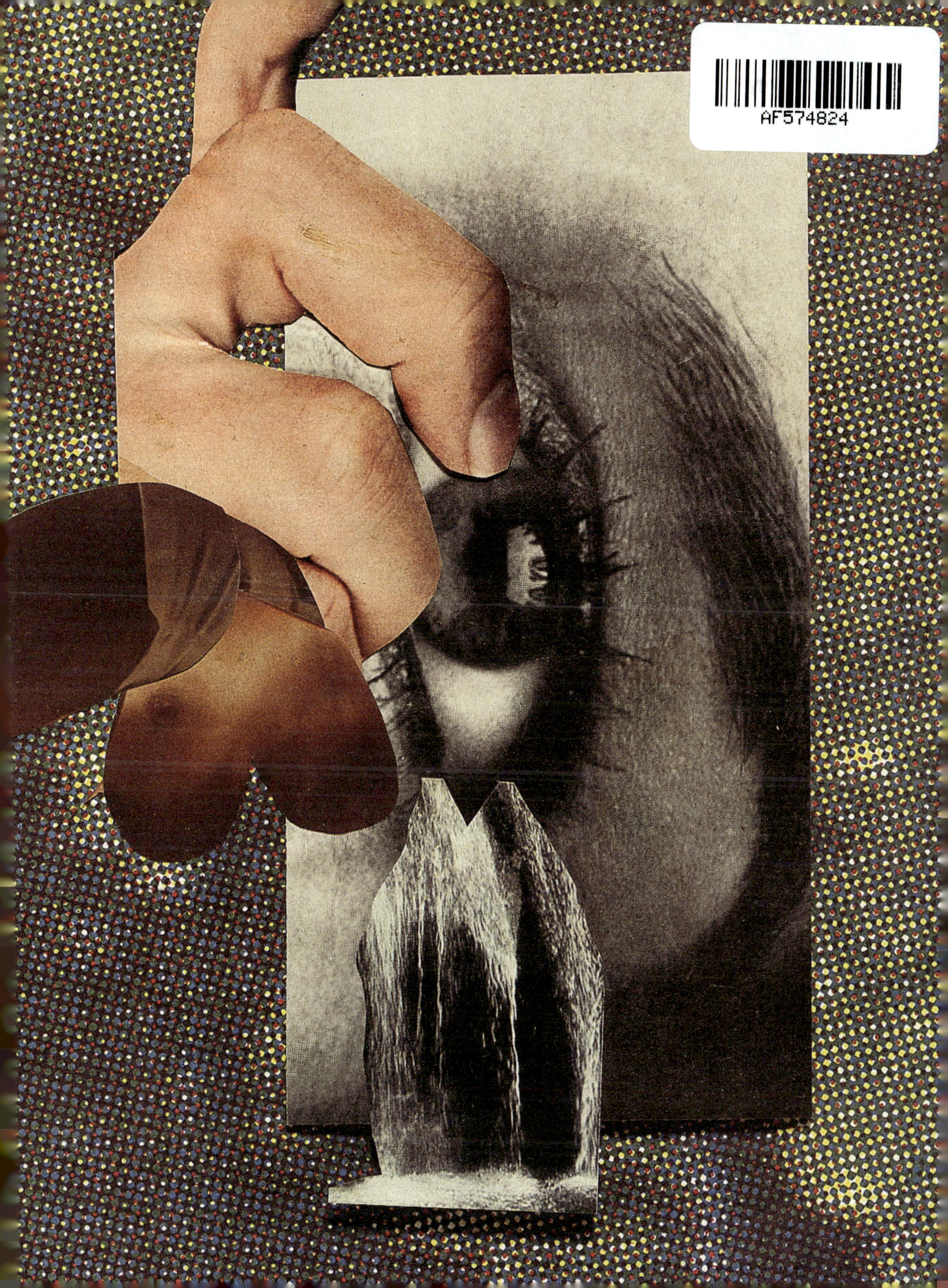

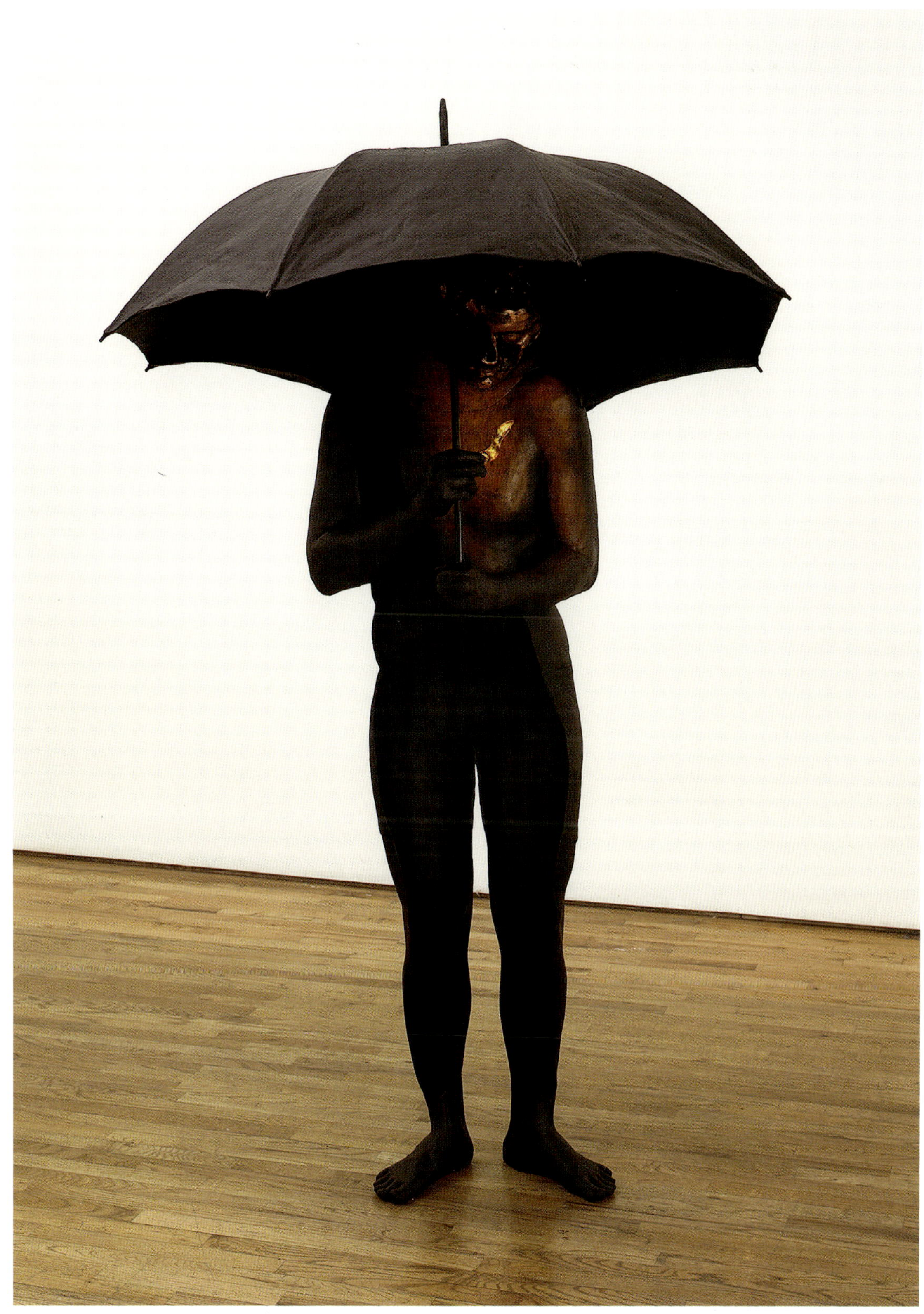

1

AMAZEMENT PARK

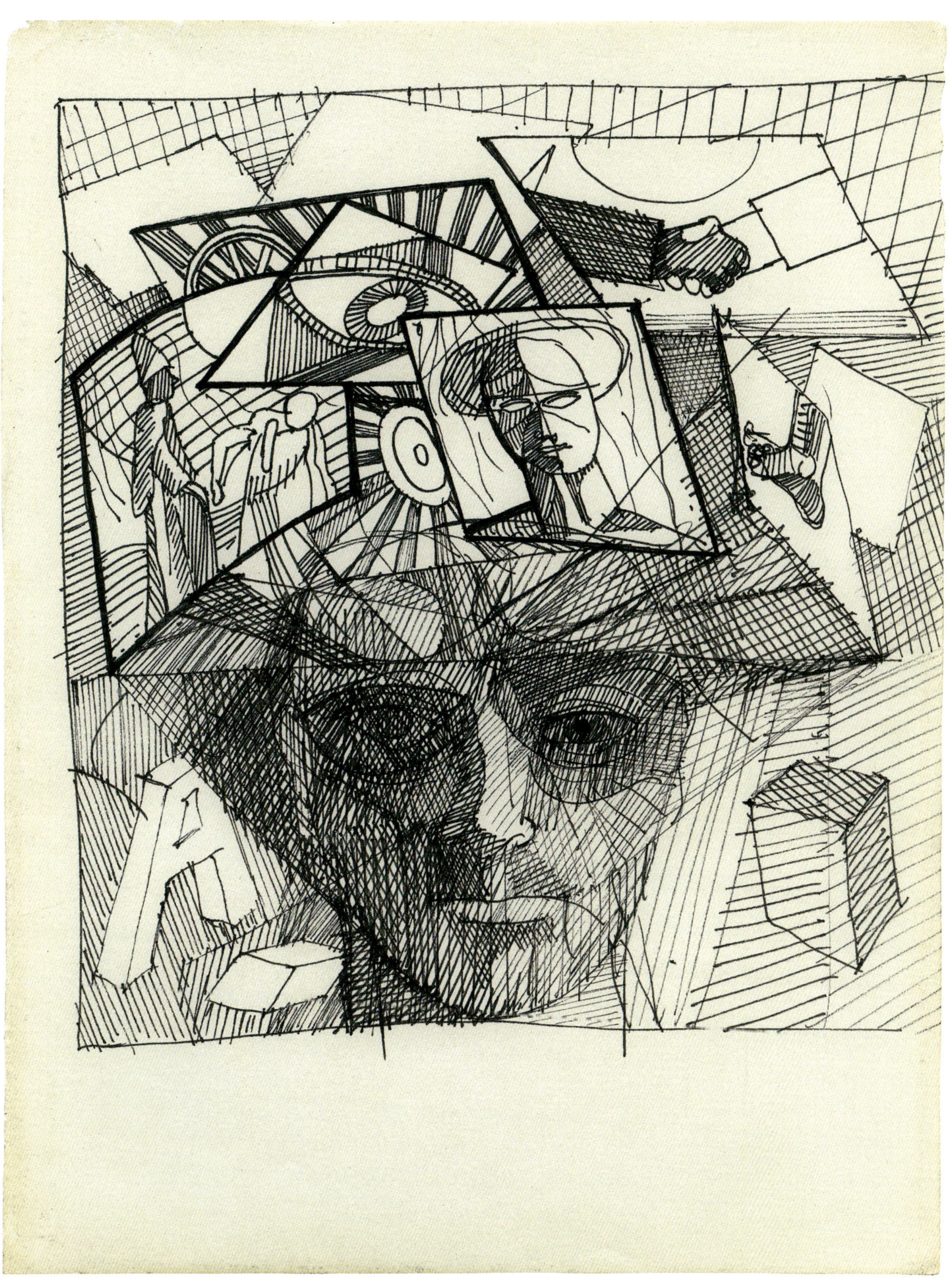

AMAZEMENT PARK

STAN, SARA, AND JOHANNES VANDERBEEK

Edited by
IAN BERRY

THE FRANCES YOUNG TANG TEACHING MUSEUM
AND ART GALLERY AT SKIDMORE COLLEGE

DELMONICO BOOKS • PRESTEL
MUNICH LONDON NEW YORK

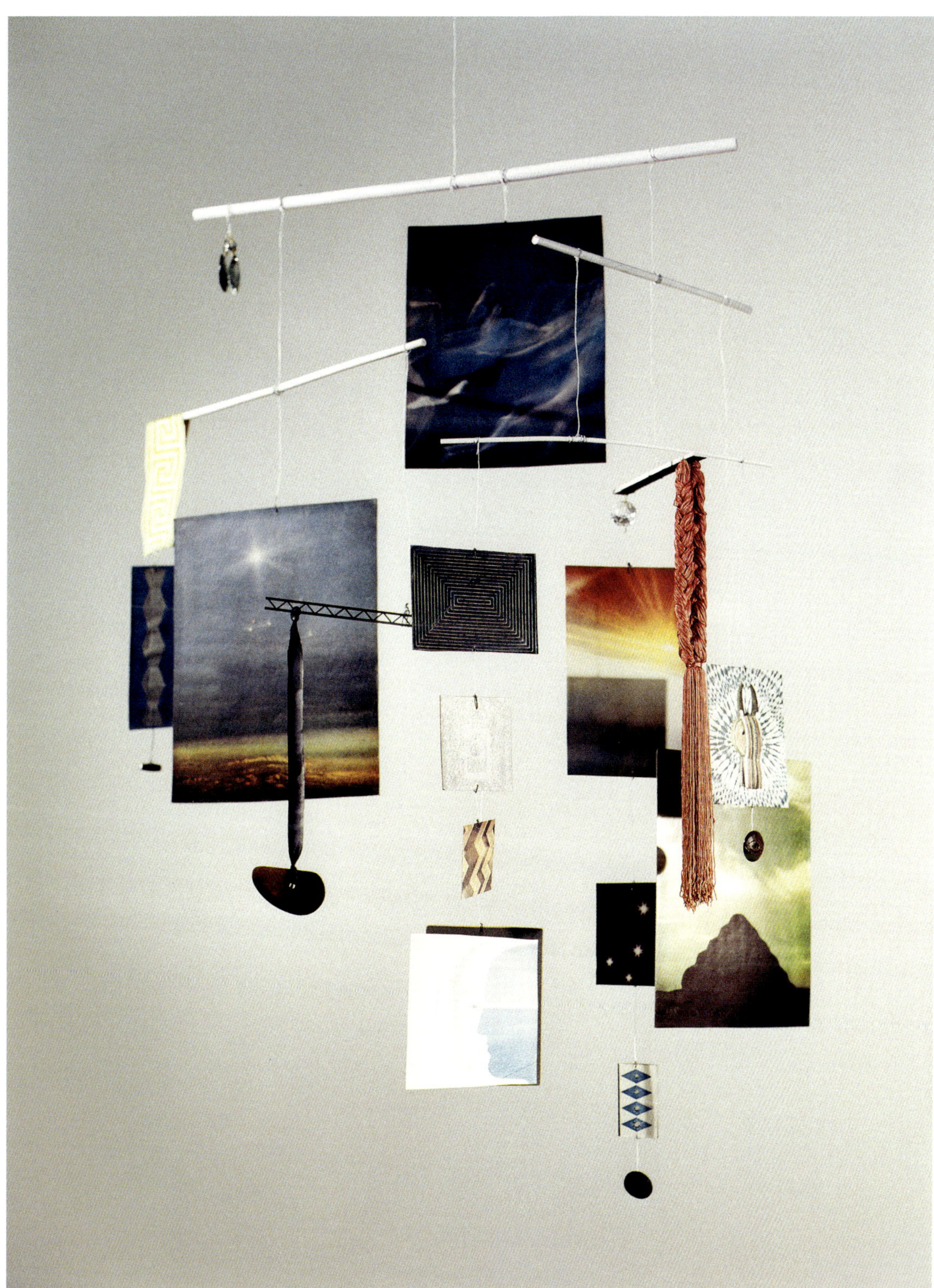

This book is published on the occasion of the exhibition
Amazement Park: Stan, Sara, and Johannes VanDerBeek

Curated by Ian Berry

The Frances Young Tang Teaching Museum and Art Gallery
Skidmore College, Saratoga Springs, New York
June 6, 2009 – May 2, 2010

Published in 2012 by The Frances Young Tang Teaching Museum and Art Gallery at Skidmore College, and DelMonico Books, an imprint of Prestel Publishing.

Prestel, a member of Verlagsgruppe Random House GmbH

Prestel Verlag
Neumarkter Strasse 28, 81673 Munich, Germany
Tel.: 49 (0)89 4136 0
Fax: 49 (0)89 4136 2335
www.prestel.de

Prestel Publishing Ltd.
4 Bloomsbury Place, London WC1A 2QA, United Kingdom
Tel: 44 (0)20 7323 5004
Fax: 44 (0)20 7636 8004

Prestel Publishing
900 Broadway. Suite 603, New York, NY 10003
Tel: 212 995 2720
Fax: 212 995 2733
E-mail: sales@prestel-usa.com
www.prestel.com

Library of Congress Cataloging-in-Publication Data
Amazement park : Stan, Sara, and Johannes VanDerBeek / edited by Ian Berry.
p. cm.
Issued in connection with an exhibition held June 6, 2009-May 2, 2010, Frances Young Tang Teaching Museum and Art Gallery, Skidmore College, Saratoga Springs, New York.
ISBN 978-3-7913-5208-4 (alk. paper)
1. Vanderbeek, Stan--Exhibitions. 2. VanDerBeek, Sara, 1976---Exhibitions. 3. VanDerBeek, Johannes, 1982---Exhibitions. I. Vanderbeek, Stan. II. VanDerBeek, Sara, 1976- III. VanDerBeek, Johannes, 1982- IV. Berry, Ian, 1971- V. Frances Young Tang Teaching Museum and Art Gallery
N6537.V329A4 2012
709.2'2--dc23
2011028403

ISBN 978-3-7913-5208-4

British Library Cataloguing-in-Publication Data: a catalogue record for this book is available from the British Library; Deutsche Nationalbibliothek holds a record of this publication in the Deutsche Nationalbibliografie; detailed bibliographical data can be found under http://dnb.ddb.de.

The paper in this book meets the guidelines for permanence and durability of the Committee on Production Guidelines for Book Longevity of the Council of Library Resources.

Edited by Ian Berry
Designed by Purtill Family Business
Printed by The Avery Group at Shapco Printing, Inc., Minneapolis

All individual works by Sara VanDerBeek: photographs by Sara VanDerBeek

All other photographs by Arthur Evans, except where noted:
Pages 1, 21, 49, 58, 127, 132–133, 157, 163: courtesy of Zach Feuer, New York
Pages 32, 45, 99, 158, 159, 160, 182–183, 197, 223: photographs by Steven Bates
Page 61: photograph by James Ewing, courtesy of the Public Art Fund
Page 63: courtesy of The Box, Los Angeles
Pages 89, 111: photographs by Cathy Carver
Pages 30, 37, 66, 68, 71, 72, 148–149, 155, 174, 175, 179, 180, 196: courtesy of the Estate of Stan VanDerBeek
Page 106–107, 122: courtesy of The Approach, London
Page 124: courtesy of Museum of Modern Art, New York
Page 162: courtesy of Brand New Gallery, Milan
Page 184–185, 189: courtesy of Metro Pictures, New York

Cover: Stan VanDerBeek, *Untitled (drawing from See Saw Seams)*, 1964, paint on acetate and paper, 10 ¾ × 13 ¼ inches (detail)
Endpapers: Stan VanDerBeek, *Untitled*, 1983, collage on billboard, 11 ¾ × 16 inches (detail)
Previous:
1 Johannes VanDerBeek, *Seeing A Man Stand Under An Umbrella From A Distance*, 2007, fiberglass, Hydrocal, umbrella, and acrylic paint, 79 × 44 ½ × 43 inches
2 Stan VanDerBeek, *Untitled*, c. 1960, ink on paper, 10 ⅜ × 8 inches
3 Sara VanDerBeek, *Ziggurat*, 2006, digital C-print, 40 × 30 inches

Contents

Ian Berry

INTRODUCTION

In 1980 artist Stan VanDerBeek (1927–1984) recalled a dream he had of the ideal exhibition space: a dark room with "projected images, movies, and stills everywhere," which he playfully referred to as an "amazement park." Suspended by a wire device, the viewer would swing through the space as "images like snowflakes…fly past." The experience would "reinforce by way of visual metaphors that the whole life experience is about sharing."

Amazement Park combines work by the influential artist and filmmaker with work by his daughter Sara VanDerBeek (b. 1976) and his son Johannes VanDerBeek (b. 1982). Taking inspiration from Stan VanDerBeek's dream exhibition, *Amazement Park* was initially presented as an experimental, studio-like gallery at the Tang Museum that changed every month for one year. The show began its first rotation in June 2009 and continued through the final installment in May 2010. Works by all three VanDerBeeks constituted each month's version of *Amazement Park*, from never-before-seen Stan VanDerBeek drawings and collages to new photographs and sculpture by Sara and Johannes.

Looking back on the project, Sara writes, "As this exhibition evolved, each hanging was a tremendous learning experience—not only about our father's work, but also about the many connections among the three of us. This process has proved a crucial exploration that has encouraged us to consider fundamental concerns of exhibitions and art in general. It was remarkable to use a room in a museum as a space for experimentation and to open our ongoing conversations to a larger audience."

Each month, in addition to presenting a new combination of artworks, I also gave Sara and Johannes a series of questions to consider. That conversation appears in this book alongside groups of images inspired by each month's theme. Sequencing of many of the illustrations reflects the juxtapositions posed in the exhibition, while new works, seen only in this publication, make the book an alternative second display space. New texts by Anne Ellegood, Fionn Meade, and Gloria Sutton add more voices to the unique character of this document.

The evolving nature of the project mirrors the spirit of their work, which shares common interests in recombination and collage, and ephemeral materials and architectural forms. Over the course of the exhibition and this book, a multilayered picture of influence and experimentation emerges.

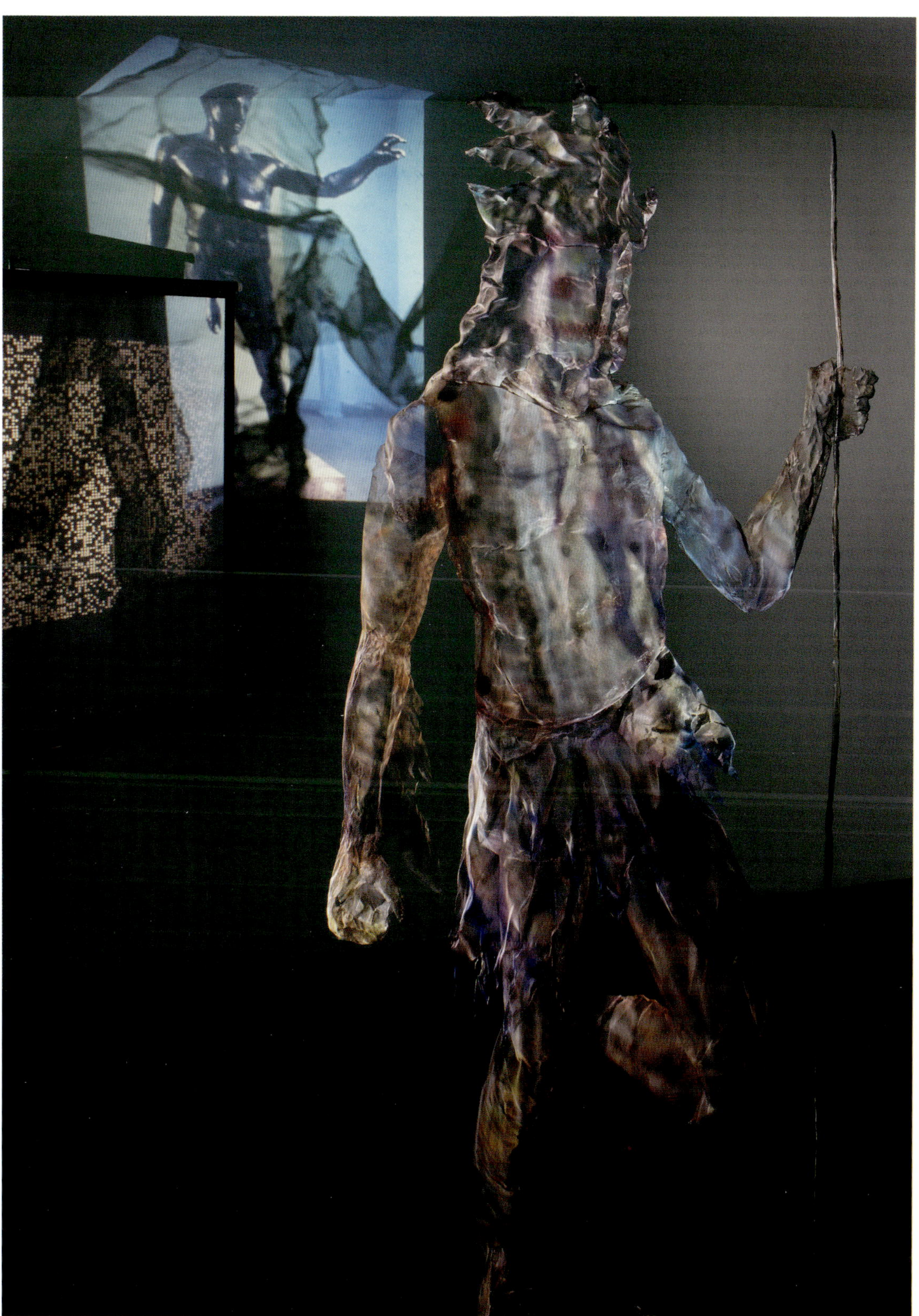

Installation view, *Amazement Park*, Tang Museum, Saratoga Springs, New York, 2009

MEANS

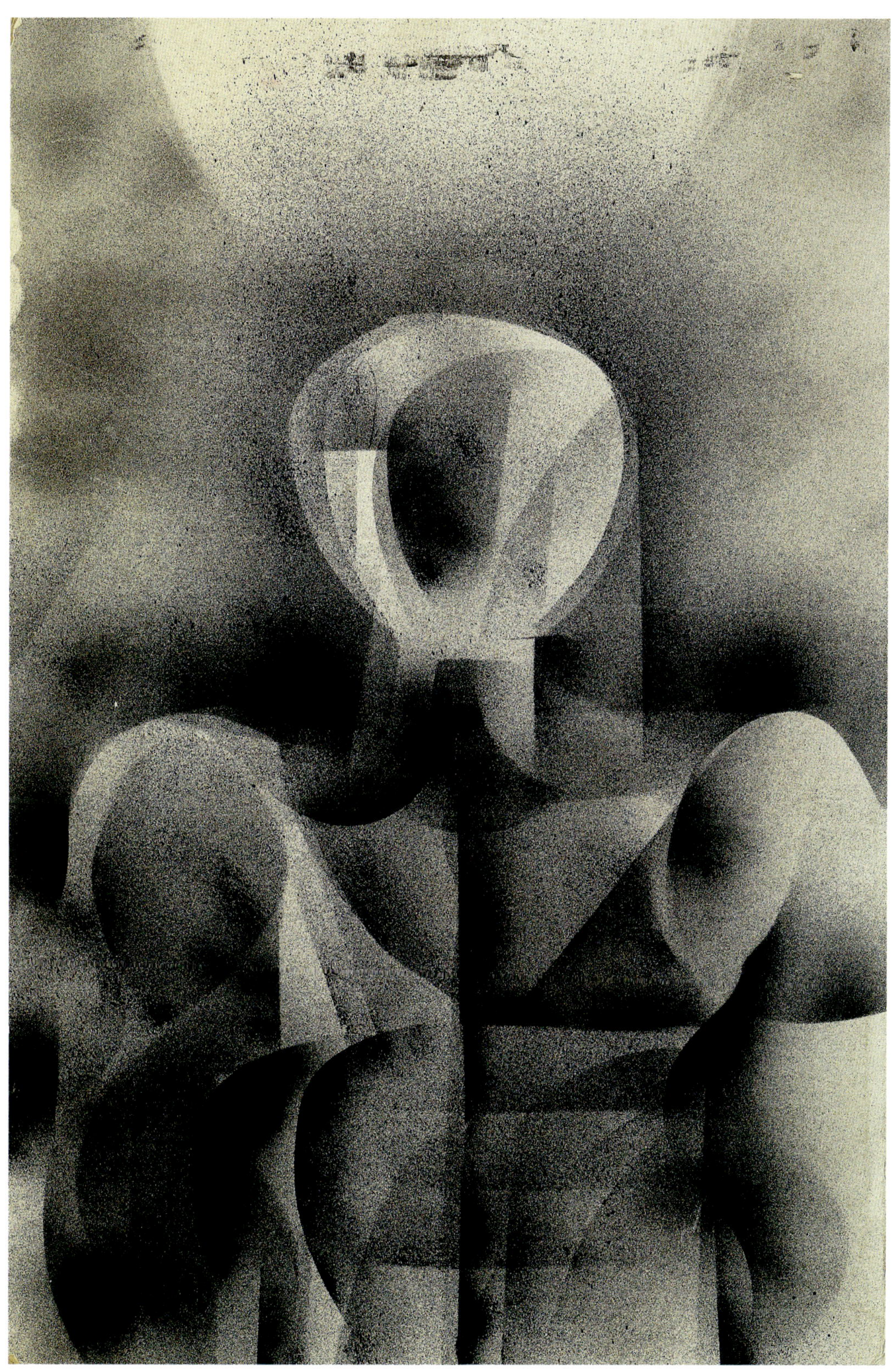

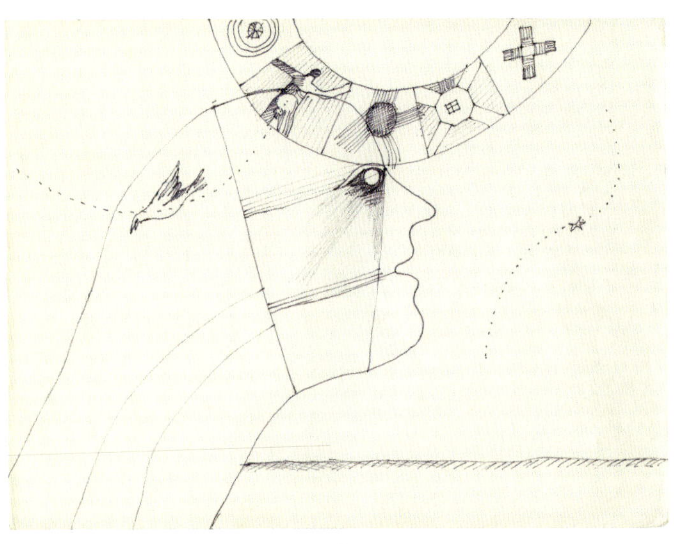

6

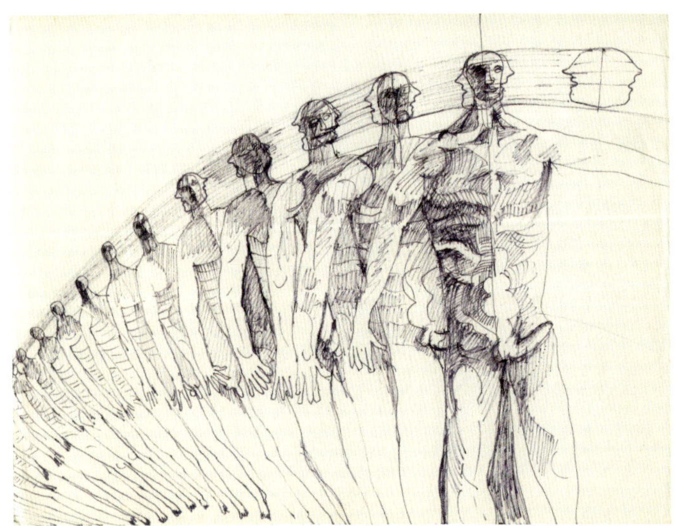

7

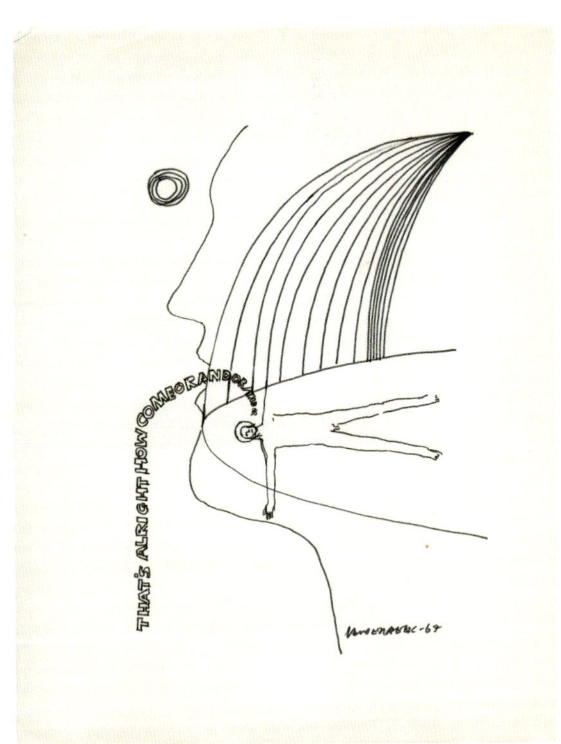

8

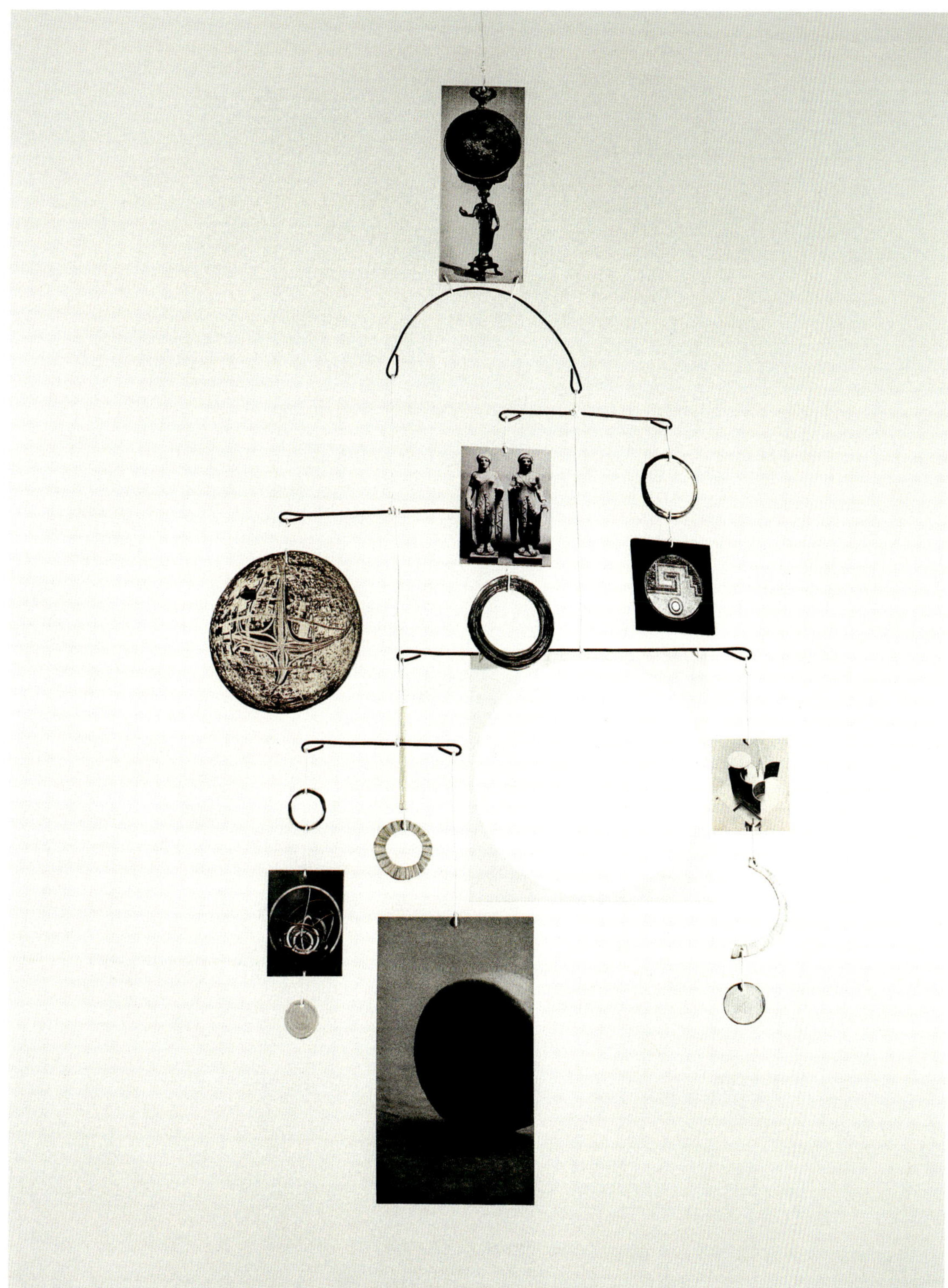

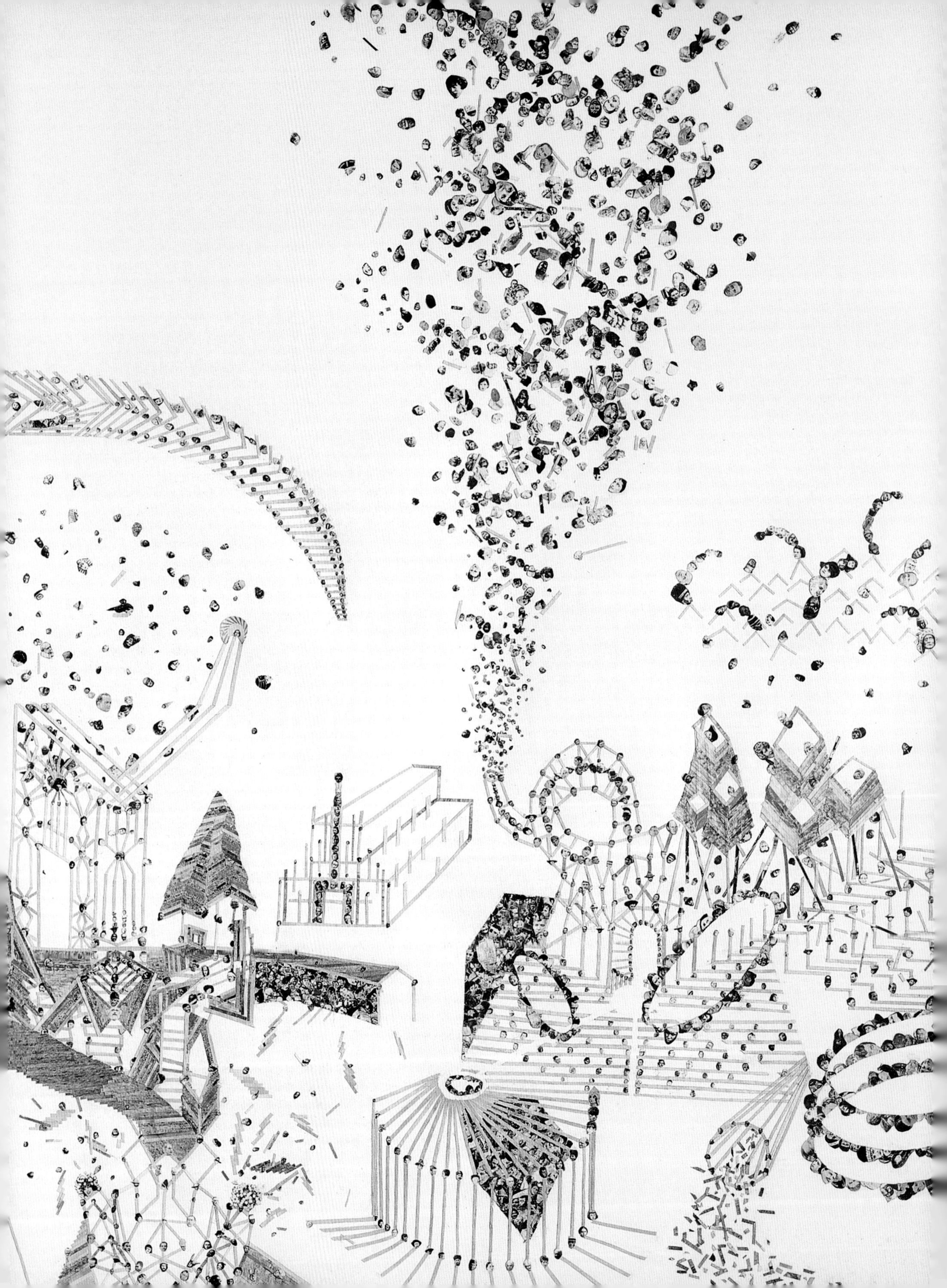

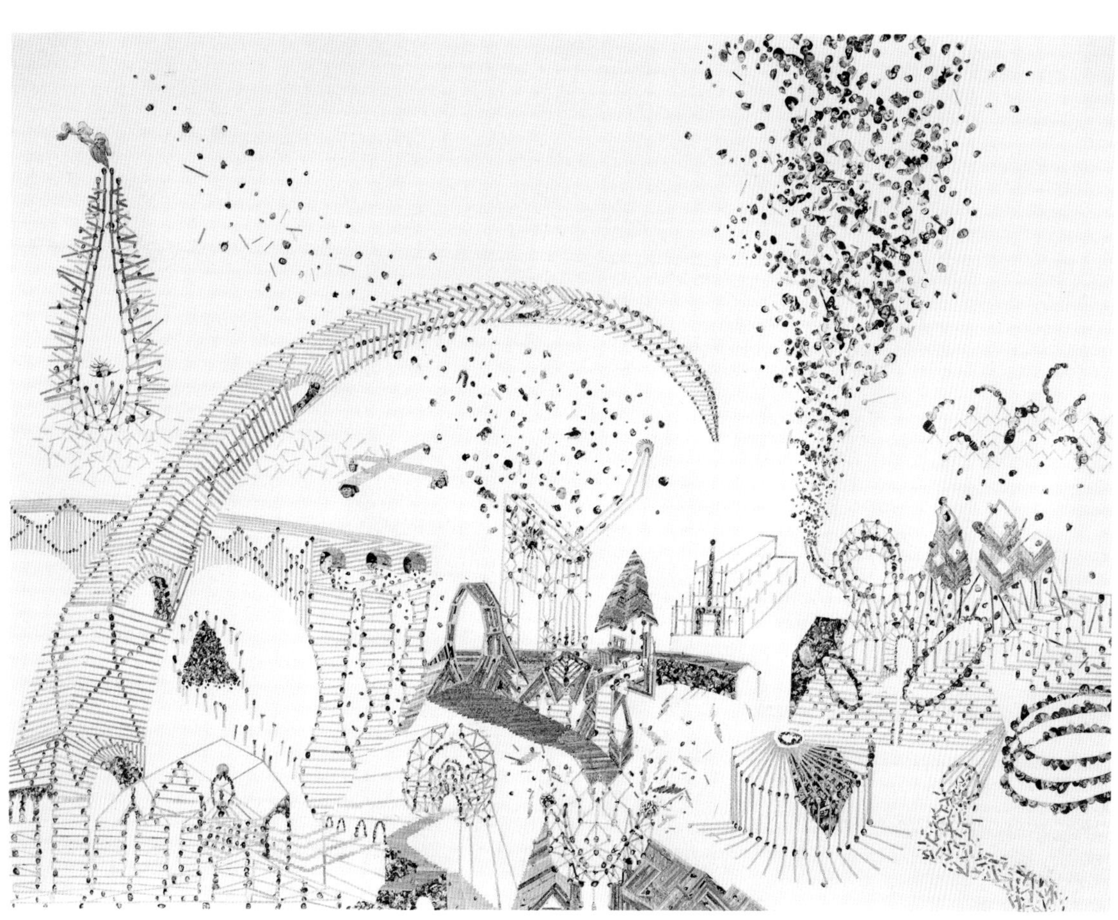

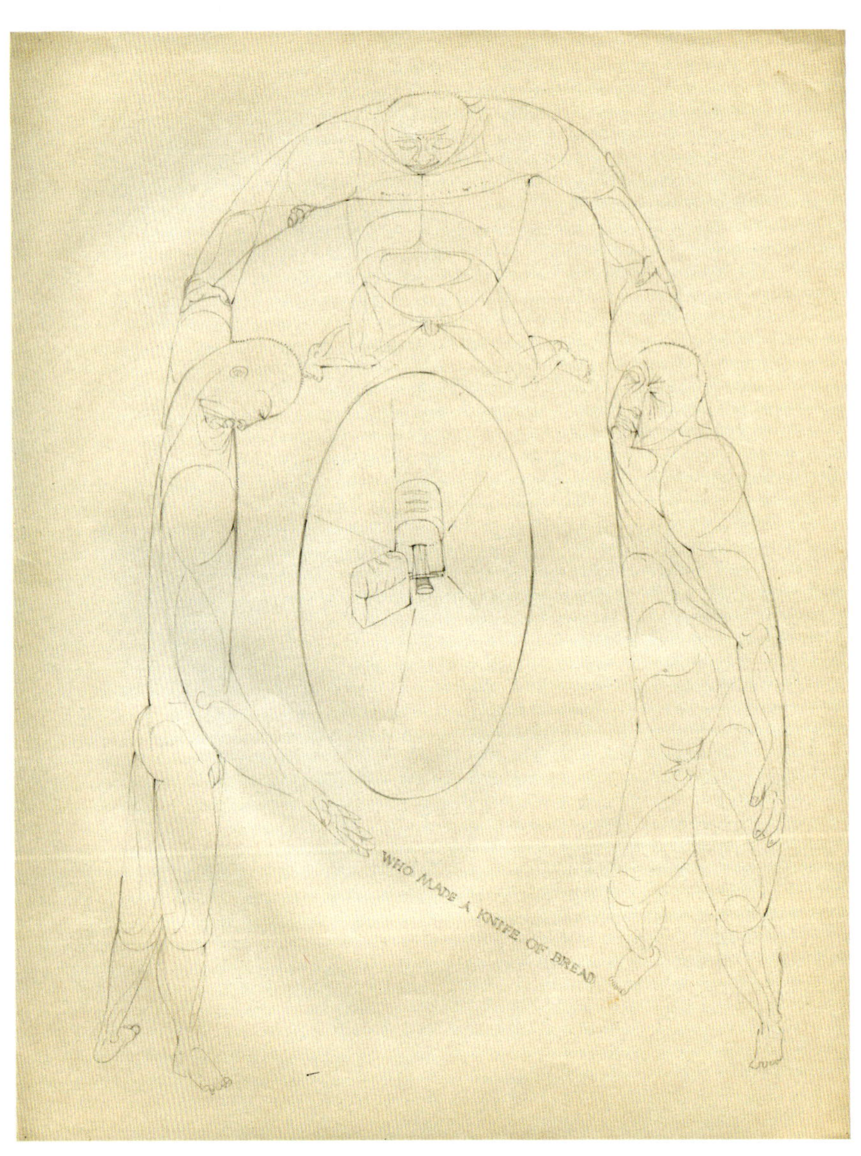
WHO MADE A KNIFE OF BREAD

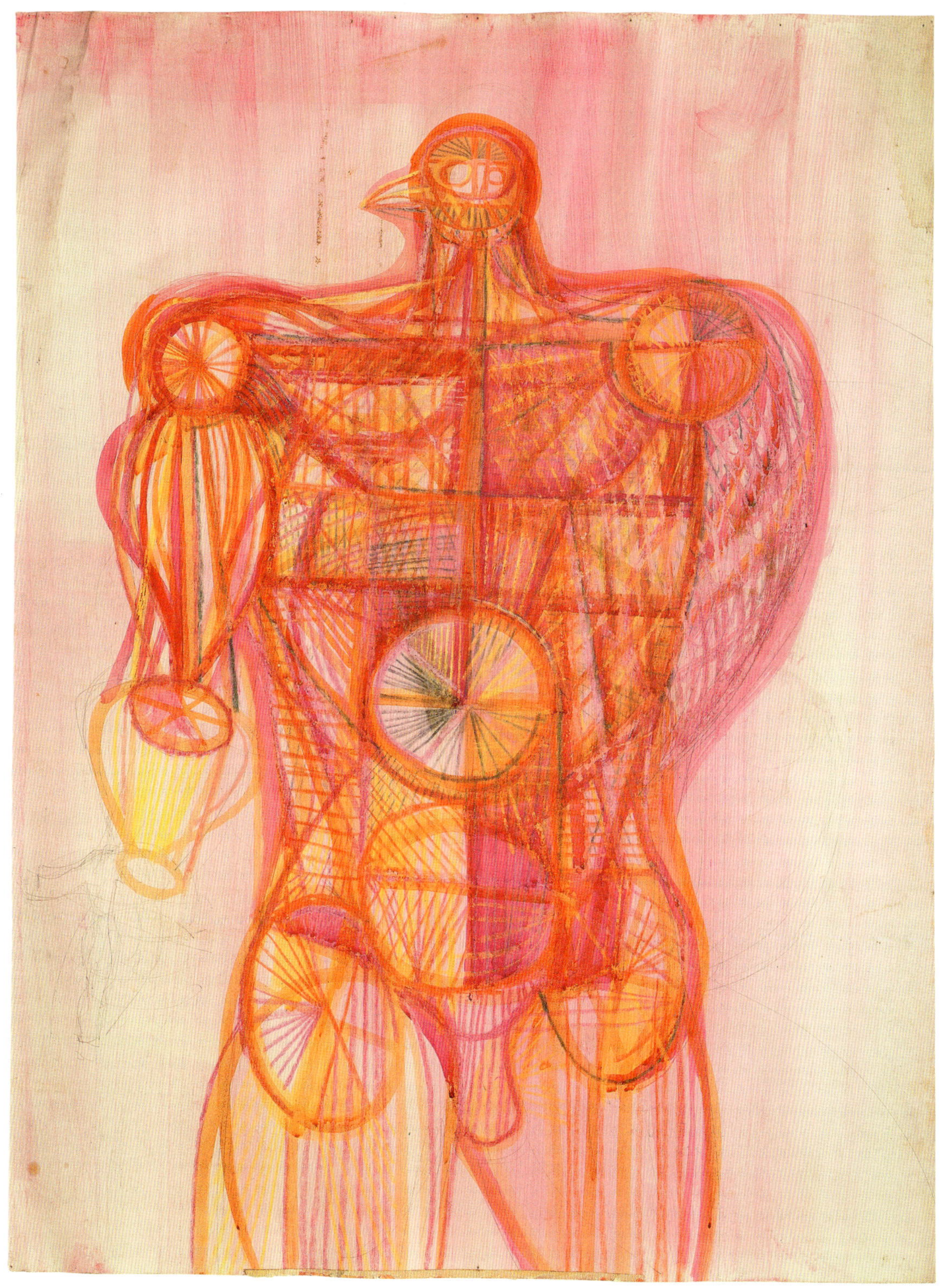

MEANS

IB: We refer to this first installation as *means*. What part of these works is elemental, like a building block, that your other works expand on?

JVDB: One way to think about the word is that the body is our only *means* of producing something outside itself. The repeated escape of ideas through our veins and bones into another medium is the pilgrimage of creation. This installation emphasized the body as it is transformed in or through art. In the different works the human frame became an ethereal chapel or a crude contraption.

The building block in my collage is the human head. I tried to treat the head as though it was a basic material like a nail or stone that can be connected with another material like a beam to produce a circus of structures. I thought about turning the process of building a collage into a sculptural challenge. I stuck to rules of tension and balance but implanted them in a white void with no real physics. This attempt to bridge the illusory depth of two-dimensional space with an absurd three-dimensional logic is something that I still aim for. With this work, I started to think about combining two illusory kinds of space, pictorial space with headspace, in actual space. This piece just approached headspace in a more literal fashion.

SVDB: My piece in this show is titled *From the Means of Reproduction*, a phrase from a Margaret Sanger speech. I came to that title because the image hanging at the bottom of the mobile in my photograph is an enlarged photographic view of the birth control pill. When it was first made publicly available it was profiled in *Life* magazine. I was drawn to the image because the pill appeared like a monolithic minimal sculpture—in its distorted scale it reflected the significant impact this small object was to have on the lives of women and society as a whole. It was also circular and throughout the work I used circles as a formal connection among many of the images. The piece moves through time from top to bottom, beginning with an image of an Etruscan hand mirror, to a statue of a Roman couple, to an image of a hanging circular construction by Rodchenko, to a fisheye view of a metropolis, to the image of the pill at the bottom. I look for echoes in contemporary society that relate to our recent and distant pasts. In this case, reproduction refers primarily to image reproduction but also to physiological reproduction in the sense of generations and the great changes that occur from one to the next. In terms of photographic reproduction, I am intrigued by the process through which an image becomes rendered and defined as historical, and how the dissemination of an image through publications, books, and the internet can lead to that image becoming a part of a collective knowledge.

IB: How do these works relate to drawing, which seems to be an elemental process for each of you?

SVDB: I often begin pieces by drawing out the idea. Mark making and a sense of the hand are really important to me. Though my final artworks are photographs, I would like the handmade nature of the object I photograph to be expressed in the image. I often paint or draw on top of the images I use, and I frequently think about the line and gesture as an element of the overall composition.

JVDB: Drawing has a permanent place as the first step in setting a perimeter around my thinking. As notions and possibilities whirl around your mind, a line can corral them into actuality. It is fitting that the first show included works that refer to drawing because it can establish this yearlong exhibition as an overarching process similar to art making. It's also fitting that we included earlier works to show our foundation as artists—rickety or sound—that we build on. Even though not all of the works were literally drawings, the use of white space bound them to drawing. The white of the page is a location with no time or inclination. All of our works presented something floating in that openness. The figure in my father's piece is a black smoke spreading into chest arches and rib cages that are evaporating into white air. My sister's mobile is a metropolis seen from above, below, and in front, dangling in a bleached light. Within this configuration, a timeline spreads through contrasting memories. My place is a scrambled agenda of progress and regress. Masses of people are used to make monuments but their meaning teeters amid a voided terrain. The white background in all of these works plays with different symbolic meanings, but a nice lingering metaphor for this installment is the means by which we move from a blank consciousness.

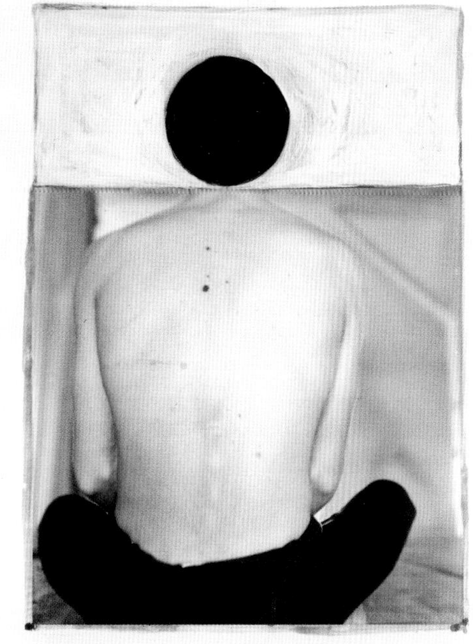

13

IB: There are some drawings of Stan's in this installation from the 1950s that haven't been shown before—where did you find them?

JVDB: Most of our father's work wound up in different

family homes. A lot of work was kept safe over the last twenty-five years by his first wife, Johanna VanDerBeek. It wasn't until a few years ago that we became aware of how much work existed, including dozens of sketchbooks and hundreds of drawings. Even in the last few months we've uncovered more work from dusty shelves in our basement in Baltimore. It's a great feeling to pick up something that looks like a dirt cake to find it's a remarkable example of mid-century collage. Unfortunately, some things couldn't be recovered, but a large portion of the estate is in good shape, given the circumstances.

IB: Do you think Stan would like his drawings being displayed in a museum? Do you know his thoughts about sketching or drawing? Was it an important part of his practice as a filmmaker?

JVDB: It's hard to say whether he would appreciate some of his most intimate thoughts being displayed. What I have taken from family stories—particularly the one from when he was eleven years old at a camp and signed his name in white paint all over the cabins—is that, like most artists, he had a healthy ego. So part of me thinks he would just be happy that his work is being seen. Particularly since so much of his work is less about the materialization of information and more about the conveyance of it, then I have to assume he would want his ideas out there. He apparently drew constantly to record ideas and plans, and his hand could barely keep up with his racing thoughts. There is so much evidence of his character in his drawings and writing that I think it's one of the truest ways to understand his dynamic creativity. At a certain point artists lose control over what gets released. It all becomes the domain of humanity, and he trusted humanity.

SVDB: Some of the drawings shown in the first installation were made while my father was at Black Mountain College. They remind me of William Blake's work, with mystical figures, and are drawn with beautiful delicate lines that are almost invisible. These works are mixed together in this installation with later drawings that have stronger marks, made with darker ink. In these you can see that he has found his way of drawing and a confidence in his ideas. I think he would have enjoyed showing the different works together. But this question brings up larger issues when we work with his archive or re-install his works from the estate. Often when we are re-creating works such as the multimedia installations, I strive to reach a delicate balance between accuracy and his vibrant and spontaneous spirit. It is difficult. All we can do is assume and interpret what he would want because he did not leave any instructions nor any organized documentation.

I recently received from a scholar who is doing research about Black Mountain College the transcript of an interview with my father about his experience at the school. The interview was conducted in 1971 while he was working

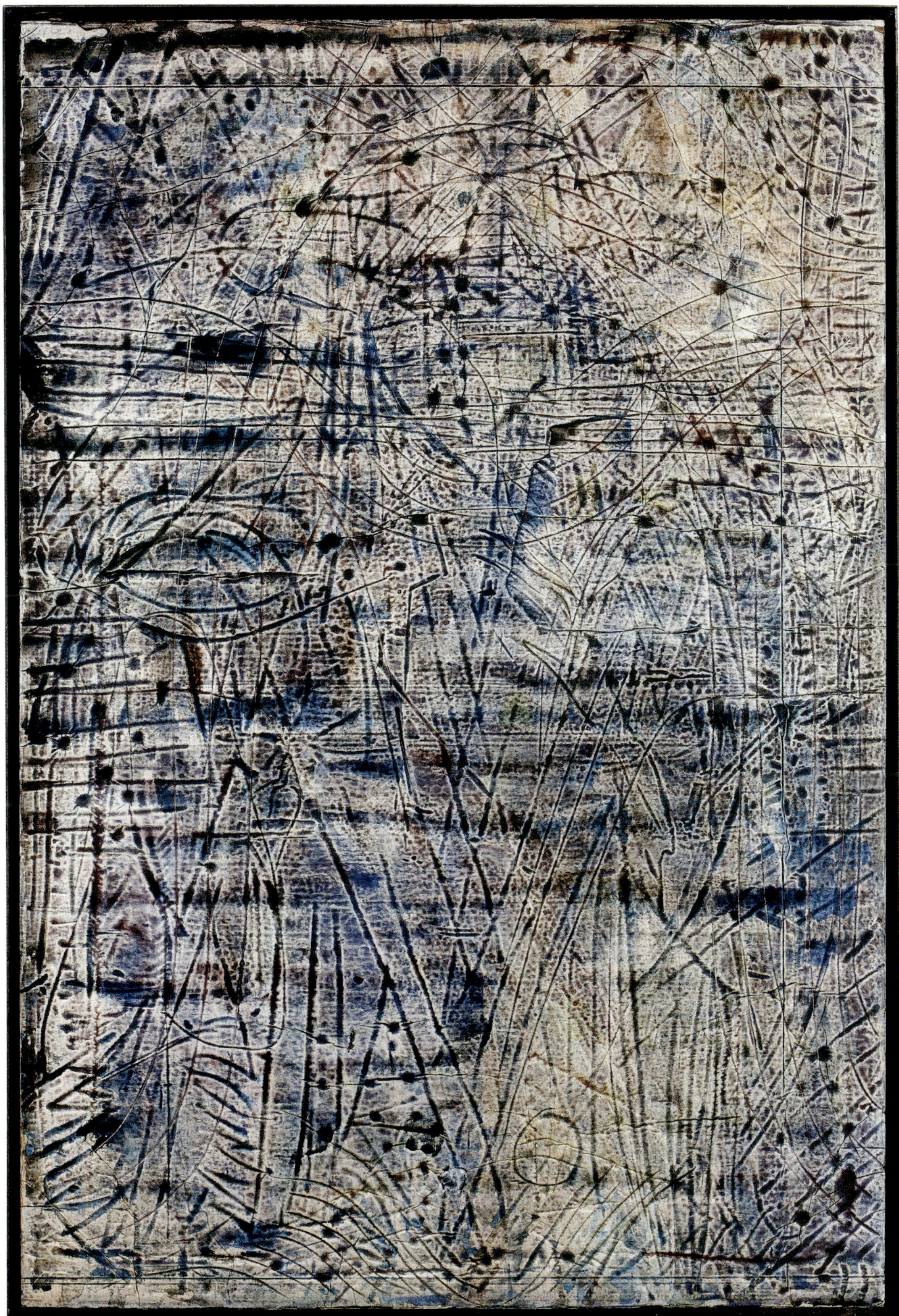

as an artist in residence at the Center for Advanced Visual Studies at M.I.T. So it was over twenty years after his time at the school from 1949–51. In this part of the interview he talks about his views on the relationship of different mediums to film and the beginning of his work in film but it also really spoke to me about how I think about my photographs. Finding and reading things like this transcript is the closest thing to having a conversation with him:

> *Actually, the crucial, key thing for me at Black Mountain was the discovery of motion pictures. And that was…well, I don't really remember anymore how exactly it happened. It started… I got interested in photography. I was always interested in it. I took Hazel's course [photographer Hazel Larsen Archer], was making still pictures, and doing a lot of drawing, a lot of calligraphy. And I was dwelling with the problems of the handmade thing versus the machine-made thing. Like photography was, you know, a difficult technique that required lots of apparatus and drawing, and literally, calligraphy—studies of fine calligraphy were just exquisite examples of hand power. So, I was always struggling between these two things and gradually took more interest in the photography and so I borrowed a camera from somebody, and made a whole bunch of completely mythological films that were never…because there was no film, I didn't have any film, which was a complicated thing I mean..*
>
> *I had a camera. And I had a girlfriend, who was a dancer, who I was making incredible movies of, whom, of course, I wasn't making any movies of, but we were going to do all these exercises with camera angles, and she was doing moves…and actually I did get around to doing some filming, but that opened my eyes to the system. And I realized that motion pictures were, you know, a special system, that they were large enough of scale to include all of the systems. They were the mythic marriage of technique. I mean, I could make movies, I could make anything out of it. I could do painting, sculpture and anything. I was then really into drawings and calligraphy and what have you—shape, color, form were all the things that I could render. And it's a technique that absorbed them—a large enough technique that absorbed all the difficult ideas I saw as individual ideas. And so that was a great union to me. You know, looking for the principle of something interested me then. I saw that the principle of motion pictures was self inclusive, or totally inclusive. Anything could be material for motion pictures. A painting was a thing that you sat here, and it went off on a wall someplace. It didn't become part of a continuum. It didn't become part of a larger media integration. I didn't really, tangibly, see it as such, I guess, at the time—only kind of after the fact. But it gradually built up to that point where I realized that it was a kind of total universal system and, as such, became the most positive and beautifully integrated system of all the systems I saw. And so I threw myself into movies….*

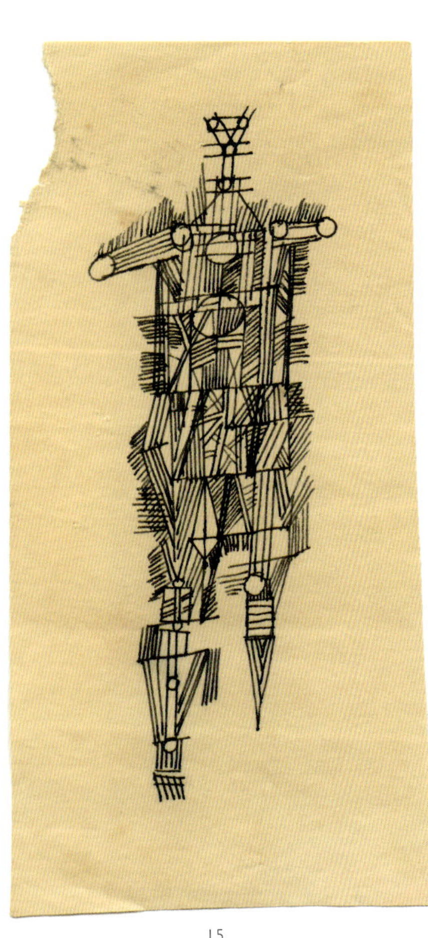

15

SVDB: Here is an excerpt I wrote about my own work many months prior to reading this transcript. It's much more formal but when I read his words, I was struck by the fact that we both referred to this visual continuum:

> *Employing images as both inspiration and form, my work often explores photography's reflexive relationship to perception and its role in the establishment of personal and collective memory. I believe the documentary action involved when taking a picture is a means of navigating the ever-expanding visual field in which we live. I am interested in how we record, view, and present images, and how that process is a mirror to our inner consciousness. The manner in which photography shapes our view of the world, the great potential of its influence and the possible shortcomings of its controlled perspective drive my continued study of the medium. In my practice I use a variety of images, both found and my own, sculptural objects, and other three dimensional forms to construct assemblages and larger multi-part installations that are then documented photographically and presented in final exhibition form as photographs.*
>
> *With each work and the image sequences within my work I hope to define a visual continuum within the larger human experience that is historically intoned yet resonant with contemporary existence.*

Means captions

5 Stan VanDerBeek, *Untitled (rolling)*, 1955, graphite and ink on paper, 29 ¾ × 20 inches
6 Stan VanDerBeek, *Untitled*, c. 1960, ink on paper, 8 ¼ × 11 ¼ inches
7 Stan VanDerBeek, *Untitled*, c. 1960, ink on paper, 8 ¼ × 11 ¼ inches
8 Stan VanDerBeek, *Untitled*, 1967, ink on paper, 11 × 8 ½ inches
9 Sara VanDerBeek, *From the Means of Reproduction*, 2007, digital C-print, 40 × 30 inches
10 Johannes VanDerBeek, *Heads and Beams*, 2004, collage on paper, 38 ¼ × 50 ⅛ inches
Private Collection
11 Stan VanDerBeek, *Untitled (Who Made a Knife of Bread)*, c. 1955, pencil on paper, 11 × 8 ½ inches
12 Stan VanDerBeek, *Untitled*, 1955, acrylic and ink on paper, 29 ¾ × 20 inches
13 Sara VanDerBeek, *Study for Four Photographers*, 2008, paint on silver gelatin print, 9 ⅞ × 8 inches
14 Johannes VanDerBeek, *Sky Impression #1*, 2011, acrylic on foam, 49 × 34 inches
15 Stan VanDerBeek, *Untitled*, c. 1960, ink on paper, 6 ⅝ × 3 ¼ inches

MATERIAL

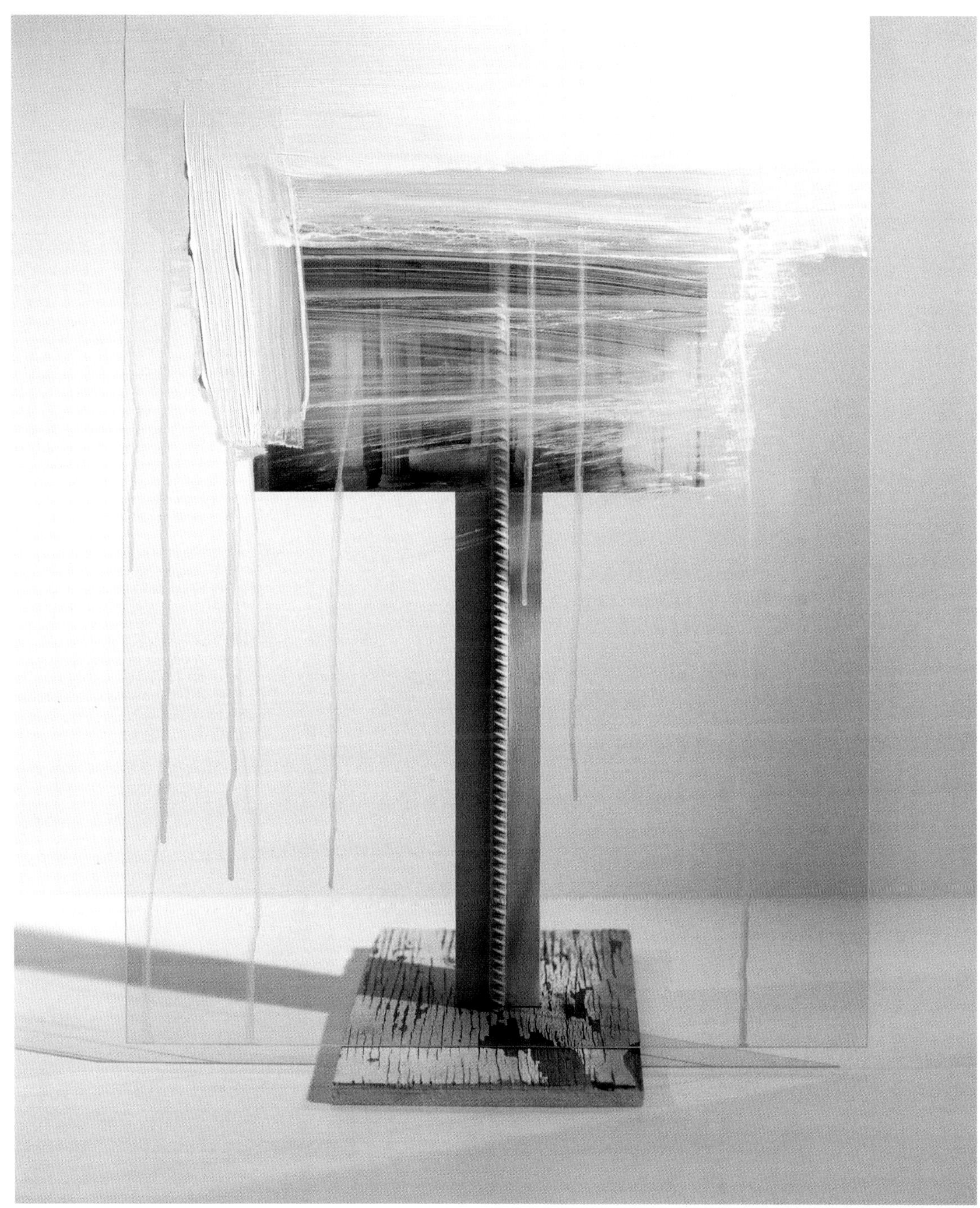

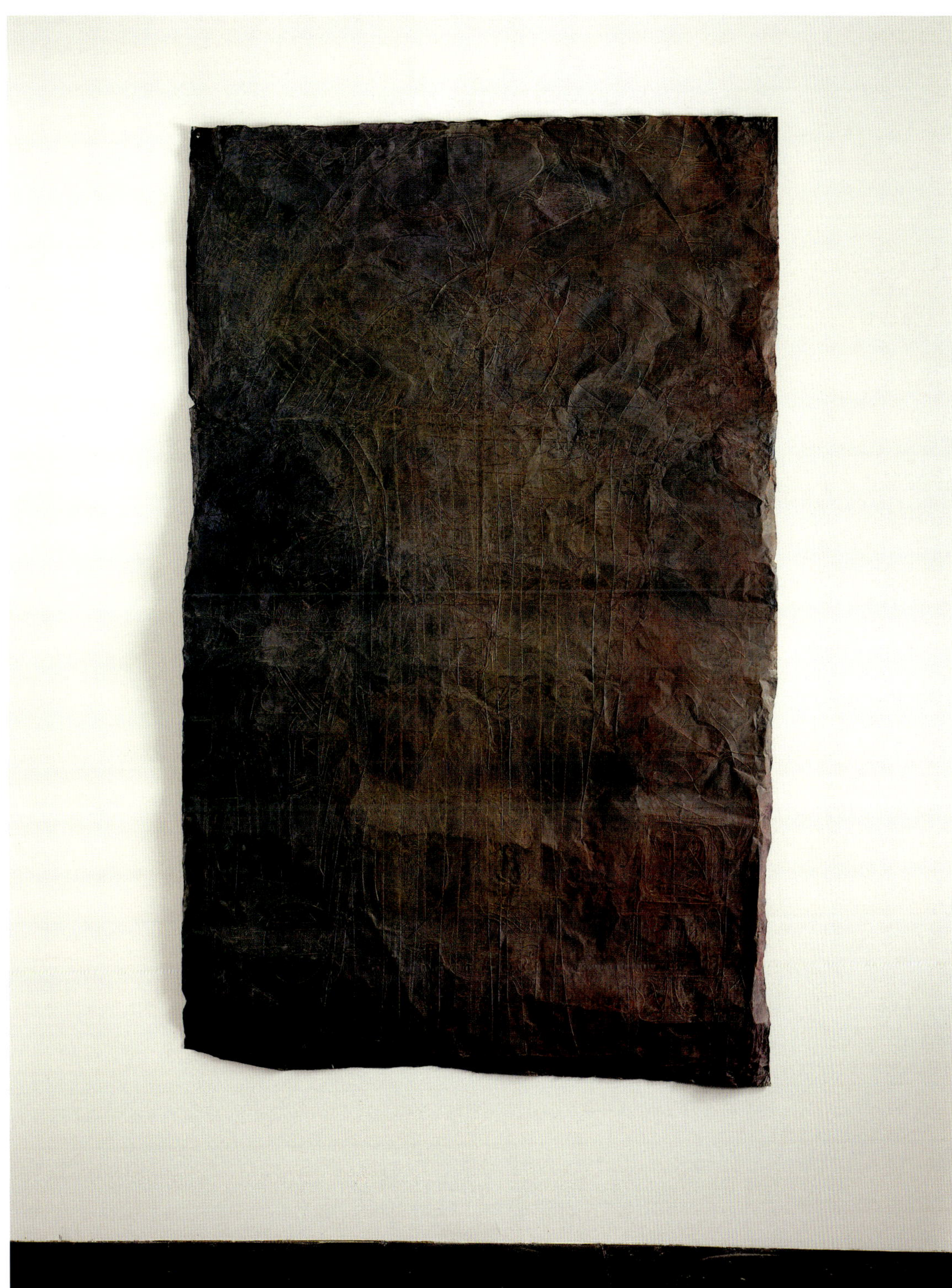

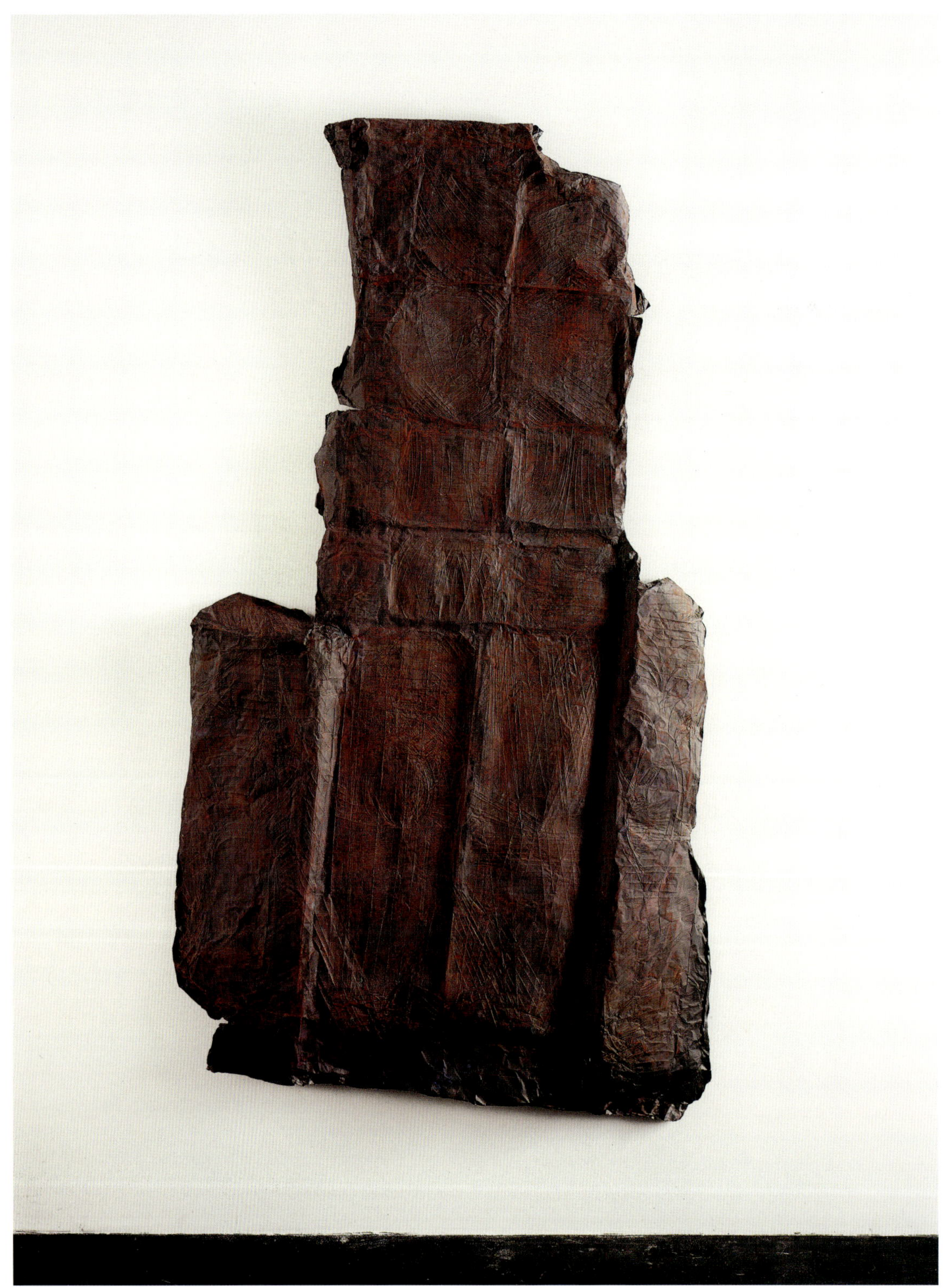

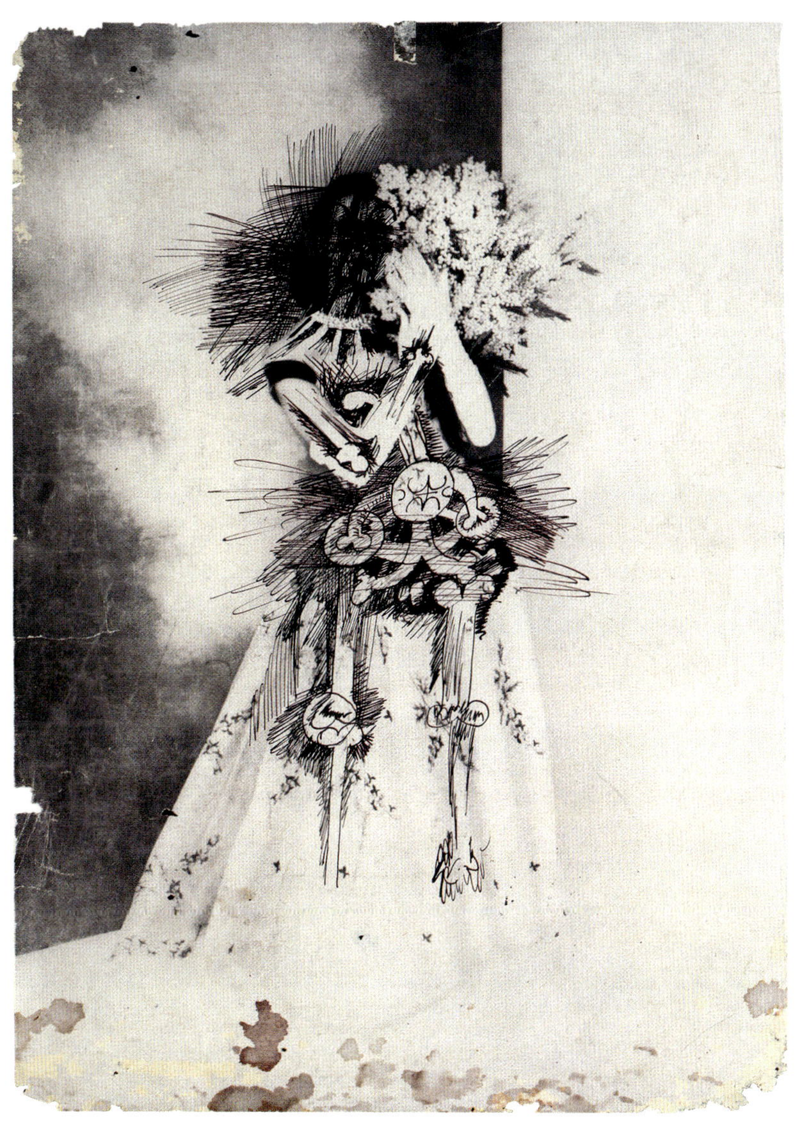

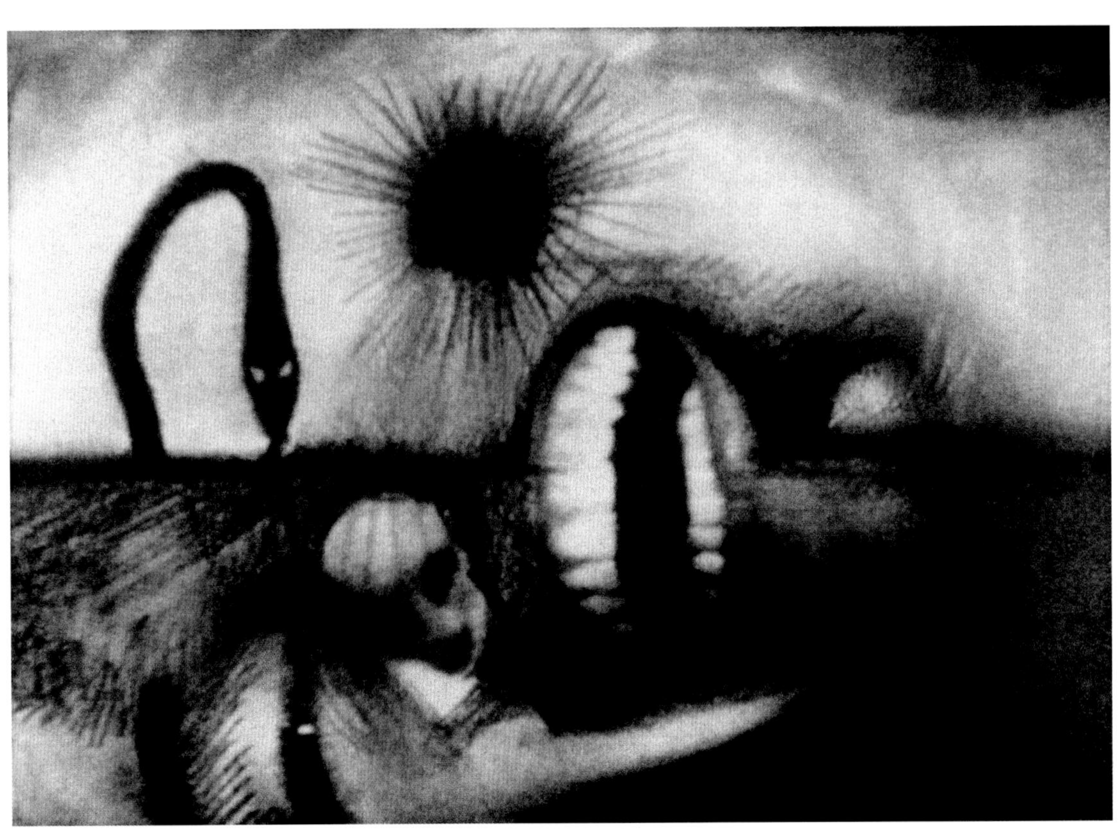

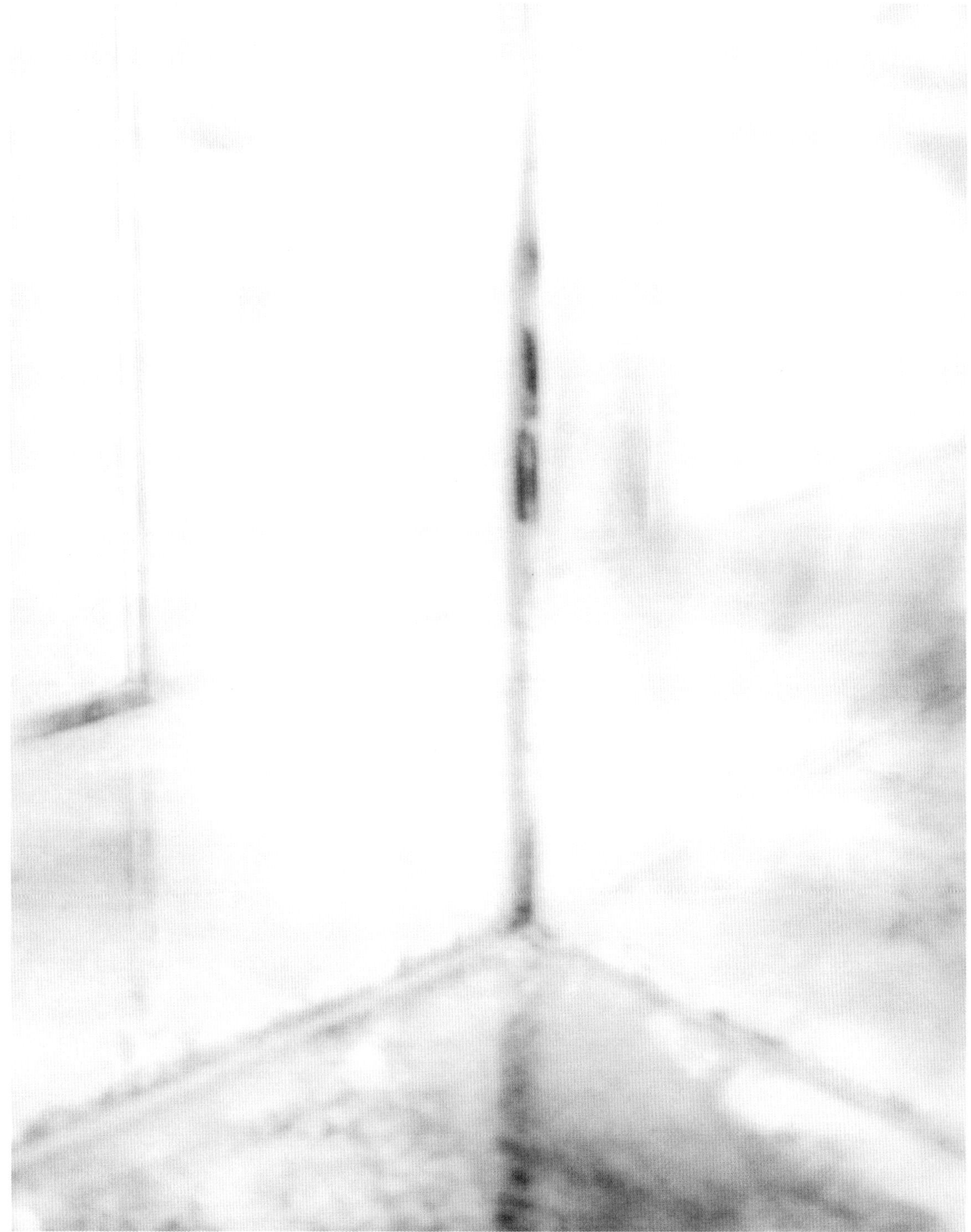

MATERIAL

IB: This month the theme is material. You are both showing new work where the material is very upfront, calling direct attention to itself. Can you start by describing your work and the material choices you made? Johannes, why such a fragile aluminum sheet, for example? What does it offer that paper doesn't?

JVDB: The aluminum foil offers the opportunity to make a more mysterious drawing surface and ambiguous object. It can be folded and creased into a clumsy rigidity, pressed into with tools from both sides to make shallow relief or protruding marks, and when it's colored with pastels it can take on an identity between stone and metal. All of these qualities aim at representing the feeling of an object from a dream or memory—something vague and vivid at the same time. In the process of recalling an object from a moment past, specifics become smoothed over through the process of recollection. The aspects that remain in focus are charged with a peculiar meaning because it is unclear why they remained. As I was making these works I pretended someone was describing something to me. I toiled with the aspects of words that reduce or elaborate details. The aluminum foil made it possible to create forms that appeared heavy and flimsy at the same time, much like the way a memory can have unclear weight in our minds. I wanted the drawings to appear on the surface like a feverish doodle or a labored etching so the properties of immediacy or permanence are more confounded, like opposing vantages. The loose approach to drawing also gets confused by the works' ancient personality and the dusty demeanor of their objecthood. I hope all these subtle contradictions would make them difficult to discern but intriguing to look at.

IB: Sara, your three photographs have a lot of different material in them—glass panes, graphite, dripped paint, peeling paint, weathered wood, and old photographs. Can you describe some of the histories associated with them—the wood from Baltimore, or the Walker Evans image, for example?

SVDB: This work is related to *A Composition for Detroit*, which focused on a city I feel is emblematic of where we are physically and psychologically as a nation. We are experiencing the last stretches of a major cultural change from

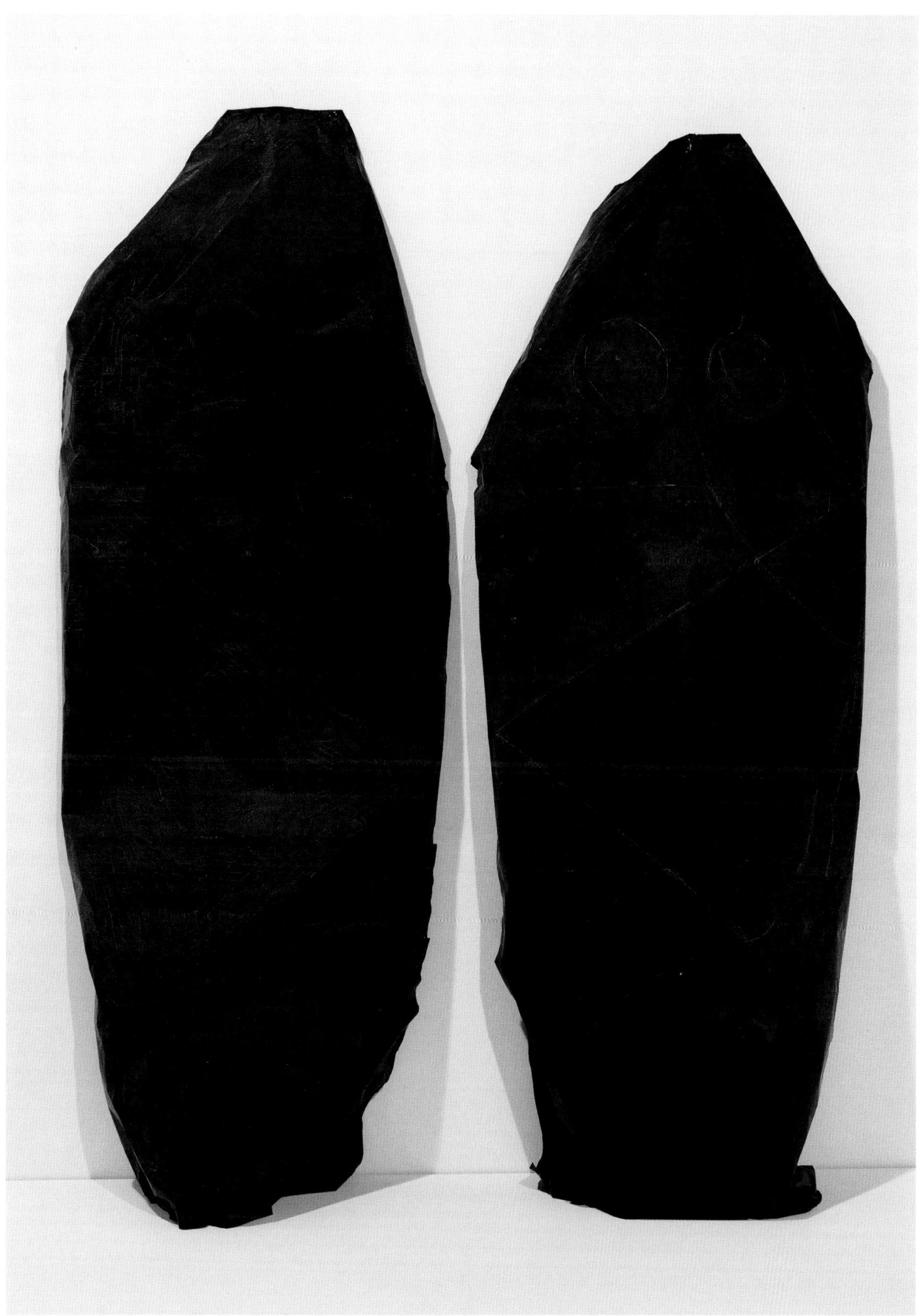

the industrial age city with a definable locus and populace to the modern, expansive, fractured city, resulting in a different way of living, communicating, and even thinking. Detroit is in some ways a dying remnant of our past, beautiful but collapsing from the inside out and in other ways a provocative social experiment representative of a new era of urban planning and politics. I was struck when I visited by how much the 1967 riots changed the city and continue to impact it. The reverberence of the riots was present in both the physical spaces of the city and the people. I thought about how, as a community, we as a nation record, react, and define tragedy. These pieces address that idea but also the history of photography and how our relationship to images has continued to evolve and inform our sense of the tragic and the historic. In *Belle Grove (Second View)*, I used Walker Evans's image of Belle Grove Plantation, in Louisiana. Evans worked for the Farm Security Administration and created *Let us Now Praise Famous Men* with James Agee, a book about

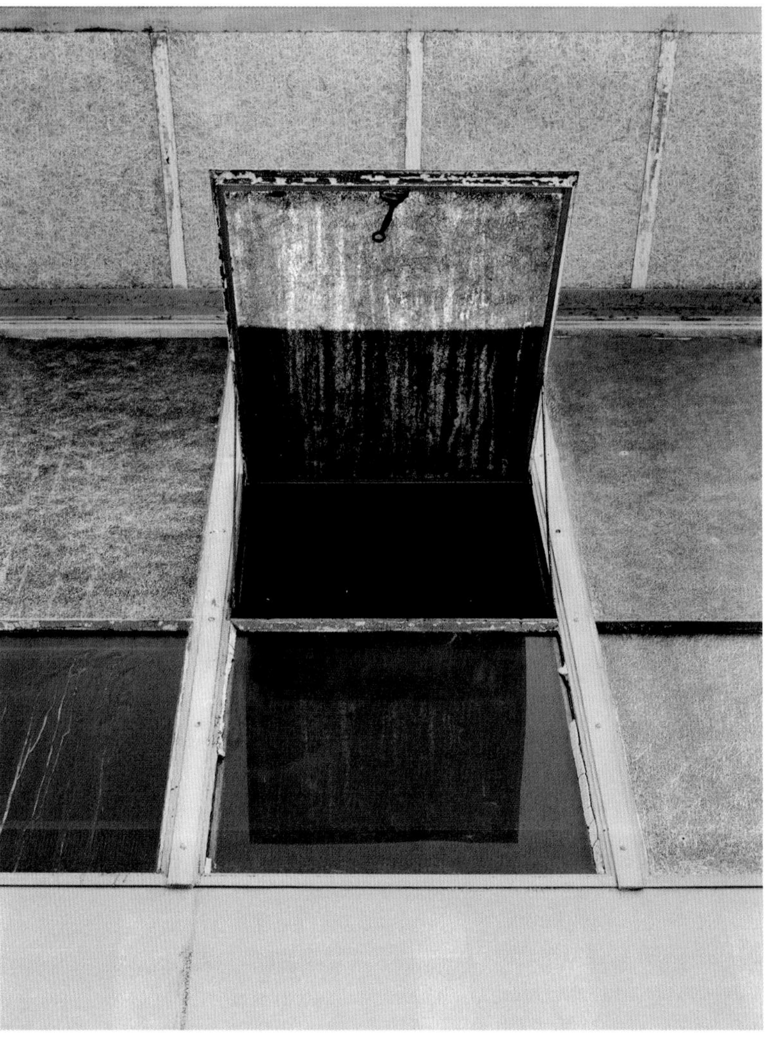

24

poor sharecroppers in the South during the Depression. Though we are not currently in an economic depression, we live in a similarly difficult and challenging time, with people experiencing anxiety, pain, and sadness, and I wanted to communicate this moment as an artist.

My use of these images and my emphasis on the materiality of the paint and the worn wood—that feeling of whitewashing something aged and worn—was a response to the tangible textures and sense of place in Agee's writing and Evans's images, but it was also about conveying the sense of ruin from within.

I'm hoping this new combination of works will describe a loose narrative as it moves along the wall. They have a sense of ruin, both physical and emotional, like the fading away of old Hollywood in *Mirror, Hollywood Boulevard*, or the wrecked Southern plantation with its strange and problematic history. Belle Grove was a plantation photographed by many well-known photographers, like Evans, Edward Weston, and Clarence John Laughlin, but also by the U. S. Government as an important historical building, which is how I got the image I used in the larger *Belle Grove* work. The government documented it in the thirties and forties when it had gone to ruin, and about twenty years later it burned down, so it no longer exists physically, only in images. Painting over it was an act of erasing or disrupting the image, but my use of the light was also a form of erasure. The image of the room was there, but just barely, and the graphite line I colored in on the edge of the wood in which the glass is resting provides a visual and metaphorical resting point, almost as if it all balanced on a moment. The graphite line is like the moment of change, there is before and after.

IB: We are projecting Stan's *Breathdeath* large on the wall this month. Did you think of his work when you made your new pieces?

SVDB: My pieces are part of a new body of work that involves different approaches to image making, including both studio and location based photography. *Mirror, Hollywood Boulevard* is a Polaroid I shot in Los Angeles of a small, empty, dirty-mirrored display window on Hollywood Boulevard. The flash on the Polaroid camera illuminated the mirror, and like *Belle Grove*, it feels as though it is simultaneously appearing and disappearing.

Breathdeath has a similar sense of opposites: breath symbolizing life, light, and motion while death is addressed with darkness and stillness. The film flips back and forth between these manic dances of imagery to haunting still images. There is a scene in *Breathdeath* where Harry Truman' s face appears, and on top of it my father draws lines that make him look trapped in a corner. A chair appears in front of him, and the lines fill and fill the space until they cover Truman. It's funny but also pointedly critical of his administration, and it invokes the anxiety of his time. In another scene, an image of a bride from a fashion magazine is erased and drawn upon so half her body becomes skeletal and then disappears. That combination of erasing and mark making strikes me as an effective means of altering an image. Both additive and subtractive, the flash of light erases, but the grit leaves lines like pencil marks.

JVDB: I thought a lot about the film's undertones and overall mood and used them as an impression to work from. *Breathdeath* peers into the annals of history with a lampooning telescope. It reflects life as a persistent push and pull between opposing forces such as light and dark, magic and marauding, hips and moustaches, fevers and levers, and so on. I've always felt it was a culmination of the avant-garde collagist approach that brought him notoriety in the art scene and expanded cinema movement, and yet it remains accessible through its humor and beauty. It captures a film noir atmosphere with flashes of the occult and our dance with inevitable death, but traces them in a genuinely entertaining arc of cinema. The slowed-down version of Screamin' Jay Hawkins's "I Put a Spell on You" as a soundtrack gives the scenes a lurching locomotion. In one scene a woman (my father's first wife) swoons on a bed over a figure made out of clothes with a TV as a head. That seems to be a fitting portrait of my father's personality. As a kid it was the film I looked forward to because it made me want to dance and be proud.

Material captions

16 Sara VanDerBeek, *Belle Grove (Second View)*, 2009, digital C-print, 24 × 20 inches
17 Sara VanDerBeek, *Belle Grove*, 2009, digital C-print, 40 × 30 inches
18 Johannes VanDerBeek, *The King*, 2009, pastel and ink on aluminum foil, 73 ½ × 49 × 2 ¼ inches
19 Johannes VanDerBeek, *It*, 2009, pastel and ink on aluminum foil, 75 × 42 × 3 inches
20 Stan VanDerBeek, *Untitled (from Breathdeath)*, 1963, ink on found photograph, 12 ¾ × 9 ⅛ inches
21 Stan VanDerBeek, Still from *Breathdeath*, 1963, black and white film with sound, 14:33 minutes
22 Sara VanDerBeek, *Mirror, Hollywood Boulevard*, 2009, digital C-print, 20 × 15 ½ inches
23 Johannes VanDerBeek, *Former Presidents*, 2010, pastel and ink on aluminum foil, each, 68 × 26 × 11 inches
24 Sara VanDerBeek, *Tremé School Window*, 2010, digital C-print, 20 × 15 ¼ inches
25 Stan VanDerBeek, Still from *Breathdeath*, 1963, black and white film with sound, 14:33 minutes

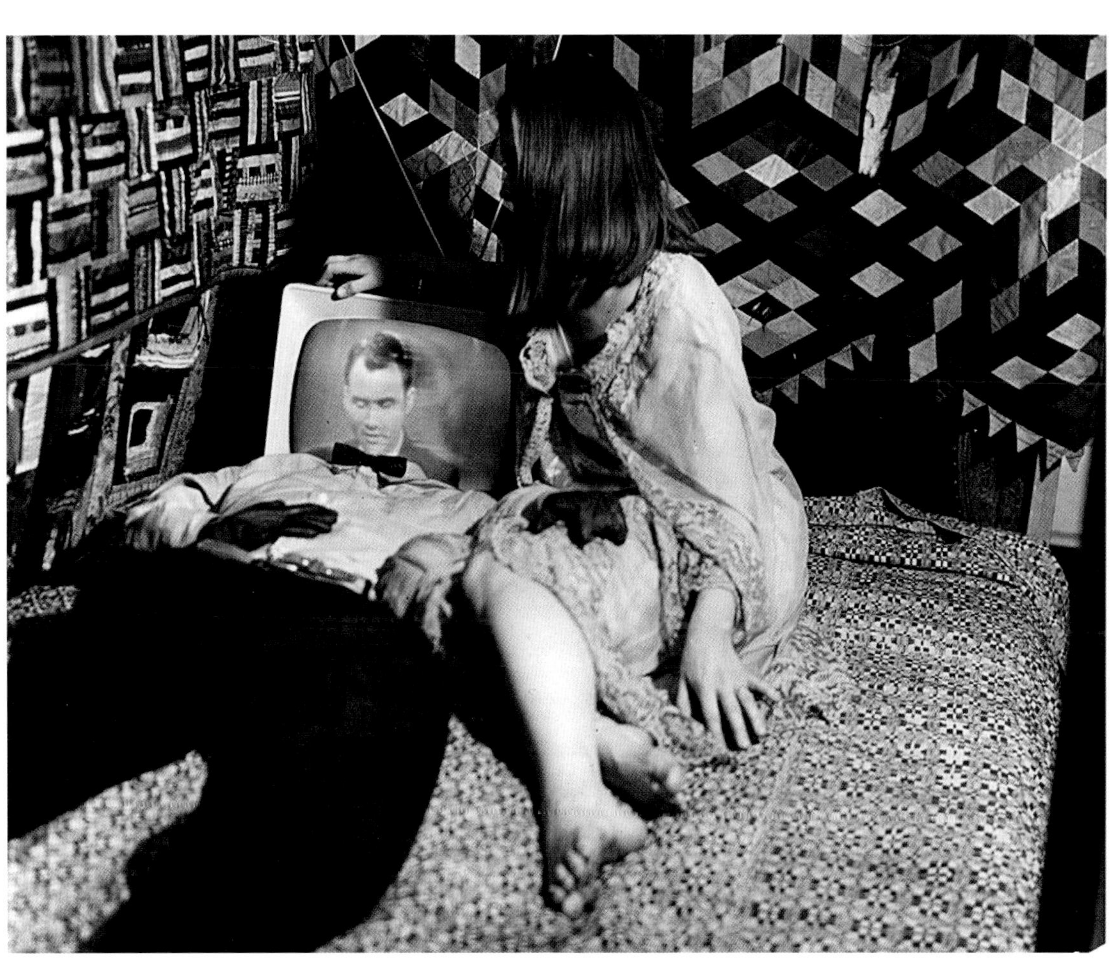

WHEEEEELS

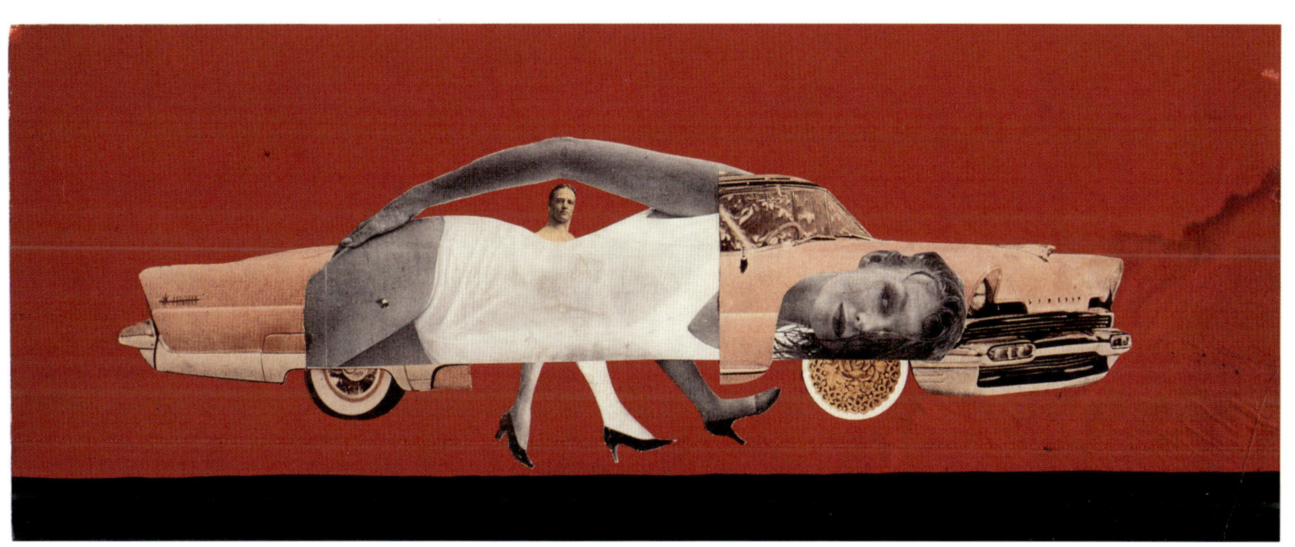

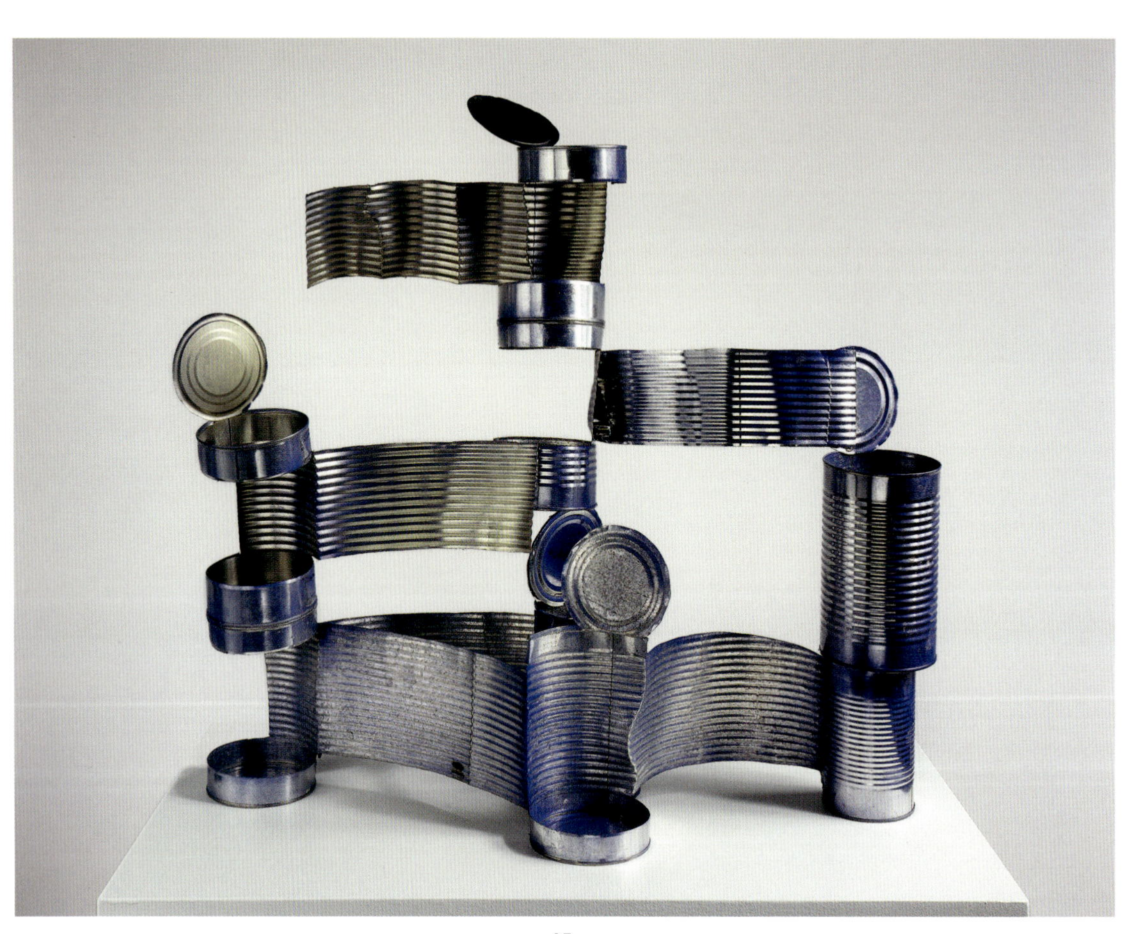

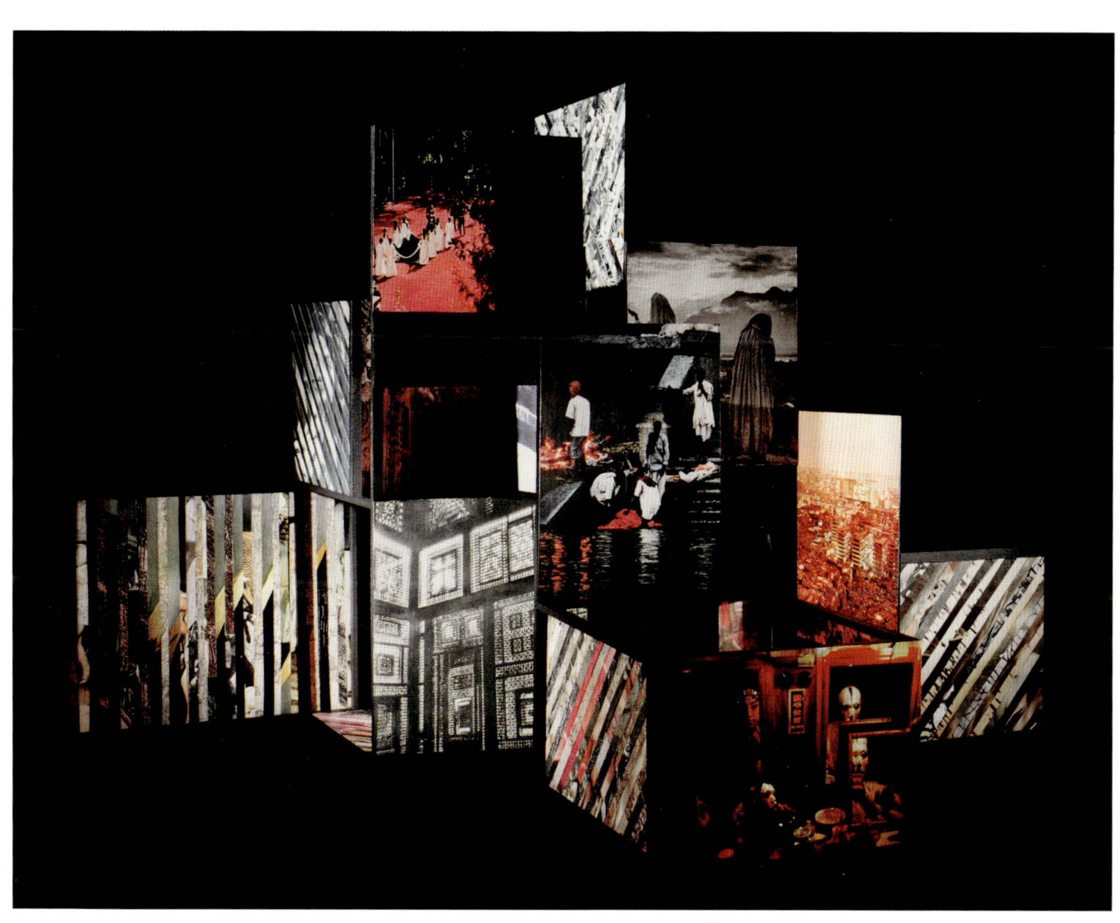

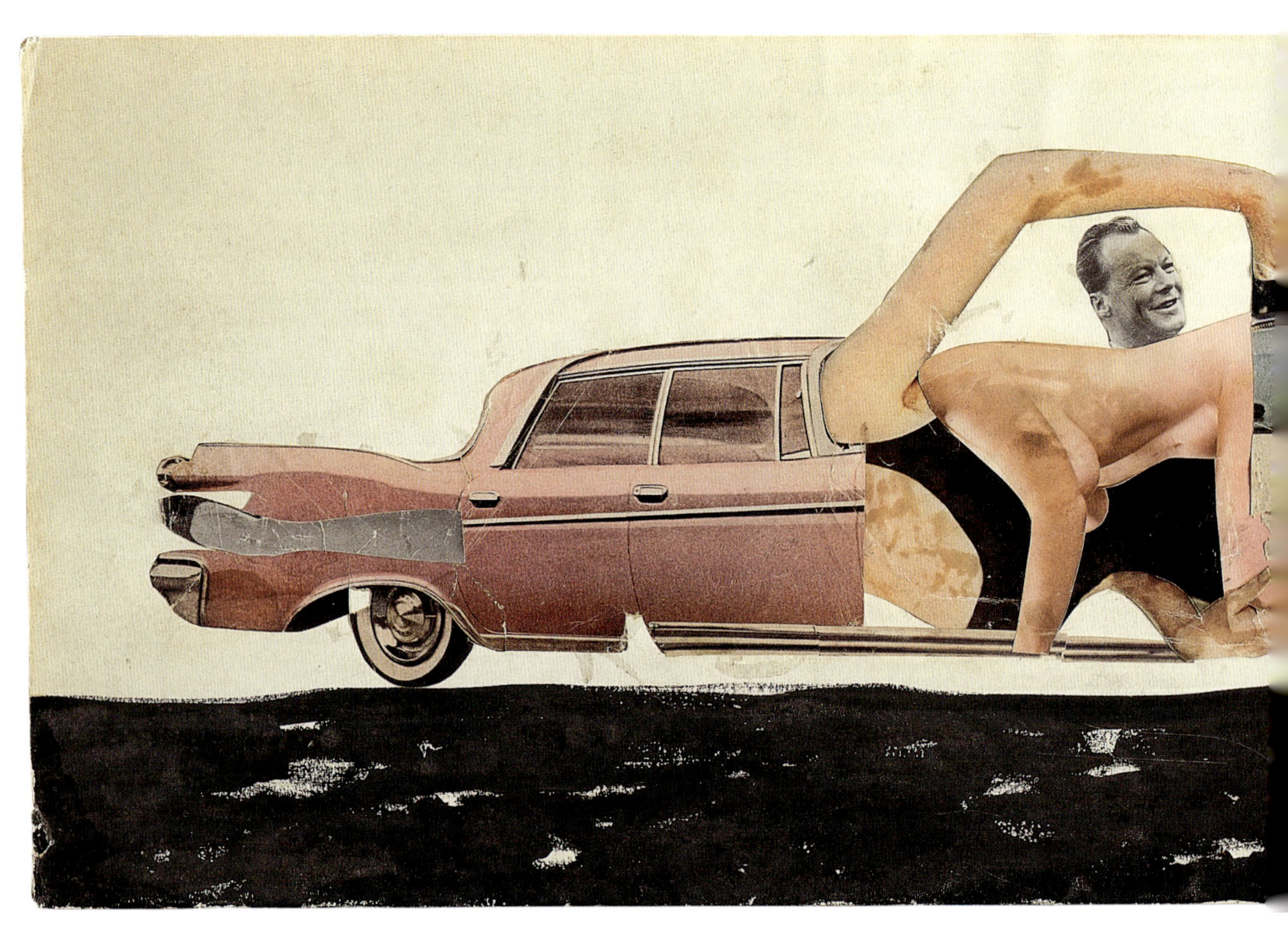

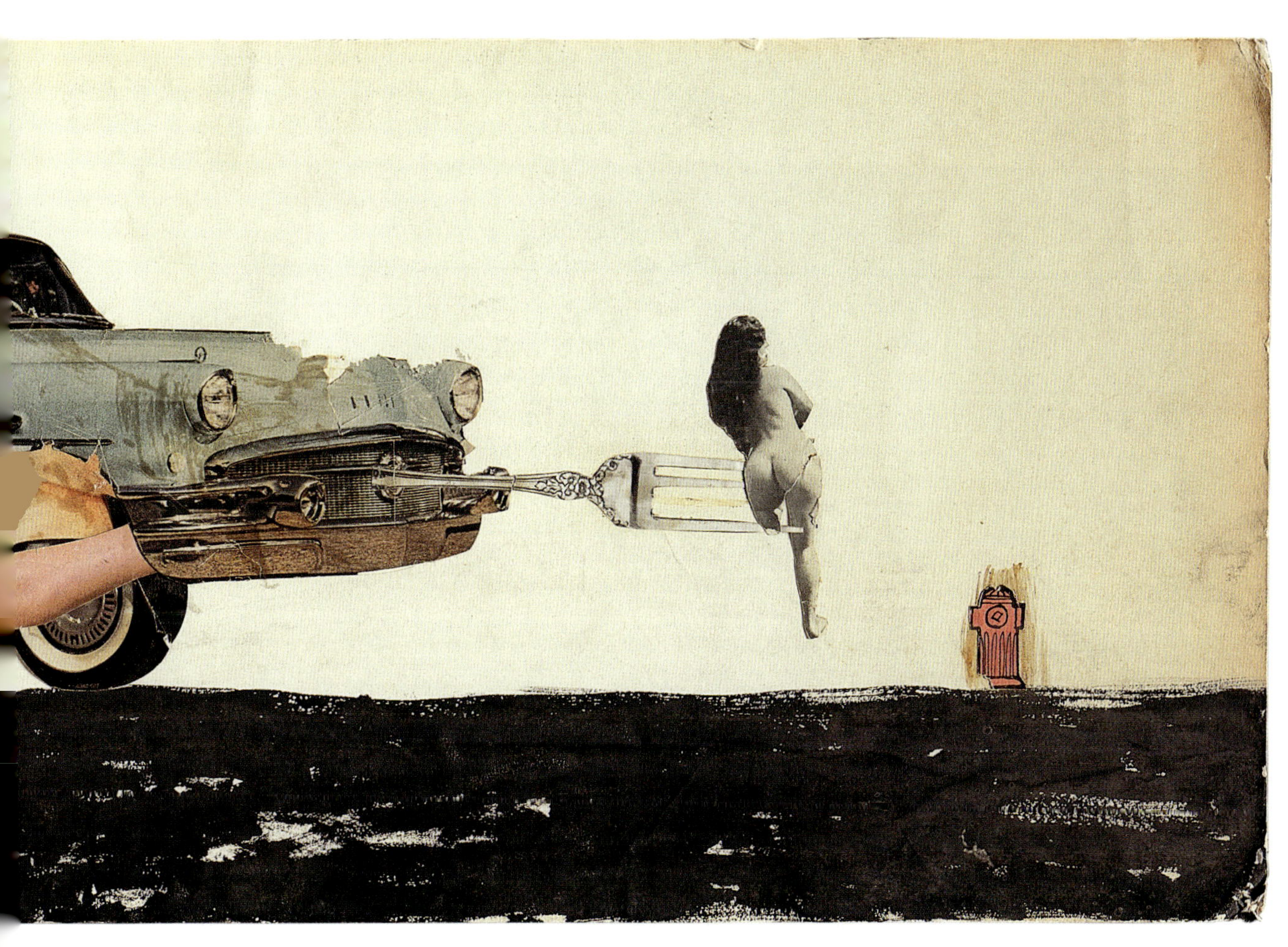

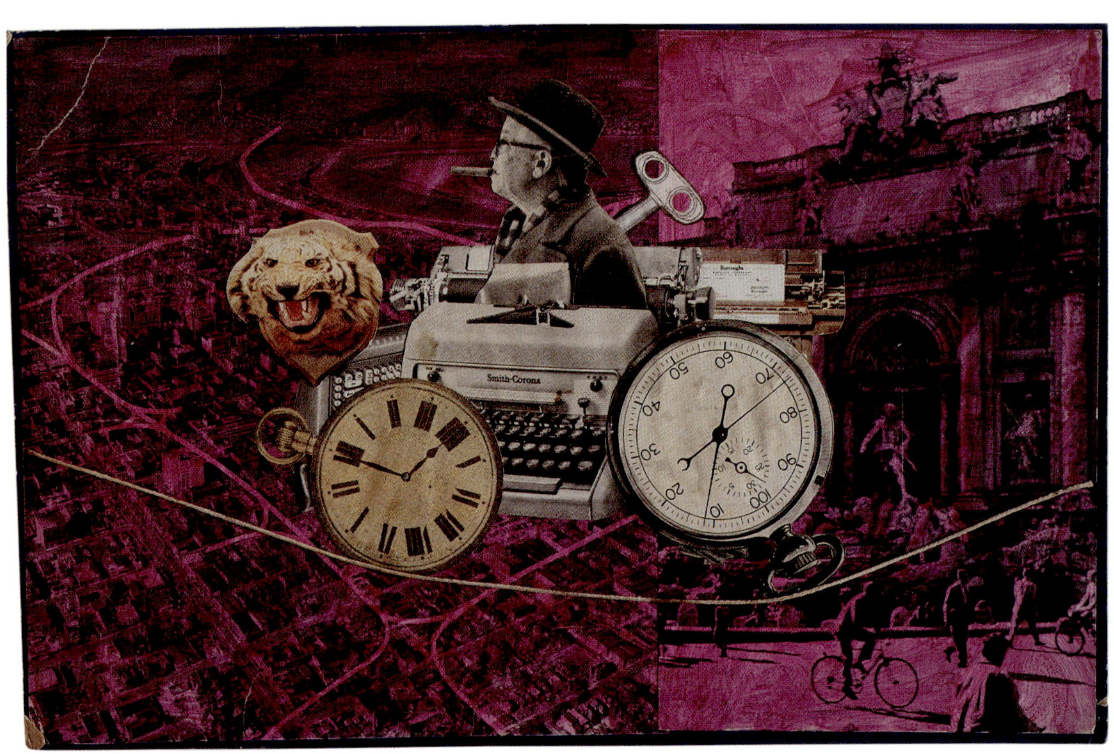
Smith-Corona

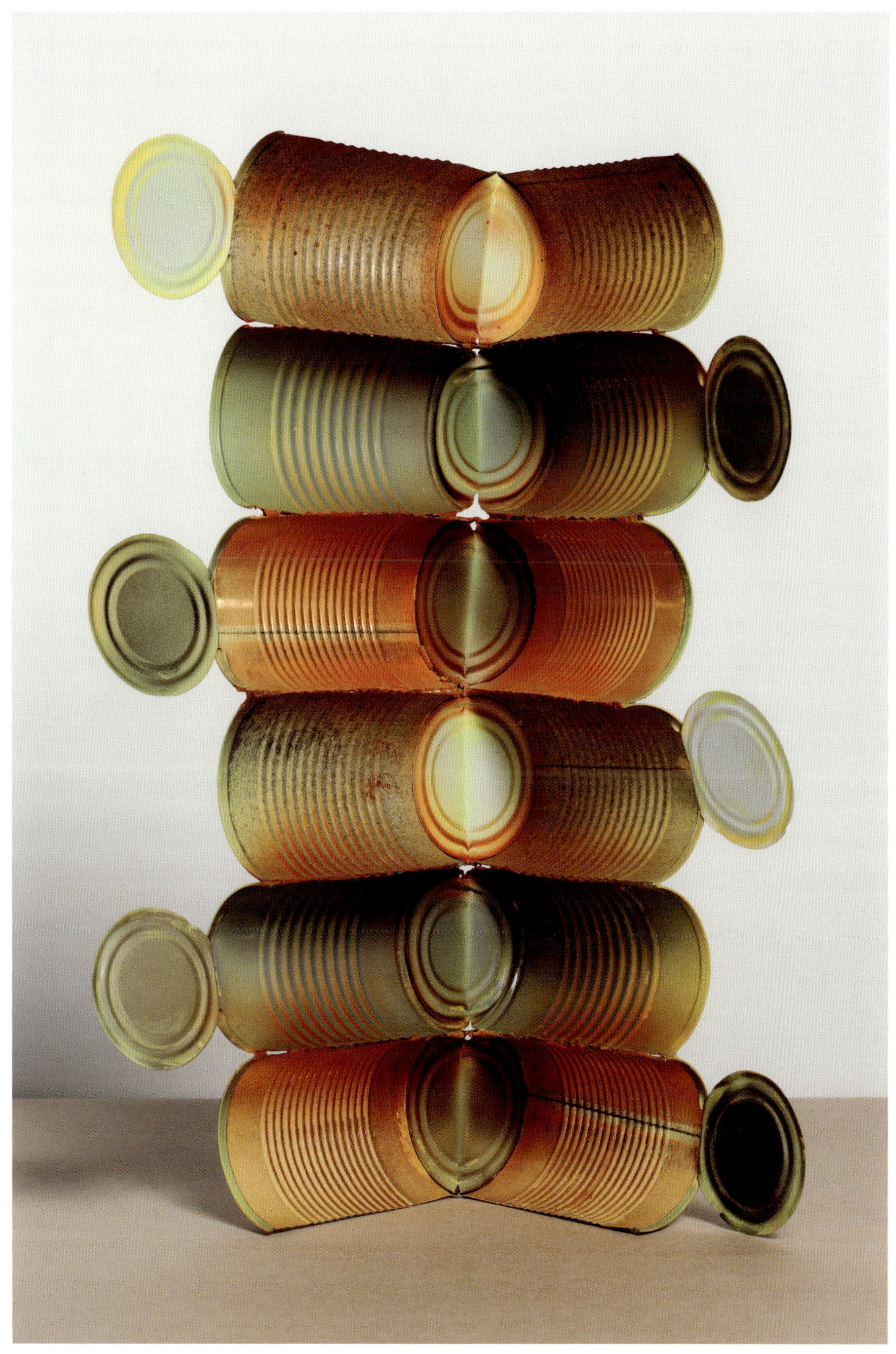

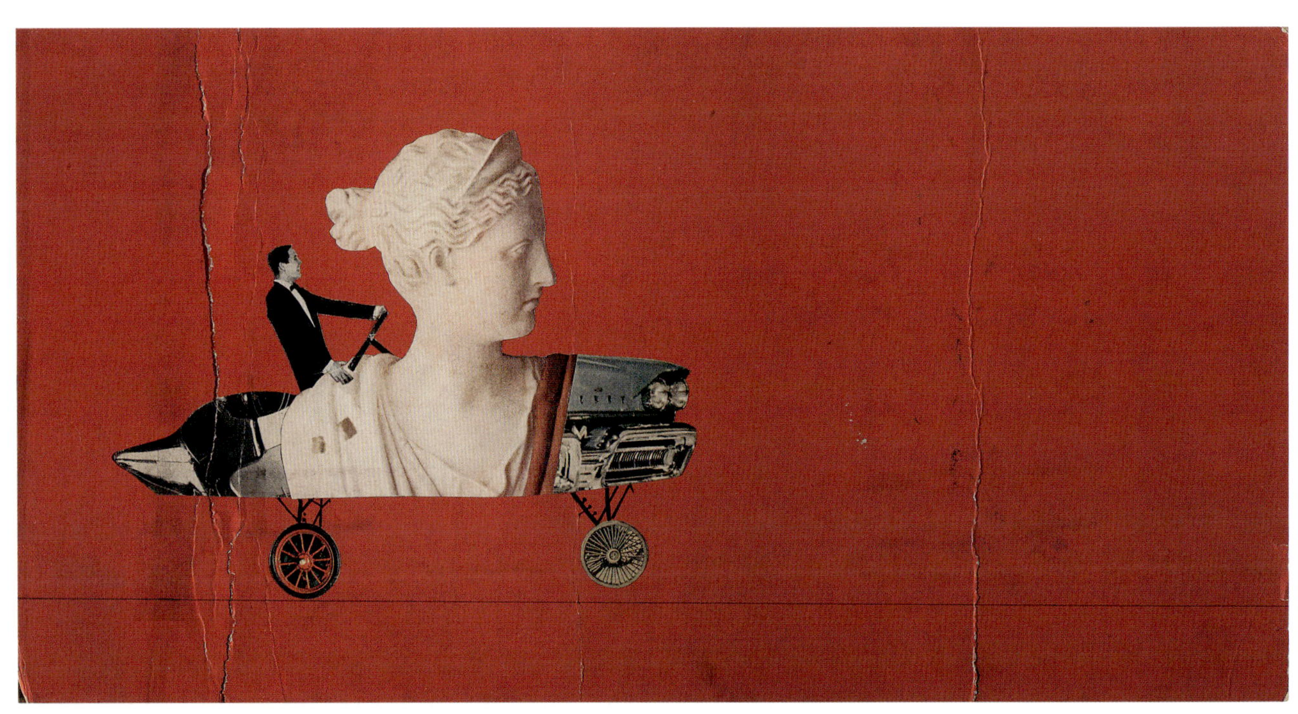

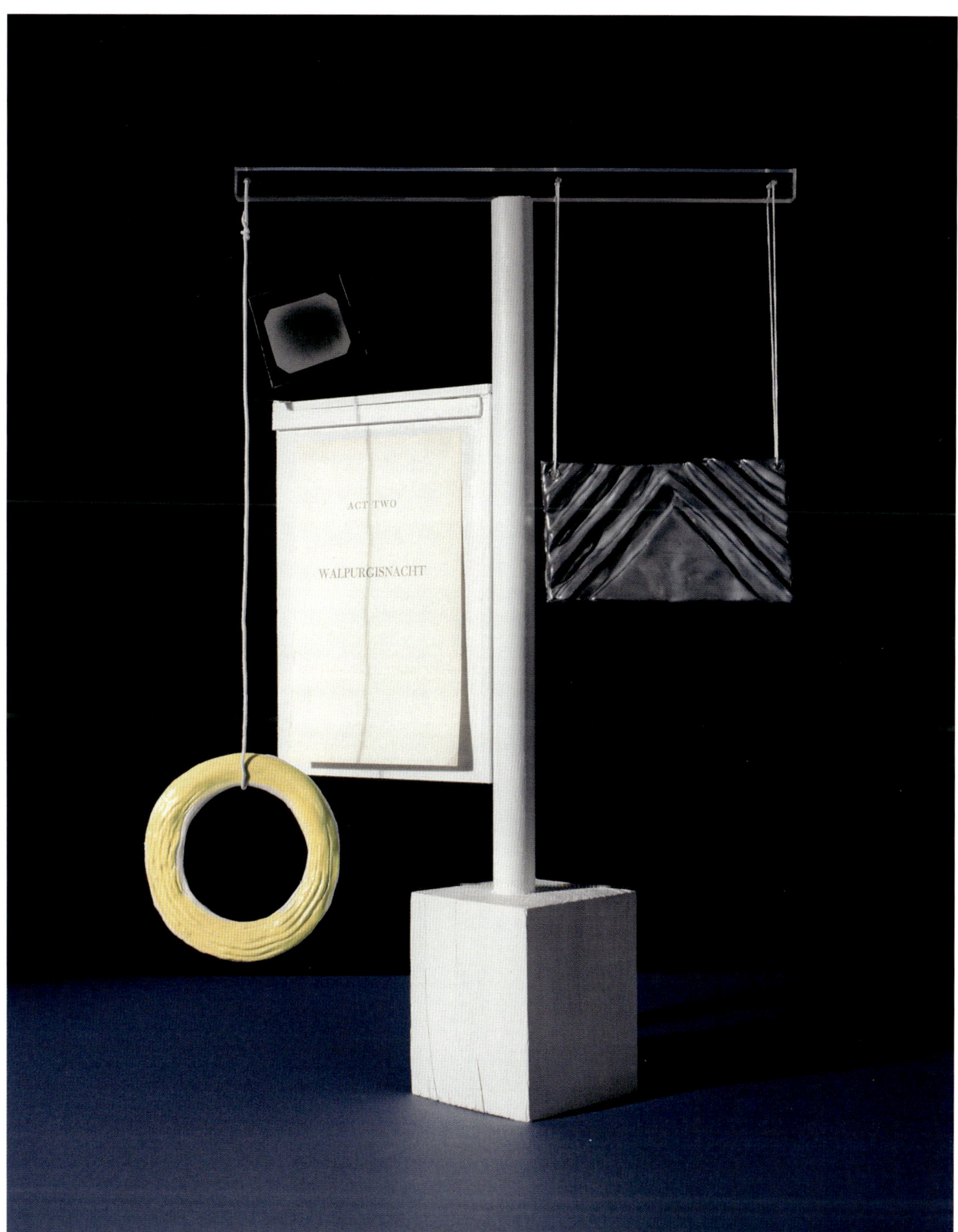
ACT TWO
WALPURGISNACHT

WHEEEEELS

IB: We crafted a more playful installation this month that features collages your dad made for a film called *Wheeeeels*. Each one shows a different contraption made of mixed-up body parts and car parts. Mechanical action is at play here. Do you think of Stan as an inventor?

SVDB: Yes. He held several patents and was constantly inventing things in order to make his work. He designed and built his home in Stony Point, and towards the end of his life he mentions building an Imax camera.

JVDB: It's fair to consider him an inventor, but with certain disclaimers like "Do not sit on a chair he invented because it might turn you into a floor." It was said he couldn't be trusted with a hammer when it came to traditional building endeavors but that only highlights that he had his own way of doing things, which is more important. What he lacked in factual understanding he made up for in empirical zeal. He had a great deal of insight into the potential of things, both mechanically and aesthetically, and he could propel the purpose of a device or form through a leap of creativity. He wrote in one of his early drawings, "Leap Before You Look," a sentiment that I'm sure landed him in a tangle of wires and duct tape but also led to daring visions. I appreciate that instinct because in order for invention to occur on any level you need to have a combination of technical knowledge and the spirit to go beyond predetermined limits. He is truest to the spirit of an inventor in that way, because he never stopped concerning himself with the future. He was simultaneously worried and in awe of the path ahead. He also realized that the best solutions come through the collaboration of dynamic people. He made sure to work with individuals with better technical understanding, but he provided them with a sense of unbound curiosity.

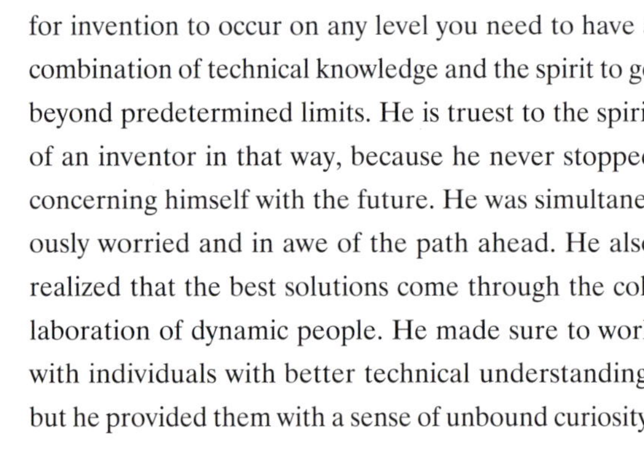

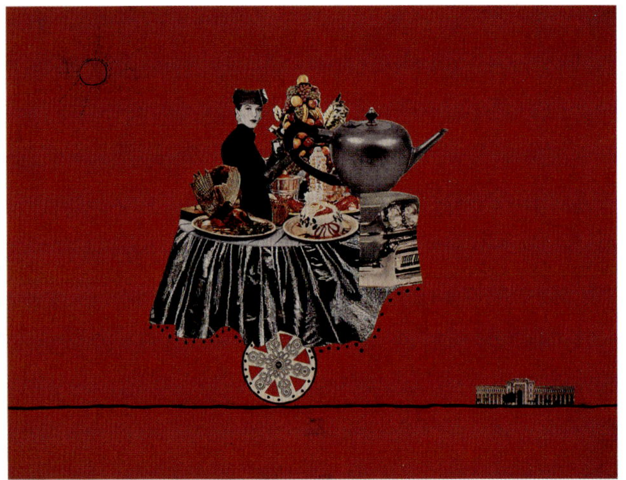

34

IB: How do you think your works intersect with his?

SVDB: In many ways, but the use of images is probably

the most obvious. I share his great ambitions for art to communicate beyond the gallery wall, for it to become an implement for social change and a universal connection amongst all people. I want my work to be effective within an exhibition space, but I would also like to consider how it could engage with the concerns of our larger society. Though I work within conventional modes of presentation, and my work doesn't lead me to the mass media venues that my father was continually trying to use, effect or disrupt, I share his interest and desire to understand and interpret media. He dreamed of sky projections and would probably be bored and disappointed that home computers screens weren't holographic already—suffice to say he thought and worked large. I hope my work as it functions within a more personal scale and space encourages viewers to consider what it means to observe, capture, and convey meaning, through images. And then they can move out from there to consider the role of images within the expansive and ever-evolving visual environment in which we live.

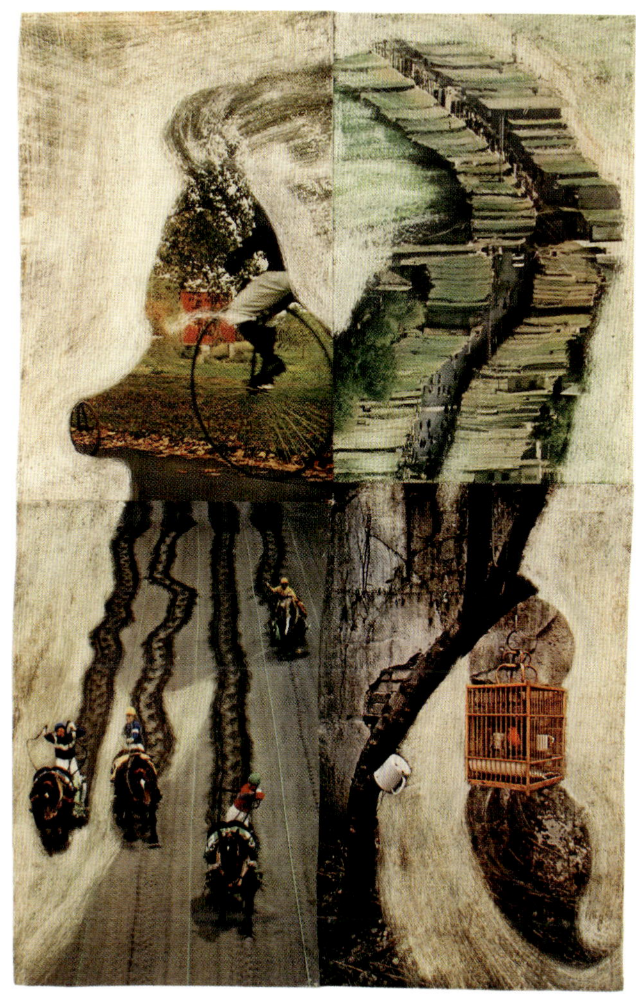

35

I realize it's a lot to ask of the viewer. Other artists and individuals who are able to achieve these goals are always an inspiration, my father being a primary figurehead in this pantheon. He is a like a totem or a shaman. Imagine a combination of both with a mustache, wearing striped shirts wielding a Bolex, a Sharpee, duct tape, and a notebook and you'll have a good sense of my inner vision of him.

With his work with the Movie-Drome, Expanded Cinema, and WGBH-TV in Boston, he was attempting to directly influence the masses. He was aiming for a direct engagement with a large public audience, and he sought to encourage a dialogue among them that would then extend back to him. He had a lot of interactive elements in his work, such as in *Violence Sonata* (1969–70), where viewers were asked to call into the station with their responses to his programming.

My first middle name is NEA—he gave it to me after he missed a very important meeting of the National Endowment for the Arts because of my birth. My role in co-founding Guild & Greyshkul, an artist-run gallery that operated in New York from 2003 to 2009, grew out of my desires to be active outside of my practice and engage in the larger community, as he so frequently did.

IB: In what ways has he influenced you, Johannes?

JVDB: Well, unfortunately or fortunately (depending on your perspective), I inherited his ad hoc sense of physics and his dreamer mentality of assessing time and gravity as always being on your side. Sometimes you think your spirit is invisible glue and that asserting your pure belief about a matter binds it to abide by your will. People like us are not always willing to accept that larger motions are at play, and very real factors such as money, space, and politics are also part of the dream. Despite leading to occasional misjudgments, seeing through a distorted lens can make reality seem truly bendable. Since reality is so expansive, I try to have my work recognize its breadth. It can be maddening to confront your insufficiency, but the struggle of wrestling with an expansive reality can at least make a compelling story. I sense that Dad also spent his life looking for new methods to capture the expansion of our existence. He continued to experiment with new forms throughout his entire life and, unlike many artists of his generation, he never settled on a single medium. That urge to push forward through experimentation is inspiring. I struggle to find the right forms and material to express ideas, and I feel eager to move onto new approaches rather than stew over old ones, sometimes to a detrimental degree. I often rely on my hands to get out of a mental rut. I believe he and I share a similar conviction toward the human hand as the ultimate tool. It is inevitable that we share certain formal relationships, such as the way we articulate lines or construct shapes, because those aspects come from the hand. The hand is the receptor of intuition and logic guided through instinct. Instinct flows through the fiber of our being, and since I come from his being, our instincts are bound to be similar.

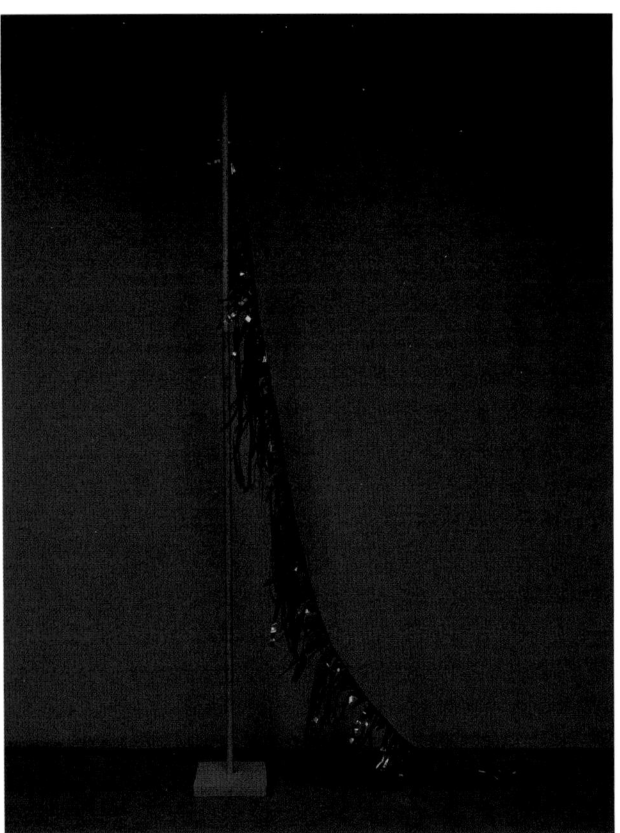

36

SVDB: I frequently draw inspiration from artists' works of earlier generations, and I think this reverence for artists and artworks of the past grows out of my relationship to my father's work. I am very interested in art movements of the nineteenth and twentieth centuries, such as the Bauhaus and its development in Europe, and its movement across to America during and after World War II. At the core of these movements were driven individuals who were idealistic about a total way of living and truly felt their principles and discipline could change the world. Facing the adversity of rising fascism in Europe, they dreamed of utopias.

A Depression-era baby, and first generation son of two immigrants, my father was very much like these enterprising individuals, always resourceful and always having to figure out how to create his ambitious projects with very little means and no commercial support. As an active member of the postwar New York art scene, he has always been a great conduit for me to this generative and influential time. The artists that he met while at Black Mountain and in New York are some of the most influential to my practice, such as Ray Johnson and Robert Rauschenberg. The Cooper Union, the art school that all three of us attended, was based on a Bauhaus model, and I liked that training and approach to art education. But like my father, I am interested in where art education and therefore art could go in the future if we move away from historical and Modernist approaches.

My father was a great collagist. His early films are made of collages. His multi-projection and multi-screen works are incredible immersive moving collages. I return often to my deep want to speak to him when I am building one of my pieces or planning a show. I would be interested to see what he would think about everything happening in contemporary art and life. He was simultaneously a great believer and a great skeptic of technology and I would be so curious to see what he thought of the Internet and the significant place computers have taken within our lives. When I look at my computer screen covered with different images I'm working on, jpegs I'm sending, the multiple open documents and web pages, I think of his multi-screen pieces and how prescient he was—they are the visual precursor to the way we live and work now. In the end, if I had to choose his most important influence upon me (and I hope upon others), it is that because of him I look at things differently. His astute eye and deft combination of images has helped shape my way of seeing.

Wheeeeels captions

26 Stan VanDerBeek, *Untitled (from Wheeeeels)*, 1959, collage and ink on paper, 8 ¾ × 21 ⅞ inches
27 Johannes VanDerBeek, *Blue Cans*, 2009, tin cans, acrylic, and epoxy, 26 ¼ × 27 ¼ × 13 ½ inches
28 Sara VanDerBeek, *The Principle of Superimposition*, 2007, digital C-print, 30 ⅝ × 40 inches
29 Stan VanDerBeek, *Untitled (from Wheeeeels)*, 1959, collage and ink on paper, 9 ⅞ × 29 ⅞ inches
30 Stan VanDerBeek, *Untitled (from Science Friction)*, 1959, collage, paint, and string on paperboard, 9 ½ × 14 ¾ inches
31 Johannes VanDerBeek, *Sun Split*, 2010, acrylic and epoxy on tin cans, 18 ½ × 12 × 7 inches
32 Stan VanDerBeek, *Untitled (from Wheeeeels)*, 1959, collage on paper, 10 ⅛ × 20 inches
33 Sara VanDerBeek, *Walpurgisnacht*, 2007, digital C-print, 20 × 16 inches
34 Stan VanDerBeek, *Untitled (from Wheeeeels)*, 1959, collage on paper, 11 ⅝ × 15 ⅜ inches
35 Johannes VanDerBeek, *Untitled (God Head)*, 2007, sanded magazine pages, 19 ½ × 12 ½ inches. Private Collection
36 Sara VanDerBeek, *Streamers*, 2010, digital C-print, 60 × 45 ½ inches

SUPERIMPOSITION

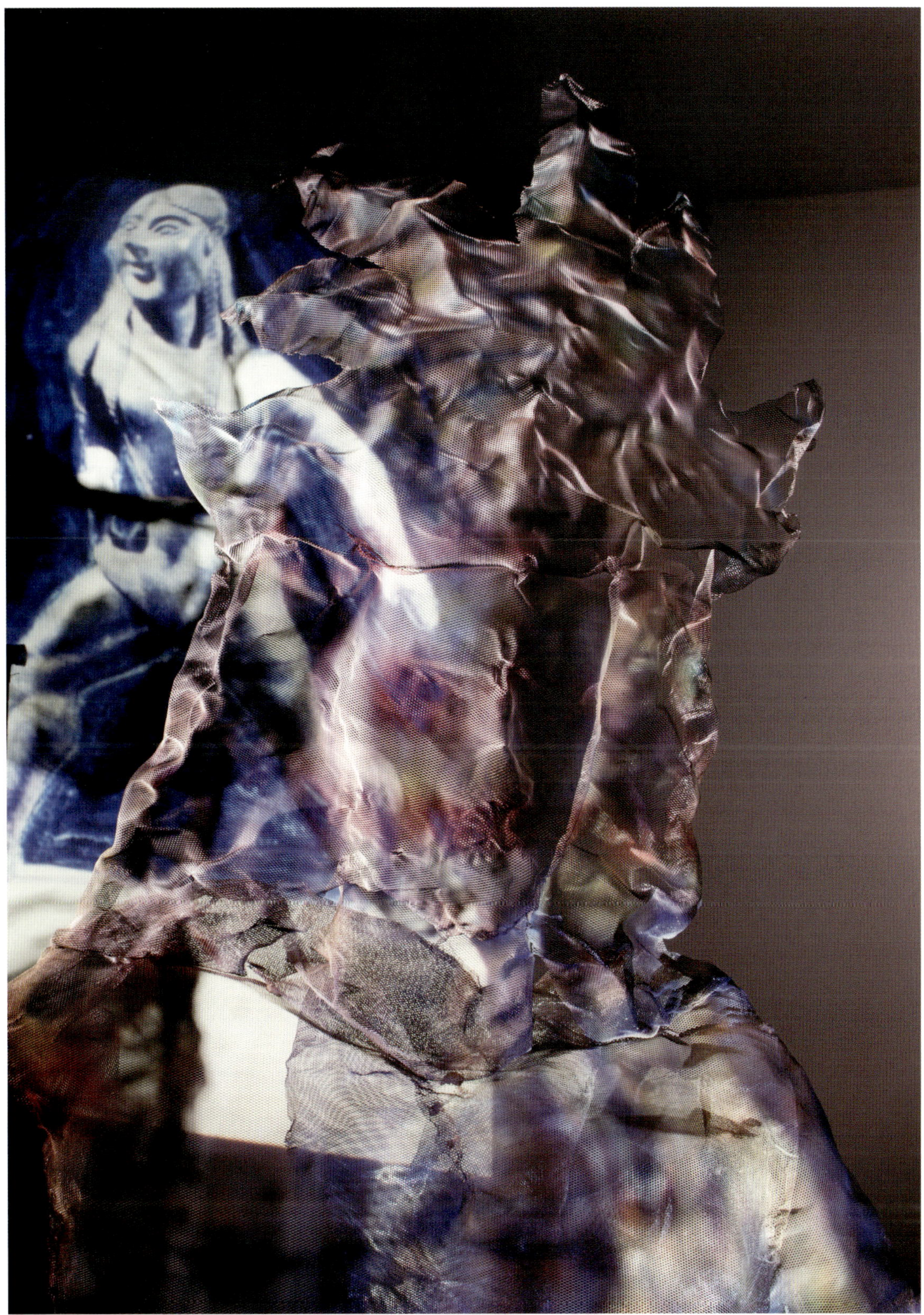

37, 38 (following)

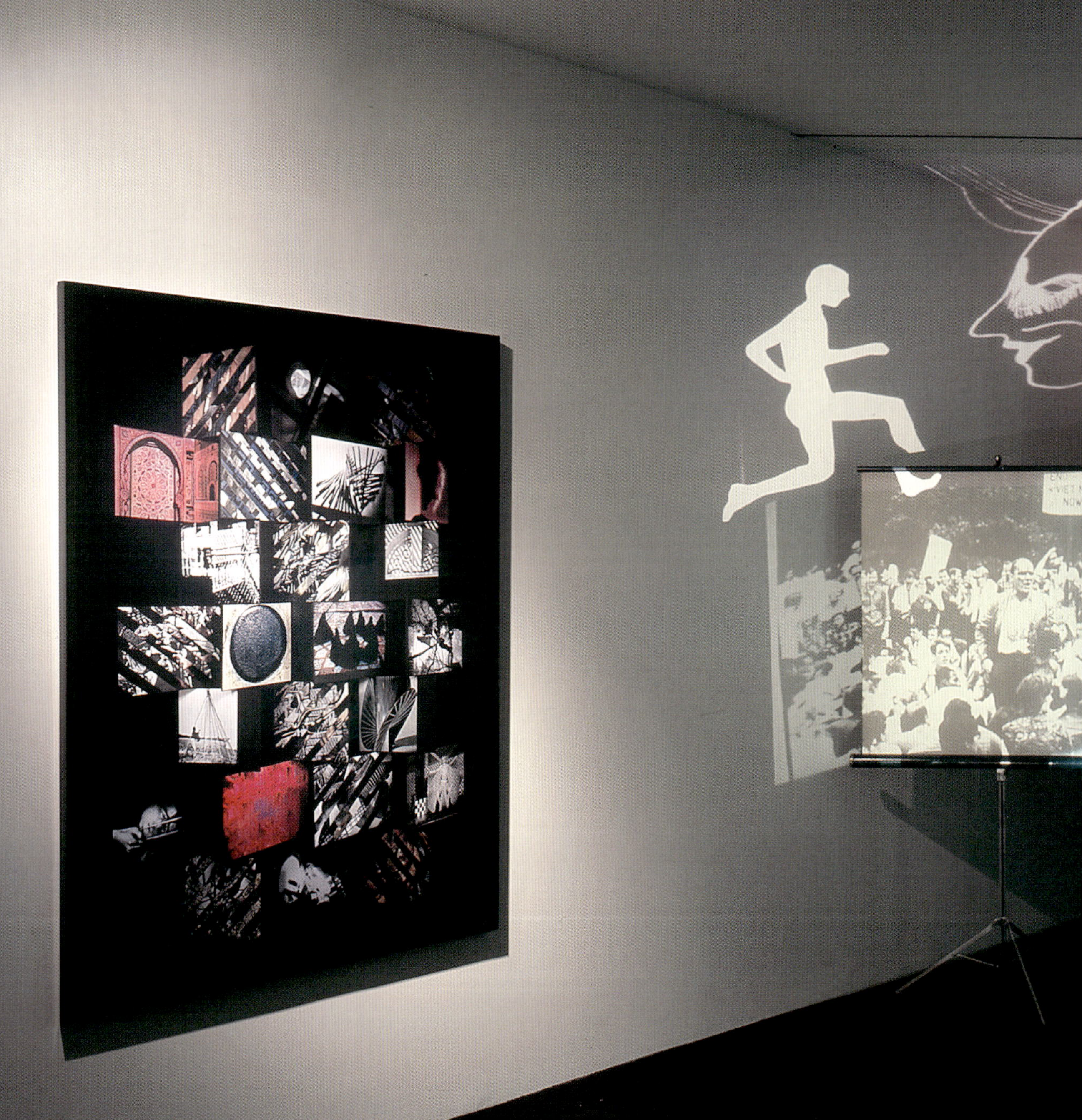
NOW

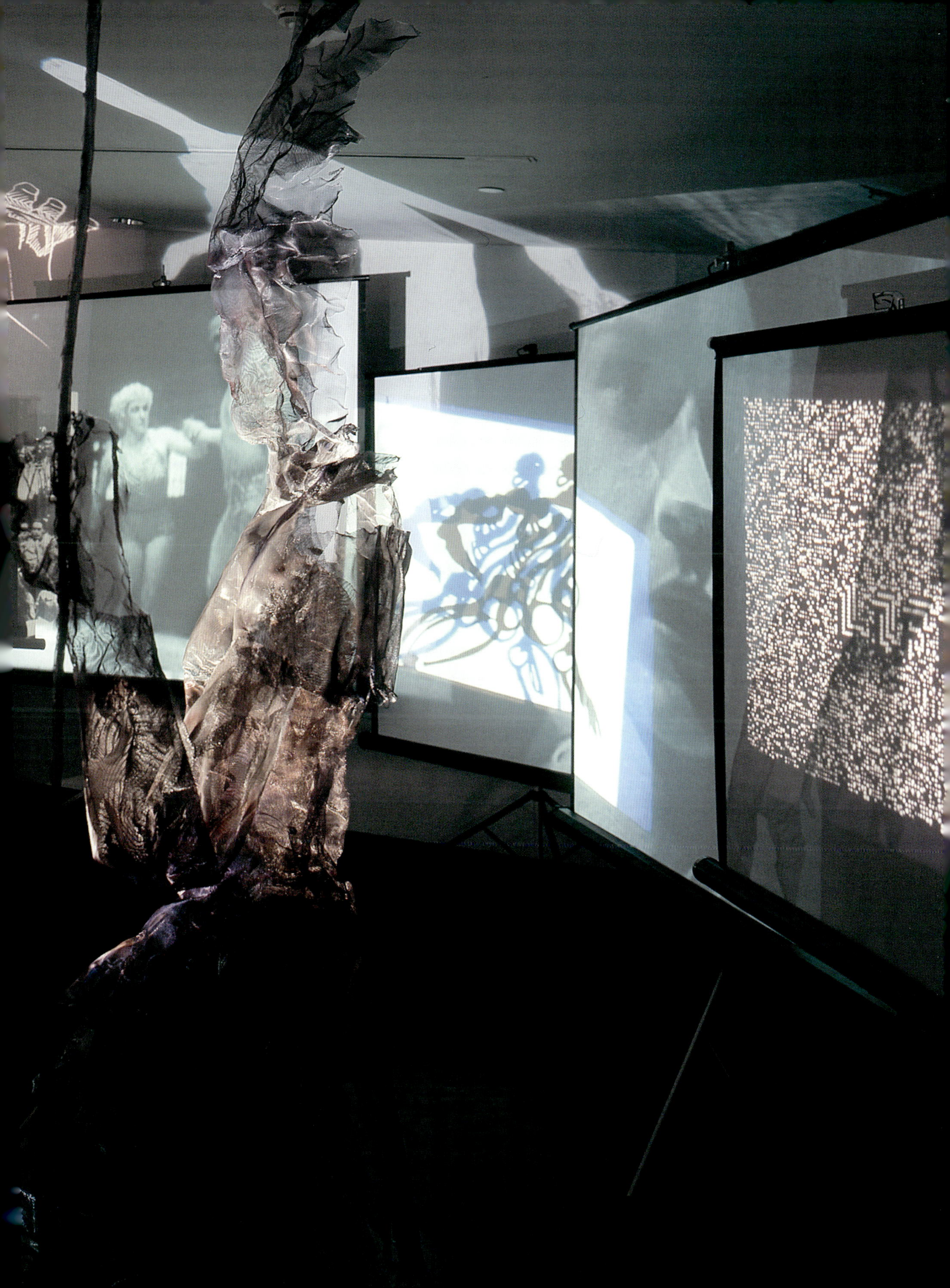

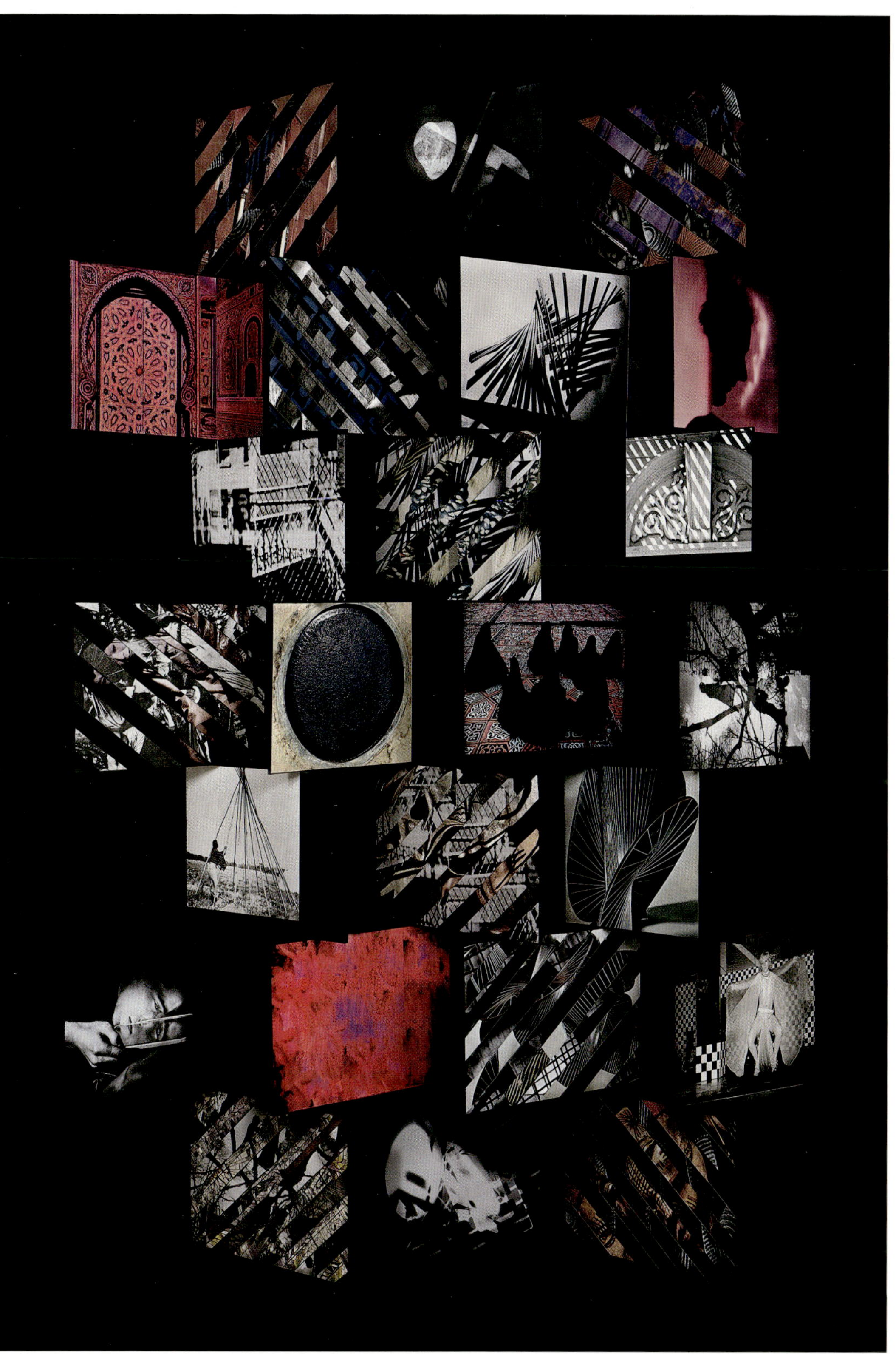

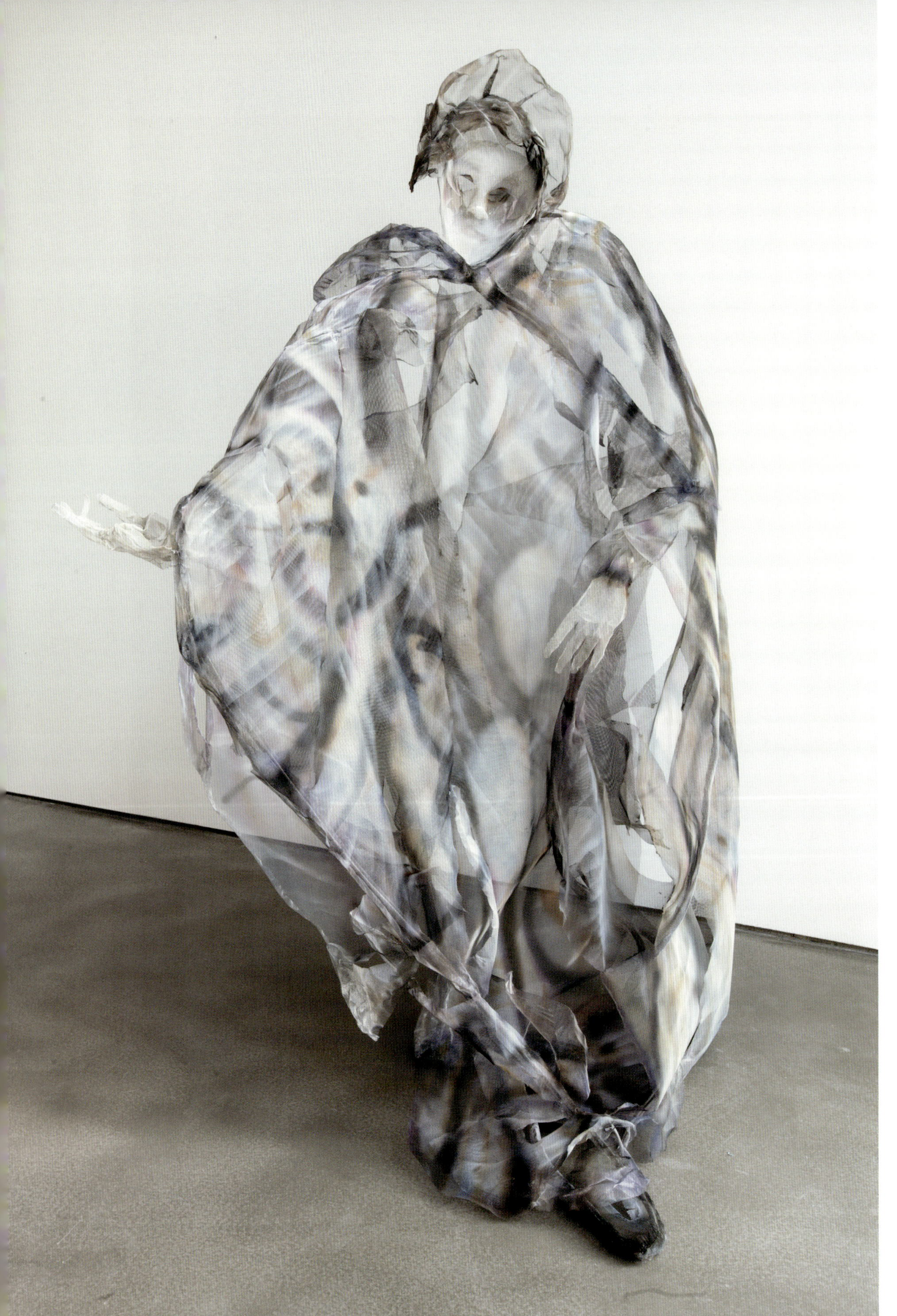

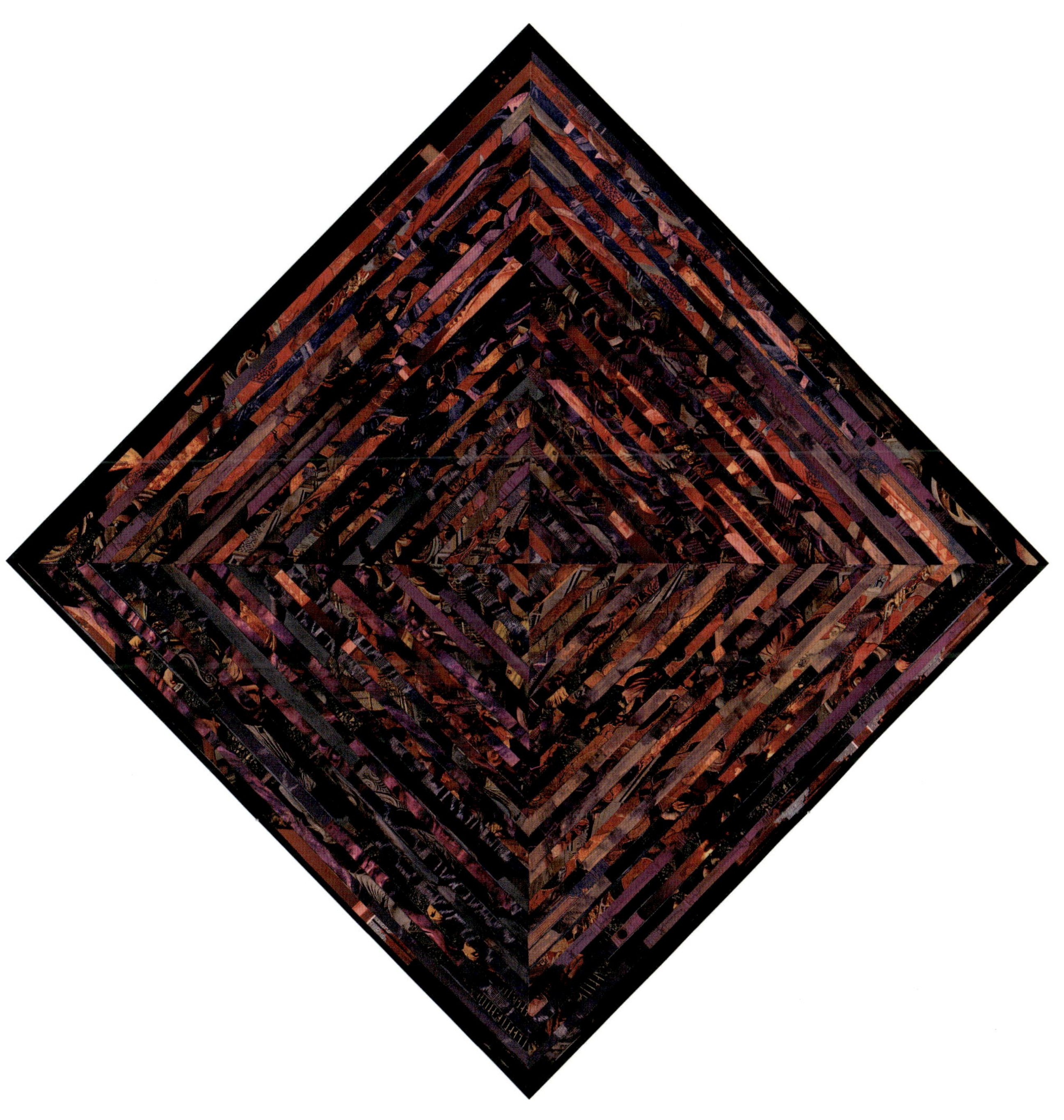

SUPERIMPOSITION

IB: Images are an important part of all your works. This month we foreground images and the layering that you each employ. Johannes, can you talk about how you developed the image of the *Indian Ghost*?

JVDB: I found the source image on the internet after doing a general search for Native Americans. The sculpture is not very close to the original but both are standing on one leg. I have always been drawn to Native American stories. I like their ways of looking at the world, its creation and flow. Their version of formalism is anchored in direct meaning through spiritual practice, and no color or shape is used aimlessly. Each aspect of their art and ceremony is grounded in a story that, in turn, is grounded in a mythology. It's a haunting fact that they created an alternate reality, then were simply overtaken by aggression and nearly made to vanish due to greed. Perhaps because they are still here but treated like phantom people, it seemed appropriate to make a ghost sculpture from the image of a proud figure staring outward. A lot of psychological charge results when people peer into an invisible vessel.

IB: Sara, can you talk about the individual images in your photograph? Where did you find them? How did you construct this work?

SVDB: For *The Principle of Superimposition II*, I created a large freestanding screen structure comprising twenty-four image panels. Its design is inspired by Eileen Gray's work. The layering of collage throughout the structure presents multiple perspectives at once—I wanted to get a sense of simultaneity and movement within a still image.

For one panel, I spliced an image of a fifteenth-century Chinese ceramic vessel adorned with a simple geometric pattern reminiscent of modernist design into a Leni Riefenstahl photograph of a Kau man painting his face in an equally graphic manner. The photogram images, as well as a few others throughout the structure, come from László Moholy Nagy's book *Vision in Motion*. The woman in profile against the pink background is a detail of a 1950 Erwin Blumenfeld fashion photograph. The black-and-white image in the third row down, far left, is a still from a Stan Brakhage film commissioned by Joseph Cornell—he asked

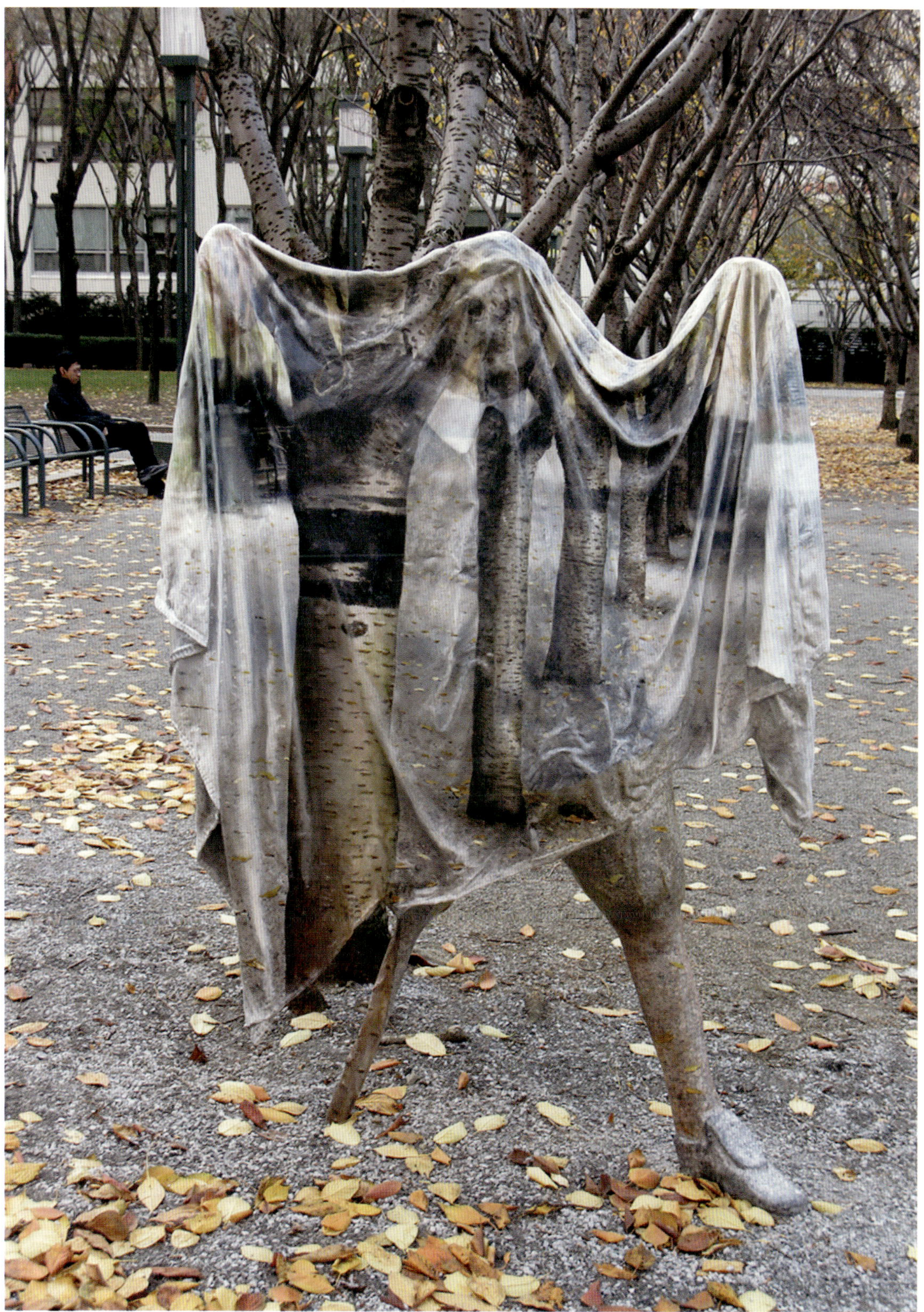

Brakhage to create a film about the last elevated train in Manhattan, which ran along the Bowery.

The geometric patterns spliced into several panels come from a book of images of ancient Chinese ceramic vessels, as well as enlargements of images of African masks photographed by Walker Evans, when MoMA organized an exhibition on African Art in 1936.

The image of the women in the black burkas on the patterned carpet is from a *Time/Life* book on photography. It was more a technical guide but I was drawn to the contrast of the dark figures against the bright color and pattern and to the contemporary quality of the image. The image in the fifth row down, to the right, is of an Antoine Pevsner sculpture that was taken from a book called *The Dimensions of the 20th Century*, which in its design and language spoke to my thinking behind this piece.

IB: There are hundreds of different images in Stan's installation. Can you describe the elements in this display?

SVDB: This particular piece is based on his *Movie Mural* presentation and the show he did at the School of Visual Arts that was called, *Panels for the Walls of the World*. *Movie Mural*'s original date of creation was 1968/69. This staging included two 16mm film transfers to DVD: *Panels for the Walls of the World* (1967, 7:57 min) and *Super-Imposition* (1968, 30:30 min): six 35mm slide projectors, including single still slide projections; individual computer-generated images; and a drawing taken from a series of drawn images by him entitled *You Do, I Do, We Do*.

Also included is a carousel of computer generated imagery on slides, a carousel of mixed Art History slides, a carousel of Edweard Muybridge cutout figures, and a carousel of graphic black and white historical images, including Martin Luther King, Lyndon B. Johnson, Viet Cong soldiers, etc.

IB: Do you know how many of these were actually put together at one time by your dad? Where did he find his images?

JVDB: I know he would ask people to send him any slides or pictures they had lying around. He was a scavenger who frequented flea markets, yard sales, or companies going out of business to amass a personal library of stock imagery. He would also make his own slides, make drawings on overhead projectors, or incorporate films he had made, creating a dense layering of public content with his own imagery. He was trying to build a ubiquitous image bank that charted the entire progress of humanity from the Egyptians to the Hippies. The sequence was not chronological, but instead a mosaic of our past that showed continuity and division through visual information rather than words.

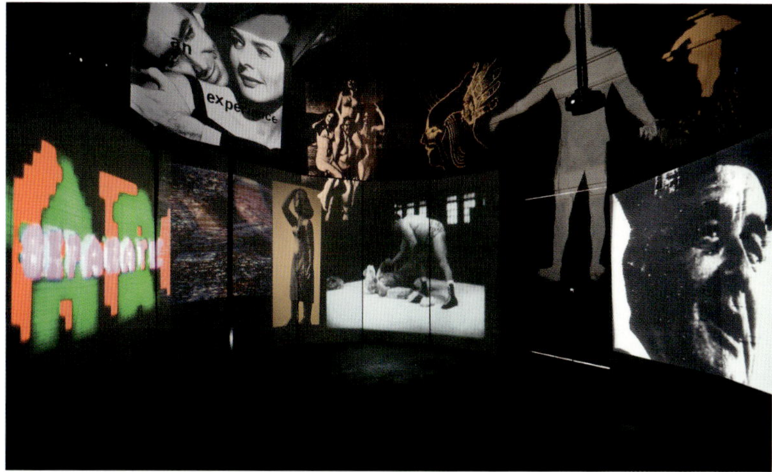

43

SVDB: For every multi-image performance he recombined the images in different ways so it was an ongoing moving collage that shifted and changed per situation. The images we have chosen are based on photographs documenting several different installations he did throughout the 1960s. The best known and most heavily layered of these was the Movie-Drome. He worked on this project for several years and always viewed it as a prototype for Movie-Dromes he envisioned around the world—the imagery would be beamed in via satellite and video rather than via the projectors he was using at the time, and it would be universal but also locally specific, reflecting issues of the community where each dome was located. His manifesto *Culture Intercom* speaks about his desire for the establishment of a universal visual language and about his plans for the dome. These installations represent his experimentation and desire to expand the filmic experience beyond that of a singular theatrical presentation. They are immersive, cacophonous and remarkable in the many narratives and thoughts they initiate, or rather instigate, in their constant combining of images. He was often given slides, or films or projectors, and also put a call out for anything that was image or sound-related for the dome in 1965 when he was nearing its completion.

IB: Sara, when you layer images, what are you hoping will happen? Are you interested in those individual source images remaining legible? Or do you focus on the new image created with these found patterns? Near the top of your photograph there are some striped images, not unlike partially seeing the images in Stan's work, or the Johannes figure that we see flickering in and out of focus. What do you gain by only partially seeing something?

SVDB: Like frames in a film, if you were to look at the strip itself rather than the projected image, my work implies a sense of movement, yet each image is static and still. In my series and multipart works, the memory of one image follows to the next. The placement of images and repetition of forms (such as circle, square, and rectangle) within the photographs move the viewer through the work and around the room. Through the use of collage, I want the works to have a feeling of filmic movement, like images fading from one into the next as in a dissolve.

The individual images in Edward Steichen's *Family of Man* exhibition, as well as the overall design, were things I kept returning to and looking at while making *The Principle of Superimposition* works. I also watched and thought about my father's film *The Human Face is a Monument* while making several of my pieces, like *Faces* and *Delaunay*. In New York, I am constantly stimulated by a world of images, and as I travel through the city I mentally gather fleeting glimpses, fragments of faces, texts, objects, situations, and patterns. The scale and construction of the *Superimposition* works, with the images spliced and fragmented and then assembled into larger patterns, are intended to feel like environments unto themselves.

I think a great deal about the process of looking at a photographic image. Viewing an image of something can affect your understanding of scale, your sense of time, and, as a result, memory.

IB: Johannes, you literally put a semi-transparent sculpture in front of your dad's projections. This makes for some amazing combinations and distortions as we see his images through yours, and see your sculpture on his projections. The wire mesh seems to mimic pixels, or ben-day printing dots. Is your figure a kind of screen for projection?

JVDB: Yes, I wanted to see if a three-dimensional object could appear more like a projection or hologram. I knew the room would be filled with beamed light, so rather than have an object block the light, I thought a form that light could move through would interrelate more strangely and almost become a solid illusion. I anticipated that the images projected on the figure would have a weird effect, but I was happily surprised by how much the images compressed into one another and made a fluid field between actual surface and projected surface. Even without the projections, these ghost sculptures are very hard to see because the painted metal mesh fluctuates in color and density as you move around it. I try to enhance this aspect by painting them like afterimages—when light burned onto the retina leaves a brief impression. The dots of color are scattered and fleeting and the hues shift in and out of balance, much like an inner sight. I call them ghost sculptures mostly because I see them as a lasting image from another time period.

IB: What does superimposition mean to you and how do you use it?

SVDB: Superimposition occurs when one element rests in front of the other. I interpret it as layering, or combining images, and making the transitive moment concrete. In my work the space created by superimposition is very shallow, like a filmic space.

JVDB: I consider a superimposition to be a composition that shows the direct overlap between two distinct periods of time. Whether the separation is only a matter of seconds or two millenniums, in order for a superimposition to occur two or more moments need to be conflated. The notion of a superimposition does not seem fathomable without the advent of photography and film, which capture time more crisply than any other medium. But when I started thinking about a real-life instance of superimposition, my thoughts drifted toward ghosts. I believe I saw a ghost when I was a kid, so for me they are as real as anything else, but to most people they are a figment of the imagination. Even as a figment they are a commonly accepted idea, and as such they become a real unreal. The commonly accepted construct of a ghost is an emanation of a person from the past. Usually as an image it is somewhat transparent because it is halfway between the present world and its point of origin. This led me to consider them as walking superimpositions. Their silhouette resembles a changing camera, constantly capturing a different composition between the foreground of the past (the ghost itself) and the background of the present (the environment where they are witnessed). I wanted to represent this interesting visual situation in a sculpture. There are admittedly a lot of foggy lines between an image of a sculpture, a sculpture of an image, or a photograph of an image, but superimpositions have the most impact at those hazy boundaries, when they give equal gravity to various spaces simultaneously.

Superimposition captions

37 Johannes VanDerBeek, *Indian Ghost*, 2009 (detail), acrylic on aluminum mesh, 85 ½ × 39 × 19 inches. Installation view, Tang Museum, Saratoga Springs, New York, 2009

38 Installation view, *Amazement Park*, Tang Museum, Saratoga Springs, New York, 2009

39 Sara VanDerBeek, *The Principle of Superimposition II*, 2008, digital C-print, 64 ½ × 44 ½ inches

40 Johannes VanDerBeek, *Bohemian Robed Ghost*, 2010, acrylic on aluminum mesh, aluminum wire, and glue, 70 × 53 × 41 inches

41 Sara VanDerBeek, *Continuum Red*, 2008, digital C-print, 40 × 40 inches

42 Johannes VanDerBeek, *Pilgrim Ghost*, 2009, oil and varnish on aluminum, 68 × 53 × 17 inches. Installation view, *double take*, Metro Tech Center, Brooklyn, New York, 2009

43 Stan VanDerBeek, *Movie Mural*, 1967/2009 (detail), 16 mm DVD transfers, 35 mm slides, overhead transparency projections, dimensions variable. Installation view, The Box, Los Angeles, California, 2009

Gloria Sutton

Stan VanDerBeek

I think we're opening a new idea of the dynamics of things. I like to call it the aesthetics of anticipation, which compared to the nineteenth century's idea of an aesthetics of meditation, is a very important change in our culture....

—Stan VanDerBeek, 1965

In 1949, as part of the first photography class at Black Mountain College led by Hazel Larsen Archer, the school's first full-time photography teacher, Stan VanDerBeek, contributed to the class's one and only student publication, *Five Photographers*. Produced in a limited edition of twenty-five copies, the hand-bound book included individually printed photographs and statements from each of the five students participating in Archer's photography course that year. VanDerBeek's brief and pointed text was titled "Towards a Definition of Photography." For an artist whose entire practice was motivated in no small part by a desire to push image-making outside established patterns and procedures of traditional media, attempting to delimit photography seemed a bit out of joint, even for a student assignment. Of interest then is how VanDerBeek's treatise suggested that the "definition of" and "solution to photography" are both bound up in what he outlined as the problematics inherent in the medium, including "the use of the camera as an external eye" that "deals with space yet interprets and controls it two dimensionally"; the notion of the photograph functioning as a type of "excerpt, an isolated area recorded and removed from context"; and the mechanical and technical aspects of photography "prescribing its working area."[1]

VanDerBeek's perceptive observations as a student learning to wield a camera in the mountains of western North Carolina led him to the conclusion that photography was essentially "an expression of movement—movement towards an understanding." The black-and-white prints that he chose to include suggest two epic leitmotifs—the human figure and the natural world—that not only appeared in his photographic works, but also populate the range of drawings, writings, and collages that for the next thirty-five years he circulated in his animated and computer-generated films, his multiscreen projection environments, and his videos. Beyond the subtle play of light and shadow that VanDerBeek learned to use, bringing a male figure into relief against a darkened background in one photograph and highlighting the texture of an apple tree's bark in the other, the fragmentary compositions of both photographs reveal that VanDerBeek did not endeavor either to capture a moment or render a complete portrait. Instead an accretive model of image making emerges, a process by which images take shape through accumulation, what can be thought of as the residue of interactions. This nonlinear working process is abundantly documented in the shifting installations and comingling of his films, drawings, and collages in *Amazement Park*, alongside Sara and Johannes VanDerBeek's recent work. In the cosmos of the Tang Museum's exhibition, which ran from June 2009 through April 2010, personal associations and fragments of cultural history fused with the formal qualities of photography, film, and sculpture, not in a derivative manner, but rather in dialogue with one another.

Within VanDerBeek's own body of work, his accretive model of image production becomes most evident in the films he produced during the late 1950s and early 1960s, after he returned to Manhattan from Black Mountain. Born in the Bronx in 1927, VanDerBeek studied art and architecture at Cooper Union. After serving in the U. S. Navy, he continued to pursue a host of visual media under the GI Bill at Black Mountain College between 1949 and 1953. VanDerBeek's time at the renowned school fortuitously overlapped with that of fellow student Robert Rauschenberg and, most notably, John Cage, Buckminster Fuller, and M. C. Richards, who all taught at the school and would become VanDerBeek's lifelong intellectual interlocutors. Besides learning the mechanics and gaining an understanding of still photography with Hazel Larsen Archer, VanDerBeek also picked up his first film camera in her class after the college acquired a 16 mm Bolex.[2]

In 1954 VanDerBeek returned to New York City and quickly established himself within the burgeoning experimental film scene while supporting himself with a design job at CBS. Many of the stop-animation techniques and editing skills that he applied to his early award-winning 16 mm films such as *What Who How* (8 minutes, black and white, 1957) and *Mankinda* (10 minutes, black and white, 1957) he acquired through his employment on the hit television show *Winky Dink and You*. What can be described only as a proto-interactive children's program, *Winky Dink and You* encouraged children to apply a special clear vinyl mat to their television screens at home and, using special crayons, draw along with the host of the program.[3] VanDerBeek often used the studio's editing equipment after hours to work on his own nonnarrative films, which frequently combined his figurative drawings and paintings with collages made from magazine advertisements and news articles. Many of these hand-painted cels, which used white, dry brushwork to animate a male figure, appear in *Amazement Park*.

Stan VanDerBeek, Still from *What Who How*, 1957, black and white film with sound, 8:00 minutes

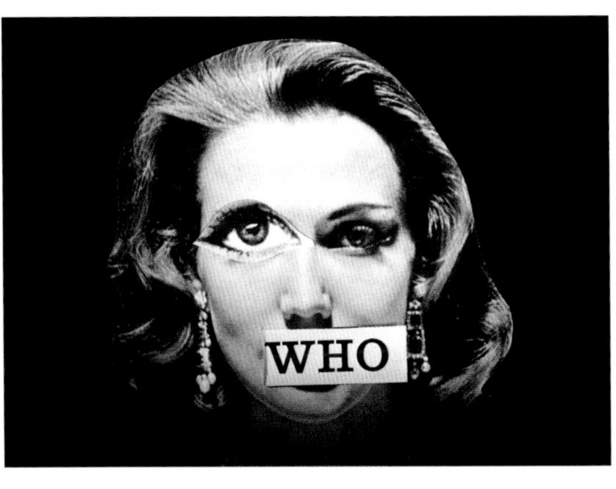

The titles from this period, such as *Wheeeeels No. 1* (16 mm, 8 minutes, black and white, sound, 1958) and *Science Friction* (16 mm, 10 minutes, color, sound, 1959), reflect VanDerBeek's lifelong proclivity for puns and alliteration. *Science Friction* was VanDerBeek's initial trial with color and sound and also represents what would become a persistent theme in his films: the use of unexpected juxtapositions to generate critical commentary. The quick-paced film intersperses images of muscle men and mad scientists in a satirical commentary on the American and Russian obsession with rockets and the race to the moon. These early collage films helped garner VanDerBeek's celebrated reputation as a part of the New American Cinema, alongside filmmakers such as Jonas Mekas, Shirley Clarke, and Ed Emshwiller, all of whom shared an interest in developing new techniques for filmmaking and are often called the progenitors of independent cinema. The works produced by the New American Cinema look quite different from what is labeled as independent film today. Not only were the films low budget, nonnarrative, and idiosyncratic in nature, they were also often created by a single artist working directly with an editor, emerging from the modest milieu of an artist's studio.

To date, VanDerBeek's reputation rests on these technically inventive films and animated shorts produced in the late 1950s and early 1960s. While he continued to produce films in this manner, VanDerBeek also engaged in a stunning array of collaborative multimedia projects during the 1960s, which brought him together with other artists experimenting with film and performance, such as Claes Oldenburg, Lucas Samaras, Carolee Schneemann, and Robert Morris. At the same time that VanDerBeek was making films of Oldenburg's Ray Gun theater events and collaborating with Schneemann and Morris to produce *Site* (1964), a six-minute super-8 mm film distributed on a reel by the multimedia publication *Aspen* (5–6, Fall–Winter 1967), his interest in digital media and computer programming led him to seek out the expertise of engineers such as Ken Knowlton at the Bell Telephone Laboratory in Murray Hill, New Jersey. Starting in 1964 the pair created a suite of films called *Poemfields* using BELFIX, a computer program written on punch cards. By 1969 VanDerBeek had produced eight different *Poemfields*, the last two completed on equipment at the Massachusetts Institute of Technology's Center for Advanced Visual Studies. Each *Poemfield* offered a five- to ten-minute formal treatise on language and movement. Taken as a whole, the films melded

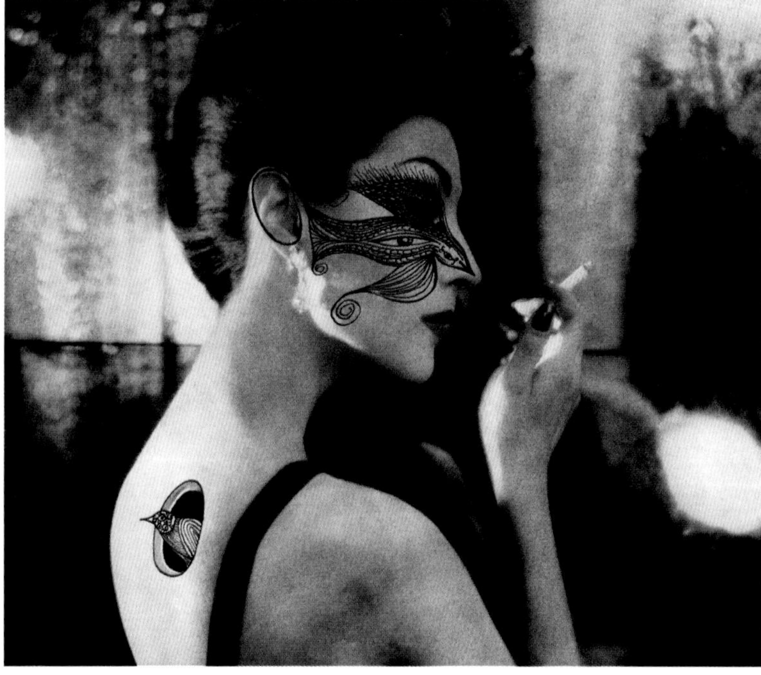

Stan VanDerBeek, Still from *A La Mode*, 1957, black and white film with sound, 6:18 minutes

the syntax of concrete poetry with the programming mechanics of early computing to generate a new type of animated film that presented poetry in cinematic time. Further media experiments from the 1960s into the early 1980s included novel uses of audio- and visual-projection systems, planetariums, and digital-image processing, presaging the visual arts' current focus on architecturally scaled video and film installation.

As the credits for his films indicate, VanDerBeek was resourceful in cobbling together grants to support his work and looked for opportunities to gain access to large-scale computer processing and editing equipment, often necessitating his affiliation with universities rather than galleries. Until his death in 1984 from complications of stomach cancer, he held a variety of professorships and residencies at universities and public-television studios, which facilitated his prolific output. He also pushed the model of the artist in residence to new dimensions by managing to forge positions at NASA and CBS. In 1970 VanDerBeek was one of the first artists in residence at the Boston public-television station WGBH, where he orchestrated a project called *Violence Sonata*, broadcast on two public-television channels and designed for viewing on two sets at once. Between each of the three "screen acts," home viewers could telephone live studio panelists with responses to questions and thus participate in a discussion about violence in America.

While VanDerBeek's reputation as filmmaker has ensured that his work has its place in the history of experimental film, he has yet to be fully recognized for his deep influence as a visual artist who worked at the center of the various radical aesthetic movements and phenomena that exploded in New York in the late 1950s and early 1960s. These movements include Fluxus, "Happenings," Judson Church dance performances, and the minimal music of John Cage and David Tudor, who, with VanDerBeek, lived with their families in an artist's cooperative called the Land, in Rockland County.[4] VanDerBeek's practice differed from that of his colleagues in that, in addition to the aleatory strategies of the historical avant-garde, VanDerBeek was also keenly involved in the burgeoning field of communications theory that imagined art interfacing with a new type of audience model, addressed by television, video, and computer networks.

The selection of VanDerBeek's works in *Amazement Park* traces these developments, from his early photographic experiments at Black Mountain, seen in the black-and-white image of two dancers, the vibrating outlines of their bodies pointing to photography's fraught relationship with movement, up through the bit-mapped, computer-generated forms that appear on the stills from *Poemfield #2* (16 mm, color, sound, 1966), which served as screen projections for *Found Forms*, and which VanDerBeek called "electric assemblage," mixing 35 mm slides, 16 mm film, and overhead projections. An inclusive, leveling metanarrative emerges from VanDerBeek's use of many media sources for transmitting images—discrete films, stills, individual animation cels, handmade 35 mm slides, and films transferred to digital video. The question of how we absorb the world around us recurs as a subject. Most significantly, the inclusion of VanDerBeek's films as digital projections and single-channel videos in the installations reinforces the formal links and visual references between his 16 mm animated films and his works on paper, reaffirming that he was a visual artist who made art with film.

Viewed from start to finish, the selection of VanDerBeek's films shows a visual history of postwar art unfolding before the viewer's eyes. They cleverly allude to a Dadaesque sense of the absurd and a Surrealist engagement with dreams and transmogrification. The Futurists' fascination with the mechanical gives way to Pop art's intermingling with consumer culture. The opening sequence of the 1959 *Science Friction*, for example, with its rotating concentric circles, directly refers to Marcel Duchamp's film *Anemic Cinema* (1926), signaling the Surrealist word games and puns underlying VanDerBeek's work, while the film's later collage of consumer advertisements with rocket imagery presages the billboard-scaled work of James Rosenquist's *F-111* (1964–1965), made five years later.

While transferring celluloid to video was anathema to many of his peers, such as Stan Brakhage, Jordan Belson, and John and James Whitney, VanDerBeek was not a film purist. He was drawn to working with film precisely because it could encompass other media and, more importantly, because it remained a variable medium. In a 1967 interview with Willard Van Dyke, then the director of the Museum of Modern Art's Department of Film, VanDerBeek alluded to the problematics of photography first outlined in his 1949 statement in *Five Photographers*. Extending his visual-art practice to include film and computer animation provided a means of contending with what he regarded as the "new sense of dynamics of art: motion and space."[5] Recognizing "the limitations of the four walls of theater" and the "visual boundaries" of painting and sculpture, VanDerBeek sought a medium that would "move beyond optical representation and deal with motion and time while accommodating all of the other ideas of painting, sculpture and theater."[6] Additionally, his method of making films often eschewed the creation of a final or master cut. Instead he considered everything a work in progress, often completing films only to appropriate them into other films. Sometimes this process involved splicing copies of certain sequences into new films or using his own films as found footage in his multiscreen projection environments.

These idiosyncratic multiscreen programs never adhered to a playlist and were conceived not for wide screens or movie palaces, but for ad-hoc, intimate settings that dotted New York's experimental-film scene. Places like the Film-makers' Cinémathèque, on Lafayette Street and the Bridge played host to many of VanDerBeek's expanded cinema experiments such as *Move-Movies*, first done in 1966. True to its title, in *Move-Movies* VanDerBeek and about five volunteers walked up and down the aisles of the Cinémathèque with handheld projectors, aiming found footage of street parades and the like onto the surrounding audience, while three 16 mm film projectors stood in the back, projecting a selection of VanDerBeek's films onto three screens. While he continued to adapt his multiscreen experiments for festivals and temporary screenings across the United States, Japan, Europe, and the Middle East, traditional theaters were never the ideal setting for his multiscreen works. He developed a conceptual theater called the *Movie-Drome*, which he outlined in aphoristic terms in *Culture: Intercom and Expanded Cinema: A Proposal and Manifesto*, published in 1966.[7]

The thirty-one foot-high metal dome VanDerBeek built on the Land between 1965 and 1967 was a prototype for a communications system VanDerBeek imagined,

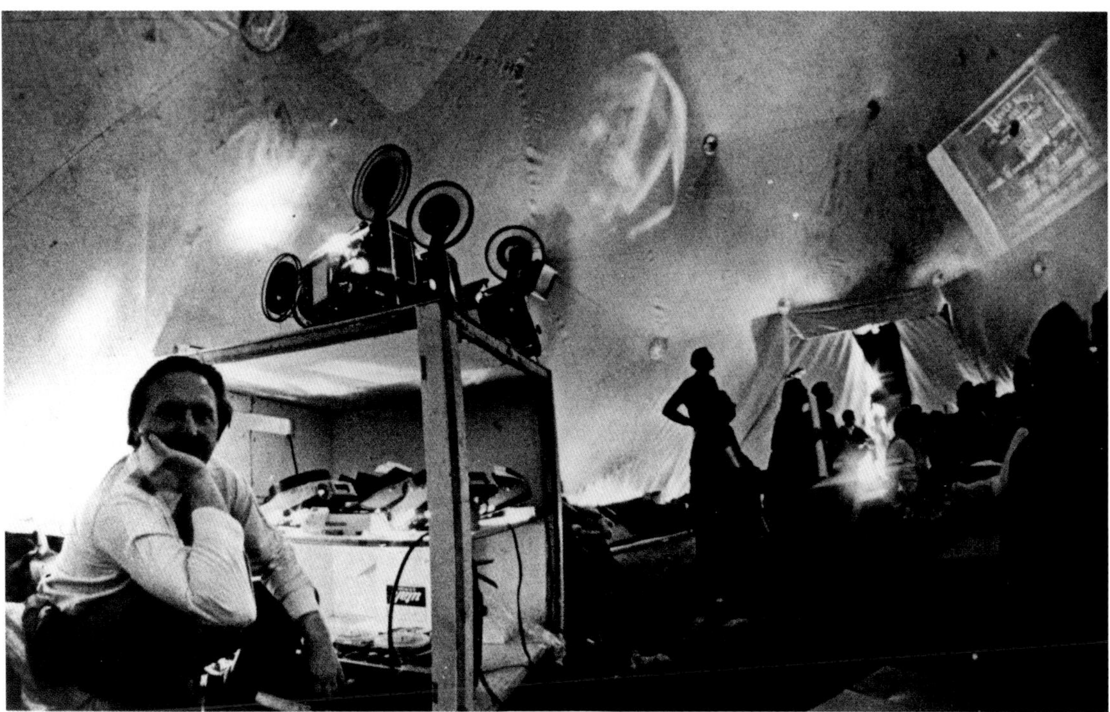

Stan VanDerBeek in *Movie-Drome*, c. 1966, the Land, Rockland County, New York

in which several dromes would be positioned throughout the world, each linked to an orbiting satellite that would store and transmit images among the various sites. Through the *Movie-Drome* VanDerBeek sought a model for a real-time, programmable communications system. He referred to the image content projected onto the curved interior of the *Movie-Drome* interchangeably as "image libraries, newsreels, and feedback," presaging today's Internet networks for sharing and distributing art and information.[8] In a 1965 interview he explained the telecommunication aspects of the project:

> *in the future similar* Movie-Dromes *could receive images by satellite from a worldwide library source, store them, and program a feedback presentation to the local community. Dialogs with other centers would be likely, and instant reference material via transmission television and telephone could be called for and received at 186,000 miles-per-second from anywhere in the world.*[9]

VanDerBeek's conceptual framework for viewing and experiencing information over a network and through multiscreen projections demanded a spatially and temporally specific subject not yet addressed by conventional cinematic forms but more in tune with the types of viewing conditions associated with contemporary forms of multimedia installation.[10]

In further experiments, VanDerBeek emphasized audience participation even more as the subject of the work. This priority became most evident in *Cine-Naps*, a four-hour-long event staged first at the Fels Planetarium in Philadelphia in 1971, in which the planetarium's astrophysical program was replaced by VanDerBeek's computer-generated films, surround-sound sequences, and colored lights, using the planetarium's sophisticated projection system. From the outset, the audience was encouraged to sleep during the event. Afterwards, they received a handout with a local phone number as they exited and were asked to call in over the next few days to recount their dreams on a proto-answering machine set up by VanDerBeek.

What further distinguished VanDerBeek as a visual artist was how prolific he was as a writer. He regularly contributed to *Film Culture*, the *Village Voice*, *The Filmmaker's Newsletter*, *Film Quarterly*, and the *Tulane Drama Review*, among other publications. In 1961 he wrote an article called "The Cinema Delimina," in which he coined the term "underground cinema" and pointed to the limitations of film as defined by the commercial film industry.[11] He would go on to produce manifestos, and many of his articles took on the form of his collages. VanDerBeek's writing projects a sense of urgency in its tone, and a recurring theme in the essays is the issue of artists taking a stand and directly addressing the audience. By 1965, when VanDerBeek had made many of his films and had a working prototype of the *Movie-Drome* in operation, Marshall McLuhan's book *Understanding Media: The Extensions of Man* had been in circulation for less than one year. But its sensationalistic reception by the popular press and academia alike had already catapulted terms like "global village" into the popular imagination. In a 1965 conference featuring both VanDerBeek and McLuhan as speakers, the latter's talk pushed for the recognition of the "reader" as an active agent who must contend with the current "invisible environment" of propaganda. He offered the example of the standard daily newspaper to demonstrate the process by which "the reader becomes the publisher within the current age of decentralization."[12] "The reader of the news," McLuhan suggested, "enters the new world as a maker. There is no 'meaning' in the news except what [the reader] makes—there is no connection between any of the items except the instant dimension of electric circuitry.

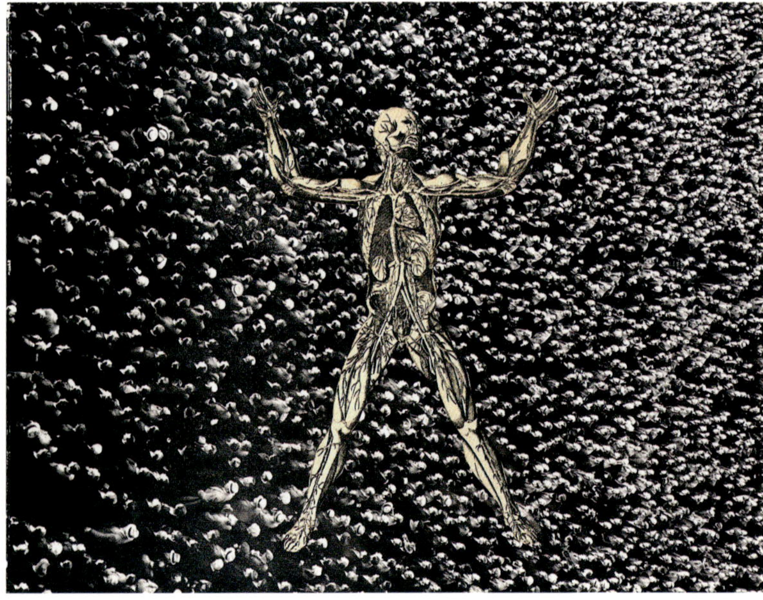

Stan VanDerBeek, *Untitled (from See Saw Seams)*, 1964, collage on found image, 8 3/8 × 11 inches

News items are like the parts of a symbolist structure. The reader is a co-creator."[13] To explicate this claim, McLuhan singled out VanDerBeek's work: "The newspaper is also very much like the delightful films of Stan VanDerBeek: the world of multiscreen projections is the world of the newspaper where umpteen news stories come at you."

In contrast to McLuhan and other "media visionaries" of the 1960s, VanDerBeek did not ignore the dystopian cultural dangers of technology and media. VanDerBeek's films, such as the more somber visuals and score for *See Saw Seams* (1965), react against the alienating impulse of computer and telecommunications technology within the political and cultural milieu of the civil-rights movement, the Vietnam War, and the rhetoric of the space age. His emphasis on two-way communication, feedback, and data transfer speaks to visual art's transformation from the industrial to the information age. Ultimately, VanDerBeek's work establishes a new interpretive framework for understanding media art, not just as an accretion of film and computer technology, but also as a critical means of engaging the effects of mass media on cultural experience.

Notes

1 Stan VanDerBeek, "Towards a Definition of Photography," *Five Photographers* (Black Mountain, NC: Black Mountain College, n. d.), unpaged. In addition to work by VanDerBeek, the publication includes photographs and statements by Hazel Larsen Archer, Vernon Phillips, Andrew Oates, Jr., and Nick Cernovich. A copy of *Five Photographers* is in the research library of the Museum of Modern Art, New York.

2 For a description of Archer's photography course and the introduction of film at Black Mountain College, see Mary Emma Harris, *The Arts at Black Mountain College* (Cambridge, MA: MIT Press, 2002), 182–201, especially 188.

3 Both *What Who How* and *Mankinda* were awarded a Bronze Medal from the 1958 Brussels International Experimental Film Competition, which ran concurrently with the 1958 Brussels Worlds Fair. *Winky Dink and You* originally ran on Saturday mornings on CBS, from 10 October 1953, through 27 April 1957.

4 VanDerBeek's work as a filmmaker is highlighted in the following important studies on experimental film: David James, *Allegories of Cinema: American Film in the Sixties* (Princeton: Princeton University Press, 1989); Wheeler Winston Dixon, *The Exploding Eye: A Re-Visionary History of 1960s American Experimental Cinema* (Albany: State University of New York Press, 1997); John G. Hanhardt, ed. *A History of the American Avant-Garde Cinema* (New York: American Federation of Arts, 1976); Sheldon Renan, *An Introduction to the American Underground Film* (New York: Dutton, 1967); Parker Tyler, *Underground Film: A Critical History* (1969. Rpt. New York: Da Capo, 1995); Gregory Battcock, *The New American Cinema* (New York: Dutton, 1967). Notably VanDerBeek's work also figures largely in key books by U. K. artists Malcolm Le Grice and David Curtis. See Malcolm Le Grice, *Abstract Film and Beyond* (Cambridge, MA: MIT, 1977) and David Curtis, *Experimental Cinema: A Fifty-Year Evolution* (New York: Universe, 1971).

5 Adrienne Mancia and Willard Van Dyke, "Four Artists as Film-Makers," *Art in America* (January 1967), 70.

6 Ibid. See also Stewart Kranz, *Science and Technology in the Arts. A Tour through the Realm of Science and Art* (New York: Van Nostrand Reinhold, 1974), 237.

7 First published in *Film Culture* 40 (Spring 1966), 15–18, *Culture: Intercom and Expanded Cinema: A Proposal and Manifesto* was reprinted in *The New American Cinema: A Critical Anthology*, edited by Gregory Battcock, (New York: Dutton, 1967),173–179, as well as in *Art and the Moving Image: A Critical Reader*, edited by Tanya Leighton (London: Tate, 2008), 72–74.

8 VanDerBeek, "Culture:Intercom," *The New American Cinema: A Critical Anthology*, edited by Gregory Battcock, (New York: Dutton, 1967), 175.

9 Janet Vrchota, "Stan VanDerBeek: Technology's Migrant Fruit Picker," *Print* (March/April 1973), 49.

10 For further discussion about the *Movie-Drome*, see Gloria Sutton, "Stan VanDerBeek's Movie-Drome: Networking the Subject" in *Future Cinema: The Cinematic Imaginary After Film*, Jeffrey Shaw, Peter Weibel, eds., Cambridge, Mass.:MIT Press, 2003, 136–143.

11 Stan VanDerBeek, "The Cinema Delimina: Films from the Underground," *Film Quarterly*, no. 14 (Summer 1961), 5–13.

12 Marshall McLuhan, "The Invisible Environment: The Future of an Erosion," *Perspecta*, no. 11 (1967), 166.

13 Ibid.

MASKS

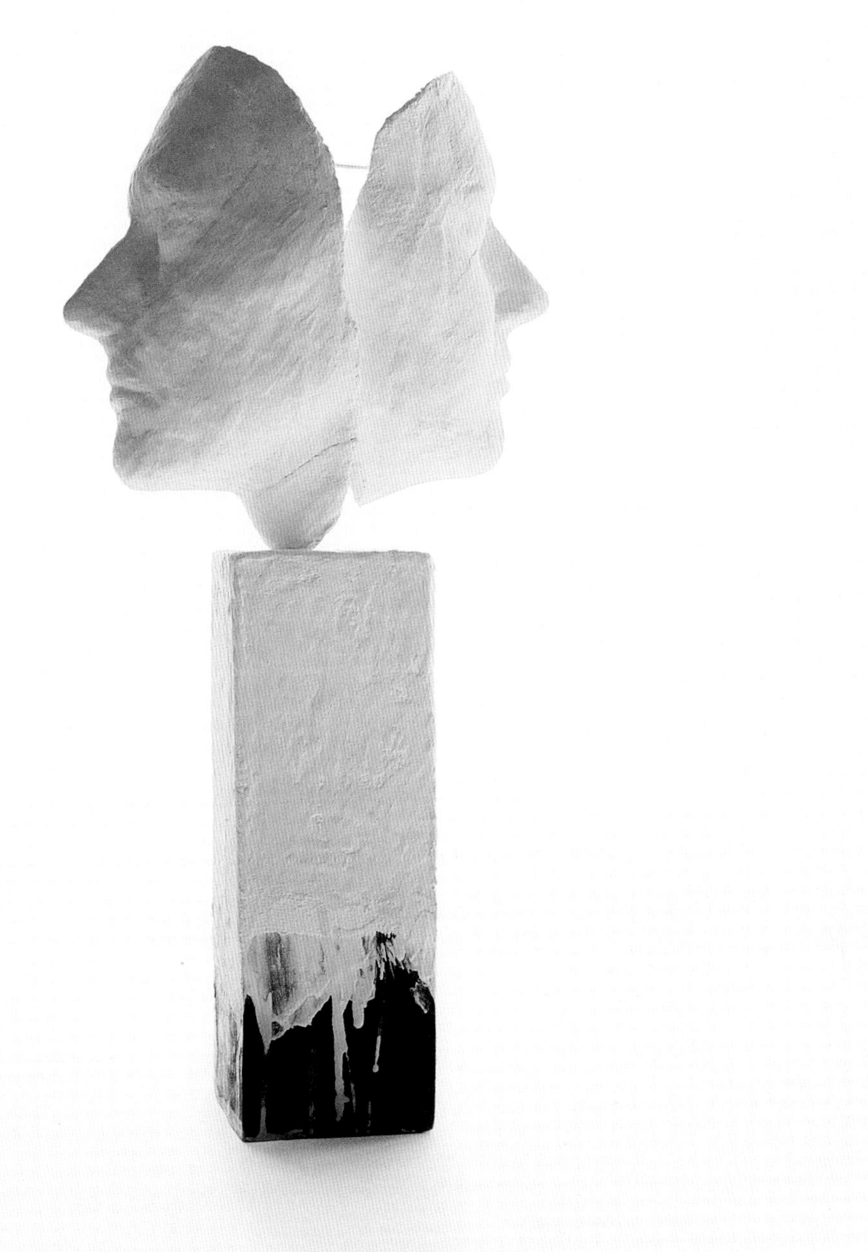

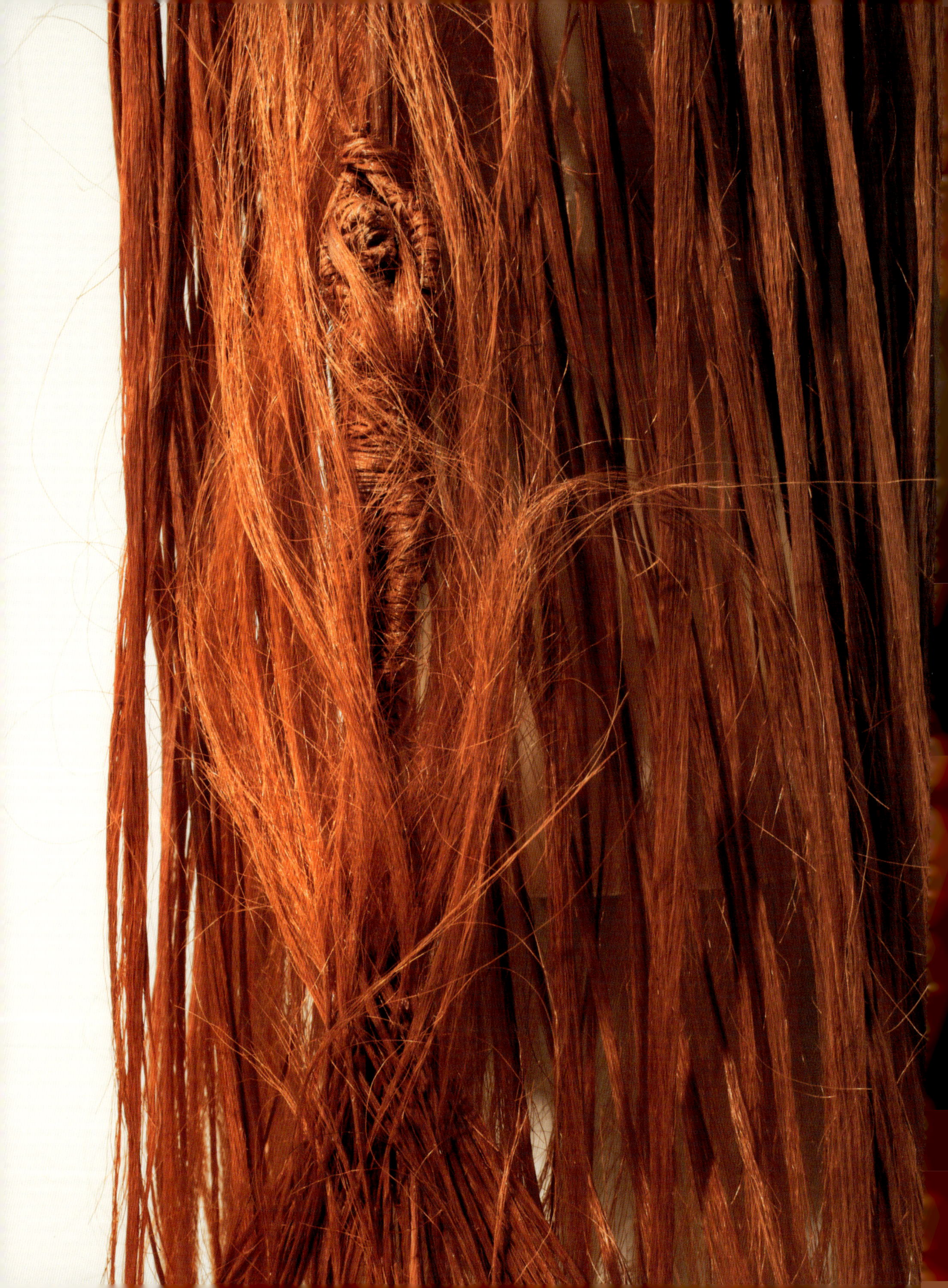

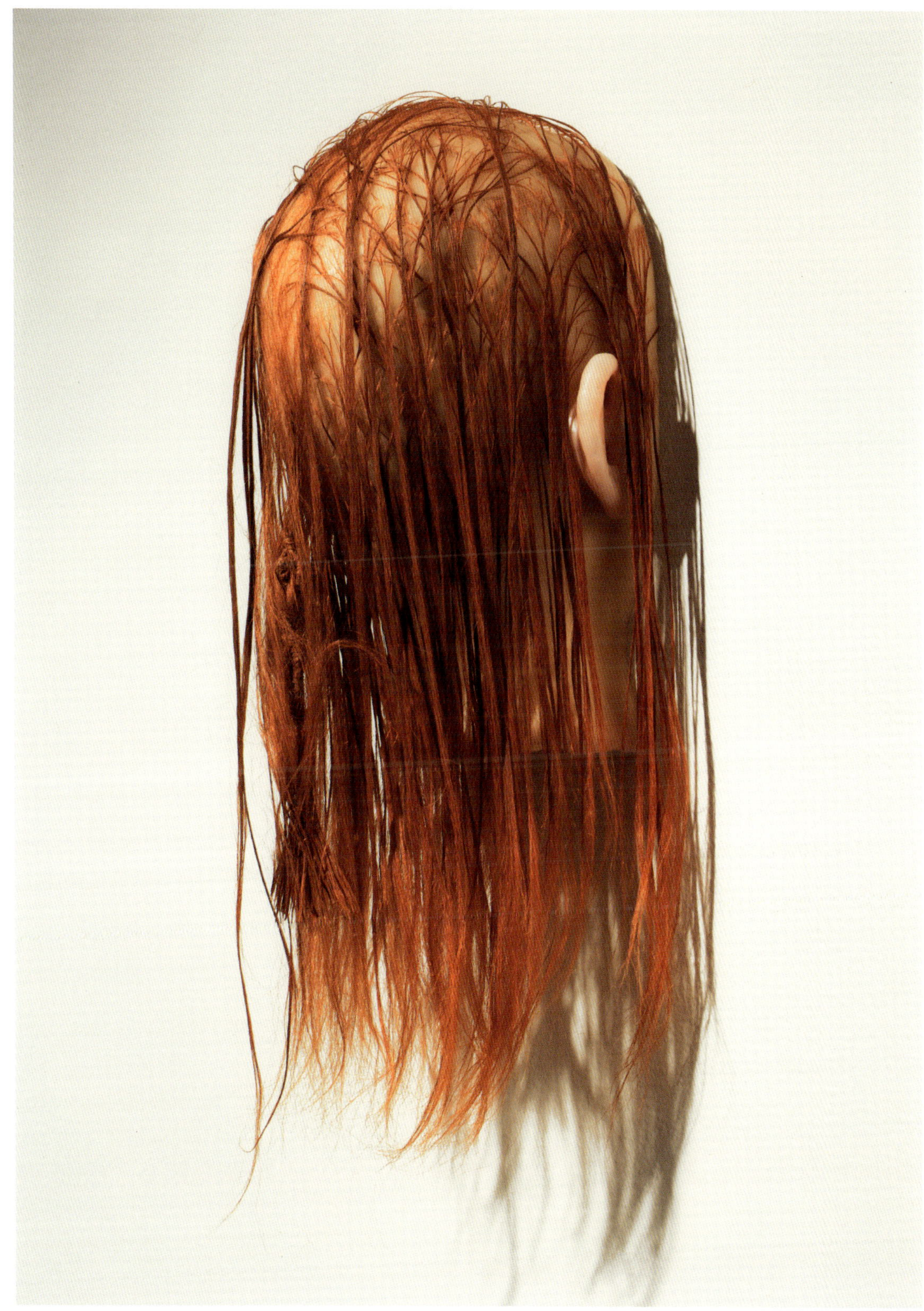

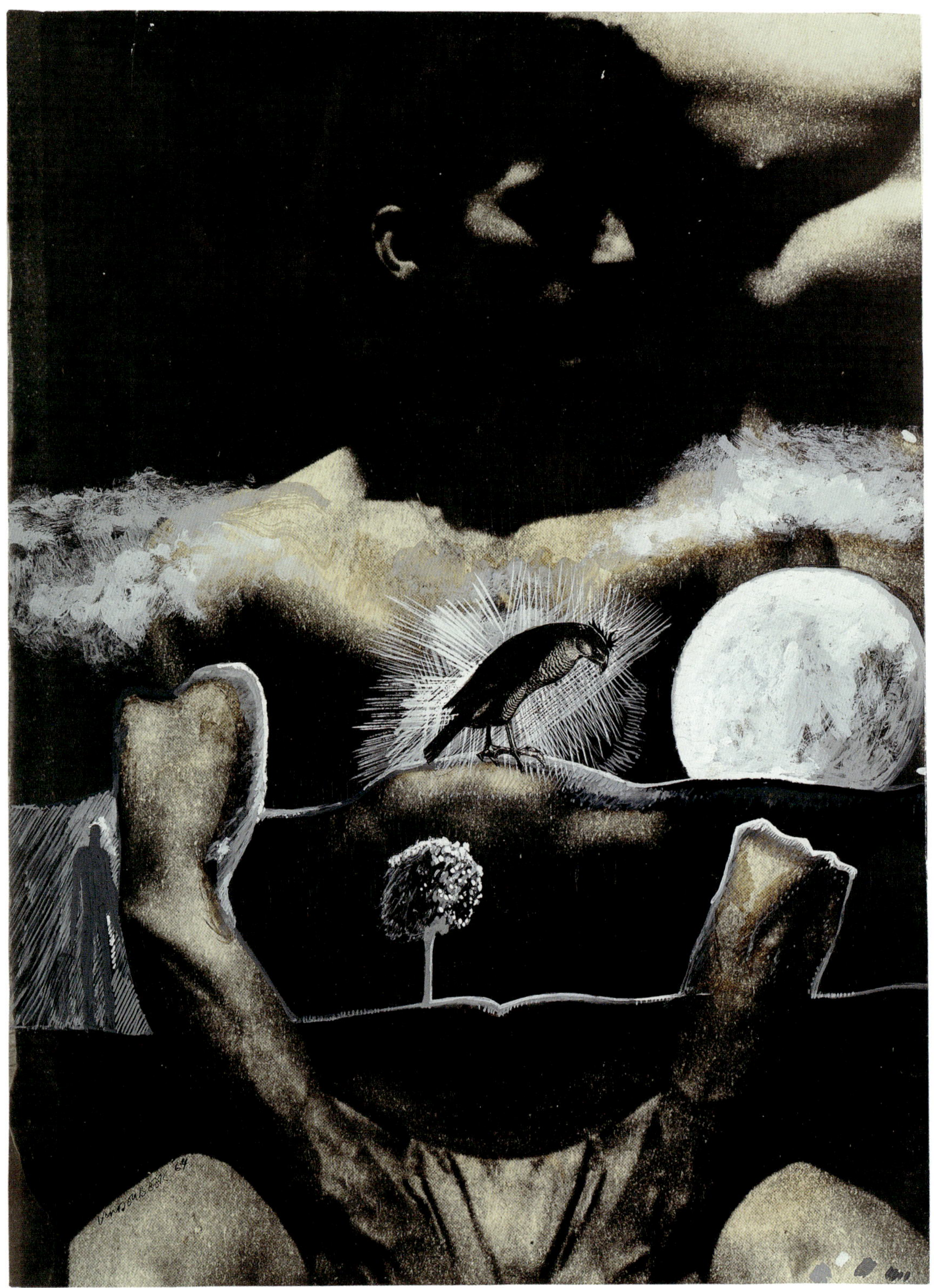

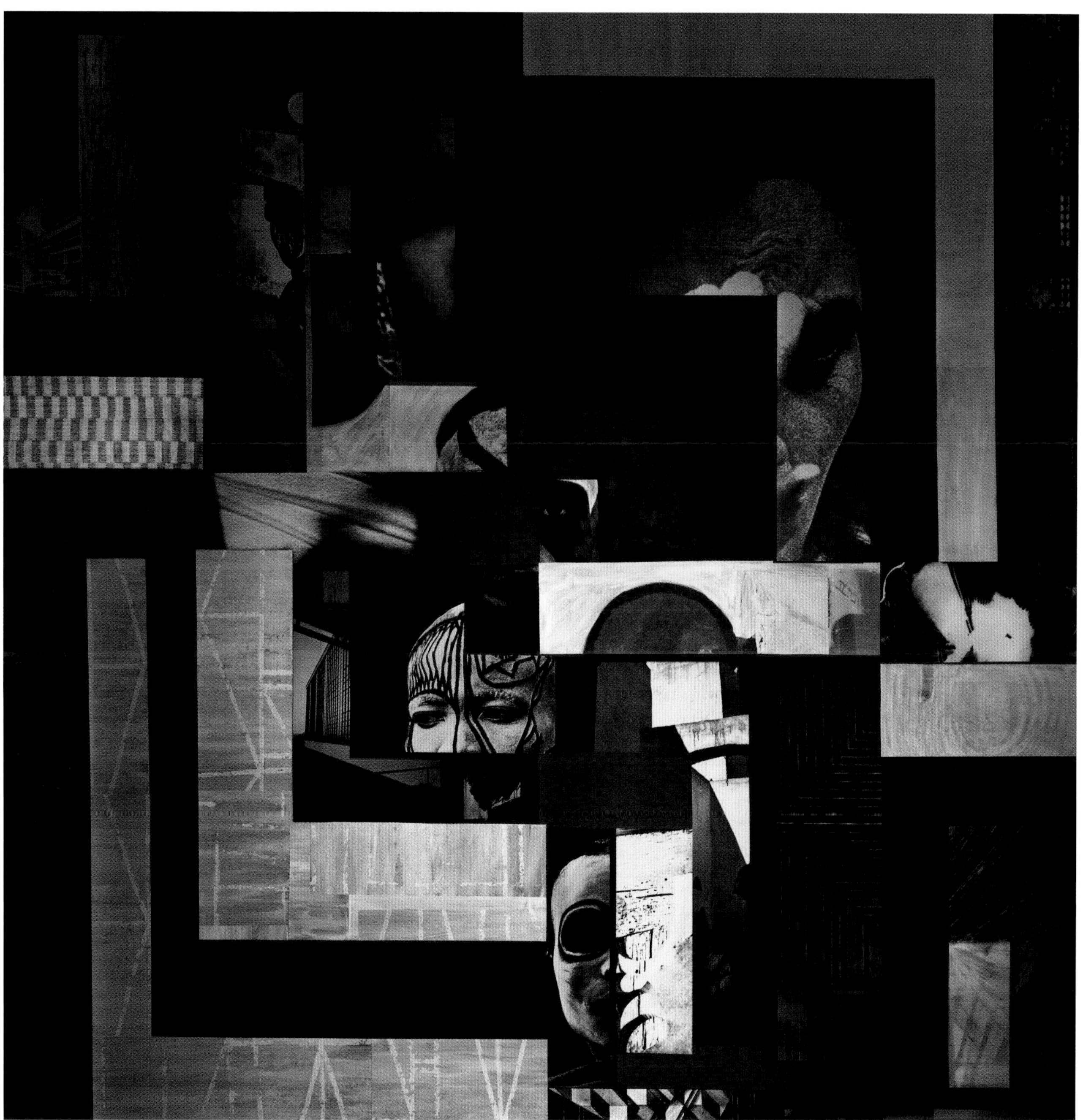

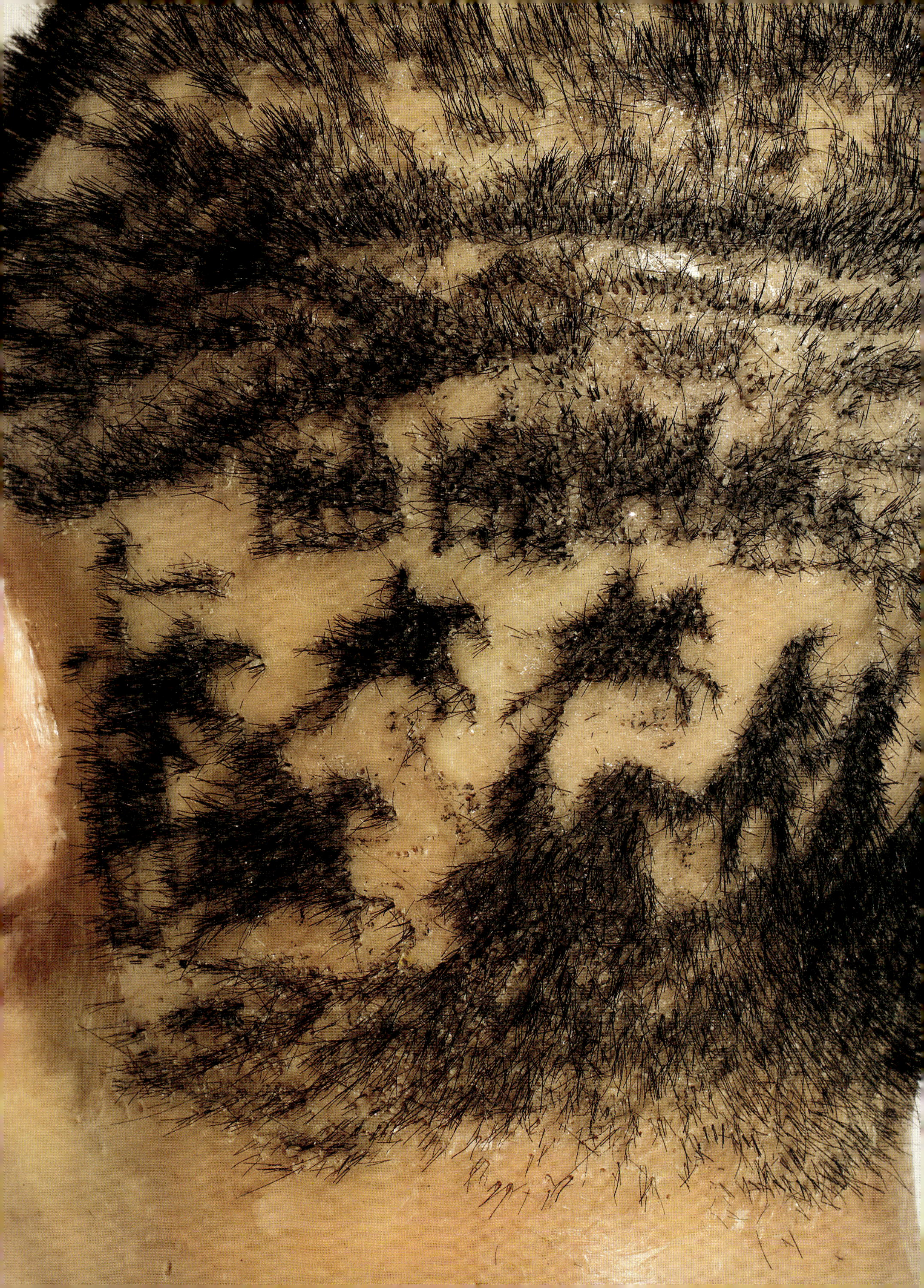

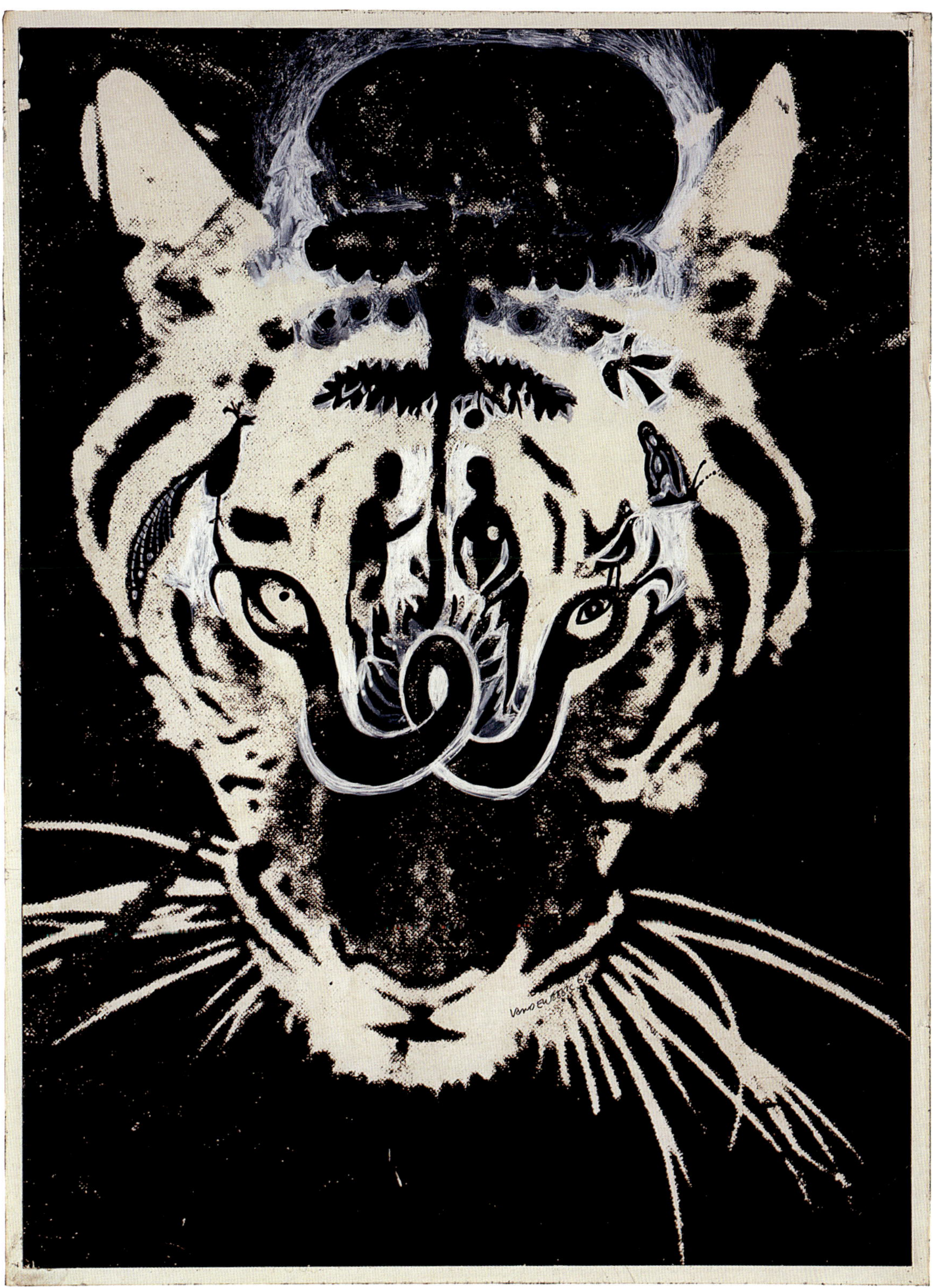

48 (opposite), 49

MASKS

IB: This month's installation includes many details of covering and uncovering. Faces hide behind veils, peek out from behind patterns, appear buried in the walls, and are cut out and missing. Can you talk about anonymity—about hiding specific identity in your work?

SVDB: In a work like *Delaunay* the black of the shadows is meant to hang over the structure like a curtain or a cloth, concealing and revealing images. But it's more about specificity and control than ambiguity or anonymity.

IB: Do you mean for us to recognize these people or to see them as formal building blocks?

SVDB: Both. I am drawn to who they are but also to the formal and visual qualities of the image. Depending on which image I am working on, the person depicted can become very important. In *After*, for example, the subject is the photographer Lee Miller, and it's important that she is recognizable.

JVDB: We seem constantly compelled by what's waiting around the corner. Once we see what's there, it may not hold our interest because it becomes too real. Without the prospect of possibility we have to confront the actual limits of being in a place or state. The unknown is a template for our interior selves to move outward more freely. At the same time it enables us to delve inward and sense our tendencies. Our personalities become chiseled through our confrontation of mystery. I find it appealing for a work of art to capture an aspect of an undefined reality so it can potentially remain in the flux between actuality and possibility. In other words, art is the building block that constructs a corner people want to see around.

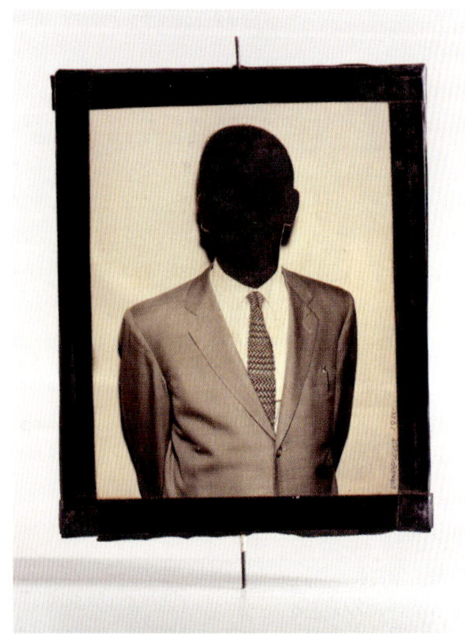

50

IB: When you appropriate a certain image or object, do you want to obscure it so that it becomes yours?

JVDB: I want to obscure it so it's not so specific. It's better if it can lend itself to multiple causes. Certain images are open enough or can be altered in ways that make them a more vacant mirror. In that type of space, viewers can fill the picture with their own questions or desires. I often erase expressions or gestures that lean the image heavily in one direction or another. The prospect of an image becoming everyone's rather than exclusively mine is much more appealing.

SVDB: I used an image of a sculpture by Giacometti in *A Composition for Detroit* not only because I admire his work, but also because the sculpture conveyed an emotion—its face is screaming upward—that I was looking for. Having completed the work, I began to reflect upon the process of removal that occurs with my use of this image, and I felt it spoke to the process one goes through when experiencing a significant event in life.

As for my use of reproductions of artworks, I think about it as representing a movement in time away from the original event—the image of the Giacommeti sculpture is many steps removed from his original action of putting the clay onto the armature, or to take it even further, his initial thought of creating the sculpture. It has been cast, placed in an exhibition space, lit, photographed, then reproduced in a book. Then I take that image, enlarge it, paint on it, include it in my composition, and re-photograph it. With so many layers of mediation, the original scream of the sculpture grows muted, and that's the point. After a significant event, whether personal or collective, positive or tragic, you refer back to that moment. As time passes, you move further and further away from it, and it becomes diffuse. My compositions are designed in the way I think we think, in glimpses or flashes, images and ideas constantly shifting.

IB: Is it important for viewers to recognize that the images came from a specific *Time* or *Life* magazine, or from a Walker Evans image, or from a specific movie still?

SVDB: I don't think the viewer needs to know these details. I do choose images for their content and their provenance, but also for their color and shape. When *Life* magazine was at its height in circulation, it was a major news source. It was the way a large portion of our country received news of the world. In that way, its images, layout, and reporting shaped our history. Formally, *Life* images have a beautiful quality—heavy blacks and saturated colors that are now even more interesting due to fading over time and changing impermanent inks. But they are also large, and I like their texture; they feel fragile and imply in their style and form a passage of time.

JVDB: In certain instances I will show where an image came from so viewers can understand how I have changed it. Then why I changed it can become another focal point. You have to show the base or beginning of an image or object for the transformation to become prominent. Viewers can't understand a transformation if they can't recognize the starting point.

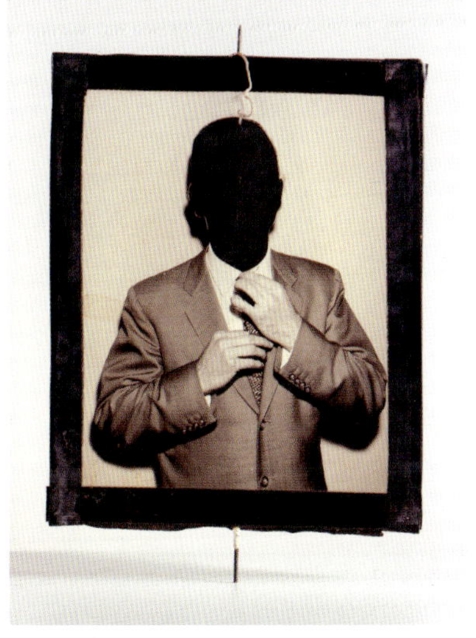

50

IB: Stan re-used images all the time. Some of his faces are very recognizable like Martin Luther King or Richard Nixon. How do you think he would answer?

SVDB: Life magazine was important to him because it was cheap and ubiquitous, something he could find on the street for free. It was also a major example of mass media at the time and provided him with images of all the political and cultural figures that he used in his collage films. Films like *A La Mode* or *Skullduggery* were jabs at the media establishment in addition to the political establishment. It was very important that the political figures were recognizable. He knew that because they were iconic their images immediately triggered certain feelings, particularly in Nixon's case when in *Breathdeath* a foot comes out of his mouth.

JVDB: In some instances it is appropriate to keep the subject recognizable. Collage gains a lot of its persuasion from the fact that it takes a recognizable image and forces viewers to change the way they interpret it. That's both an inherent strength and weakness of appropriation. To take a symbol of power like Nixon and show a foot coming out of his mouth suggests a whole span of political views in one simple action. However, for someone who does not recognize Nixon, it is simply a goofy gesture. Dad would be happy with both interpretations, but artists need to be cautious of assuming people share their base of knowledge. Sometimes appropriation can seem like insider trading or a secret verse. If people don't know where you're jumping from or even what type of pole you are using, you might catapult off into infinity where no one cares.

IB: Do you think your father's work looks dated?

JVDB: Some of the techniques and materials look dated but that's inevitable. We have grown conditioned to look at digital images rather than film, so anything with the gritty remnant of film processing looks like a relic from the last century. Stylistically you could put a piece of his in a show now and it could pass as a contemporary work. That says a lot about his relevance and a little about current trends in art-making. But he appears most anchored to his time in his continual reference to the atomic bomb and the tension that seeped into the planet's psyche as it rested on a razor's edge. Only people of that time could genuinely put that anxiety in their work.

What ensures artists' relevance over time is the integrity of their intentions. Our dad was ahead of his time in many ways—his use of computers, his satirical animations, his intermedia output—but his overall approach to creation was wholeheartedly earnest, inquisitive, whimsical, comical, spiritual, and cerebral, and it's hard to imagine a time when those characteristics are not relevant.

SVDB: I don't think his work looks dated. In *Poemfield #7*, the poem is about war; I screened it last year and felt it spoke to exactly where we are now. You can't deny echoes of Vietnam in Afghanistan. Sadly, this comparison highlights for me the apathetic indifference of many of our citizens toward Afghanistan, its casualties, and its outcome. I can't help but wonder at the cause of this lack of engagement and protest and how even within myself I am not addressing this further in my work and my political activity. This questioning comes to mind particularly when I see his films. He was so ahead of his time, he was often waiting for the technology and the audience to catch up. The programmer who worked with him on the *Poemfields* series at Bell Labs said he always felt exhausted after working with my father because he pushed him and the machines beyond their capabilities. I found an interview from 1983 where he seemed a little rueful that his work and others from experimental cinema could not consistently reach mass audiences. He had done works for WGBH and had asked CBS in the 1960s if he could be an artist in residence, which didn't happen, but he mixed *Panels for the Walls of the World* at CBS, using their video mixers because they had technology that no one else had. At one point this film along with a few others appeared on the network as part of its series *Notes from the Underground*, and *Violence Sonata* aired once nationally, but that was the closest he got to a mass audience. I think he would have loved that his films are streamed on the internet; finally the audience for his films is truly universal.

IB: There is a peek-a-boo flirty quality to some of the work in this month's installation, and a horror-movie style to others. Faceless heads, burning witches, tribal-looking face paint, a burlesque performer flashing us. Can you describe these parts of the show?

SVDB: Dad had a great sense of humor and great comic timing; his work is playful at times to balance its seriousness at other times. He loved turns of words, the visual trick of the flip collages. I'm sure he created the flip collages for sheer enjoyment. He used the men with the missing faces in *Breathdeath* for an apocalyptic scene. The cutout seems aggressive and woeful, as if they were eradicated. The nuclear bomb and the horrible aftereffects leading into the Cold War always haunted my father and, I think, most people who lived during that time. I love Johannes's pieces in this show because they're totally unnerving, but beautiful and haunting at the same time.

JVDB: Well, this show is open during Halloween so it seems fitting to do a show about what hides in darkness. These pieces offered an opportunity to capture the shadowy nature of perception. Dad's film *See Saw Seems* tracks a loose narrative about things not always being what they seem. The camera moves slowly inward upon a scene, and as it gets closer the subject changes through an animated metamorphosis. Forms like the sun turn into the pupil of an eye, the eye turns into a bridge, we walk through the bridge toward a house on the hill, which is really a woman's body. On this journey one symbol acts as a mask for the next.

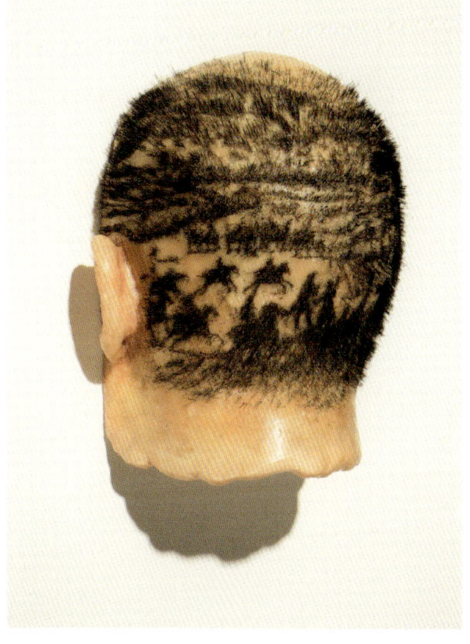

51

The other works in the show represent this slippery slope of shifting planes and surrealistic splices as ways to mirror the convoluted relationship we have to our innate narratives. Perception can either be a scientific process of deduction that moves toward actual truth or a vessel for subconscious desires that spiral us into a sprawling abyss of subjective meaning. To some people a red-headed women is the product of a rare genetic chromosome, and to others she is a sign of the devil. It is amazing how drastically elastic perceptions can be.

IB: Johannes, can you talk about what you were thinking when you made the two heads?

JVDB: The two heads were the first time I tried to make an object as though appearing through someone else's eyes. The images implanted through the manipulation of hair on the back of an anonymous head, are supposed to be the product of a fantasy. The real viewer of the object is taken into the mind of the hypothetical person seeing the Battle of Waterloo in the back of a balding man's head and a witch burning in the woods within the long red hair on the woman's head. I chose imagery that struck me as inherent to these situations, but they disclose the way my imagination works too. In the case of the male head, the patches of hair easily morphed into regiments of soldiers moving across a landscape. As for the female head, the imaginative leap stems from the cultural associations that redheads have carried throughout history. It does not seem impossible that someone seeing a redhead from behind on a bus could recall the persecution of the witch-hunts. The long strands of hair become tall trees in a forest, and a knot turns into a small woman burning in a pile of sticks. The perception animates the object into what was imagined. Sometimes traces of former traumas or events affect our interpretations. It is important to remember people do strange things even when they think they are acting upon entirely clean logic.

IB: Sara, can you talk about the images that are part of *Delaunay*?

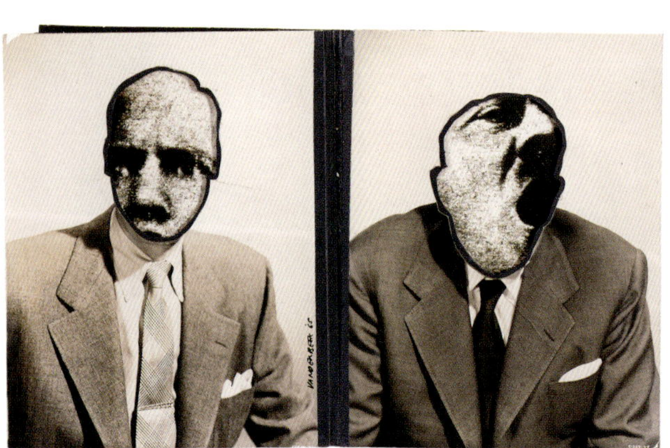

52

SVDB: The layout of *Delaunay* derives from a textile design by Sonia Delaunay, a formative figure of Modernism, who was very influential in applied arts and design. I am drawn to the evolution of Modernist ideals and what happens when these ideals meet with the everyday lives and needs of people.

I was creating this and the *Superimposition* works around the time of protests in Kenya. I saw an image of people fleeing Kenya on the cover of the *New York Times* and perceived them as constantly moving fugitives within their own country. I equated the fugitive nature of this piece with the fugitive existence of the displaced. The eye cannot rest for too long on any part of this work. It moves around, flitting from part to part, trying to recognize and connect images and create meaning. I was drawn to the *Times* image because of its color palette—the poignant contrast of the refugees' extreme suffering against the bright colors and patterns of their clothing. I also saw in this situation a larger, albeit simplistic view of the growing imbalance of social and economic power that is occurring the world over. In both developing and developed nations, the poor continue to experience instability and adversity. Their support is often undermined and their means of existence threatened. It is an endemic problem that causes great rifts within many communities. Including, with rising frequency, here in the U.S.

The two black and white images of women, to the left and right of the man, come from *Forced Out*, a book from 1989 about the lives of refugees. I use a mix of historical and current images but to focus on how the echoes of the past affect the present, and what this means for the future. The blue, somewhat abstract half circle that cuts across the central man's face is a detail of a painted house from the amaNdeble people of South Africa. This image is contemporary. Often women are the painters of these homes. I connected their striking designs, geometric patterns, and ingenuity to Sonia Delaunay's work. In contrast to the dark cycles, it felt like a positive continuum.

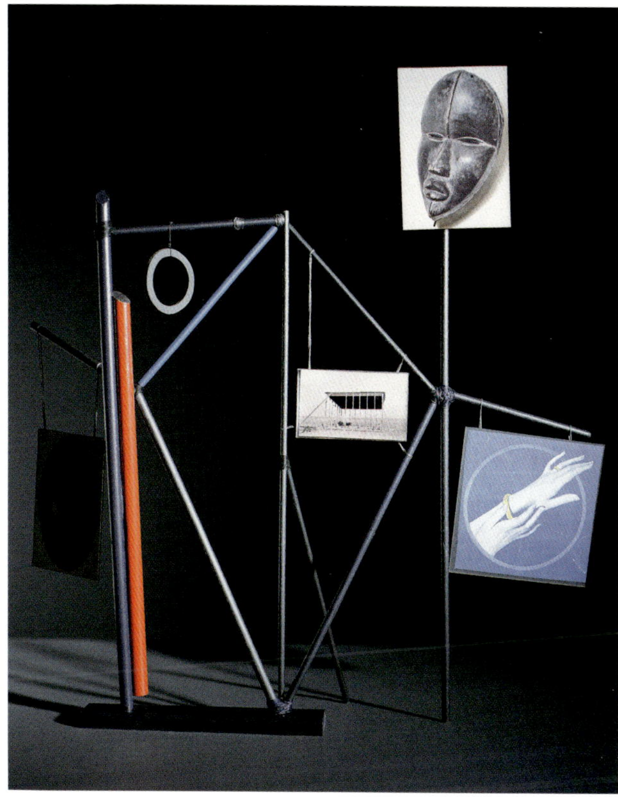

53

Masks captions

44 Sara VanDerBeek, *We Will Become Silhouettes*, 2010, digital C-print, 20 × 16 inches

45 Johannes VanDerBeek, *Burning at the Stake*, 2008, foam, wax, and human hair, 18 × 10 × 7 inches. Collection of Dennis Freedman, New York

46 Stan VanDerBeek, *Untitled (from See Saw Seams)*, 1964, ink, paint, and paper on found image, 13 1/2 × 10 1/4 inches

47 Sara VanDerBeek, *Delaunay*, 2008, digital C-print, 40 × 40 inches, The Carol and Arthur Goldberg Collection

48 Johannes VanDerBeek, *The Battle of Waterloo*, 2003 (detail), wax and human hair, 9 1/2 × 8 × 6 inches. Collection of Ernesto Caivano, New York

49 Stan VanDerBeek, *Untitled (from See Saw Seams)*, 1964, paint on found image, 13 3/4 × 10 inches

50 Stan VanDerBeek, *Untitled (flip collage)*, 1958, paper and tape on board, wire, and string, 9 3/4 × 8 inches

51 Johannes VanDerBeek, *The Battle of Waterloo*, 2003, wax and human hair, 9 1/2 × 8 × 6 inches. Collection of Ernesto Caivano, New York

52 Stan VanDerBeek, *Untitled* (flip collage from *Breathdeath*), 1965, found photographs, matboard, tape, and marker, 9 1/8 × 14 3/4 inches

53 Sara VanDerBeek, *Construction 3 (Mother Mask)*, 2006, digital C-print, 20 × 16 inches

BODY/BUILDING

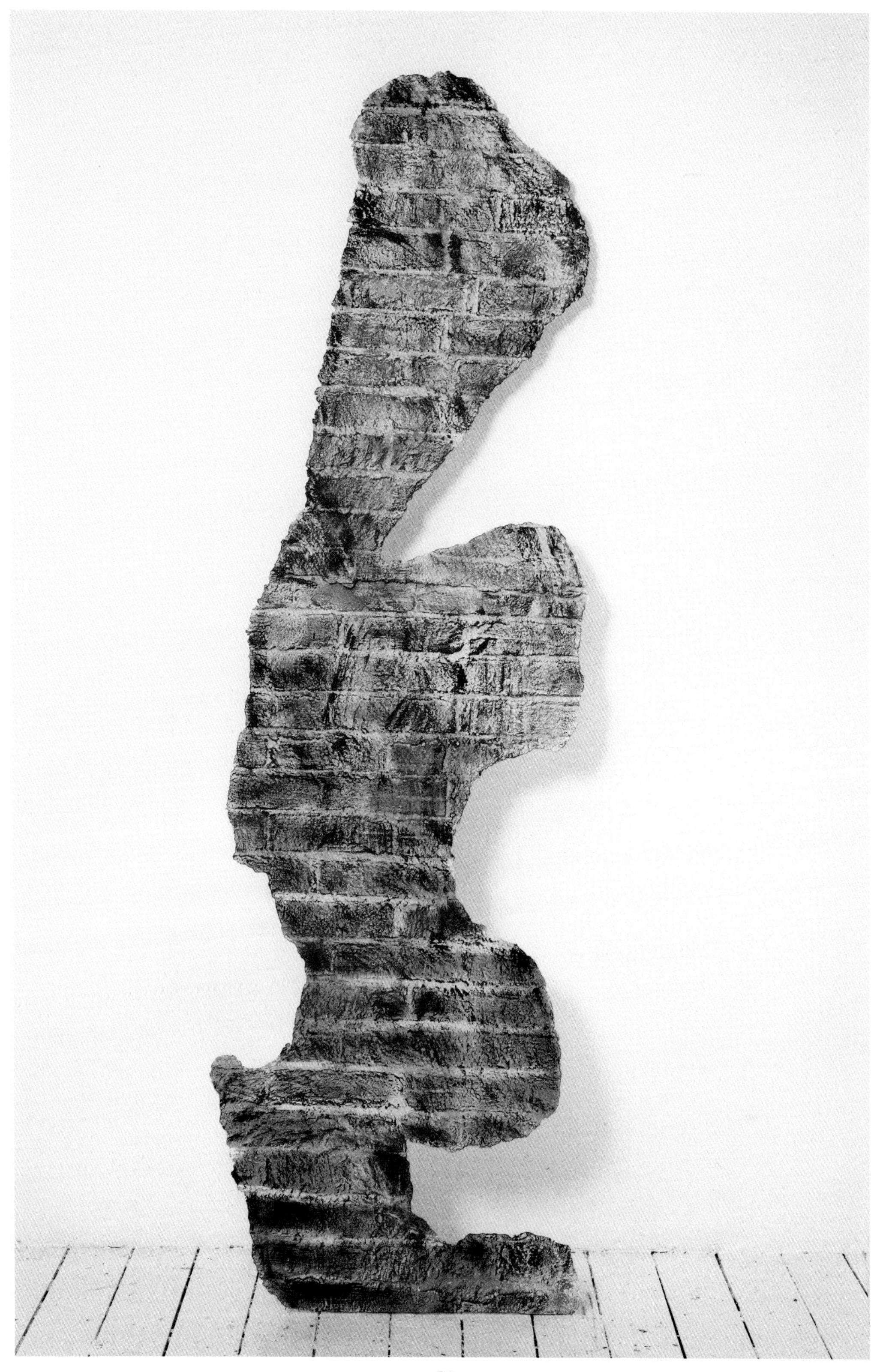

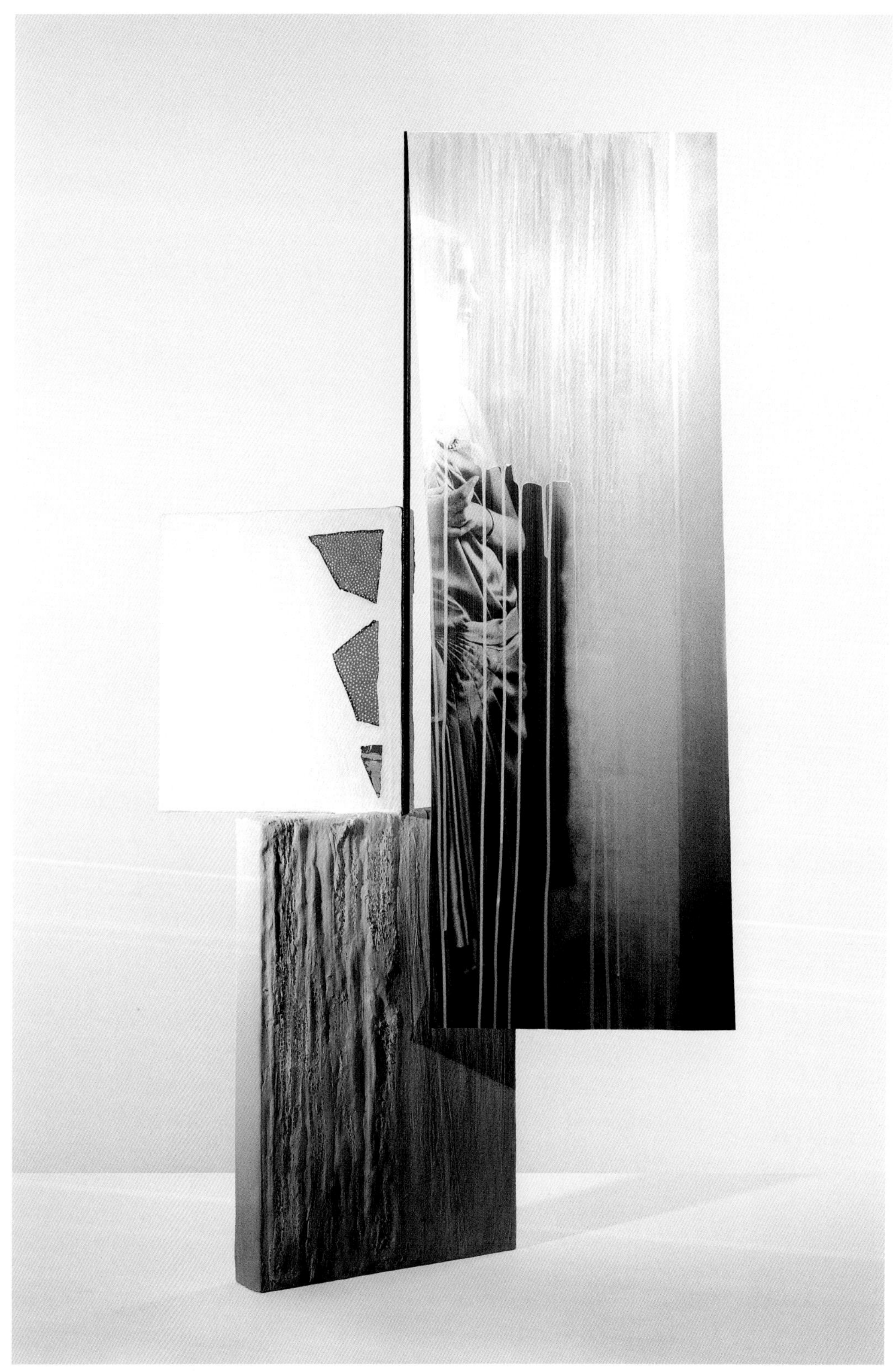

55, 56 (opposite)

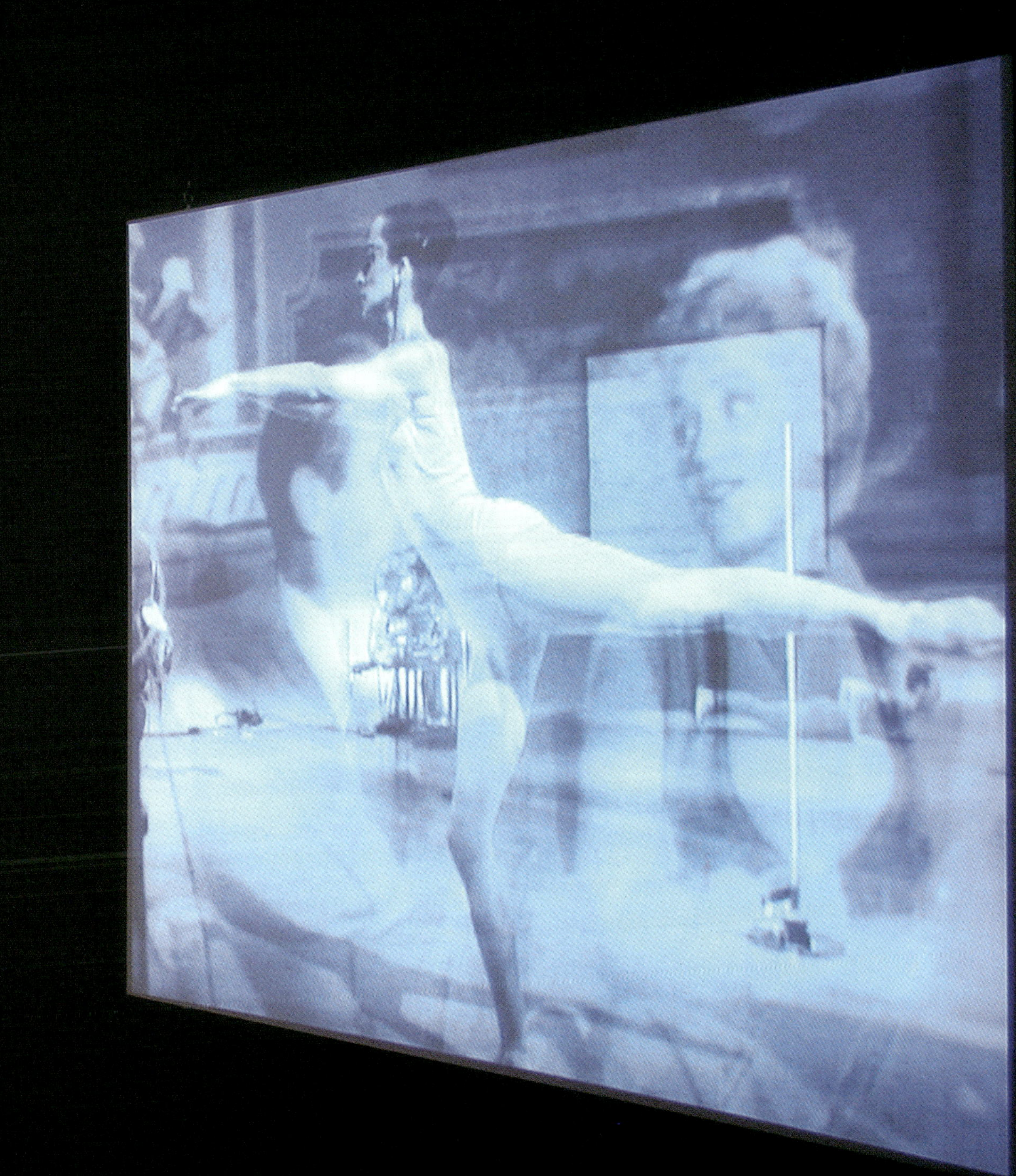

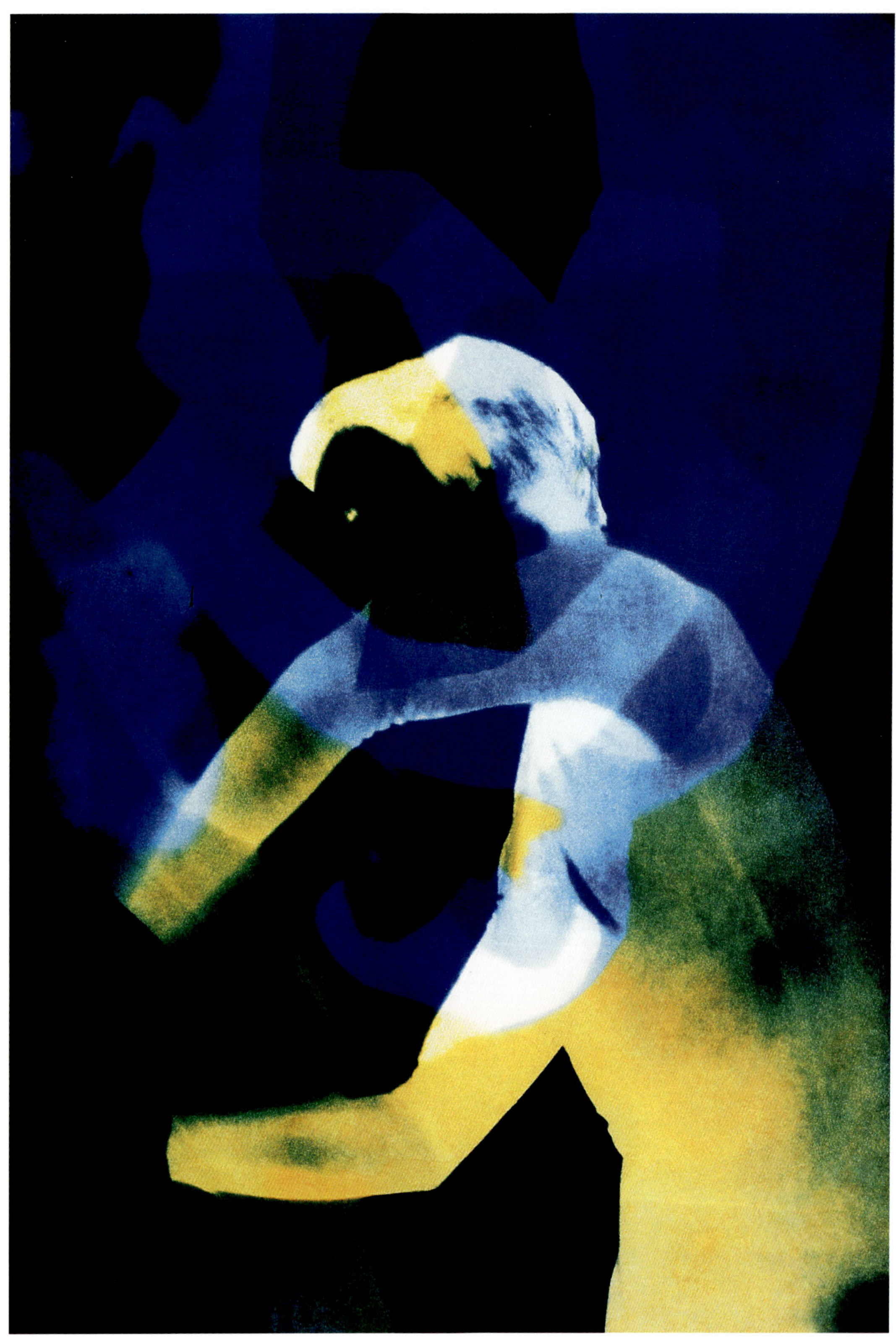

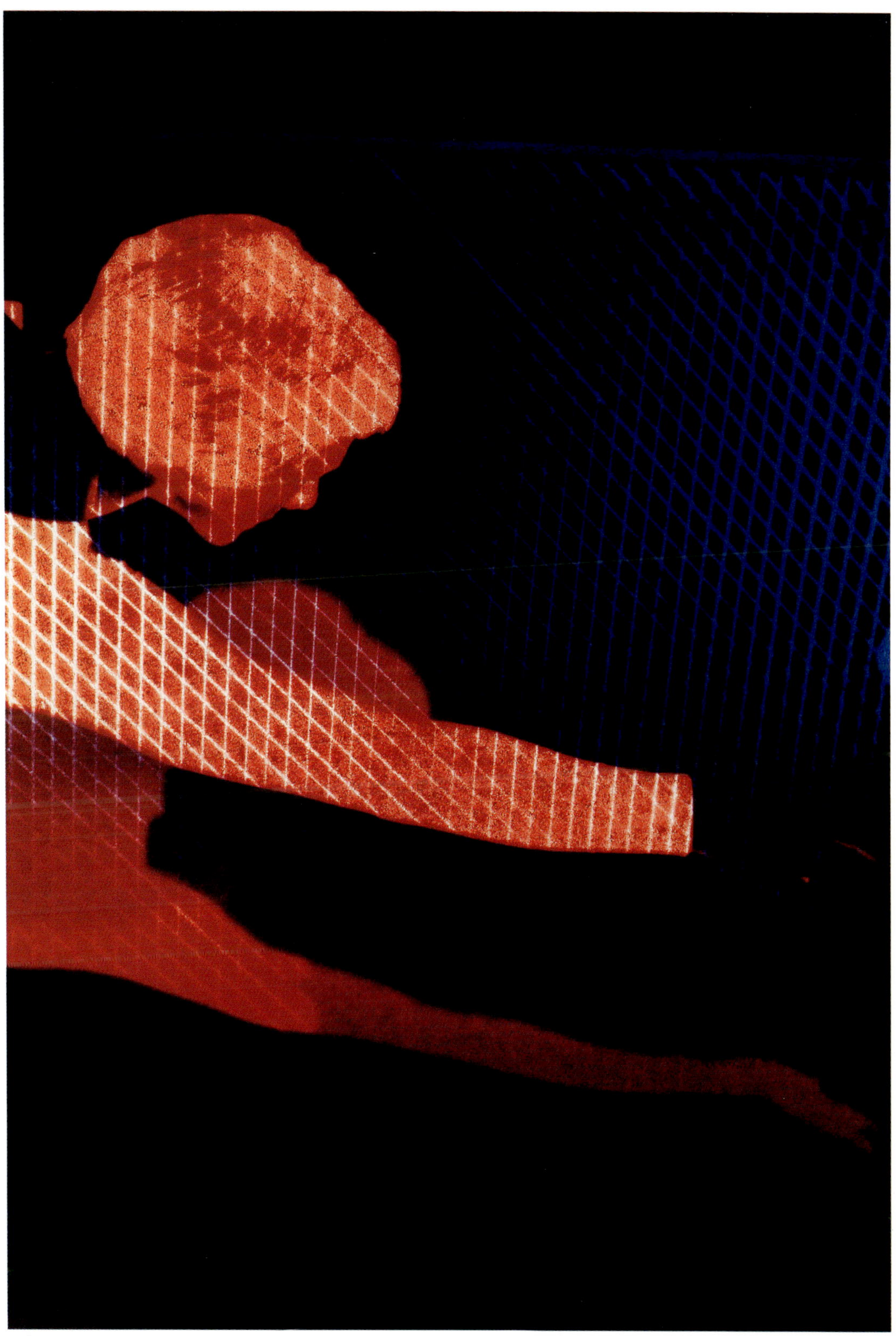

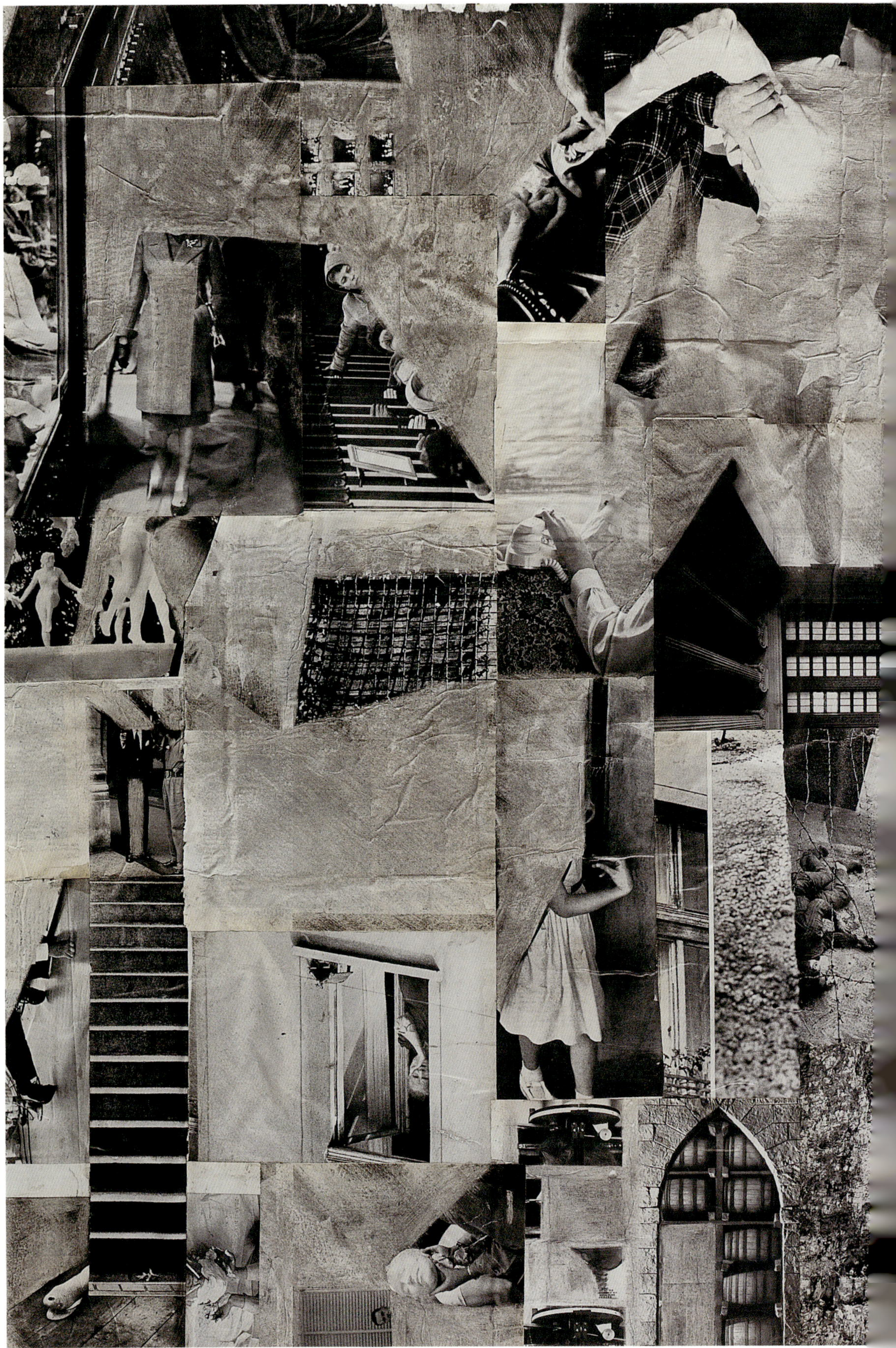

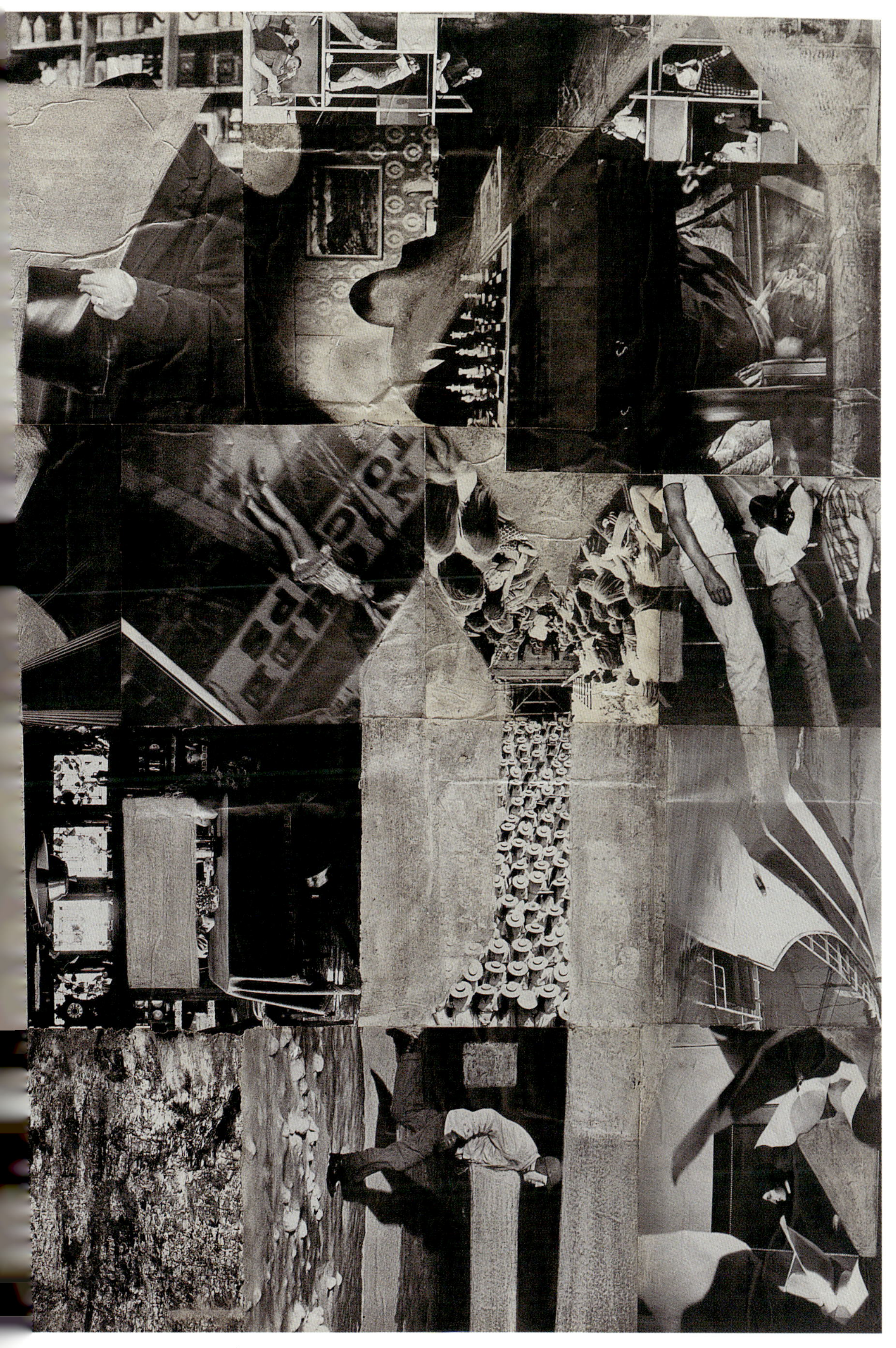

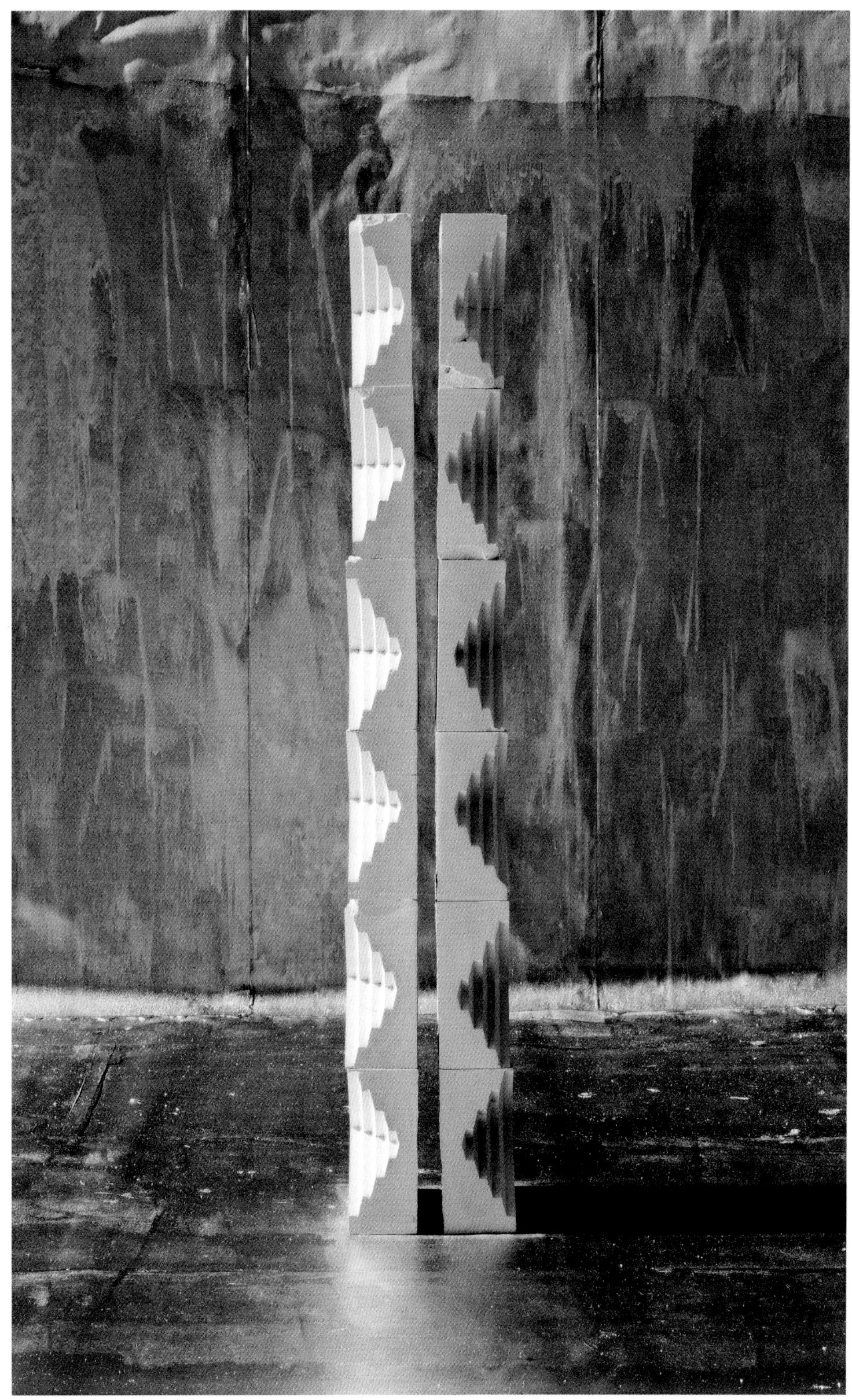

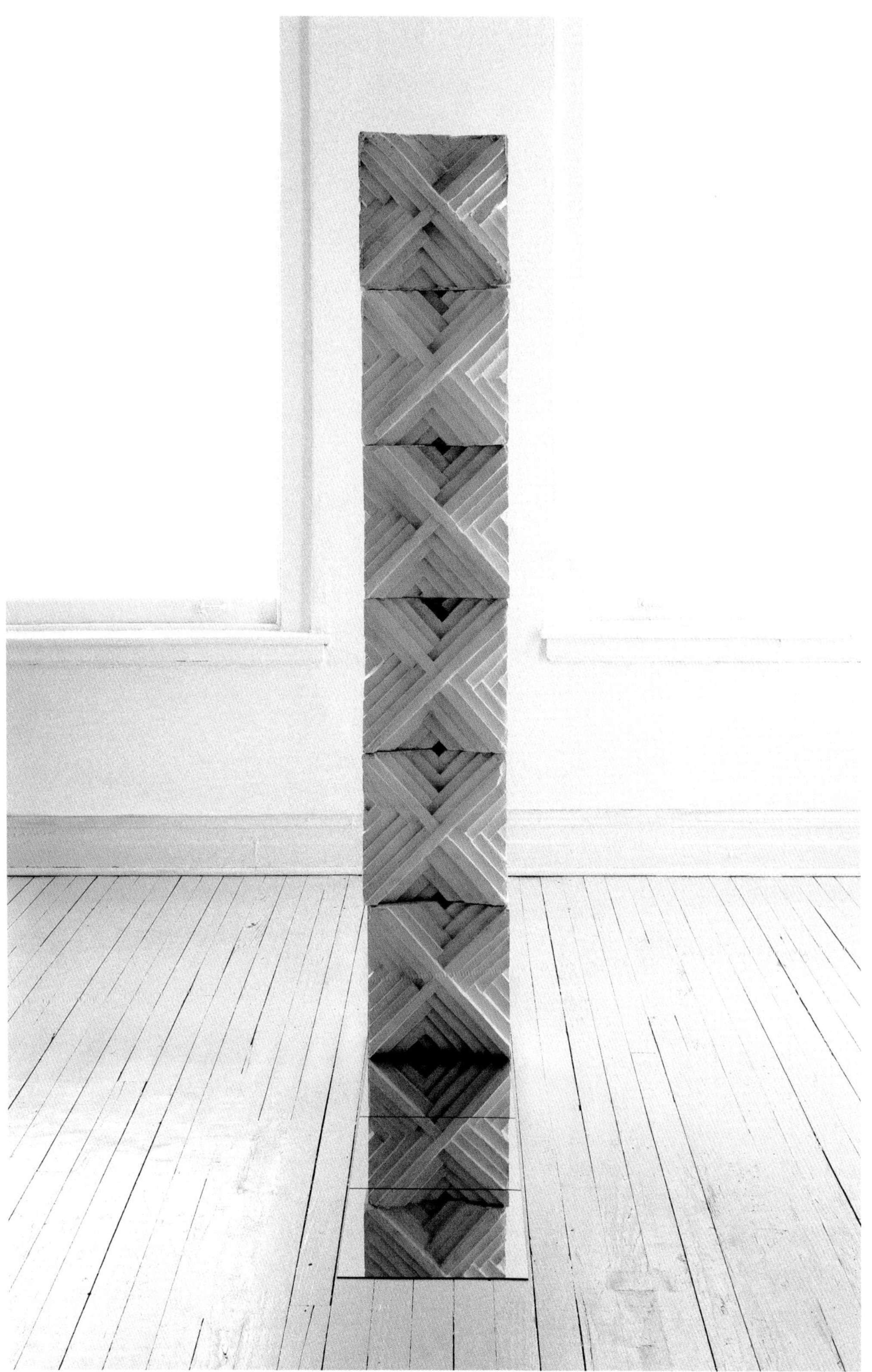

BODY/BUILDING

IB: This month features one larger work by each of you. Johannes, how did you achieve that mixture of color and texture in *Documentation of Body/Building*?

JVDB: That collage is made from sanding away the ink on a magazine page. I pushed certain pictures together whose elements would match up in appealing ways. The sanded white areas act as a unifying field and link disparate themes so they resemble one fresco. All of the pages come from 1950s *Life* magazines. The ink is probably toxic so the color you see reflects my life expectancy pluming out of my body as I breathed in all that wholesome dust.

IB: Sara, can you talk about the paint drips? Are they found or did you craft them? And what about texture in your work—what surface quality are you looking for?

SVDB: The images I have been working on recently include many painted elements with dripped paint or graphite lines heavily drawn over images. I was thinking about the images covered by these marks as a history rising to the surface. The texture and mark of the hand is important to me. Even though I like the work to feel balanced and formally resolved, and through the lighting, and printing I exploit aspects of the photographic process that can polish the image, I still want it to echo the rougher, more tactile process of its creation.

After includes an image of Lee Miller taken by Edward Steichen in the 1920s when she was a popular model for Conde Nast. Like Sarah Bernhardt and Sonia Delaunay, Miller forged a career when it was difficult for women to do so. She was an artist in her own right but also a muse to other influential artists, Man Ray in particular. A sense of theatricality permeated all aspects of her life, but she also experienced great difficulties early on, and horrific violence when she became a war photographer during World War II. I was drawn to this Steichen photograph because of the way Miller is posing. She appears inanimate, like a statue. Similarly to the men painting their faces in *Delaunay*, her stoic pose demonstrates the transition that occurs when someone is photographed: in front of the camera she has already become a static image. This Steichen image epitomizes staged studio photography: the corner

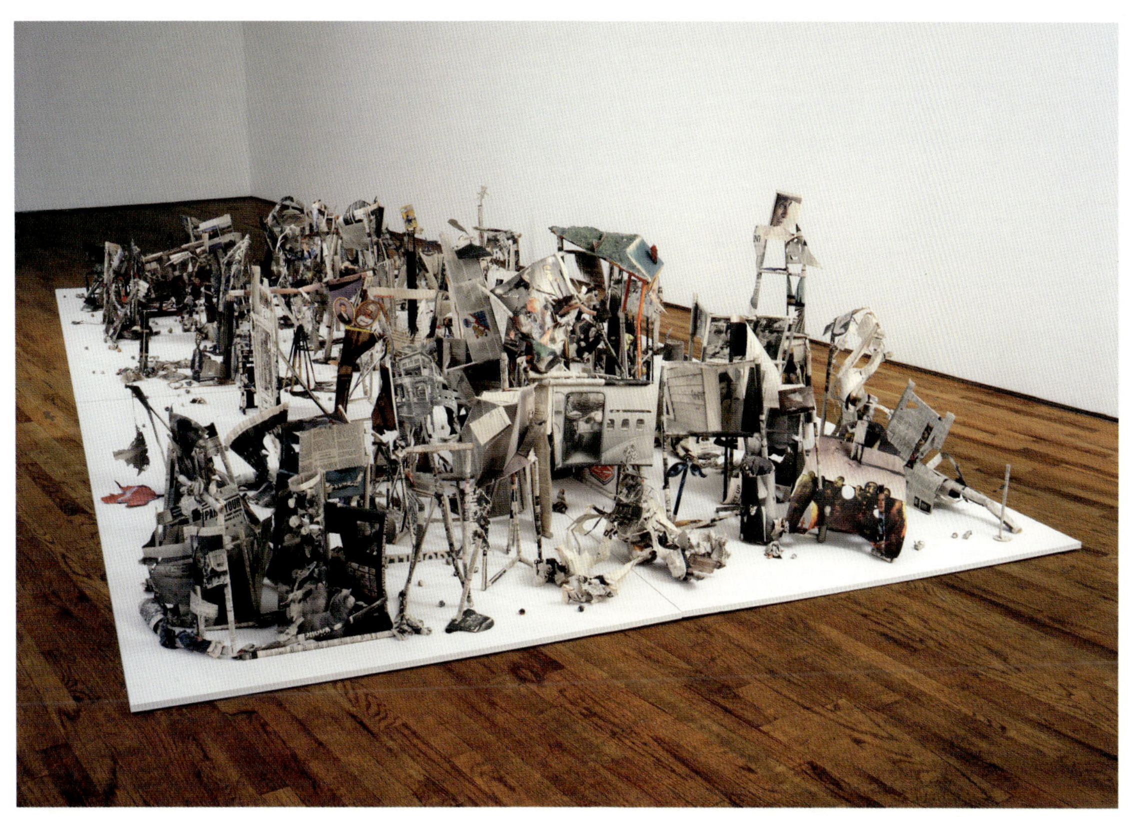

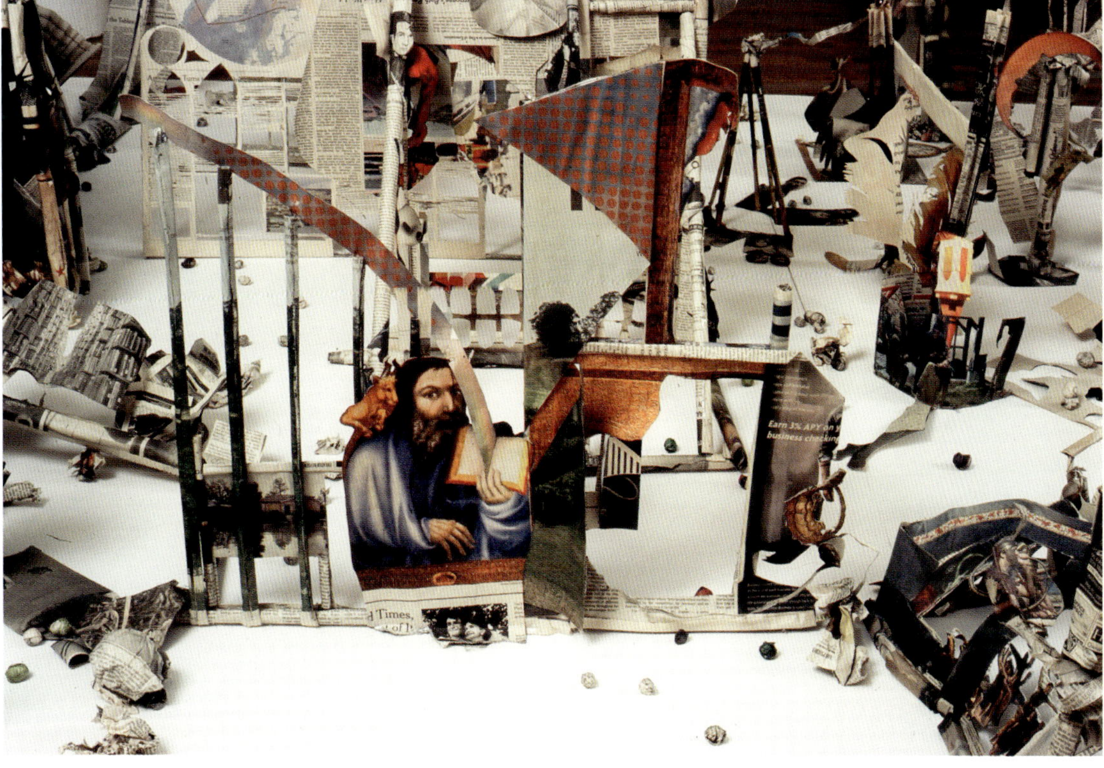
Earn 3% APY on
business checking

space in which she stands, the lighting, and the camera perspective are all very controlled. I wanted to keep elements of that control as a reference point to my work in the studio, but I am always striving to disrupt that control. This time the gesture entered in the cutting and the painting over the image.

The image of Miller hangs from a metal bar that rises from a plaster rectangle at the center of the composition. The blue/green shapes embedded within the plaster are pieces of glass I collected from abandoned factories in Detroit. I liked the texture and color of the glass and was drawn to the way the light hit it. I kept the plaster rough. In the bottom rectangle of plaster I embedded parts of a beaded dress I found in Detroit. Like the image being seen from behind the paint, it suggested a history rising to the surface.

IB: Stan's work this month is an important collaboration with the Merce Cunningham Dance Company and it involves many collaborators, including a few from Black Mountain College. Can you talk about this collaboration and where the video came from?

SVDB: The film was created for German television and is a layered documentary of a performance that was originally staged at Lincoln Center and has been restaged in the television studio for this broadcast. It is great because you get an intimate, revealing perspective on the event—one you would not have enjoyed as an audience member. The camera stays close to the performers, and in addition to projecting on screens behind the dancers, my father superimposed video images on top of the footage. Nam Jun Paik did a large portion of the video mixing. I don't know how Merce Cunningham and my father came to create this work together but I do know that dance was very important to him. He worked with dancers throughout his life. It is not shown often nor is his connection to Merce well known, but they were friends from school and I think it was Merce who first introduced my father to dance.

JVDB: While Dad was attending Black Mountain College he made an account in a sketchbook of a profound reaction to the dance performances at the school. He started taking still pictures of dancers and then transitioned to filming performances. When he discovered the possibility of capturing movement in the transpiring frame of film, he moved away from the static frame of a painting. Pieces like this with Merce Cunningham were efforts to exhale the breath of the camera as it followed the movements of a body.

IB: We hung the projection screen in the middle of the space to underline the notion of architecture and bodies in space. Can you talk about that in relation to your works?

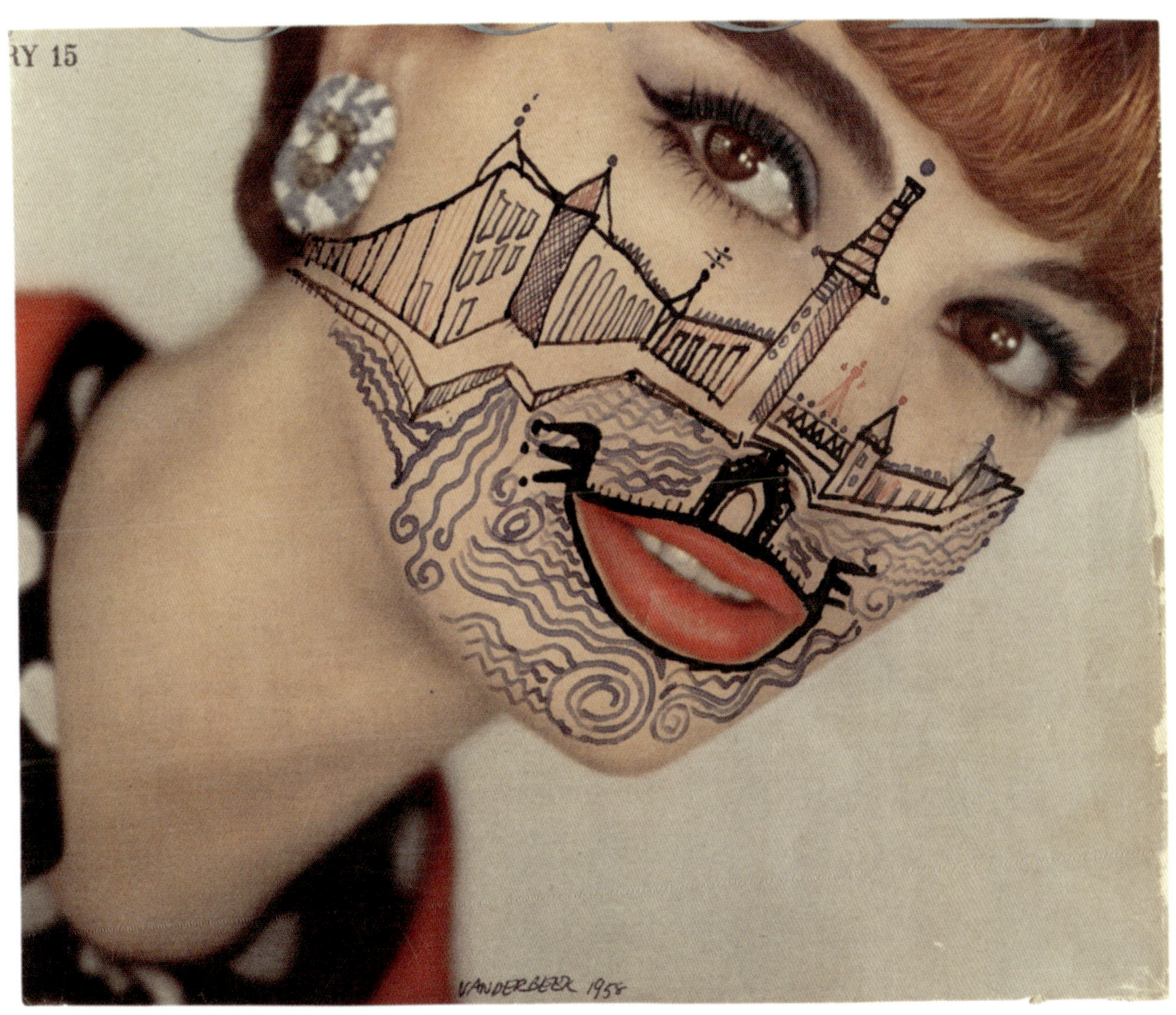
RY 15
VANDERBEEK 1958

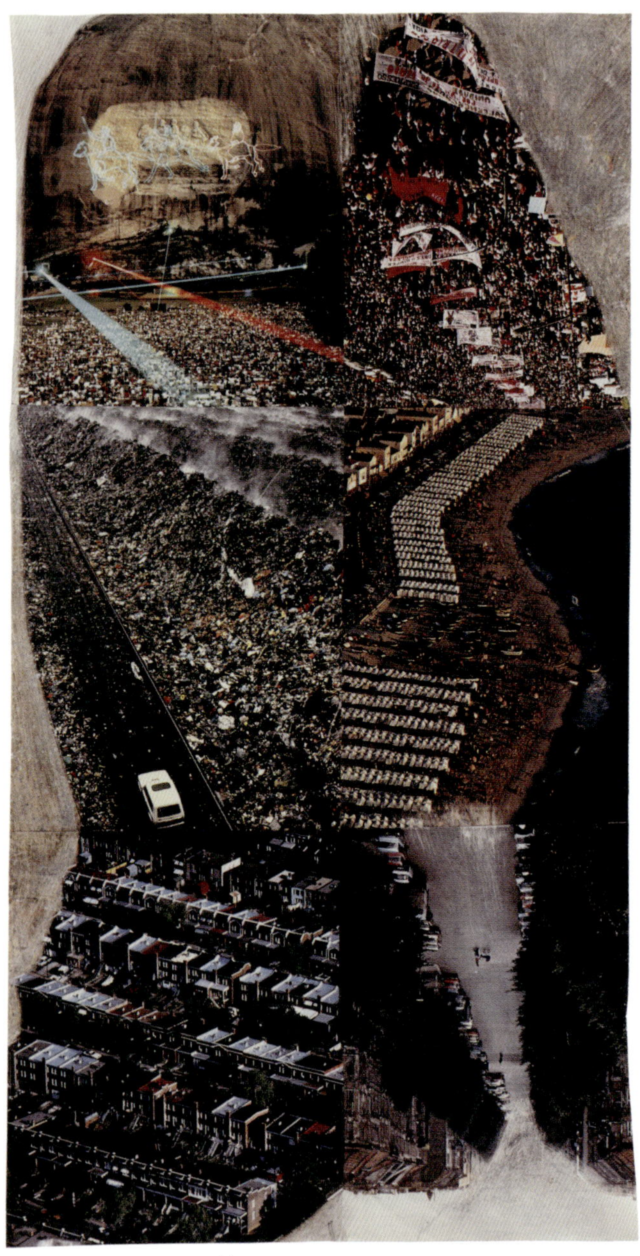

64

SVDB: I am interested in architecture because it is often a meeting of idealism and reality. I enjoy its mixture of function and form. I am drawn to architects who were somewhat utopian in their thinking about architecture, such as Le Corbusier and Frank Lloyd Wright, but I am also very interested in structures such as the painted mud houses of amaNdebele and Dogon tribes in Africa, the step pyramids of ancient Meso America, and the ruins of the industrial age that populate many American cities. Architecture of a country or city can reveal a lot about its culture, its divisions, and its strengths.

JVDB: The bodies in my collage are oriented in every possible direction that gravity encourages. The people in the pictures are suspended in actions that highlight the suspense between movement and stillness. You see bodies hanging out of windows, slumped in the gutter, descending a staircase, leaping through the air, holding a bag, kissing faces, or running on ice. Harsh angles of black and white suggest the pervasive geometry of buildings that support our nimble shape. It shows how much a body makes a space and a space makes a body.

IB: How important is installation to you? You both have experimented with hanging things low on the wall or putting work out on tables—can you describe how you approach installation?

JVDB: I approach installation with an open mind so that the artworks can fulfill their optimum purpose. This is a very intuitive process, like assembling a puzzle without a final image in mind. It becomes a negotiation with space, color, profiles, and weight. The aim is to find a positioning where each piece has its own stature but together vibrates the room.

SVDB: I often think about how the images I create are going to move across a wall or, in their grouping, define a narrative. I'd like to get a little more adventurous in my installations, possibly by considering different means of breaking up a gallery space to experiment with lighting, or try something more theatrical to really alter the exhibition space.

Body/Building captions

54 Johannes VanDerBeek, *Wall #4 (Thunder)*, 2011, fiberglass, Hydrocal, resin and paint, 80 × 28 × 1/4 inches

55 Sara VanDerBeek, *After*, 2009, digital C-print, 60 × 40 3/8 inches

56 Stan VanDerBeek and Merce Cunningham Dance Company, Still from *Variations V*, 1965. Film produced for German Television transferred to DVD, 49:23 minutes. Courtesy of The Estate of Stan VanDerBeek and Merce Cunningham Dance Company. Installation view, Tang Museum, Saratoga Springs, New York, 2009

57 Stan VanDerBeek, *Untitled (from Feedback)*, 1968/2009, C-print on aluminum, 23 7/8 × 16 3/8 inches

58 Stan VanDerBeek, *Untitled (from Feedback)*, 1968/2009, C-print on aluminum, 23 7/8 × 16 3/8 inches

59 Johannes VanDerBeek, *Documentation of Body/Building*, 2007, sanded magazine pages, 61 7/8 × 43 3/4 inches, Private Collection

60 Sara VanDerBeek, *Caryatid II*, 2010, digital C-print, 74 × 46 inches

61 Sara VanDerBeek, *Caryatid*, 2010, digital C-print, 74 × 48 inches

62 Johannes VanDerBeek, *Newspaper Ruins*, 2005, mixed media, 48 × 96 × 192 inches

63 Stan VanDerBeek, *Untitled (from A La Mode)*, 1958, ink on found photograph, 7 × 8 1/2 inches

64 Johannes VanDerBeek, *Crowded Face*, 2009, sanded magazine pages, 22 1/2 × 12 1/2 inches

65 Stan VanDerBeek, *Untitled (from A La Mode)*, 1958, ink and paper on found photograph, 6 1/2 × 7 3/4 inches

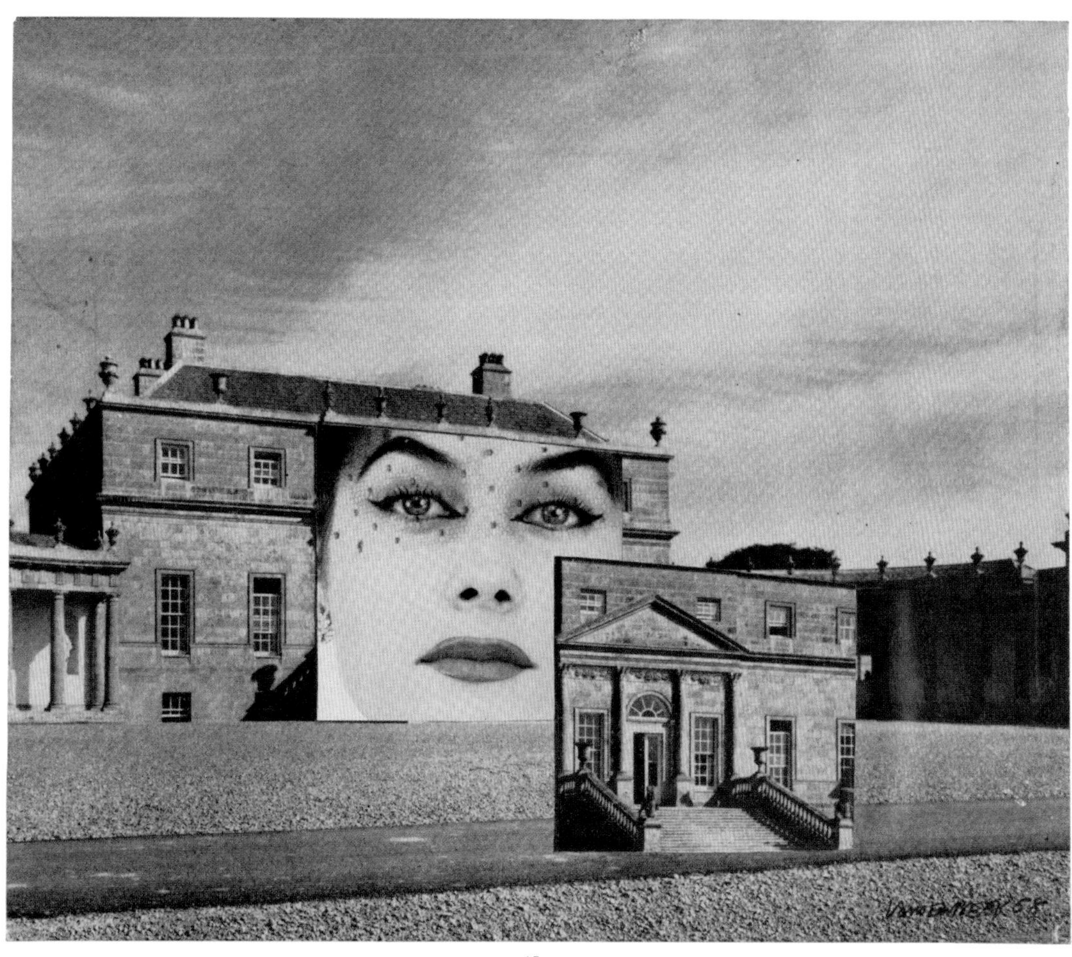

65

STUDIO

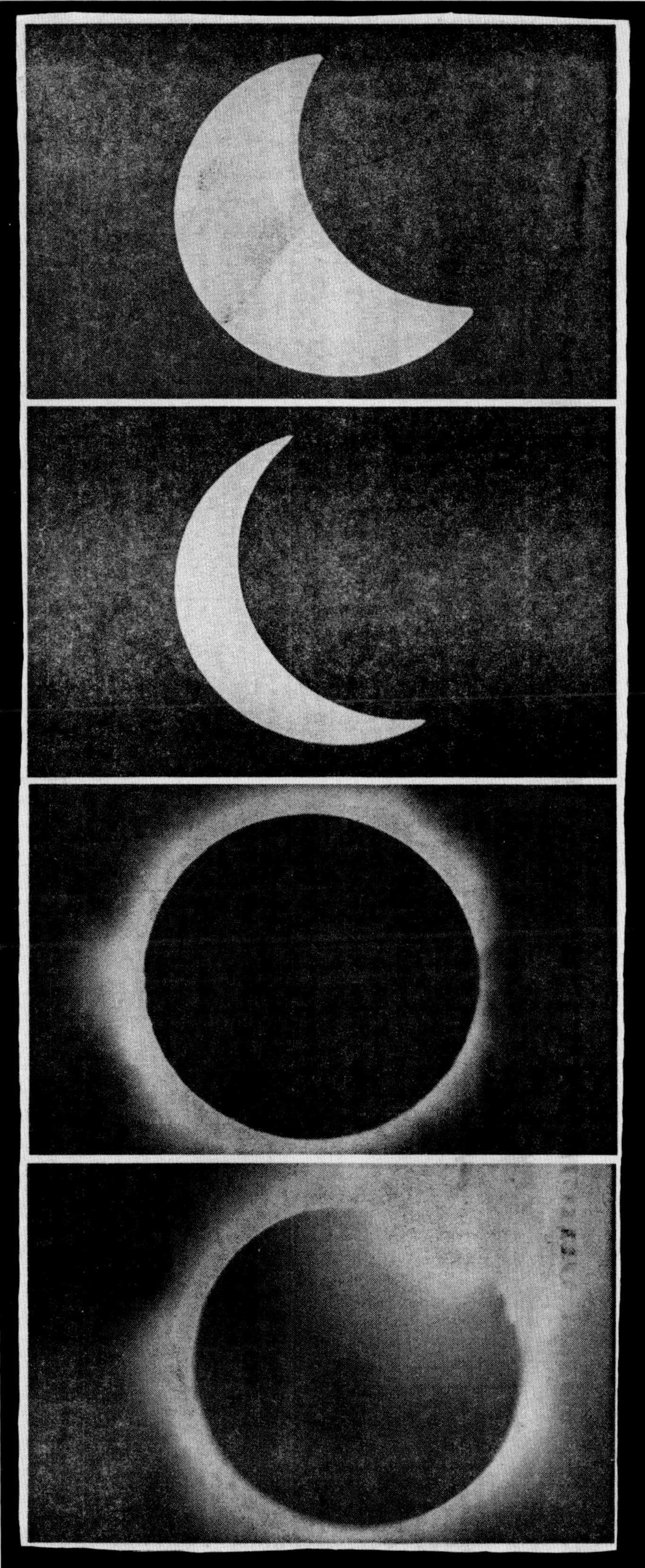

66, 67 (following)

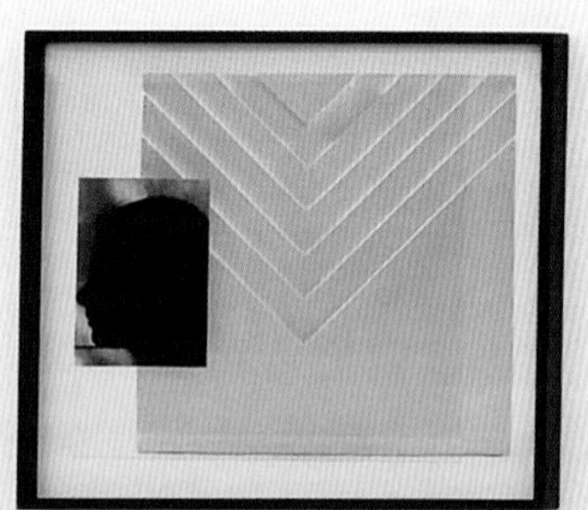

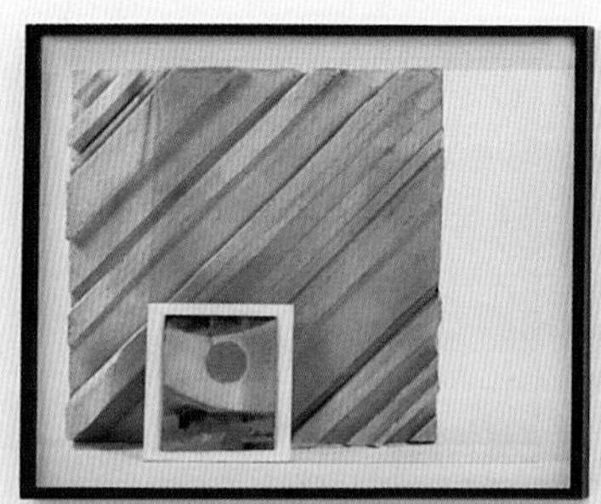

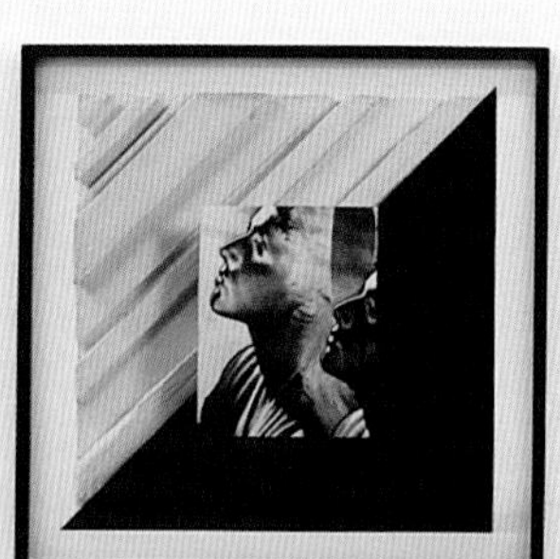

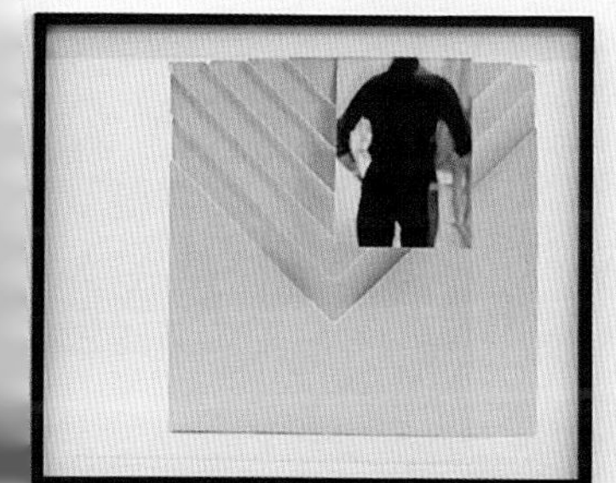
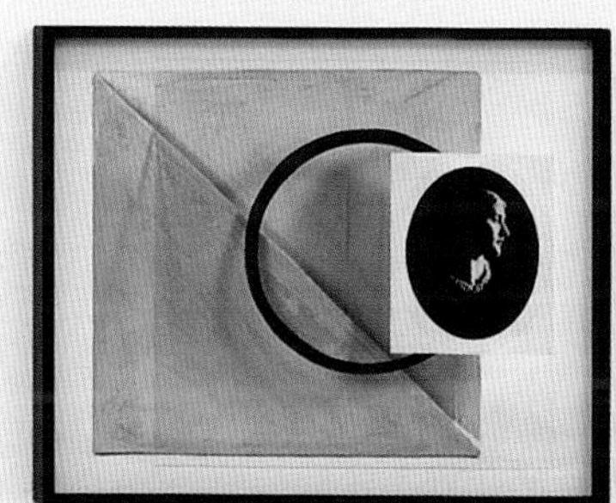
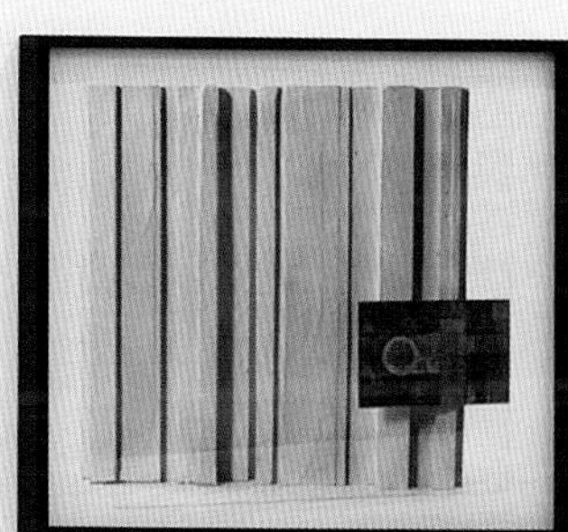

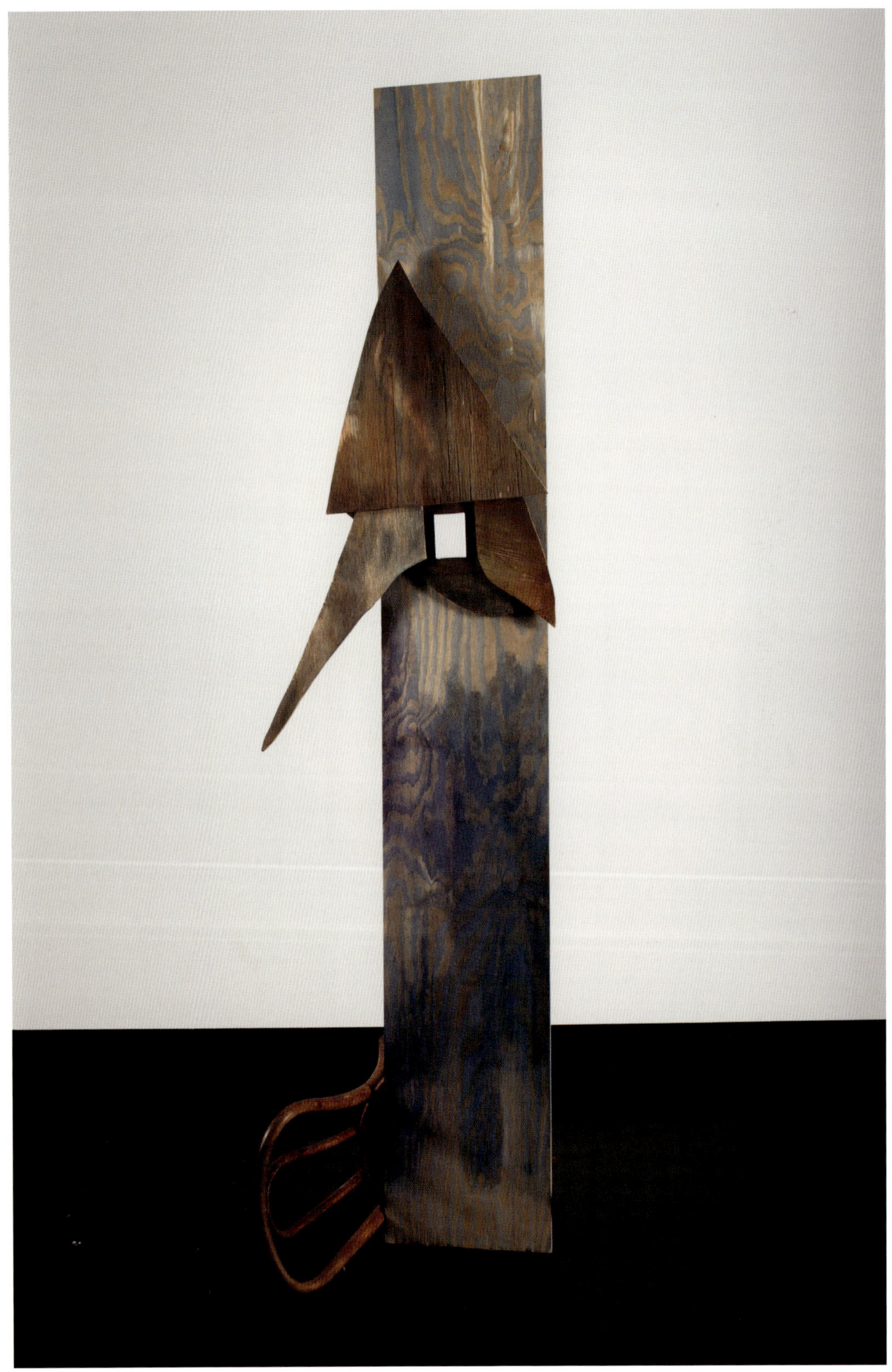

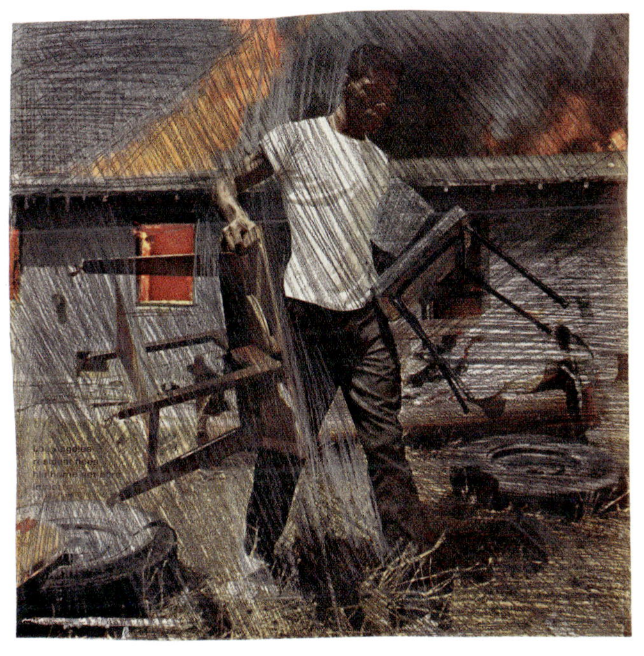

69

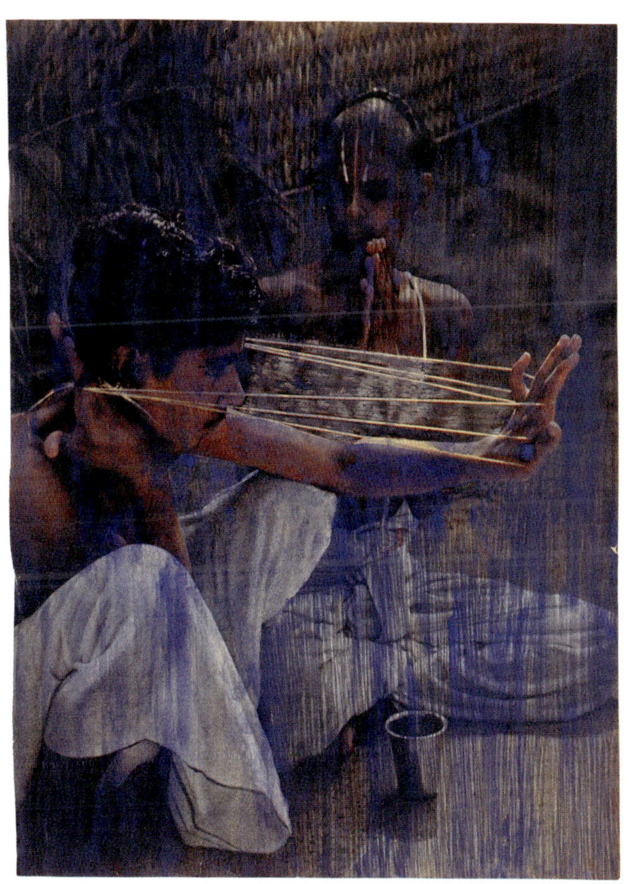

70

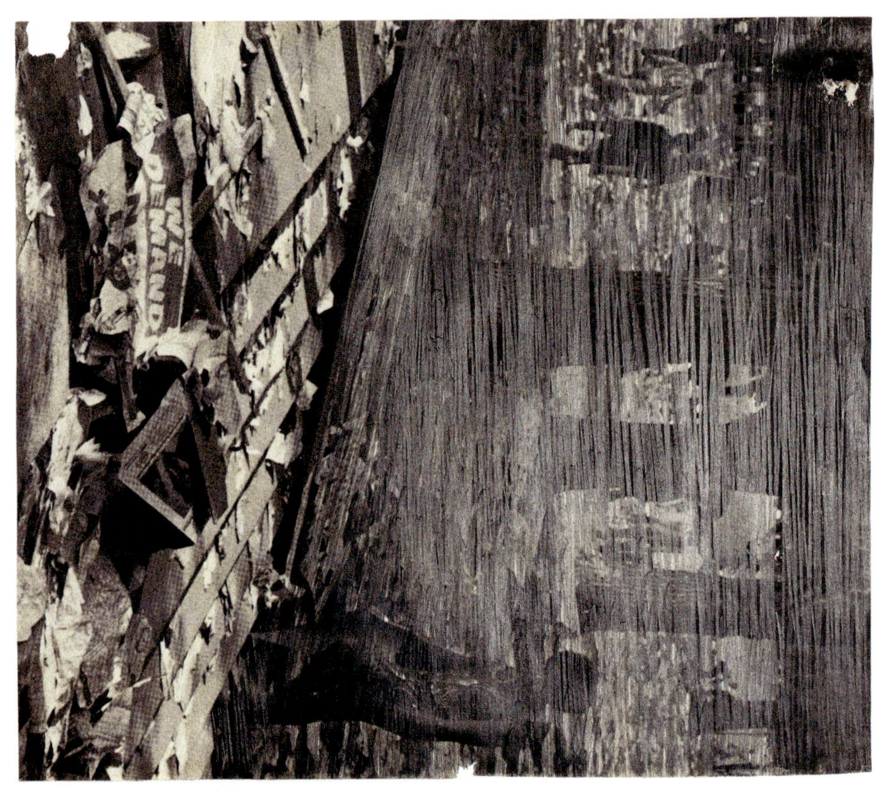
WE DEMAND

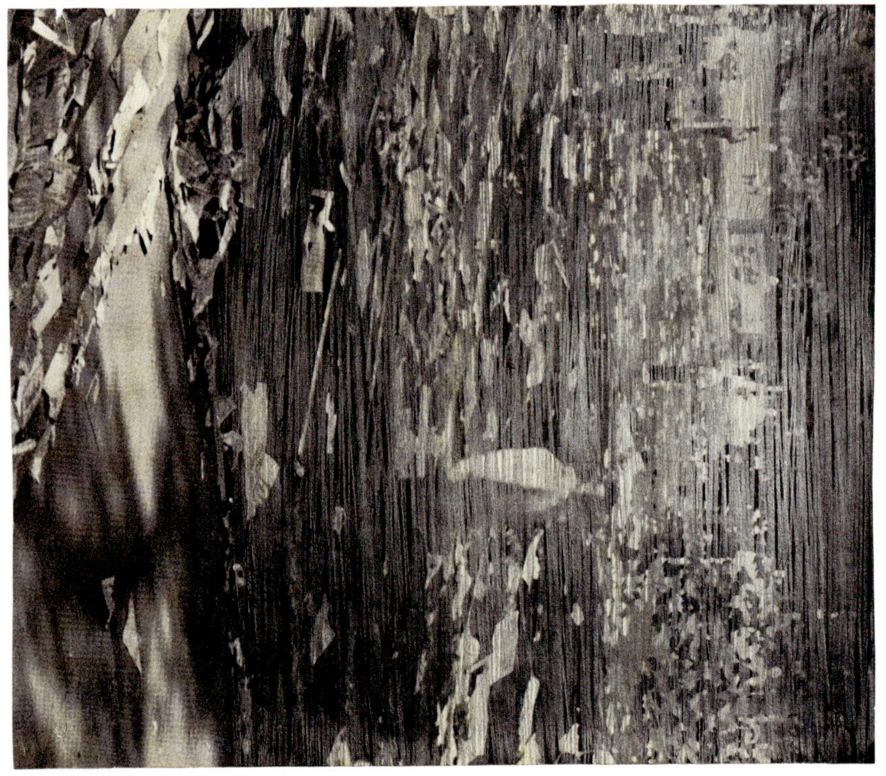

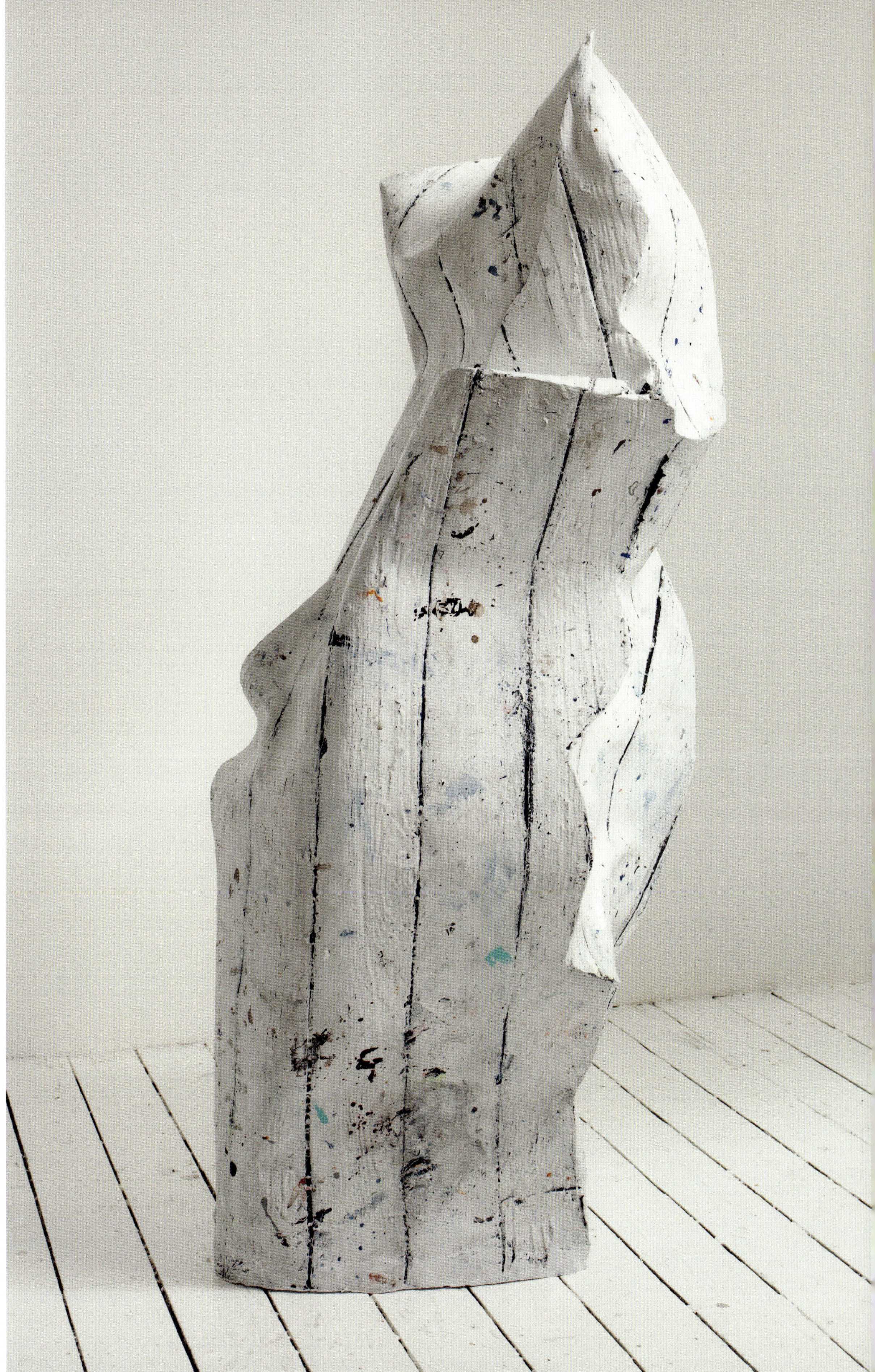

STUDIO

IB: Describe your studio. What does "studio" mean to you?

JVDB: My studio doesn't look like anything special. I'm trying to change that constantly by making it a space that reflects the tone or feeling I want my work to have. At one point, when I was thinking a lot about dreams, I decided I needed to work only in low light so nothing in the room had a hard outline, because that is how things appear to me in dreams. But that was an impractical idea. If anything, I try to make the space disappear so I don't fixate on its flaws. Sometimes, when I'm absorbed in a specific piece, I forget about my studio for a while. When I am in between pieces I start looking at the alterations I need to make. In that way it's kind of an abusive relationship because I only pay attention to it when I want something from it. I should really be more kind to it.

SVDB: Studio means process to me as much as it signifies a space in which I work. Until we opened Guild & Greyshkul with studios in the basement, I did not have a studio, or a studio-based practice. The studio can be an imaginary space, one of the mind rather than reality—an internal, deeply personal space. If the studio is working, it is as a physical realm, representative of your mind's activities. What I have appreciated about this show is a sense of experimentation that is closer to the studio process than to the finality of a show, and the quick turnover between exhibitions has encouraged a looseness and gestural quality that I'd like to strive for more in future installations.

My studio is usually a mess, and organized not in a rational manner but more in a tactile way. I collect many images that often sit in piles in my flat file. Sorting through them to find a particular image usually leads to other tangents and associations. I've just rearranged my studio so that one wall is full of shelves displaying different materials and found objects made visible for consideration in my sculptures and assemblages.

There are two sides to my practice: the messier construction side, and the cleaner, photographic side. I try to embrace and maintain a balance of both but sometimes I worry I don't retain the looseness of the building side as it transforms to the other. The final print is as significant as the creation of the sculpture or situation that I photograph. I think of the printing lab as an extension of my

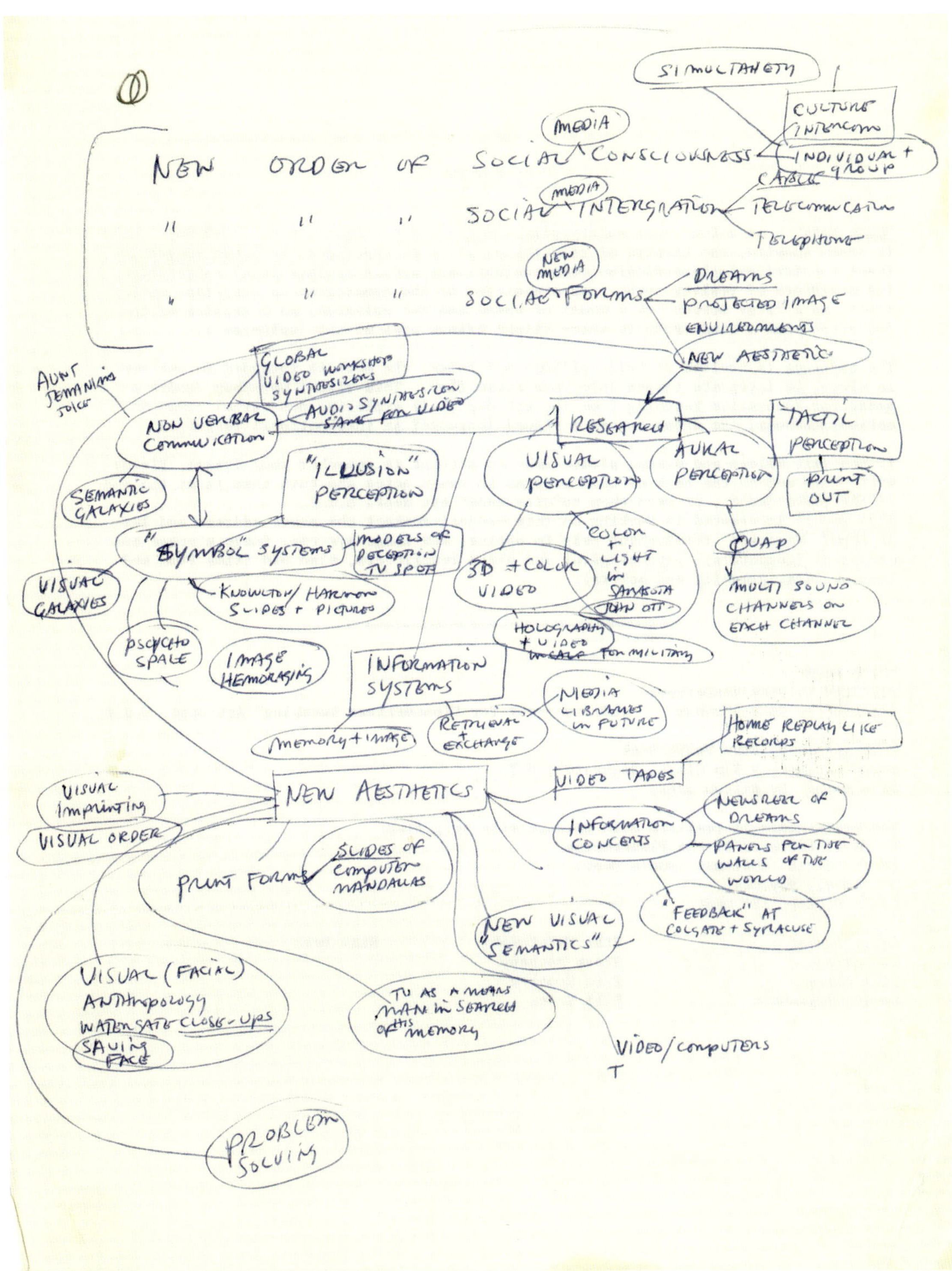
SIMULTANEITY
CULTURE INTERCOM
MEDIA
NEW ORDER OF SOCIAL CONSCIOUSNESS
INDIVIDUAL + GROUP
MEDIA
" " " SOCIAL INTERGRATION
CABLE
TELECOMMUNICATION
TELEPHONE
NEW MEDIA
" " " SOCIAL FORMS
DREAMS
PROJECTED IMAGE
ENVIRONMENTS
NEW AESTHETIC
GLOBAL VIDEO WORKSHOPS SYNTHESIZERS
NON VERBAL COMMUNICATION
AUDIO SYNTHESIZER SAME FOR VIDEO
RESEARCH
TACTIL PERCEPTION
PRINT OUT
VISUAL PERCEPTION
AURAL PERCEPTION
"ILLUSION" PERCEPTION
SEMANTIC GALAXIES
"SYMBOL" SYSTEMS
MODELS OF PERCEPTION TV SPOT
COLOR + LIGHT in SARASOTA
JOHN OTT
3D + COLOR VIDEO
QUAD
MULTI SOUND CHANNELS ON EACH CHANNEL
VISUAL GALAXIES
KNOWLTON/HARMON SLIDES + PICTURES
HOLOGRAPHY + VIDEO
FOR MILITARY
PSYCHO SPACE
IMAGE HEMORAGING
INFORMATION SYSTEMS
MEDIA LIBRARIES IN FUTURE
MEMORY + IMAGE
RETRIEVAL + EXCHANGE
HOME REPLAY LIKE RECORDS
VIDEO TAPES
VISUAL IMPRINTING
NEW AESTHETICS
VISUAL ORDER
NEWSREEL OF DREAMS
INFORMATION CONCERTS
PANELS FOR THE WALLS OF THE WORLD
SLIDES OF COMPUTER MANDALAS
PRINT FORMS
"FEEDBACK" AT COLGATE + SYRACUSE
NEW VISUAL "SEMANTICS"
VISUAL (FACIAL) ANTHROPOLOGY
WATERGATE CLOSE-UPS
SAVING FACE
TV AS A MEANS MAN IN SEARCH OF HIS MEMORY
VIDEO/COMPUTERS
PROBLEM SOLVING

studio, because the images change a great deal when I'm finalizing them. At the printing stage I have moved from the more isolated solo practice of my studio to a collaborative partnership with my printer. I try not to overwork images, though, and recently I have been leaving them rawer than some of the more polished earlier works. I like the work to feel as though it can be entered, and not so controlled and finished that the viewer remains solely on the surface.

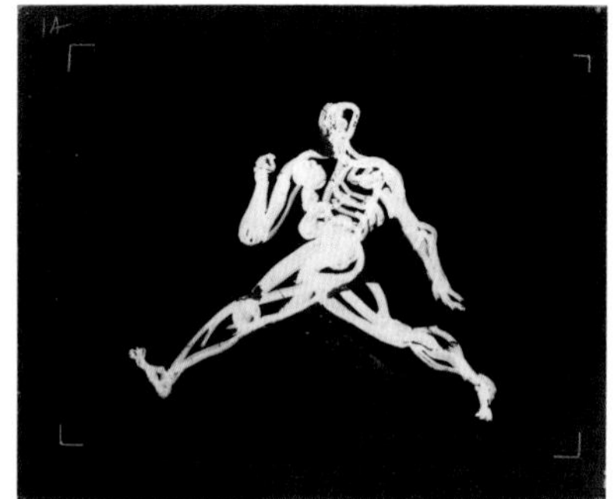

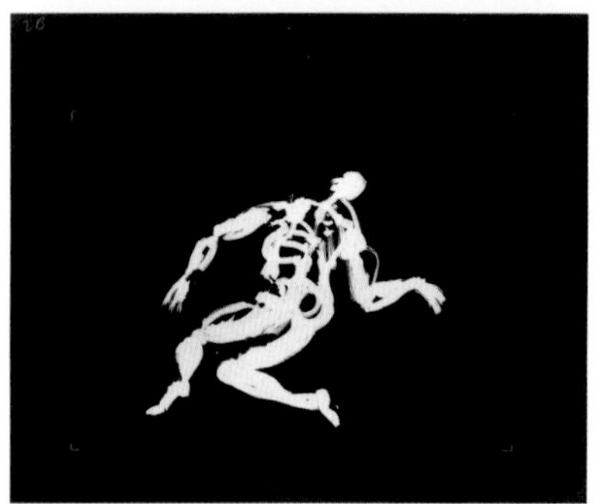

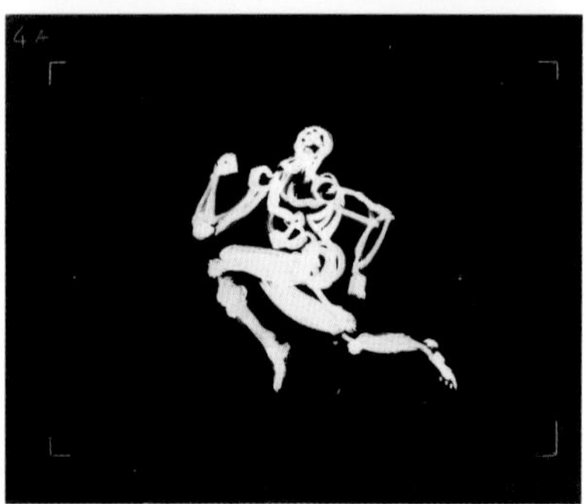

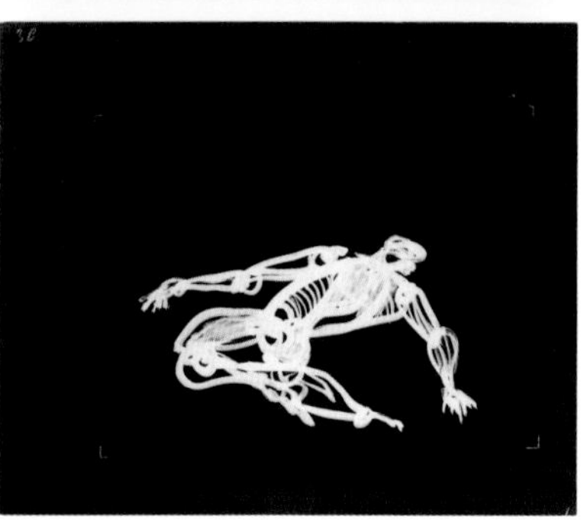

74

IB: How much do you like to reveal about your process? What value does mystery have in your work?

JVDB: I don't like to spell things out too clearly. I would like to make a career out of avoiding firm definitions because they make me uncomfortable. People forget there is no right answer in art; that its engine is fueled by intangibles like taste. The challenge is that we are an information and commodity-based society so people are accustomed to receiving an overload of explanatory content. It would be nice if individuals used their intuition to navigate their reactions to an artwork, but I understand it is not so straight-forward and that reason is on the hunt. I've been naïve in the past to think that if you put all of your effort into the way the object performs visually, then you should not have to explain it with so many words. It is a matter of balance. Keep the mystery of the object and accept it as open to interpretation—but a small point in the right direction does not hurt.

SVDB: Mystery is important because it encourages imagination. I do a lot of research when making a new body of work, and that research often influences my use of found images, objects, or spaces. When possible, I like to convey certain aspects of that decision process, but I don't want to be so authoritarian as to prevent viewers from arriving at their own ideas. It's a balance. One is continually revealing and withholding in one's work, and equally so in discussions about it. I'd like to feel that at times nothing is withheld, but I think I'm too guarded and perhaps too process-oriented to allow that. It's a good question: can photography, which in essence is a process and an interpretation of supposed "actual events," be mysterious? The purpose of the lenses, mirrors, focus, and apertures of a camera are to record in clear and distinct detail that which is in front of the camera. Can an act of capture be mysterious?

I hope it can go beyond the more obvious idea of mystery–i.e., illusion or obfuscation—and closer to the ancient sense of mystery as an almost spiritual experience. Can viewers in this world of millions and millions of images still wonder at the creation of a photographic image? Can they be curious as to how the image came to be, and what, in its creation, it says about our world? I would like my images to be grounded in this world but also to transcend it.

IB: Johannes, can you talk about the chairs in your sculpture this month. Did they come from your studio?

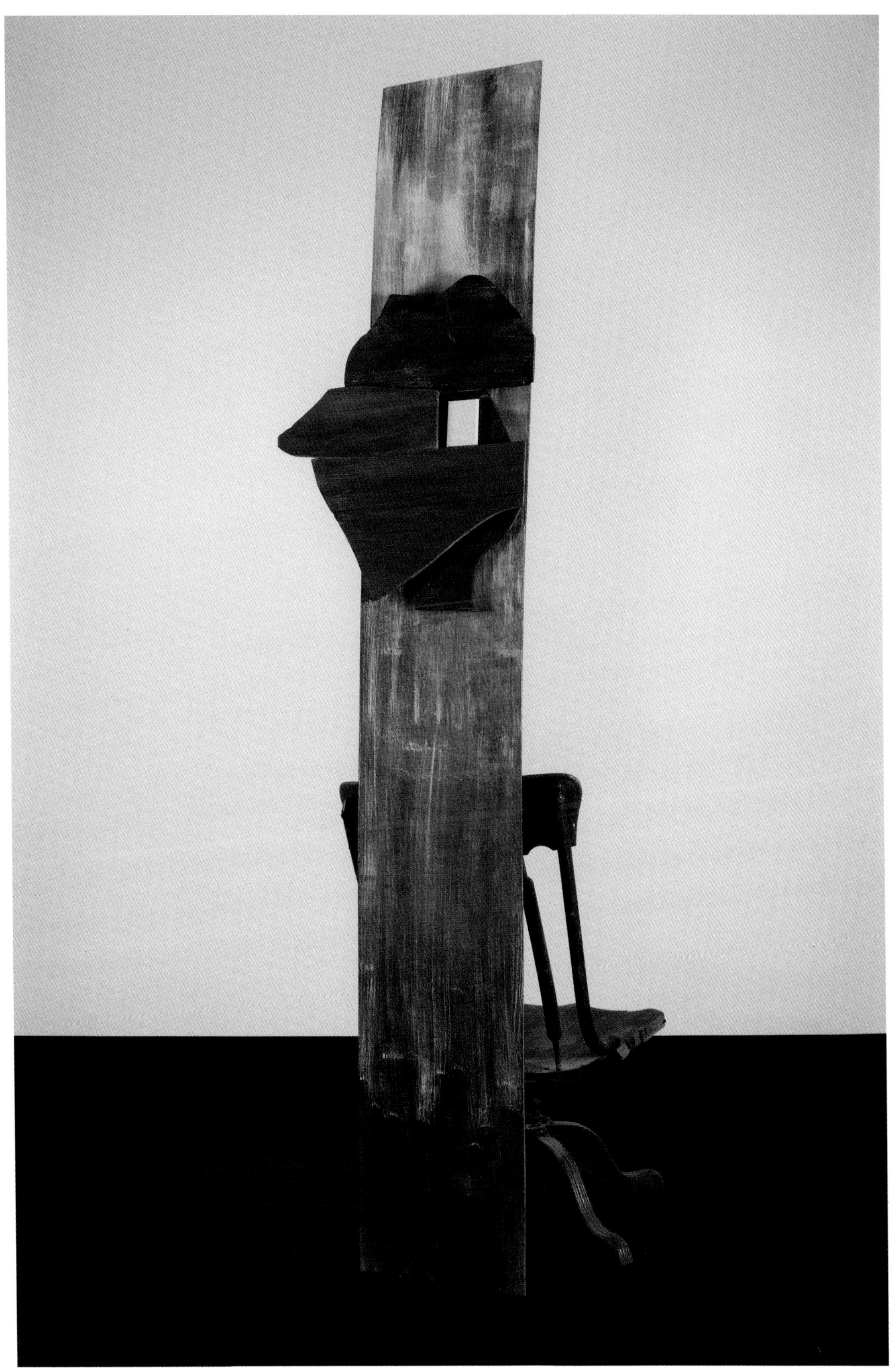

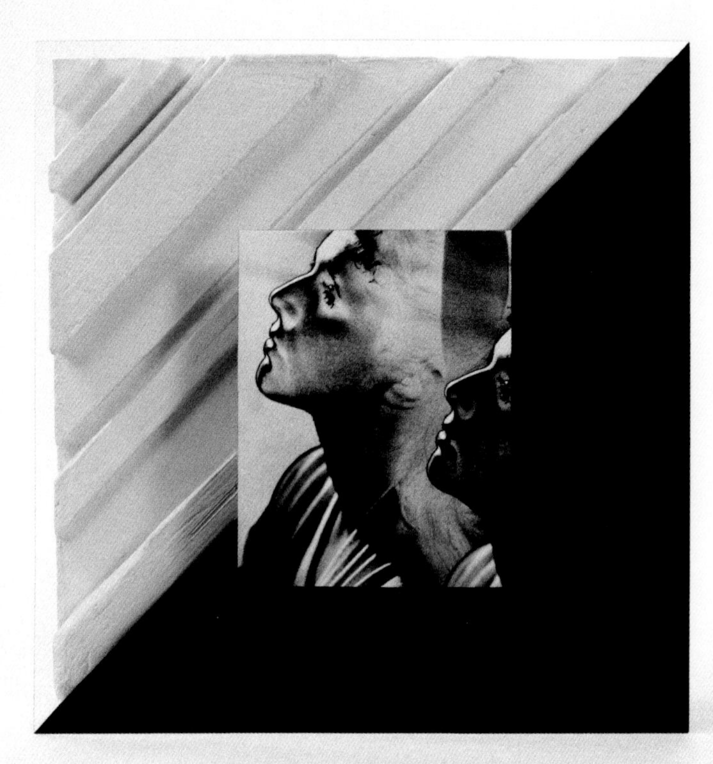

76

JVDB: I had these chairs in my studio for years and debated how to use them. One of the chairs is actually my dad's old studio chair, so I felt the reverberations of his own brainstorming held in that saddle. I figured bringing that chair back into the vicinity of his work would bring some nice poetics to the show. The planks I added stand in for the walls of my studio. The frame/face forms that I put on the planks became ambassadors for the ideas I was circulating. Then I put in the tiny blank canvas at the center to mark the empty hole that all the deliberation was aiming at. As a total object, they were partly ridiculous easels—a lot of material to hold up little canvases with nothing on them. In that way they also became a farcical model of the stages one goes through while thinking about making something. There is this buildup to a moment of decision, and when it happens it can sometimes feel as puny as those tiny canvases—and yet that little decision requires a lot of support to keep it standing firm.

IB: Sara, can you talk about the four photographers in your work?

SVDB: This is the first piece where I used plaster forms, which I have been increasingly incorporating. I made unique plaster casts for each of the six images in *Four Photographers*. I then set a glass panel on each plaster square and placed a photo or photo-reproduction on the face of the glass. I arranged both the individual compositions and the overall group specifically to evoke an architectural frieze of classical sculpture. I also mean it to imply motion and feel like a filmstrip or a contact sheet. The source images come from three of the four photographers to which the title refers. My father, while at Black Mountain, took the images of dancers, and two photographs include abstract paintings he made as a young artist in New York. I used a portrait of Virginia Woolf's mother by Julia Margaret Cameron and a solarized image by Man Ray to represent different eras of photography and its continually evolving aesthetic and conceptual aims. The women's profiles also reminded me of the horses in the Parthenon frieze, and the beautiful, now-decapitated horse's head on view at the British Museum among the Elgin marbles. I do not place myself on a level with the other artists I have included in this work, but wanting to allude to the sense of time, process, and my camera's perspective, I included myself as the fourth photographer.

Studio captions

66 Sara VanDerBeek, *Eclipse Newspaper Blue*, 2010, digital C-print, 40 × 17 inches

67 Sara VanDerBeek, *Four Photographers*, 2008, digital C-prints, left to right: 18 ½ × 20 ¾ inches; 18 ½ × 22 ⅛ inches; 18 ½ × 18 ½ inches; 18 ½ × 22 ⅛ inches; 18 ½ × 22 ⅛ inches; 18 ½ × 20 ⅜ inches. Collection of Ken and Helen Rowe, London

68 Johannes VanDerBeek, *Hair Hut Horn Head (around a small painting)*, 2009, paint on wood, canvas, and chair, 96 × 25 ½ × 35 inches

69 Sara VanDerBeek, *Study for A Composition for Detroit*, 2009, graphite on cover of *Life* magazine, 10 ⅛ × 10 ⅜ inches

70 Sara VanDerBeek, *Lines*, 2009, graphite and paint on printed image from *Look* magazine, 13 ⅞ × 10 ¼ inches

71 Sara VanDerBeek, *Study for A Composition for Detroit*, 2009, graphite on printed pages from *Life* magazine, diptych, each, 10 ¼ × 12 inches

72 Johannes VanDerBeek, *Floor #6 (Ancestor)*, 2011, Hydrocal, resin and paint, 64 × 30 × 37 inches

73 Stan VanDerBeek, *Untitled (New Order of Social Consciousness)*, c. 1960, ink on paper, 11 × 8 ½ inches

74 Stan VanDerBeek, *Untitled (from Mankinda)*, 1957, paint on paper mounted on cardboard, each, 14 × 17 inches

75 Johannes VanDerBeek, *Gypsy Hill Surgeon Chest (around a small painting)*, 2009, paint on wood, canvas, and chair, 96 ¼ × 24 ¾ × 27 ¼ inches

76 Sara VanDerBeek, *Four Photographers*, 2008 (detail), digital C-print, 18 ½ × 18 ½ inches. Collection of Ken and Helen Rowe, London

Anne Ellegood

Sara VanDerBeek

Sara VanDerBeek is an archivist, a collector, a keeper of images. Having inherited her late father's collection of photographs, and, it seems, his instincts to search and save, she regularly scours bookstores, flea markets, antique shops, and yard sales for vintage photographs, film stills, magazines, newspapers, postcards, exhibition catalogues, books on photography and design, and other publications. With her archive of thousands of images as a starting place, VanDerBeek's working process is curatorial in nature: she collects and cares for photographs from various periods, with wide-ranging subject matter, and painstakingly arranges them in precise juxtapositions that encourage associations both transparent and opaque. As Susan Sontag wrote, "To collect photographs is to collect the world,"[1] and VanDerBeek's library of images encompasses all categories, from fashion to architecture, portraiture to landscape, culture to science. Personal family snapshots from her childhood and, increasingly, her own photographs taken while traveling, visiting family, or in and around her neighborhood in Brooklyn, punctuate the many cultural, political, and historical events her collection of images touches upon. Her sculptural configurations of borrowed photographs (which have recently begun to incorporate her own photos) have included images of ancient statuary, people bathing in the Ganges River, an aerial view of a freeway intersection, African tribal masks, Marilyn Monroe, Merce Cunningham, a Viet Cong soldier, Navajo rugs, eyeballs, profiles, lunar eclipses, and a portrait of Virginia Woolf's mother, to name only a few.

While VanDerBeek's work begins with her formidable photographic archive and ends with a single photographic image—the middle stages of her process are sculptural. For each final work, she carefully assembles her photographs into three-dimensional constructions using segments of wood, panes of glass, and plaster forms. Several early constructions became mobiles that hung from the ceiling, or precarious tabletop configurations of frames or dowels held together with string and adorned with buttons, feathers, tree branches, pieces of mirror, strings of beads, crystals, glitter, macramé, and swatches of textile or lace. VanDerBeek shoots numerous photographs of each composition, selecting one print as the final work before disassembling the sculpture, returning the images to her archive, and keeping the trinkets for later works.

VanDerBeek has an acute understanding of how photography operates in the world. Her practice acknowledges photography as a ubiquitous presence in contemporary life, serving functions from the documentary to the artistic, the commercial to the personal. Photographs pop into view everywhere, perched on tabletops or hung on walls, before us as we walk or drive through our communities, when we open a web page, while we thumb through magazines or read the morning paper. Yet we are rarely fully conscious of this fact of contemporary life. VanDerBeek takes an image from the *New York Times* or a familiar photograph by Walker Evans and puts it before you *again*. Changing its context, its scale and orientation, and the photographs adjacent to it, she suggests our previous understanding of the image may be too narrow, too singular, or simply, too brief. She argues that photography's inherent reproducibility signifies its meanings multiply, too. VanDerBeek explores how photography informs our understanding of the past and how it brings history forward—encapsulating, and in many cases reducing, the complexity of earlier moments. Her work encourages us to continually recalibrate our previous understandings in order to negotiate the present.

Each of VanDerBeek's photographs becomes a permanent manifestation of her process, taking up photography's ability to capture lost gestures or moments in time. In such works as *Decorations in a Notebook* (2006) and *A Reoccurring Pattern* (2006), she explicitly takes up photography's propensity to memorialize, recalling Susan Sontag's provocative claim that all photographs are *memento mori*, tinged with an intrinsic pathos that encourages an awareness of our mortality.[2] *Decorations in a Notebook* features a black-and-white Associated Press photograph of a Viet Cong soldier decorated with National Liberation Front stars. A typewritten caption, obscuring the bottom half of the portrait, details that the photograph was found in his notebook after he was killed in battle. Adjacent to the soldier, VanDerBeek has

Sara VanDerBeek, *A Reoccurring Pattern*, 2006, digital C-print, 30 × 40 inches

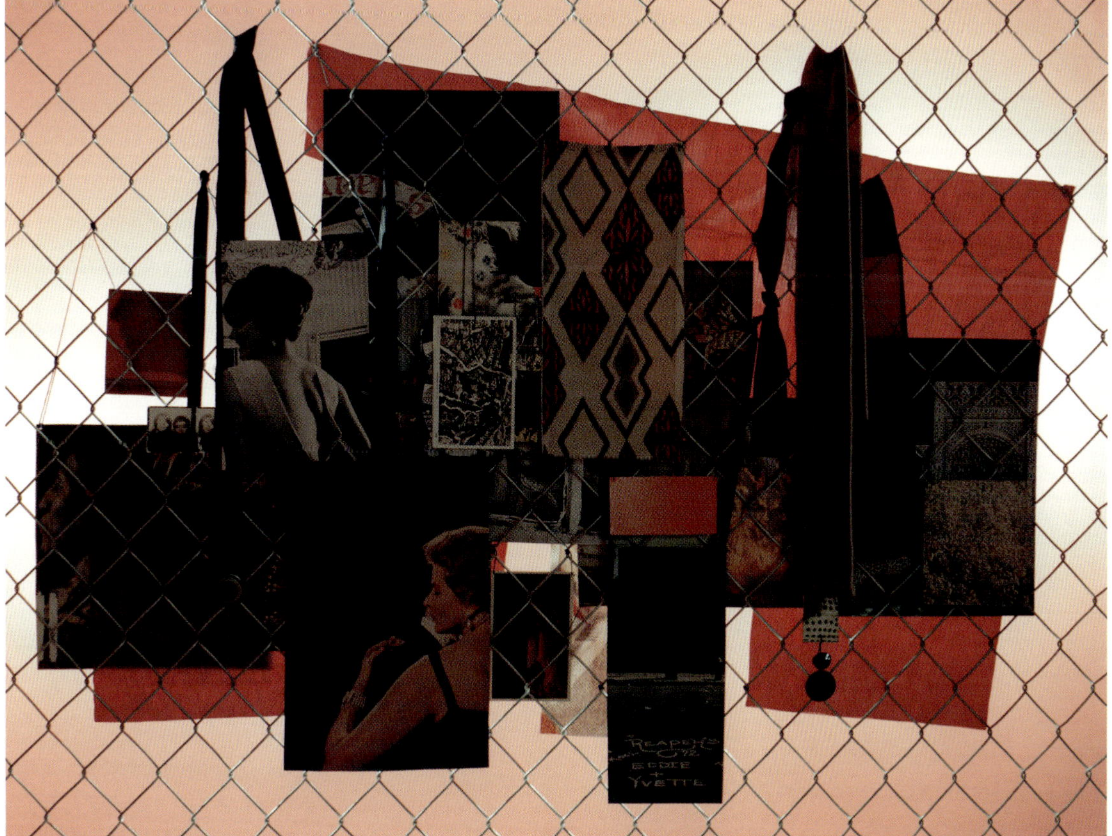

placed a found photograph of Pablo Picasso's haunting sculpture *Death's Head* from 1941, its skull form casting a severe shadow to one side. Building a dark backdrop composed primarily of black painted wood panels, VanDerBeek also uses dramatic lighting, casting deep shadows that exaggerate the theme of mortality present in her borrowed images. In the right background lurks a single eye staring out at the viewer, its glowing whiteness and dilated pupil portray the vitality of life, while its isolation within the composition suggests something more menacing. Death, VanDerBeek suggests, is both complicated and shockingly simple. It can be violent, political, and deeply distressing. And it is inevitable.

A Reoccurring Pattern conspicuously adopts the visual language of memorials. Featuring a collage of portraits and patterned textiles affixed to a chain-link fence, the composition is reminiscent of the spontaneous shrines that adorn urban streets after a fatal accident or other tragedy and were particularly prominent on the streets of New York City following the attacks of September 11, 2001. Unlike *Decorations in a Notebook*, the piece does not memorialize a specific figure but calls up a more broad sense of death, both historical and personal, on scales both monumental and intimate. A portrait of a Native American coupled with a swatch of diamond-patterned textile brings to mind the history of colonial genocide. An image of the Los Angeles riots reminds how abuses of power can serve as catalysts for eruptions of social protest, some leading to the loss of life. A striking profile portrait of Jackie Kennedy alongside diminutive photo-booth pictures of VanDerBeek's mother and a friend (taken when they were teenagers) present vivacious women who would outlive their husbands. Other images—a young girl, a gang from the Bronx called the Reapers, Ingrid Bergman, the Taj Mahal—are layered upon one another, the surface becoming a site for the accumulation and excavation of life stories.

VanDerBeek's *Extravaganza* (2006) incorporates a number of disturbing images of death—an appropriation of an already borrowed picture with the inclusion of a car crash from Andy Warhol's "Death and Disaster" series; a *Life* magazine photo of a supine woman lying dead on the ground after jumping from a building; a counter-intuitively gorgeous image of a deadly mushroom cloud; the terrible shot of Martin Luther King, Jr., collapsed on the balcony of the Lorraine Motel in Memphis; and Marilyn Monroe with her face provocatively obscured. *Extravaganza* continues VanDerBeek's examination of photography's capacity to memorialize and highlights the emotional weight of these images by, surprisingly, obscuring their legibility. Each picture is lovingly adorned with lines of silver glitter and precariously propped up against tree branches skinned of their bark. Whereas Warhol's invocation of tragic figures participated in their transform into icons—his use of repetition paralleling the numbing reproduction of photographs in the public sphere—VanDerBeek's acts of embellishment enhance the photographs' expressive quality. Eschewing repetition in favor of combining thematically linked but distinct photographs, VanDerBeek denies the viewer full consumption of the images by juxtaposing and overlapping them and adding her own flourishes, returning these images to the private sphere. Viewers must slow down in order to examine the photographs carefully, allowing the unsettling aspects of these portrayals

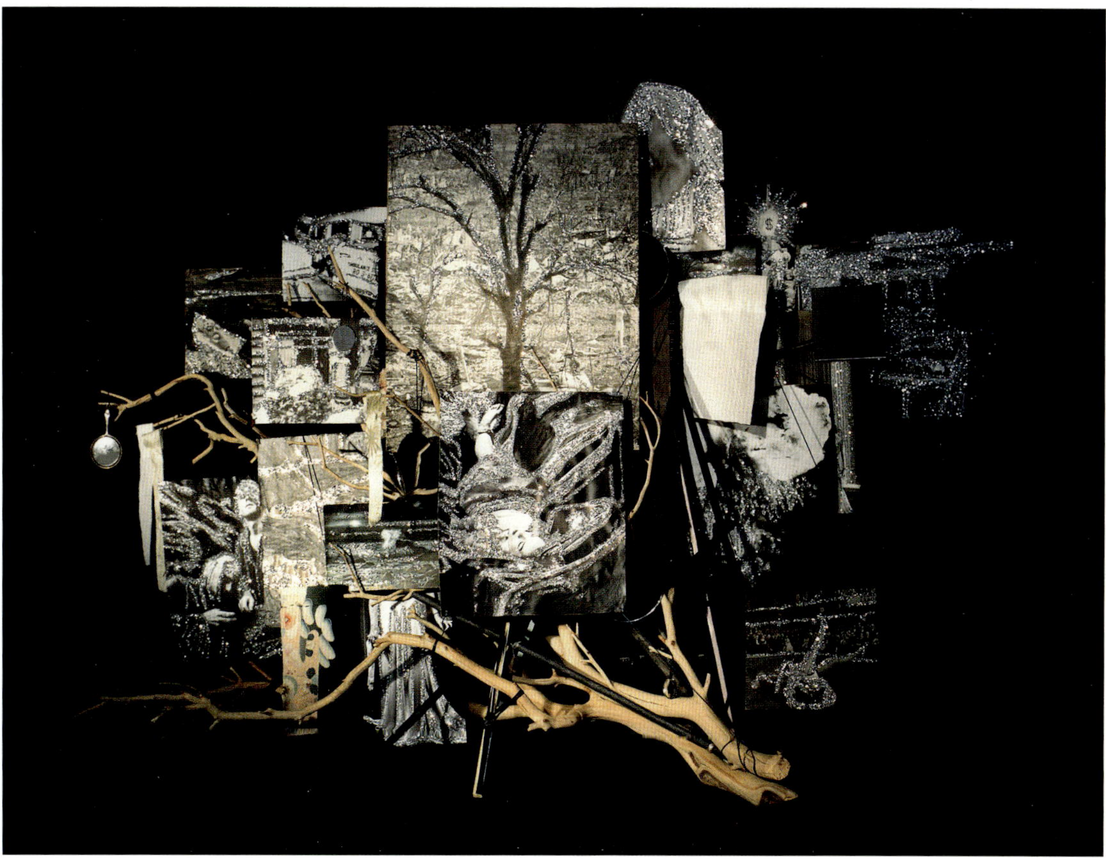

Sara VanDerBeek, *Extravaganza*, 2006, digital C-print, 30 × 40 inches

of death to reveal themselves gradually from beneath the artist's beautification, as if the documentation of each tragedy and its accompanying loving attention by VanDerBeek were itself a small memorial.

VanDerBeek repeatedly calls our attention to how photography frames its subject. By changing the perspective of her lens and layering individual photographs so that they both enhance and disguise one another, she emphasizes how each image is a detail of a larger scene, only a fraction of the story. Her selection of a single vantage point as the final work underscores the photographer's power to provide *and* withhold information. The mobile construction *Ziggurat* (2006), a study in photography's role in delimiting space, offers endless spatial and temporal possibilities. We imagine the work's images of landscapes—night skies and sunrises—extending infinitely past the photograph's edges. The top image captures dancers in motion, their blurred bodies already outside the frame. And in a nod to historic works of art that likewise explore their medium's material limits, she includes images of Constantin Brancusi's sculpture *Endless Column* (1918) and one of Frank Stella's 1950s frameless abstract black stripe paintings, both works embracing a system of repeated forms that could theoretically continue indefinitely.

Indeed, the way in which VanDerBeek pictures our world, while creating both erasures and distortions, suggests her awareness that each photograph, for all its apparent relationship to truth, is a manipulation, whether through posing, decontextualization, framing, or juxtaposition. Her attentiveness to photography's capacity for simultaneous presentation and obfuscation is evident in her selection of existing images, cropping techniques, and overlapping, and recalls poet and critic Susan Stewart's insightful assertion that collections reside somewhere between public and private space, "between display and hiding."[3] In a series titled *The Principle of Superimposition* (2007–2008), VanDerBeek builds up photographs like a house of cards, stacked at ninety-degree angles so that images in front hide all or part of those in the background. Furthermore, VanDerBeek slices some photographs into vertical or diagonal strips, piecing two images together into alternating bands. The highly decorative panels that result recall abstract patterning more than the kind of representational information we expect from photographs. The coupling of straightforward, unaltered photos with the striped alterations reveals both order (compositions inspired by particular themes that require a typological methodology and forms constructed with great balance and precision) and exhilarating chaos, bursting with imagery.

The accumulation of imagery—replacing one image with another in potentially infinite permutations—lies at the heart of *The Principle of Superimposition* series. The house-of-cards-like arrangements suggest the works may grow over time, extending far beyond the photograph's edges. Deliberately countering the notion that photography's aim is always to capture and immortalize its subject, these works argue that even while static, photographs can shift and change, their meanings slipping and rearticulating with each viewing (and with each viewer). The eye jumps from one image to the next, across the field of connections and disconnections. The experience is almost cinematic, as if a loose narrative were gradually unfolding. For this series, VanDerBeek has chosen strikingly beautiful and theatrical images. The first photograph in the group centers on rituals and acts of performance around the world—a fire ritual in the Ganges River in India; cloaked praying women seen from behind; Japanese performers preparing

Installation view, *Sara VanDerBeek: The Principle of Superimposition*, The Approach, London, England, 2008

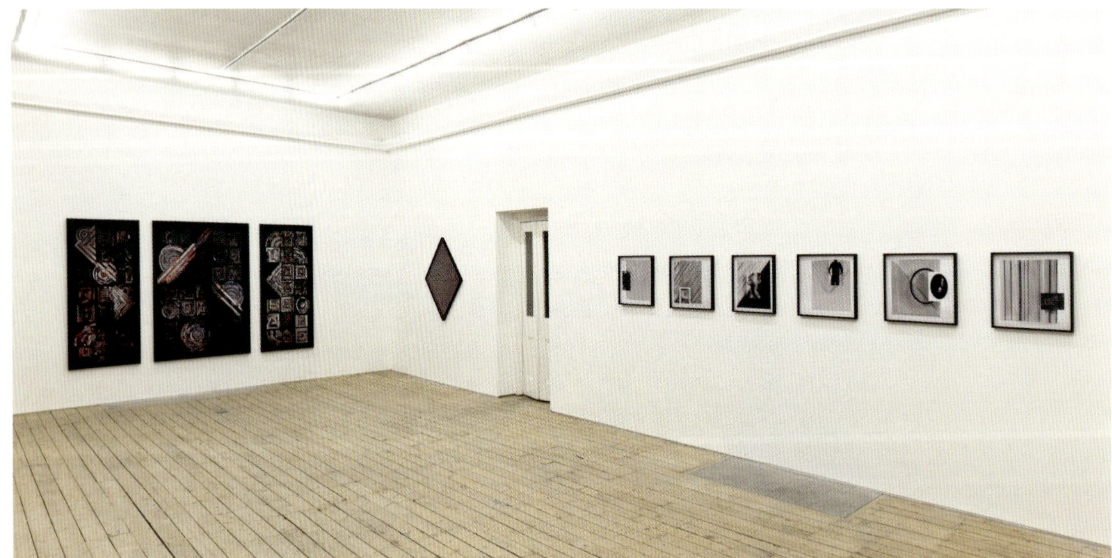

backstage; a black-and-white elaborately ornamental tiled room—creating a sensory collage that immerses the viewer in abundant details.

VanDerBeek cites the Museum of Modern Art's 1955 *The Family of Man* exhibition, organized by Edward Steichen, as inspiration for some of her image choices (Henri Cartier-Bresson's photo of the praying women, for example, was featured in the exhibition and is incorporated into VanDerBeek's piece). But the exhibition served primarily as a model for the *structure* of VanDerBeek's assemblages. The strategy of superimposition integral to the installation at MoMA (and adopted by VanDerBeek) included wide-ranging and far-reaching subjects, as Steichen described, "the gamut of life from birth to death." *The Family of Man* architect Paul Rudolph designed an elaborate hall of mirrors and presented the more than five hundred images selected by the curators on every surface. Steichen sincerely intended that the exhibition's democratic approach to selecting and displaying the work—he claimed to have considered two million photographs from around the world by photographers both famous and amateur—would bring to life the universality of human experience. VanDerBeek pays homage to this aim by choosing spiritual subjects as well as images of design and abstraction that evoke notions of shared human impulses and universal aesthetics. Steichen's optimism about "the family of man" may today feel nostalgic—and the show's leveling of important differences in experience between, say, laborers in China and gray-haired men sitting around a large boardroom in the United States is certainly problematic—but VanDerBeek mirrors these inconsistencies and curiosities in order to ask important questions about the potency of photography and its "democratic appeal." More than any other medium, photography is characterized by its accessibility—the idea that anyone can take a picture and the increasingly shared belief that we are obliged to document and memorialize our lives through photographs. Within this democratization and proliferation of photography, VanDerBeek's work reminds us of the medium's specific historical role. By borrowing photographs from the past, she recirculates images to highlight how alive they can remain, how relevant and inspiring they can be over time. In other words, VanDerBeek's work argues that photographs are not just *of the moment*; they can be timeless in their capacity for building associations, for casting light on new meanings, and, of course, for triggering memories.

At the height of the recent economic recession, VanDerBeek traveled to Detroit and took photographs. The resulting work—a four-part large-scale piece entitled *A Composition for Detroit* (2009)—was her first work in many years to combine found imagery from her archive with her own photographs, some taken in Detroit and some in her studio. The project was inspired, in part, by moments in American history when photography has played a fundamental role in making visible hidden social problems and furthering the causes of social reform. While a project like Walker Evans's Farm Security Administration-sponsored documentation of the depression-era South provides an important precedent, VanDerBeek's approach to this type of photographic investigation acknowledges both the impact of these early state-sponsored photographic essays and the limits of the camera's power to actually implement change. Photography's ability

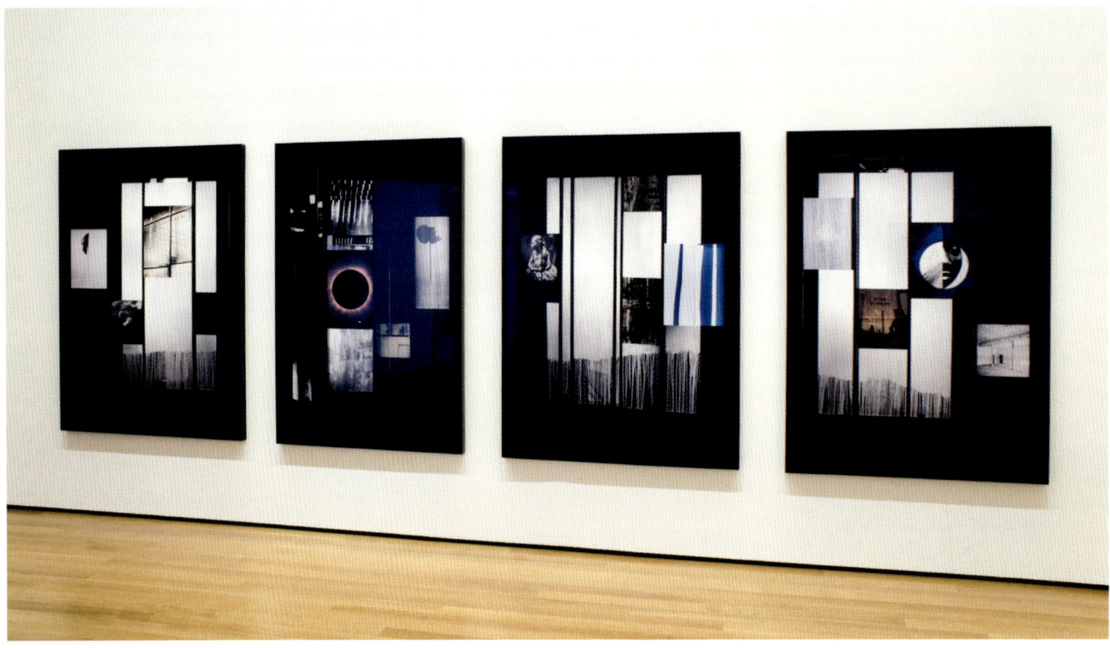

Installation view, *New Photography*, Museum of Modern Art, New York, 2009

to call attention to injustice—to present undeniable facts in order to inspire action—remains a powerful role for the medium, and yet it has lost potency over time. As a culture, we are now more skeptical of the factual nature of the photograph, prone as it is to manipulation. And yet an image can still add visual elucidation and impact to the limitations of language. In the end, it is difficult to ignore the vastness of a tragedy like the BP Gulf oil spill when faced with a photograph of a bird mired in dark viscous oil. It is a nearly impossible task to translate stories of hardships faced by residents of Detroit into visual images. We get overwhelmed by too much information instead of feeling able to connect with real, suffering people, which makes VanDerBeek's decision to shoot there feel all the more urgent. But, VanDerBeek's homage to Detroit is hardly straightforward documentation, nor does she have the same social agenda as that of the Farm Security Administration photographers. Her view into the city is far more poetic and abstracted. Yet the images of the city relate directly to the failure of the automobile industry and its abandoned infrastructure: a photograph of an empty office building, for example, its window blinds loose and hanging askew. Across the work's four panels, VanDerBeek traces time backwards and geography southward, articulating some of the historical threads of politics and human migration that helped create the Detroit of today. Alongside the largely architectural depictions of Detroit, VanDerBeek includes such found photographs as Walker Evans's portrayal of the historical southern plantation Belle Grove in Louisiana; Charles Moore's widely circulated 1963 photograph of a woman being hosed down during a civil rights protest in Birmingham, Alabama in 1963; images of the 1967 Detroit riots; and works by Tina Modotti, Matthew Brady, and others. *A Composition for Detroit* offers a portrait of a city while also reaching far beyond its geographic boundaries so that details of Detroit's complex and compelling history emerge from the shroud of the current economic downturn.

George Baker recently pointed out that two seminal essays exploring the ontology and social function of photography, Walter Benjamin's "Little History of Photography" (1931) and Roland Barthes's *Camera Lucida* (1980), both appeared in times of economic collapse. Baker describes Benjamin's nostalgia for photography's beginnings "an intellectual response to the economic crash of 1929" and Barthes's investigation a "theory of photography characteristic of the decade of the 'oil crisis.'"[4] He calls both fantasies of "photographic atavism," rooted in an impossible desire to return to the medium's earliest history. He argues that our current economic crisis is no mere crash that can be easily repaired: "The metaphor is no longer the (modernist) one of the crash, calling for strategies of disjunction, collision, and montage. Instead it is of the tsunami, a metaphorics of flow, overflow, and excess, of echoes and reboundings, of chain reaction, of inundation and flood—liquidity gone awry. It is not a question of the industrial object crumpled before us, but of the floor plan swept bare, the barren aftermath of a catastrophic clearing."[5] Given the current economy, thinking about VanDerBeek's work in relationship to Baker's metaphor of the tsunami seems apt. The photographic atavism Baker protests is also resisted by the artist, whose use of appropriation is not nostalgic or elegiac, but rather strategic and productive. She does not mourn the death or inertia of these earlier photographs, or how they functioned in society, nor does she believe they have lost their power. Rather than remove the original photograph (or, for that matter, the photographer) further and further away from its intention or presumed meaning, we might argue that VanDerBeek's re-generative processes argue for something fundamental about photography: the medium's endless capacity for repetition does not have to result in a blurring or indifference to the image; it can, indeed, make us see again in ways that articulate how an image from the past can help us understand the present.

Notes

1 Susan Sontag, *On Photography* (New York: Anchor Doubleday, 1977): 3.

2 Ibid, 15.

3 Susan Stewart, *On Longing: Narratives of the Miniature, the Gigantic, the Souvenir, the Collection* (Durham and London: Duke University Press, 1993, originally published by John Hopkins University Press in 1984): 155.

4 George Baker, "Photography and Abstraction," *Words Without Pictures*, ed. Alex Klein (Los Angeles: Los Angeles County Museum of Art, 2009): 372.

5 Ibid, 375.

TIME

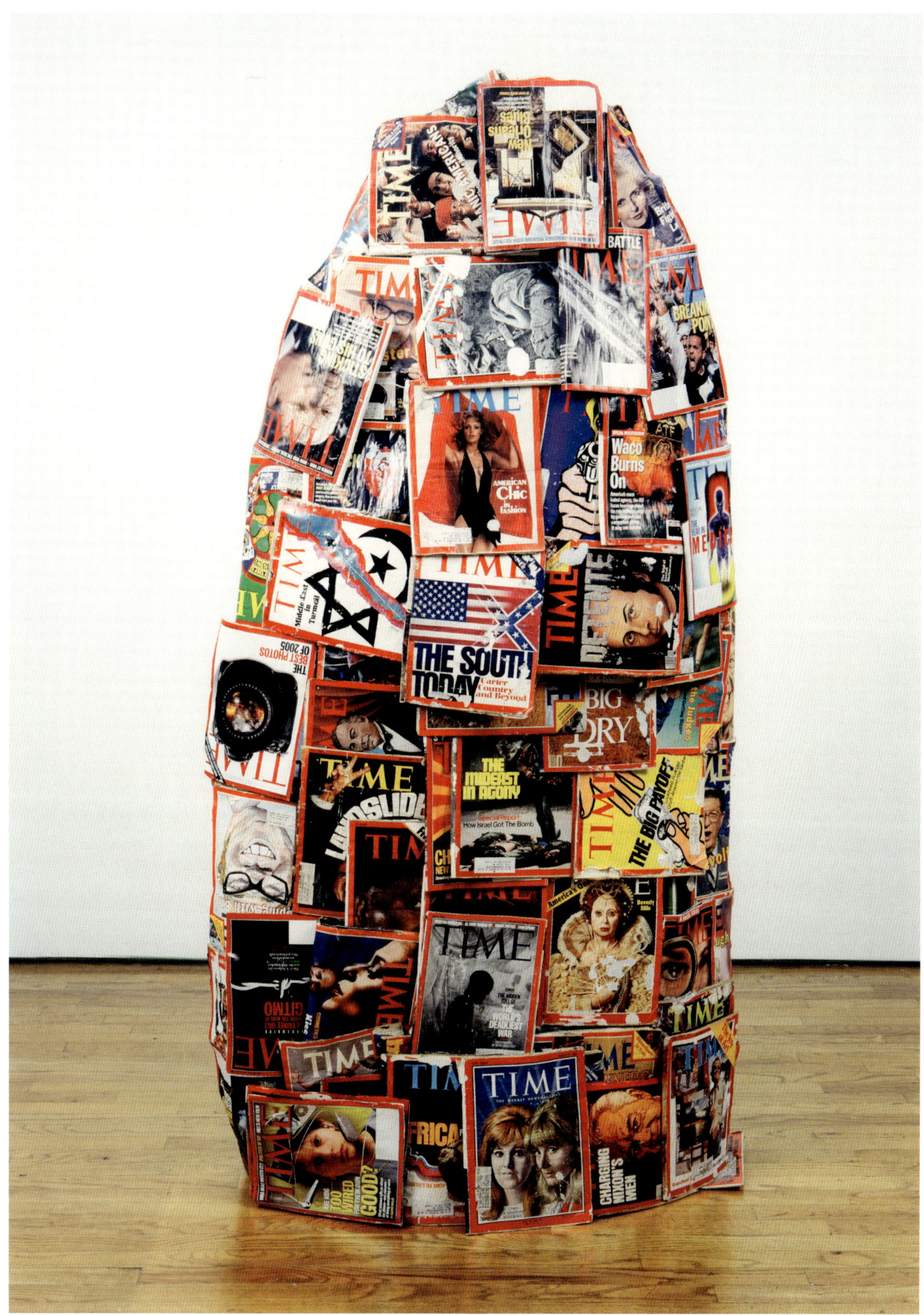

77, 78 (following)

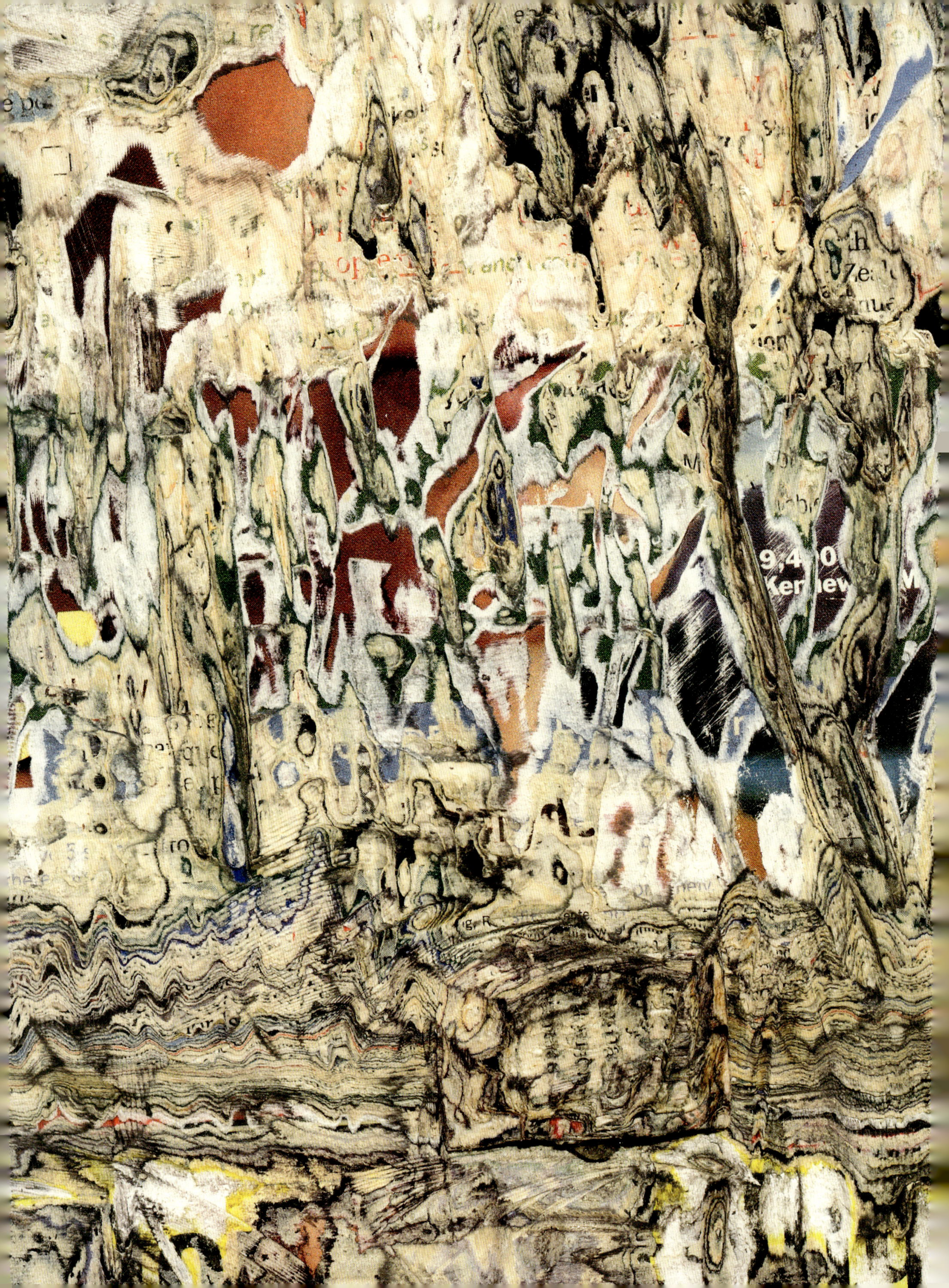

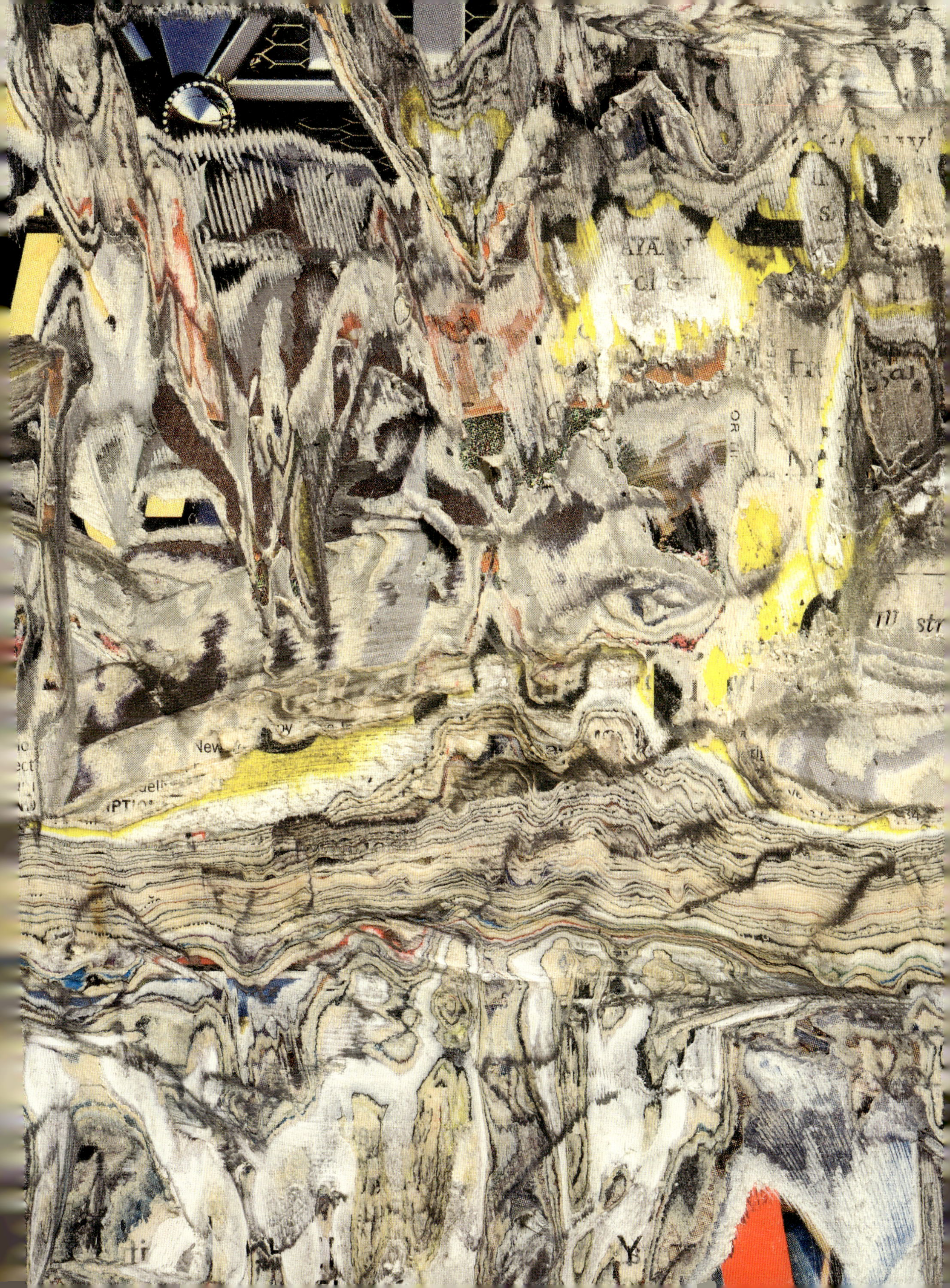

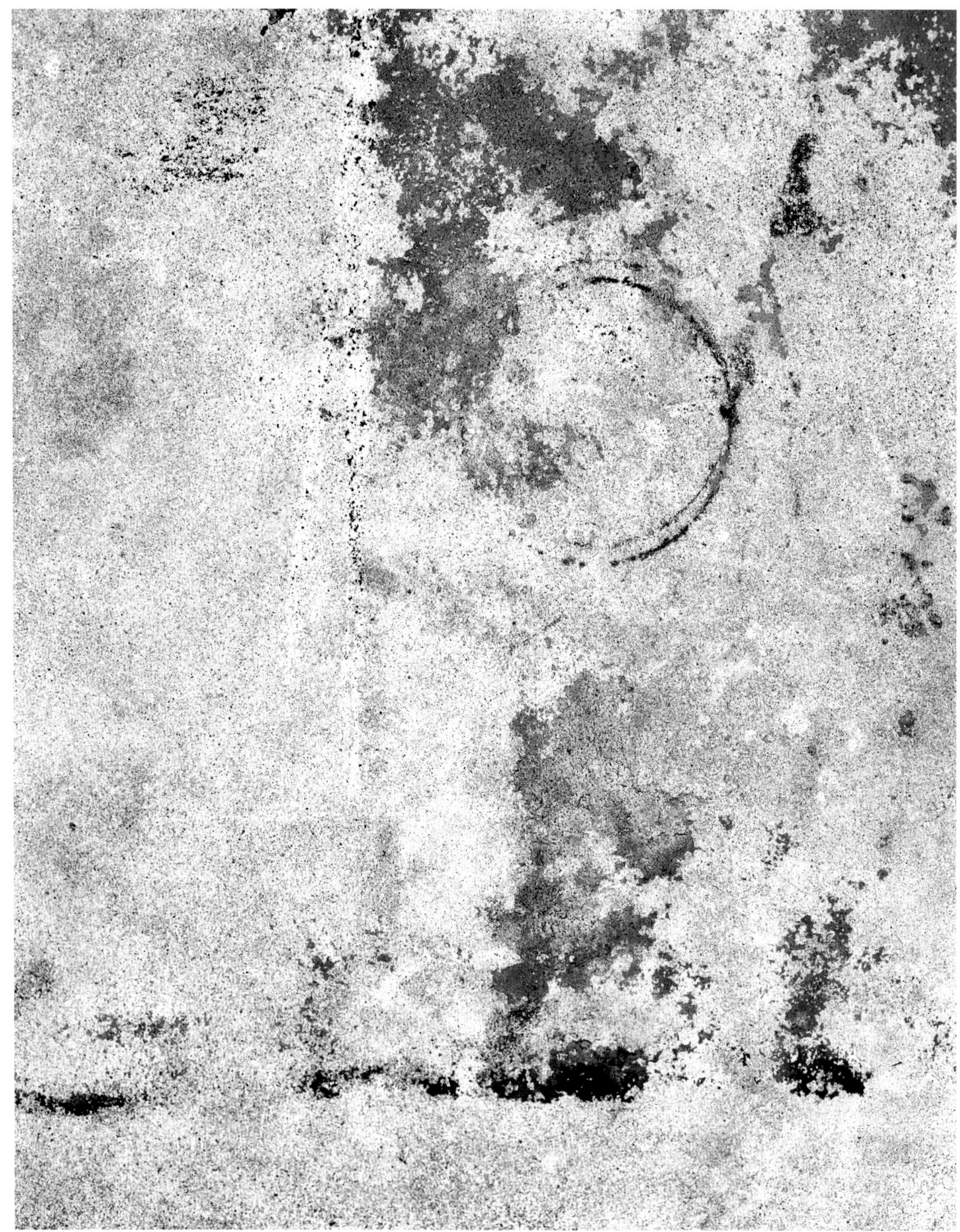

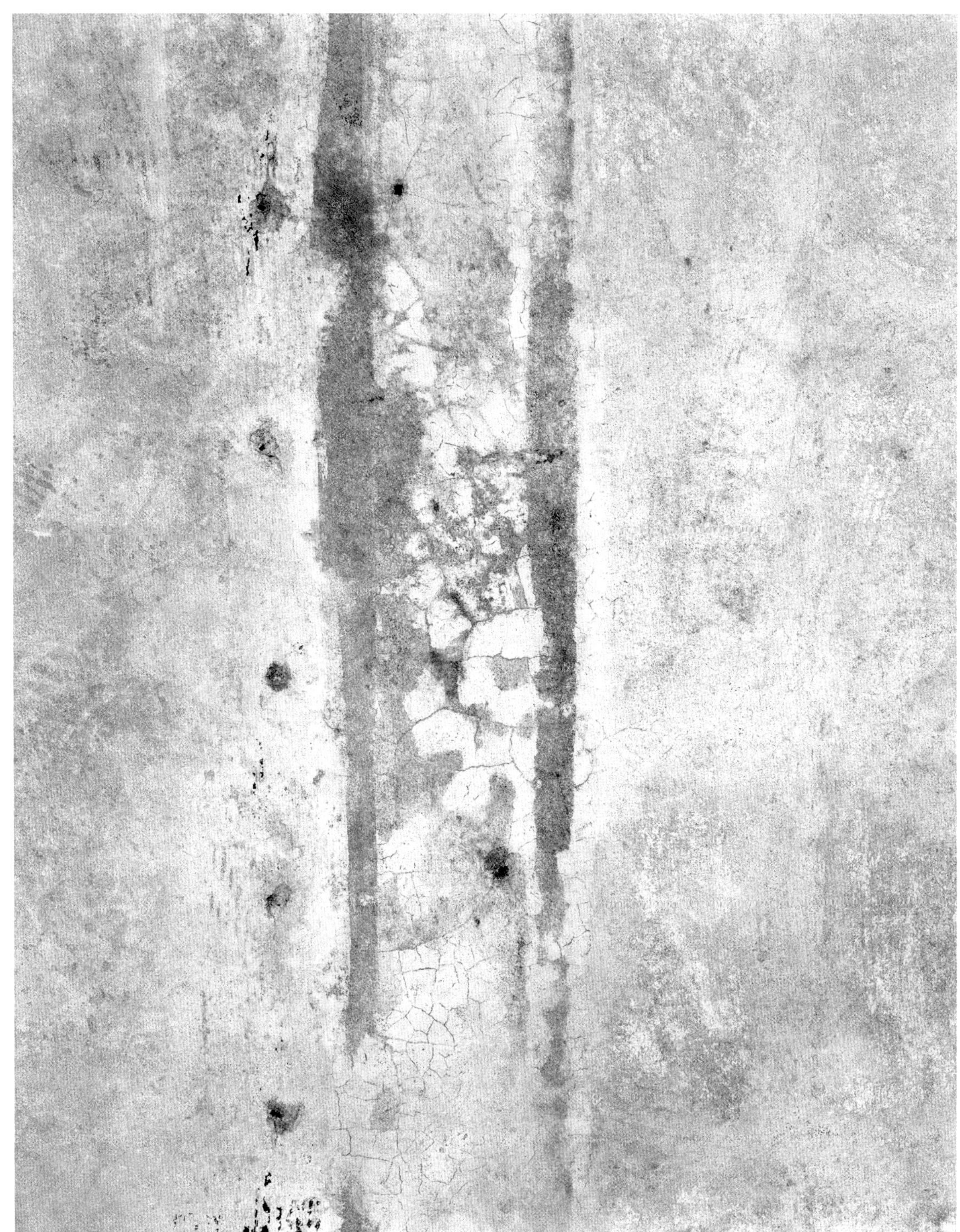

80, 81 (following)

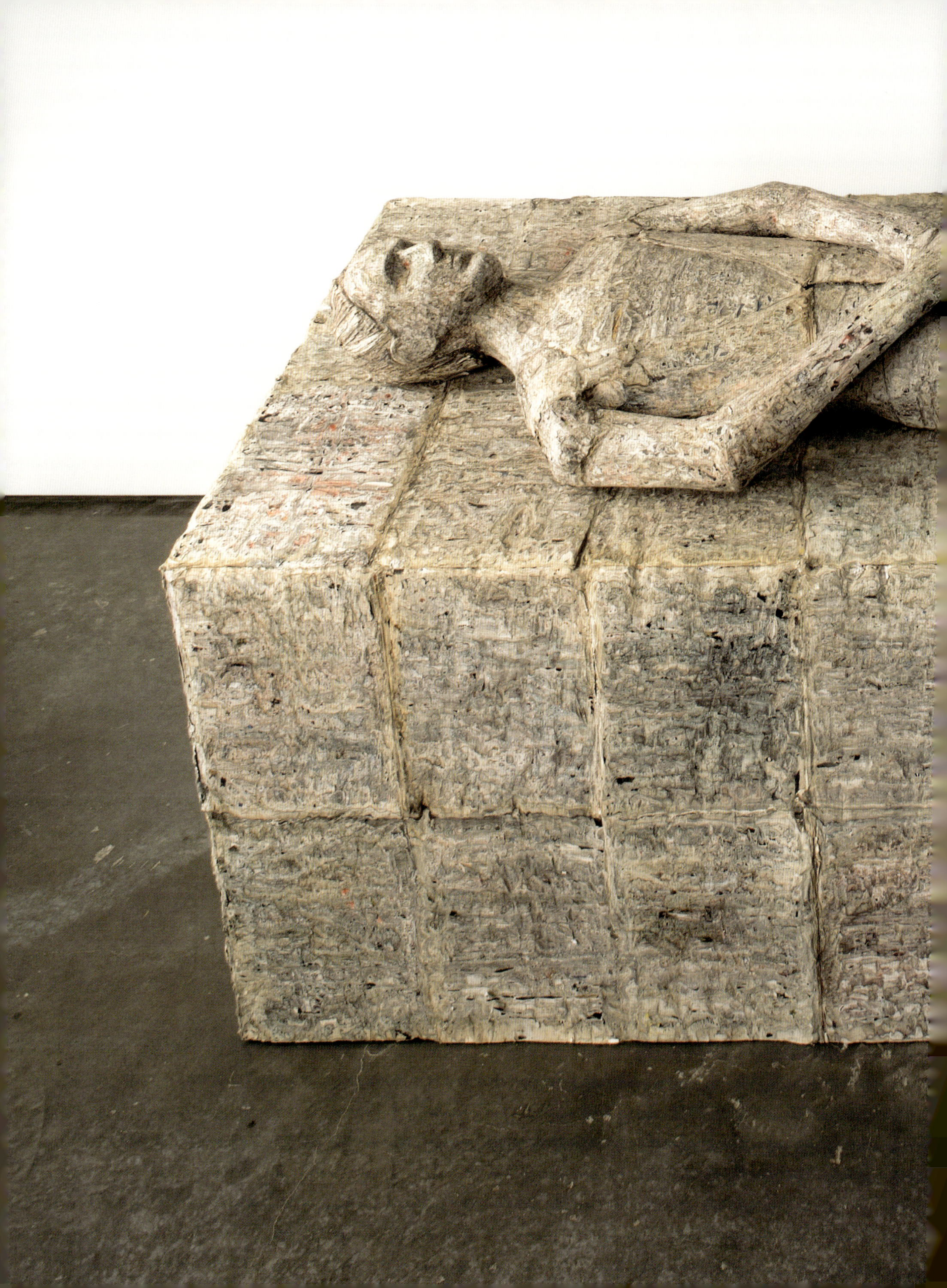

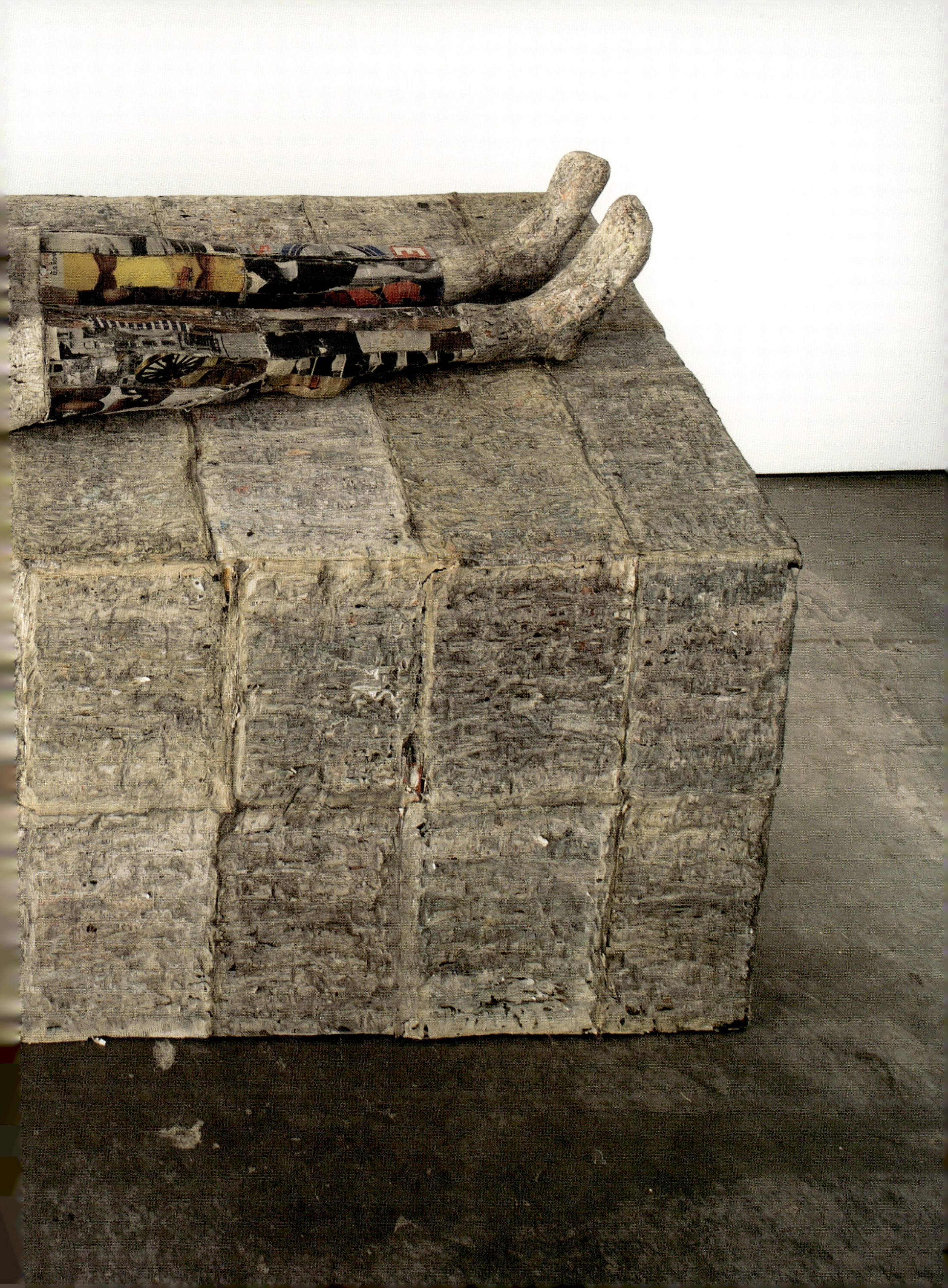

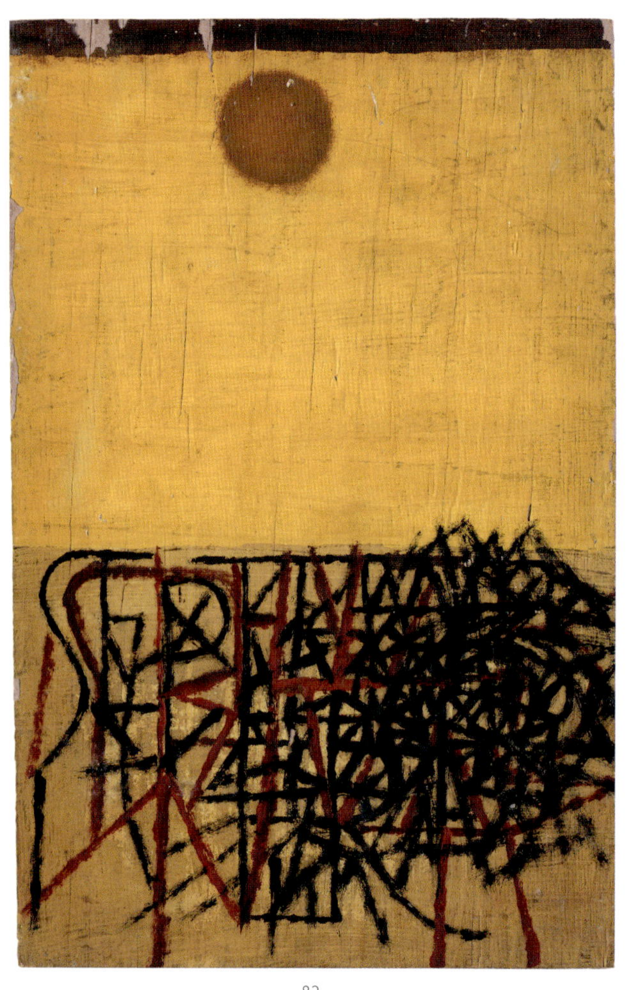

82

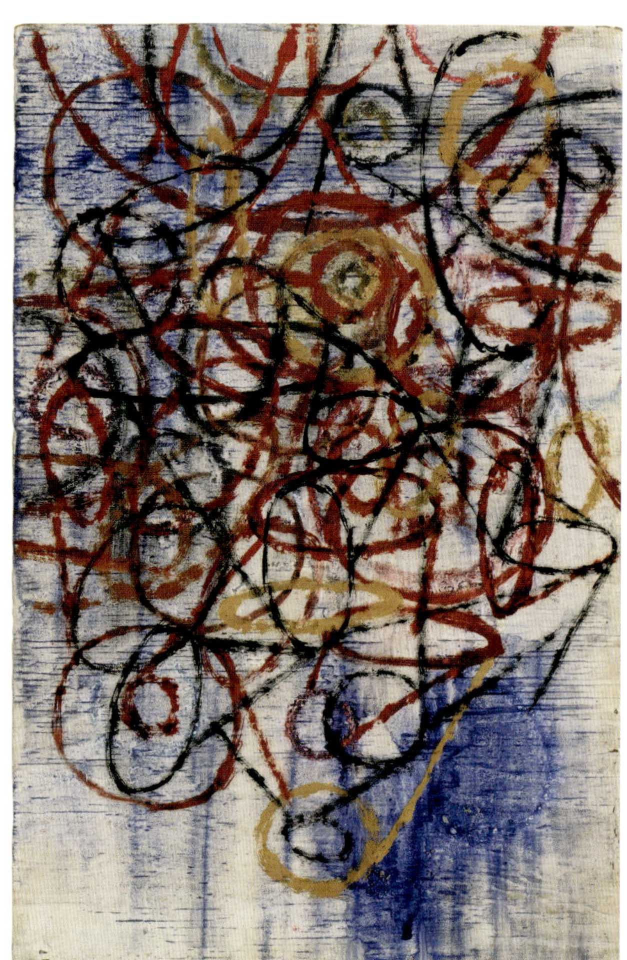

83

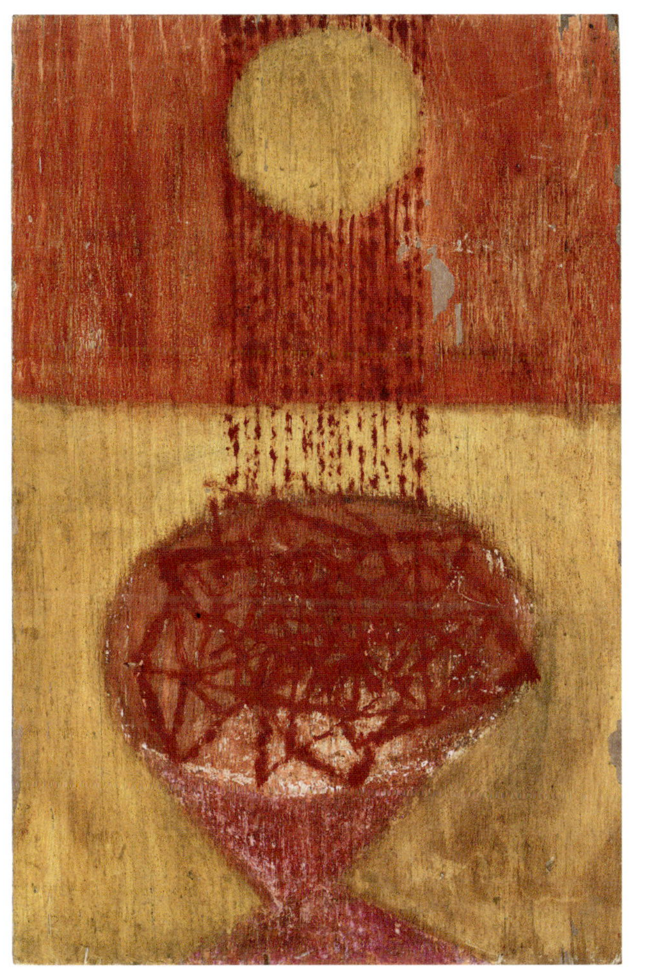

84

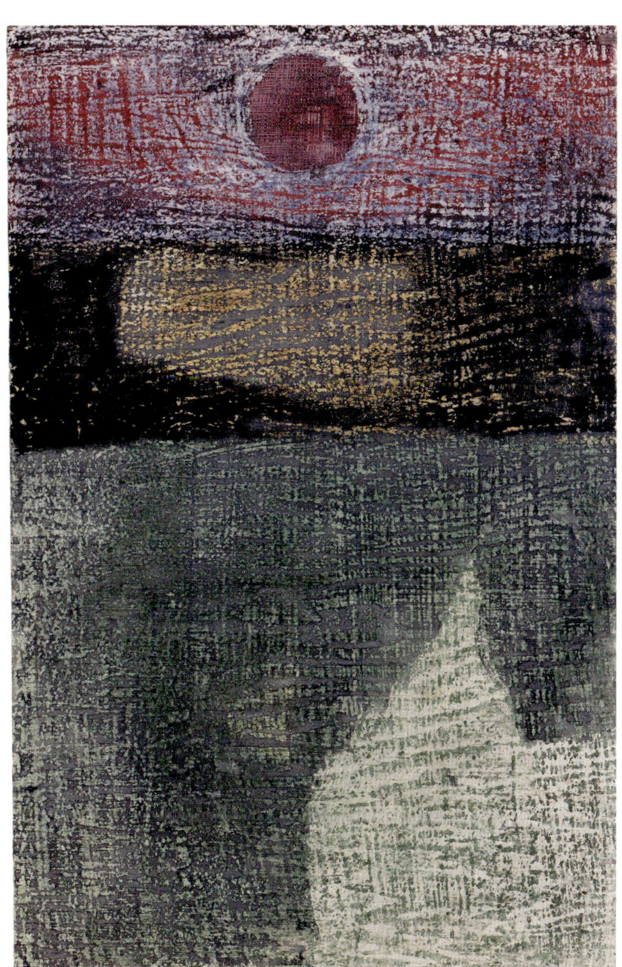

85

TIME

IB: Johannes, how did you make *It's Time!?* Did you leave it to chance what patterns and colors would be revealed or did you plan it out as a strategy ahead of time?

JVDB: I glued many pages from random *Time* magazines in a feverish campaign to mold the passage of time and form it into a physical field. I then grinded the condensed surface to scramble all the information on the pages, turning it into a portal of sorts to an indistinct past. I came up with this process a few years ago and have done several works in the same vein, including a seventeen-foot wall that looks like an ancient ruin. I'm drawn to the implications of dispersing the specific information of media and literally scrambling the continuum among distant past, recent past, and present. I also enjoy the formal potential of a material at once familiar and foreign, psychedelic and muted. It becomes a pseudo-archaeological site, where elements from former cultures mix like rivers converging. I began to think of piles of information we can no longer use as our contemporary ruins. The current of information moves so fast nowadays that something from yesterday might as well be from two centuries ago. It's equally as distant in our memory.

It's Time!? is the very first work I made using this process. I wanted to produce a fragmented narrative, an aspect I moved away from in later works. But a brief synopsis would be: a peacekeeper got stuck while walking through the portal, and before he could give the full peace sign his hand froze in a limp version of the icon. He is suspended in a state before the full physical achievement of a movement and its social significance solidify. The title's exclamation point followed by the question mark exemplifies my generation's lack of wholehearted conviction. We only partially believe in something while also maintaining an ironic distance, so we don't risk losing anything, especially ourselves. Irony becomes a shell, and the hermit inside is never happy with his home.

IB: Stan's paintings date from his time at Black Mountain College in the early 1950s. Do you know who his friends were at the time?

JVDB: He met several people at Black Mountain College who became close friends or collaborators. Merce Cunningham and John Cage opened his eyes to dance and music as forms of expression. Another important figure was Buckminster Fuller, whom he met briefly. He admired Fuller's thoughts about new-old forms in architecture that included the utopian forms of circles and domes. When he moved back to New York, he was around artists like Claus Oldenburg, Robert Rauschenberg, Ray Johnson, Robert Morris, May Wilson, Anita Steckel, Jim Dine, Andy Warhol, Allen Kaprow, Stan Brakhage, Robert Breer, and he may even have met Duchamp. His first wife, Johanna, was a full-fledged muse with an innate sense of design that made a big impact on his aesthetic. It's also important to note the company he kept in his head. He referred to Salvador Dali as his grandfather. He studied Charlie Chaplin and Buster Keaton and made homages to their gestural energy. He looked to Max Ernst for other formal advice, like how to apply paint and construct a collage. Early drawings and poems also seem to reflect William Blake, mainly in the depictions of the sun moving across a landscape, and in how the fundamental forces of nature have an effect on our tools of sleep and reason and the eventual illumination of rumination.

SVDB: It is always hard with my father's early work to place it accurately because he often gave incorrect dates for his attendance at Black Mountain College and therefore evaded sharing his real age. The years 1949-51 make the most sense, because during that time Robert Rauschenberg, Merce Cunningham, John Cage, Ray Johnson, and others were at the school. He became close with many of these people while at school and after. Cage had a place at the Land, a cooperative community founded in Rockland County by Vera and Paul Williams, an artist and an architect who also attended Black Mountain with my father. At the Land dad built his home and the Movie-Drome.

He traveled so much and was working in so many different areas that he made friends or acquaintances with a wide array of individuals. He grew close to other experimental filmmakers like Ed Emschwiller and Robert Breer. He had close but contentious relationships with Stan Brakhage and Jonas Mekas; it often seems they fell out over ideas about experimental media. He moved away from New York's underground film scene to work with the nascent technologies in computers, television and mass media, and telecommunications at M.I.T.'s Center for Advanced Visual Studies, where he was close with scientists and programmers as well as its founder Gyorgy Kepes. It might seem that there was a great deal more crossover in the arts during

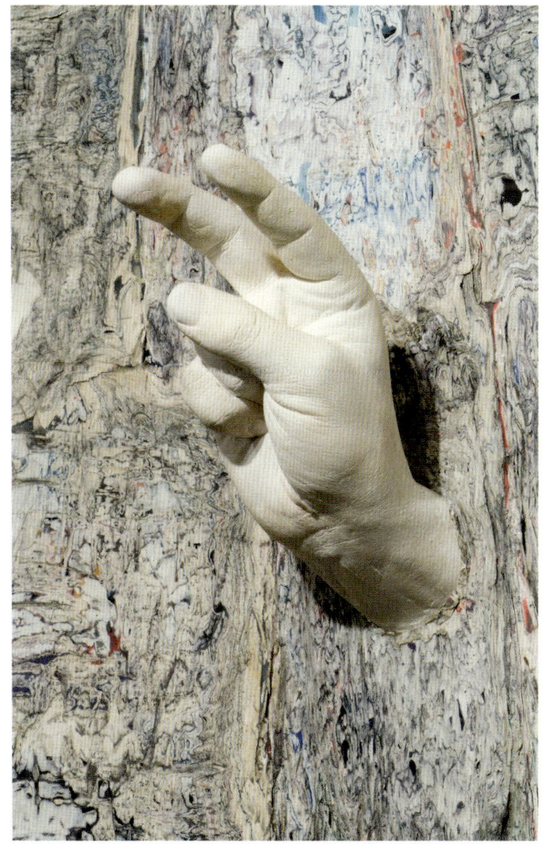

86

my father's lifetime, but I think we have begun to see a girth of performance and media works bridging many disciplines that speak to the idealist views of media pioneers like my father.

Regardless, at Black Mountain he studied with the poet and ceramist M. C. Richards and wrote a great deal of poetry. His paintings from that time have an intimate poetic quality. Some have texts and some are sequential—they feel like precursors to his later animations, and I think they are important as a foundation of his visual language. Eyes, faces, and the repeating Ernst-like sun recur as symbols, while the darkness of some of these paintings hints at his later obsession with the threat of a nuclear holocaust.

IB: Black Mountain, New York, the Land—your father continually belonged to one or another community of artists. Is it important to have other artists respond to your work?

SVDB: It's wonderful to have artist friends and I get a great deal from seeing and speaking with other artists, but I also like to connect to people outside of the arts and go beyond what can be a fairly small world here in New York. It can be easy to remain within the patois and comfort of those with similar views about the making and viewing of art. It's usually still based in art education, so it's not a complete break from my world, but I really like teaching high school students because they have a completely different perspective from mine and that of my peers. For that reason I also like speaking with artists from older generations.

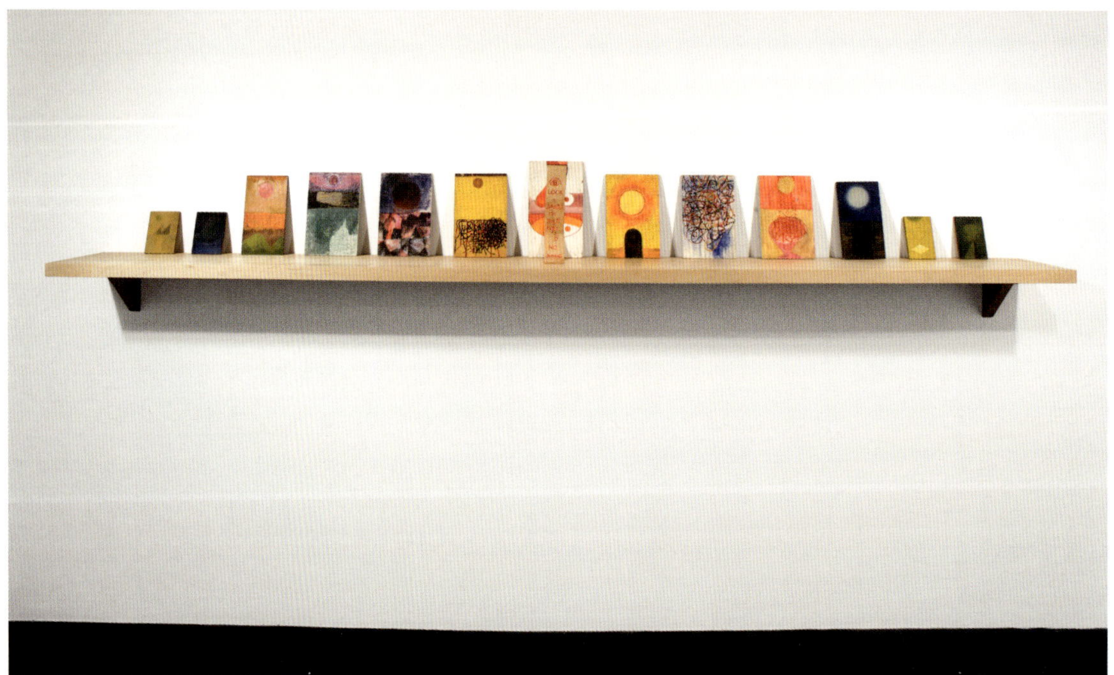

87

JVDB: My gang is a group of shapes that don't fit into the allotted holes. One friend Aaron is a holy rock that makes rebel sculptures with a minimalist bent toward Dubble Bubble and Double Trouble. Another friend, Robin, is built like a bear wearing Terminator boots but has a mind as reflective as the steel toe and as infinitely complex as the hairs growing from his body. One guy named John eats brown beans every day for dinner but makes paintings as vibrant as an invisible pyramid filled with countless facts about John Wayne and flat-bottomed john boats. A dapper fellow we call 'Max'imum Cheeks because of his name and face is true Boston Brahman with the delicate touch of a child painting a scene of a rearview mirror reflecting fleeting fog. Devon has the angst of a cerebral dolphin trapped in an ocean full of fish; his installations channel the diversity of coral reefs consisting of cartoon heads and Botticelli bodies. His wife is a steady ship that we have all at points loaded our worries upon, but the Watanabe continues to be fastest and most reliable vessel at sea. One sister is the anchor who keeps me still when I drift toward the edge of the world's stage. Another sister is the eye at the top of the lighthouse, staring, glaring, and caring with the precision of a photo falcon. Her cardinal flew from England and brought with him a glow as red as the coat he wears. Strong branches from Baltimore, Poland, Florida, and Tahiti have grown to catch the winds of words in their leaves. These and other peers provide piers to walk onto stable land in case the currents are discursive. My mom is the sage of smoke that made my globe and gave it such large dimension. But the sun that warms it all is the golden hair that rises on my pillowy landscape each day. She is the ray of friend, fiancée, and fellow that takes the tangles of lines on my face and makes them a beaming smile.

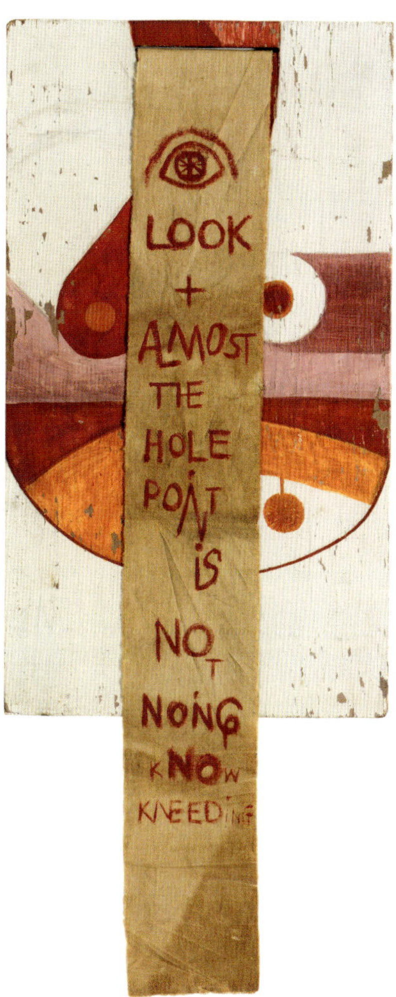

00

These are all talented artists and good people. It's vital to surround yourself with like-minded individuals who can keep your spirit afloat and be an outlet and arrow when you hit a wall. It's equally important to be around people who are drastically opposite, to challenge and extend your perception of longitudes and latitudes. No point in being an island just gathering sand and blowing palm trees. Artists need to recognize that directly engaging with the approach of other artists is another way to gain further access to your own ways. When you start to think about your life objectively, you realize it's a delicate flux of changing states. The people around you play an integral role in the consistency of your identity.

IB: Sara, did you intend to use the mirror in *Black Mirror* as a metaphor for a lack of vision?

SVDB: I shot this piece in California under the strong diagonal light of the desert. It's one of the first times I set something up in a location outside of the studio. The piece of fabric hanging down is a cuff from a dress, probably from the 1940s. It felt like a fragment of a costume and had an aged, tattered Hollywood glamor. The dark mirror does not fulfill its usual purpose of reflection. Black is a dense color, there and not there. Being there and not there constitutes a photographic perspective. When creating an image, the photographer exists at once in the moment, capturing it, but also outside of it, thinking about its creation, its composition, and its realization as an image. Sometimes even considerations surrounding the image's circulation or its final presentation may enter at this early point. This simultaneous engagement and removal then translates to the viewing and reading of an image. Photography is a self-reflective medium, equally so is the experience of viewing it, which is fitting given that the camera, at least as it exists in its traditional form, is centered upon a shifting mirror.

The mirror was also like a black sun or an eclipse, the opposite of what it should be. Like the sun in my father's paintings, I return often to the circle as this primary—and mysterious—shape.

Time captions

77 Johannes VanDerBeek, *It's Time!?*, 2006, *Time* magazines, plaster, wood, and glue, 73 × 38 1/4 × 11 5/8 inches. Collection of Zach Feuer
78 Johannes VanDerBeek, *It's Time!?*, 2006 (details), *Time* magazines, plaster, wood, and glue, 73 × 38 1/4 × 11 5/8 inches. Collection of Zach Feuer
79 Sara VanDerBeek, *Foundation, Alabo Street*, 2010, digital C-print, 20 × 16 inches
80 Sara VanDerBeek, *Foundation, Deslonde Street*, 2010, digital C-print, 20 × 15 3/4 inches
81 Johannes VanDerBeek, *Ruins (Culture Pants)*, 2007, *Life* magazines and glue, 41 × 77 × 29 inches
82 Stan VanDerBeek, *Untitled*, 1955–1957, paint and mixed media on wood, 11 × 7 1/4 inches
83 Stan VanDerBeek, *Untitled*, 1955–1957, paint and mixed media on wood, 11 × 7 1/4 inches
84 Stan VanDerBeek, *Untitled*, 1955–1957, paint and mixed media on wood, 11 × 7 1/4 inches
85 Stan VanDerBeek, *Untitled*, 1955–1957, paint and mixed media on wood, 10 3/4 × 5 7/8 inches
86 Johannes VanDerBeek, *It's Time!?*, 2006 (detail), *Time* magazines, plaster, wood, and glue, 73 × 38 1/4 × 11 5/8 inches. Collection of Zach Feuer
87 Installation view, *Amazement Park*, Tang Museum, Saratoga Springs, New York, 2010
88 Stan VanDerBeek, *Untitled*, 1955–1957, paint and mixed media on wood, 18 3/4 × 7 1/4 × 1/4 inches
89 Sara VanDerBeek, *Black Mirror*, 2009, digital C-print, 20 × 15 3/4 inches

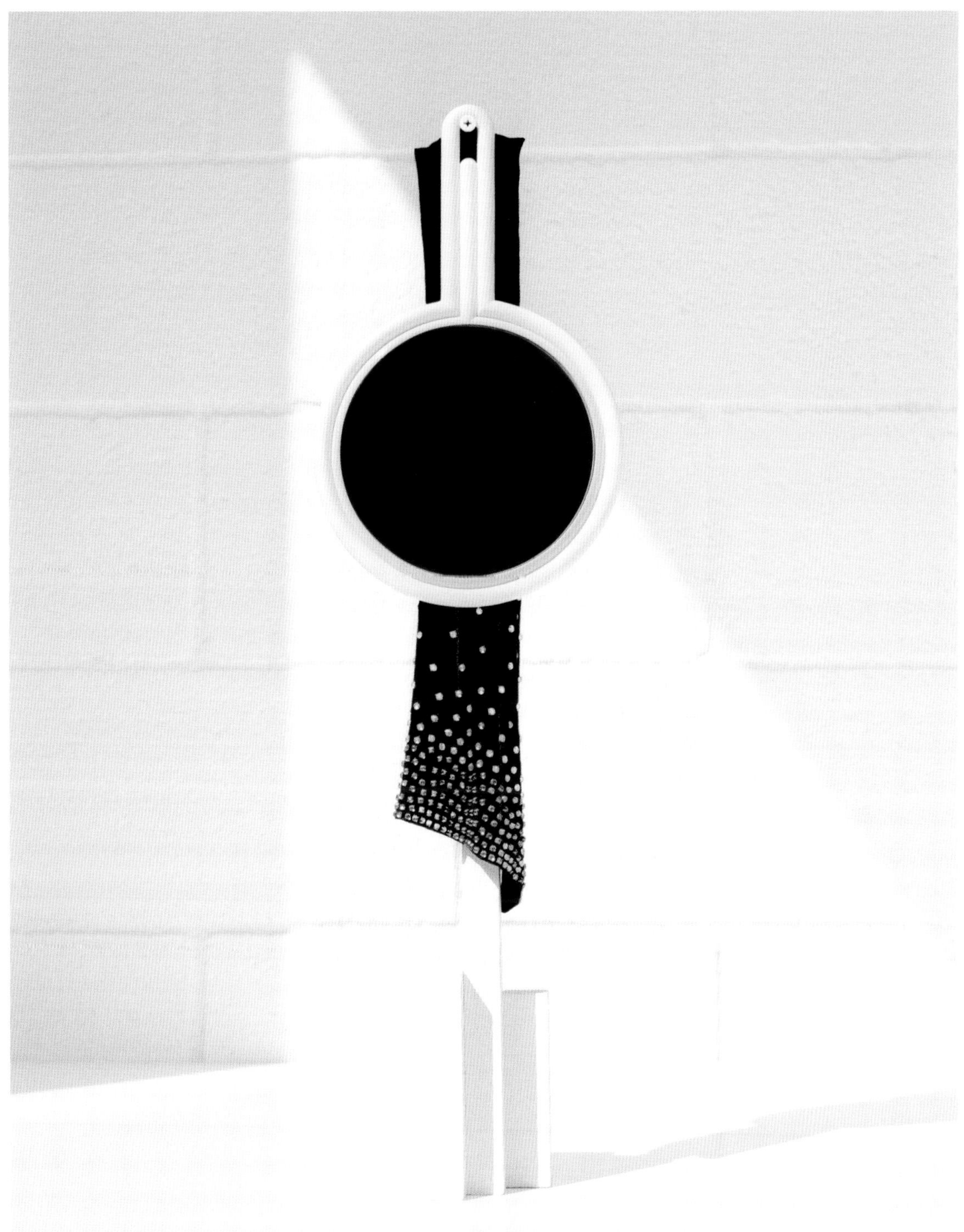

VIOLENCE

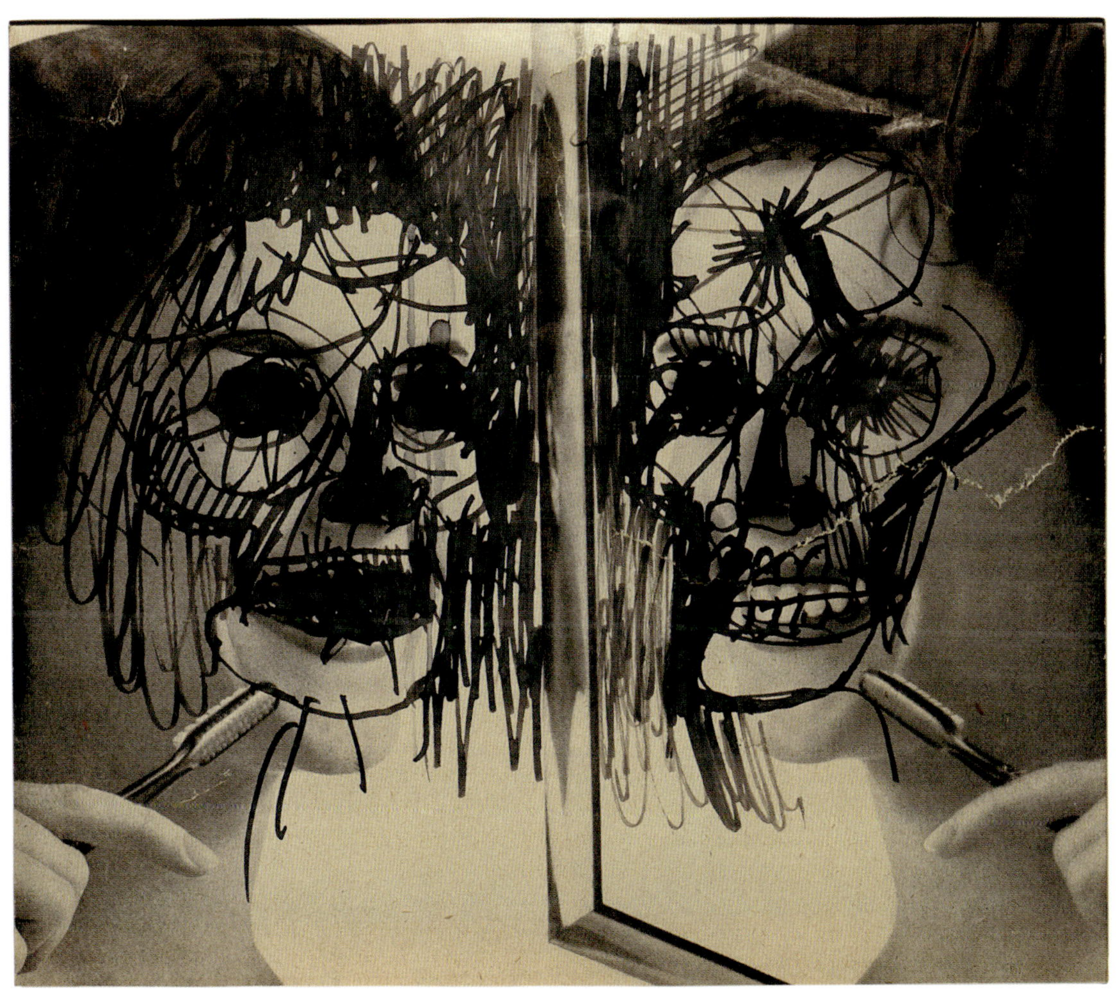

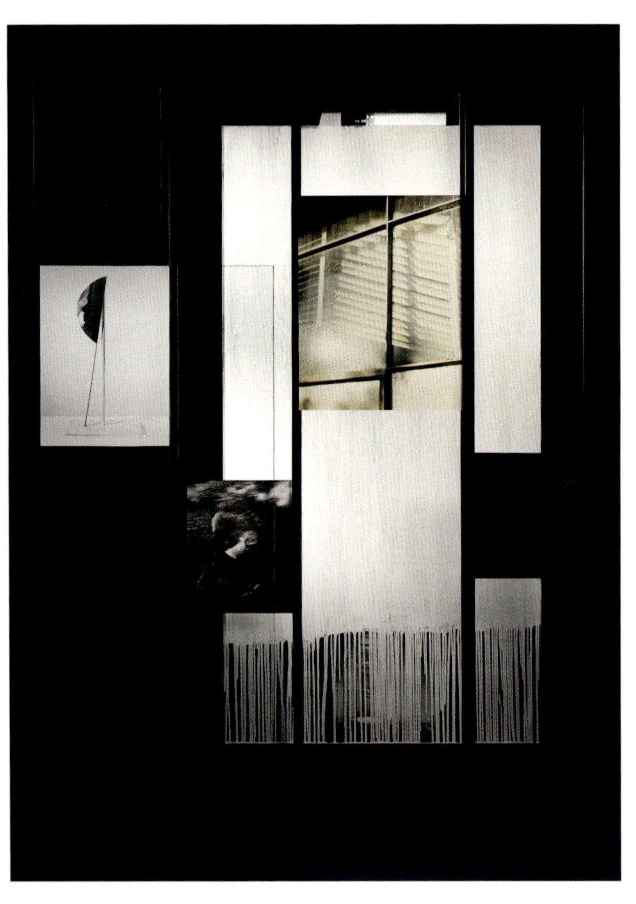
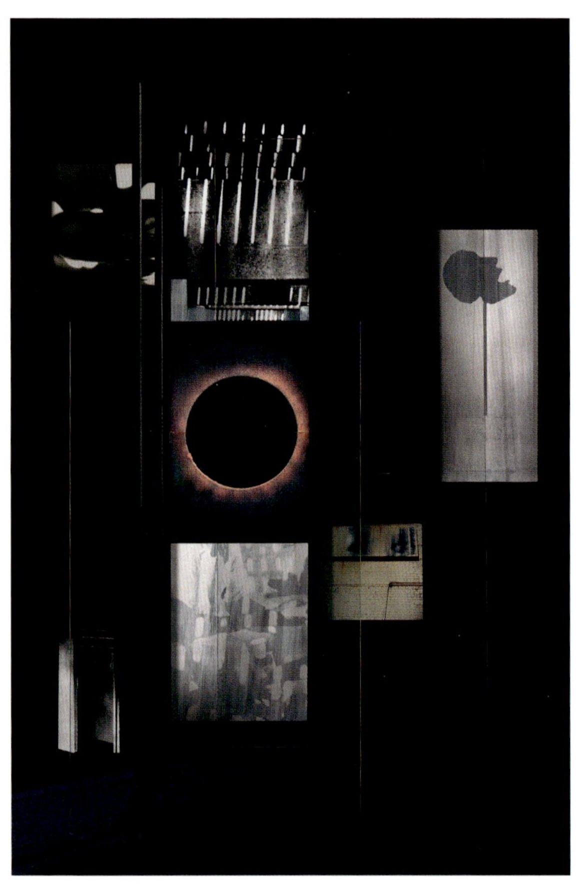

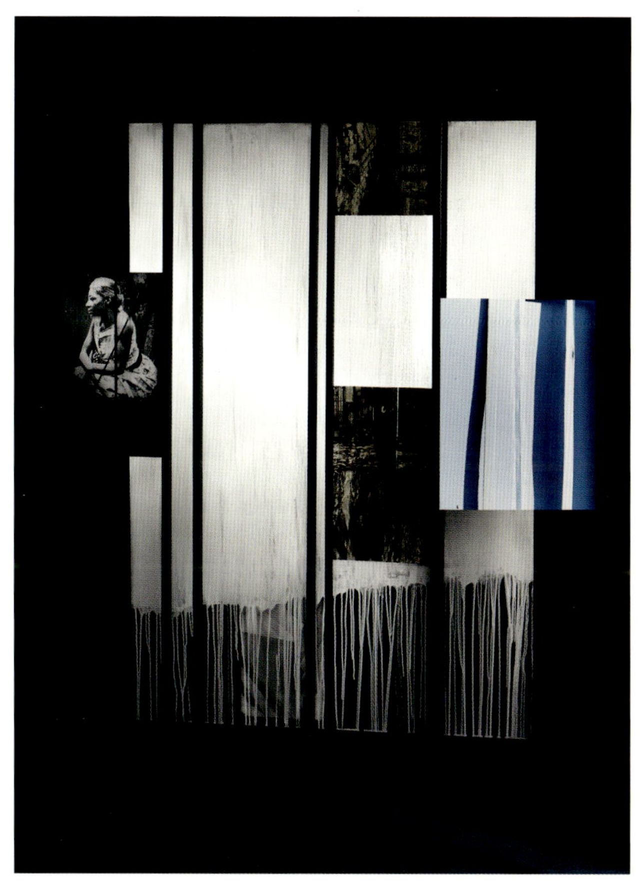

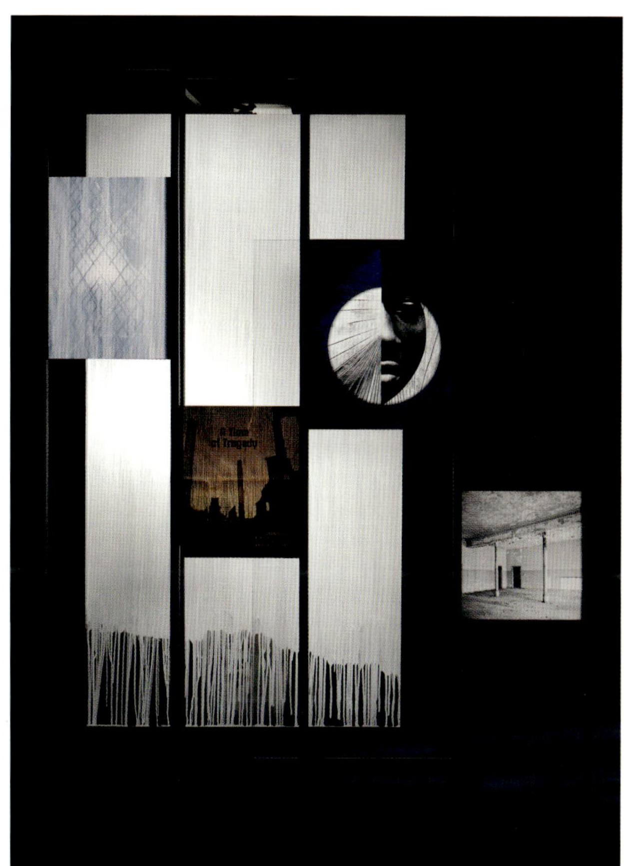
A Time
of Tragedy

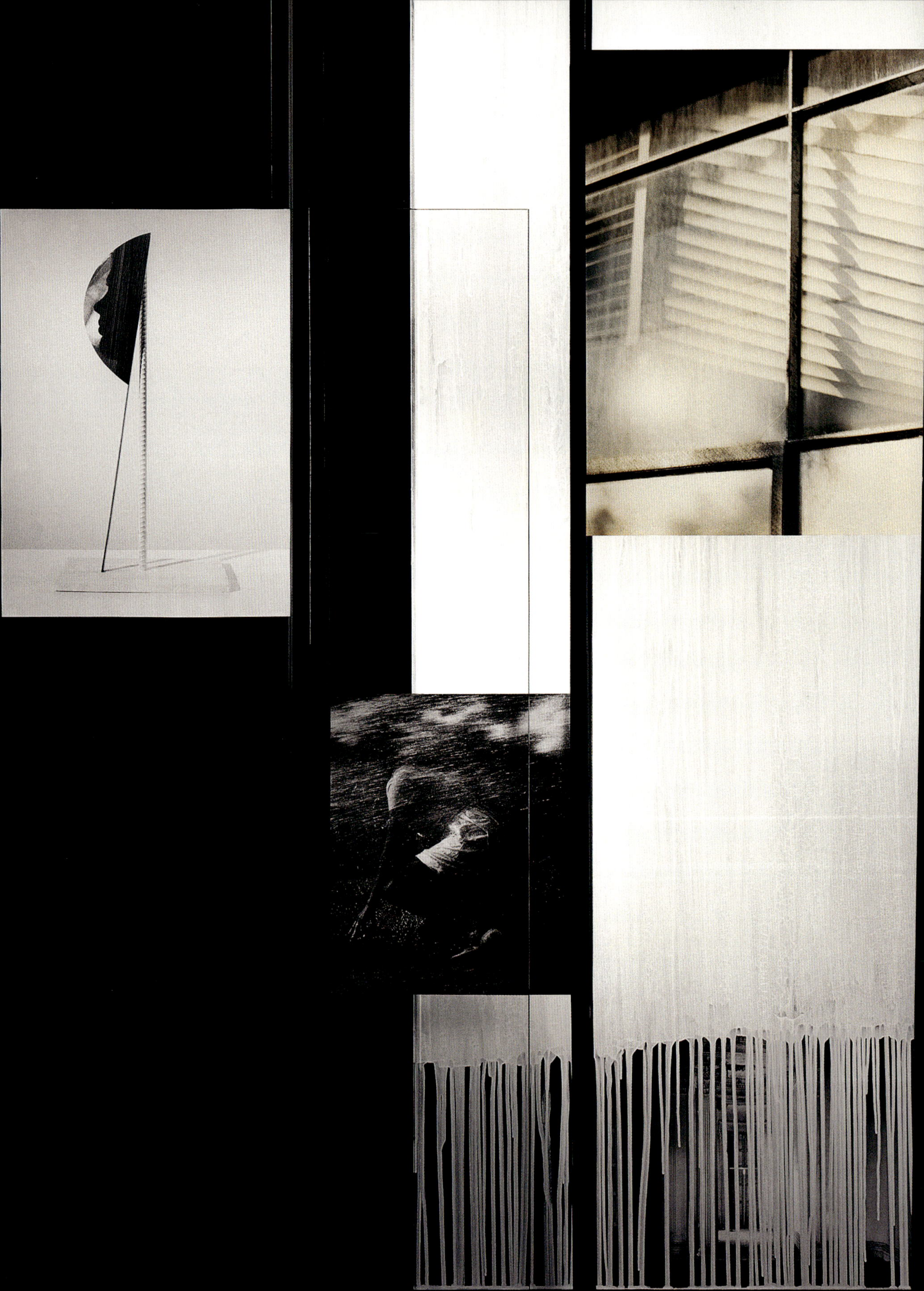

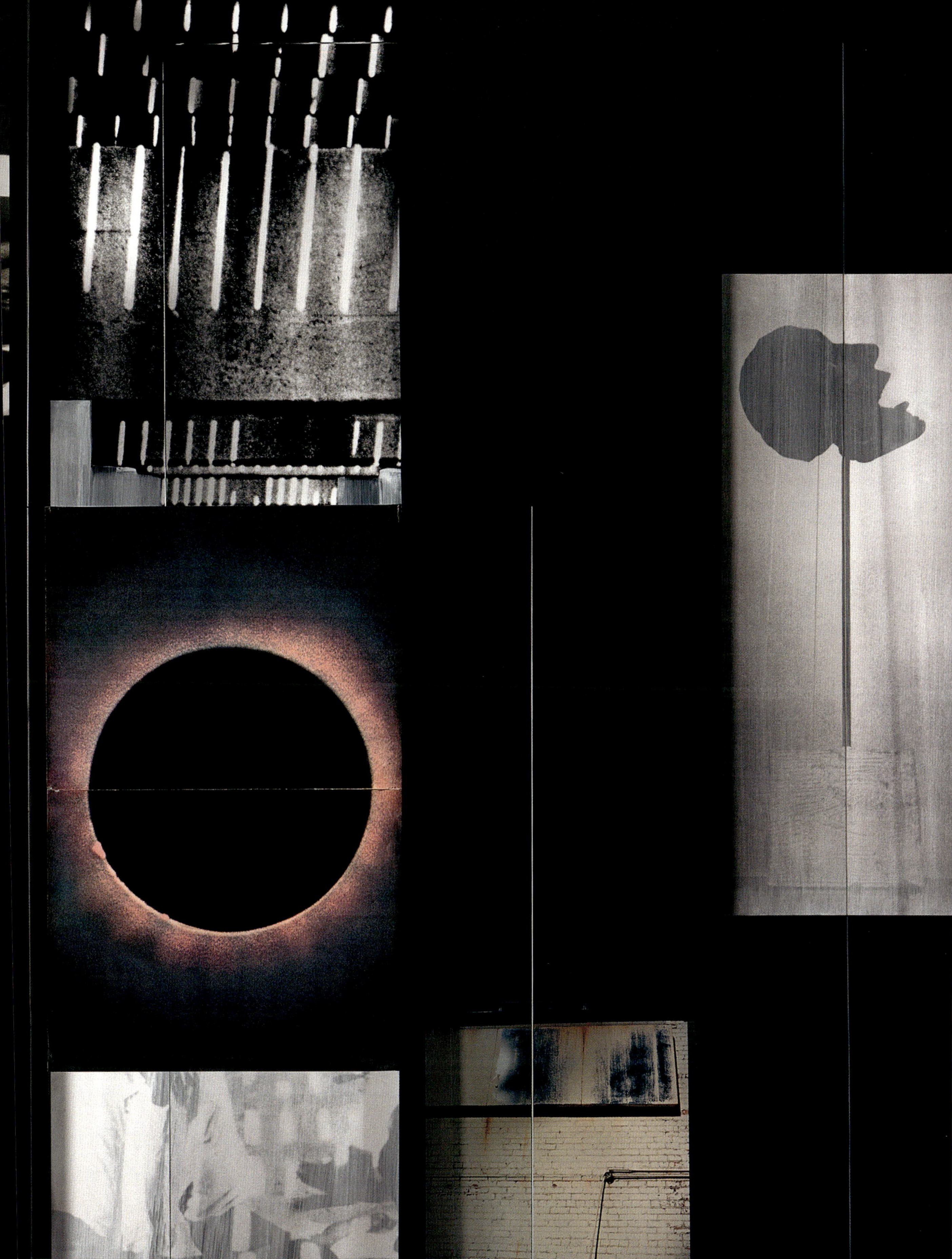

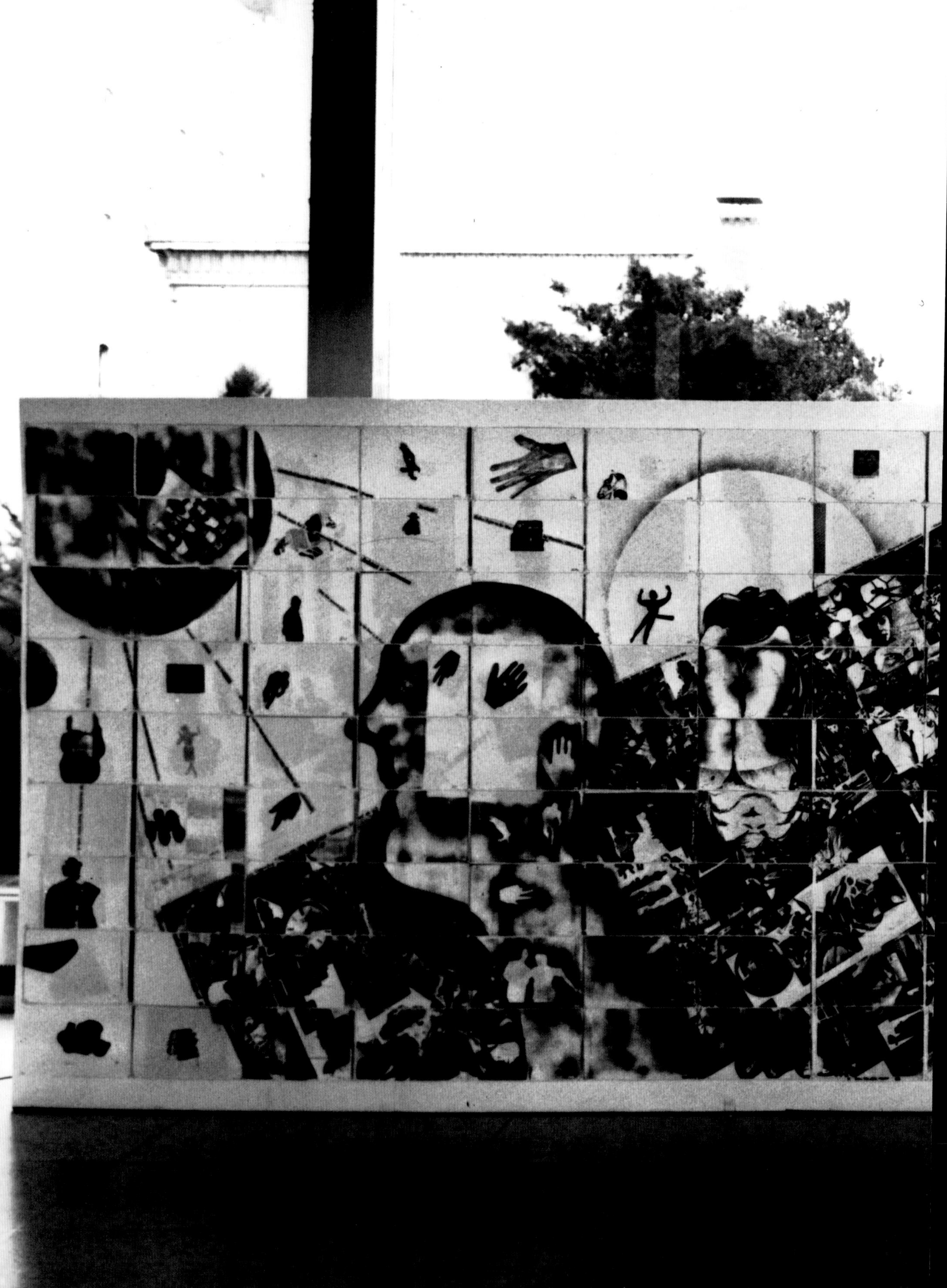

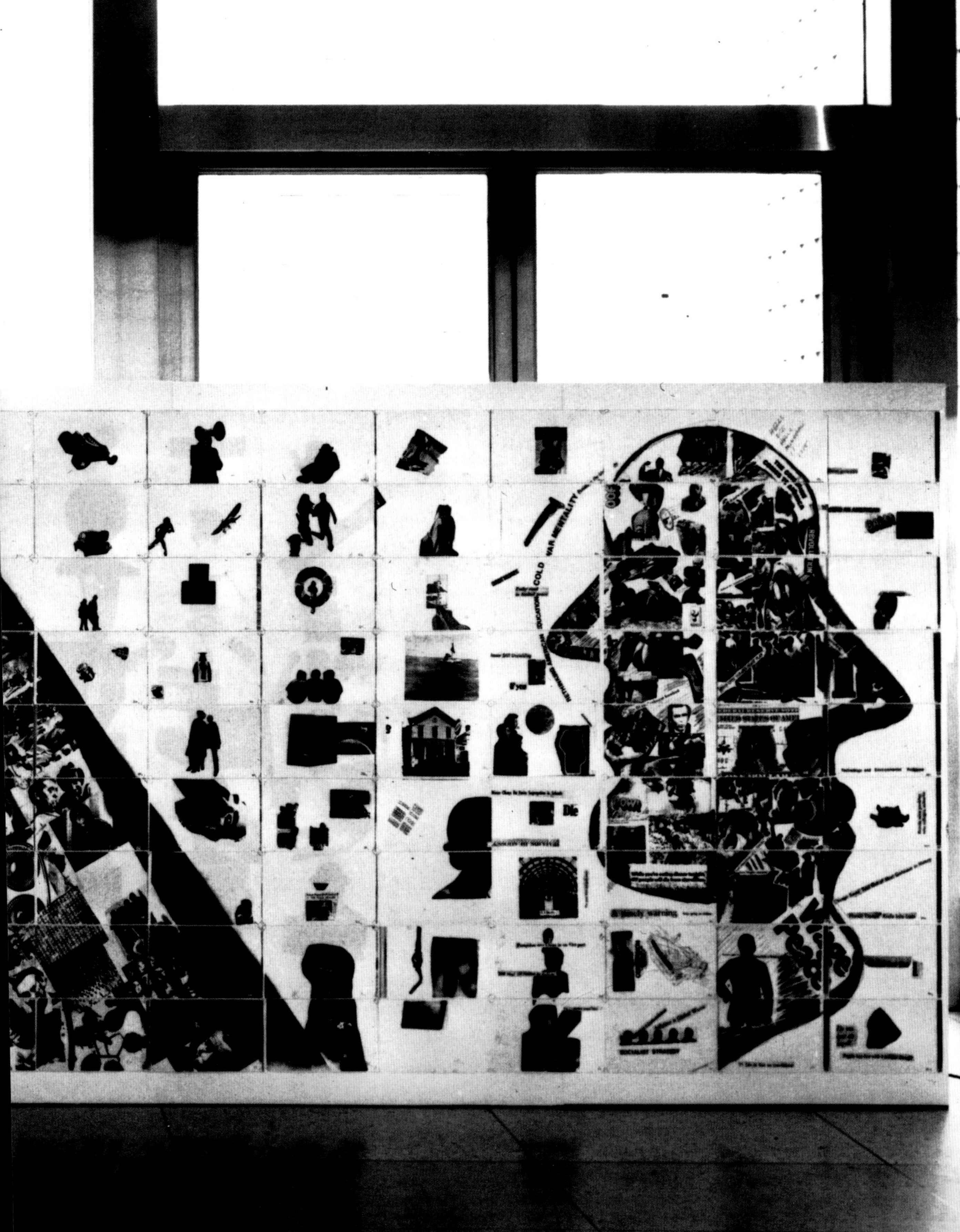
COLD WAR MENTALITY
Die

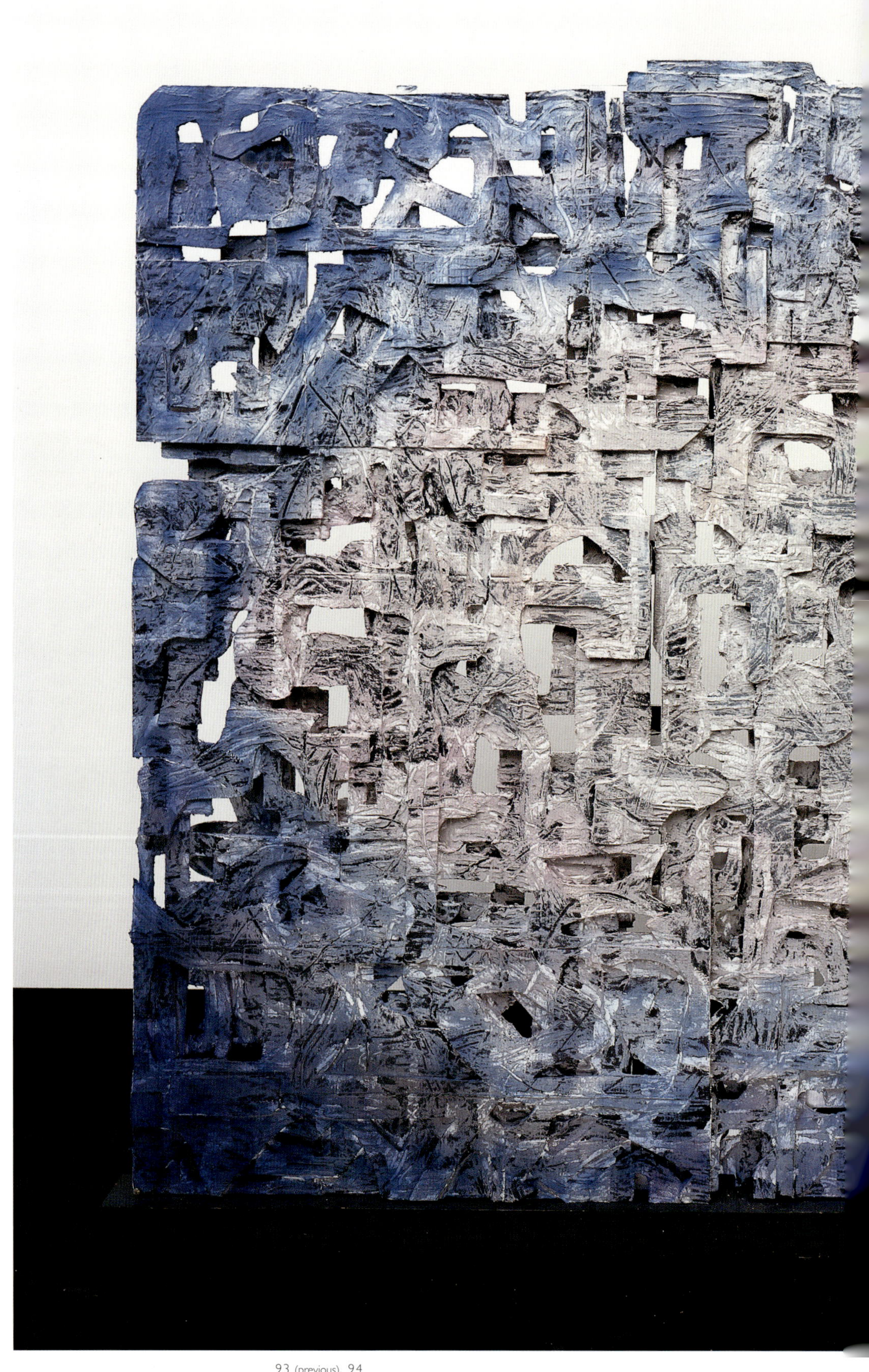

93 (previous), 94

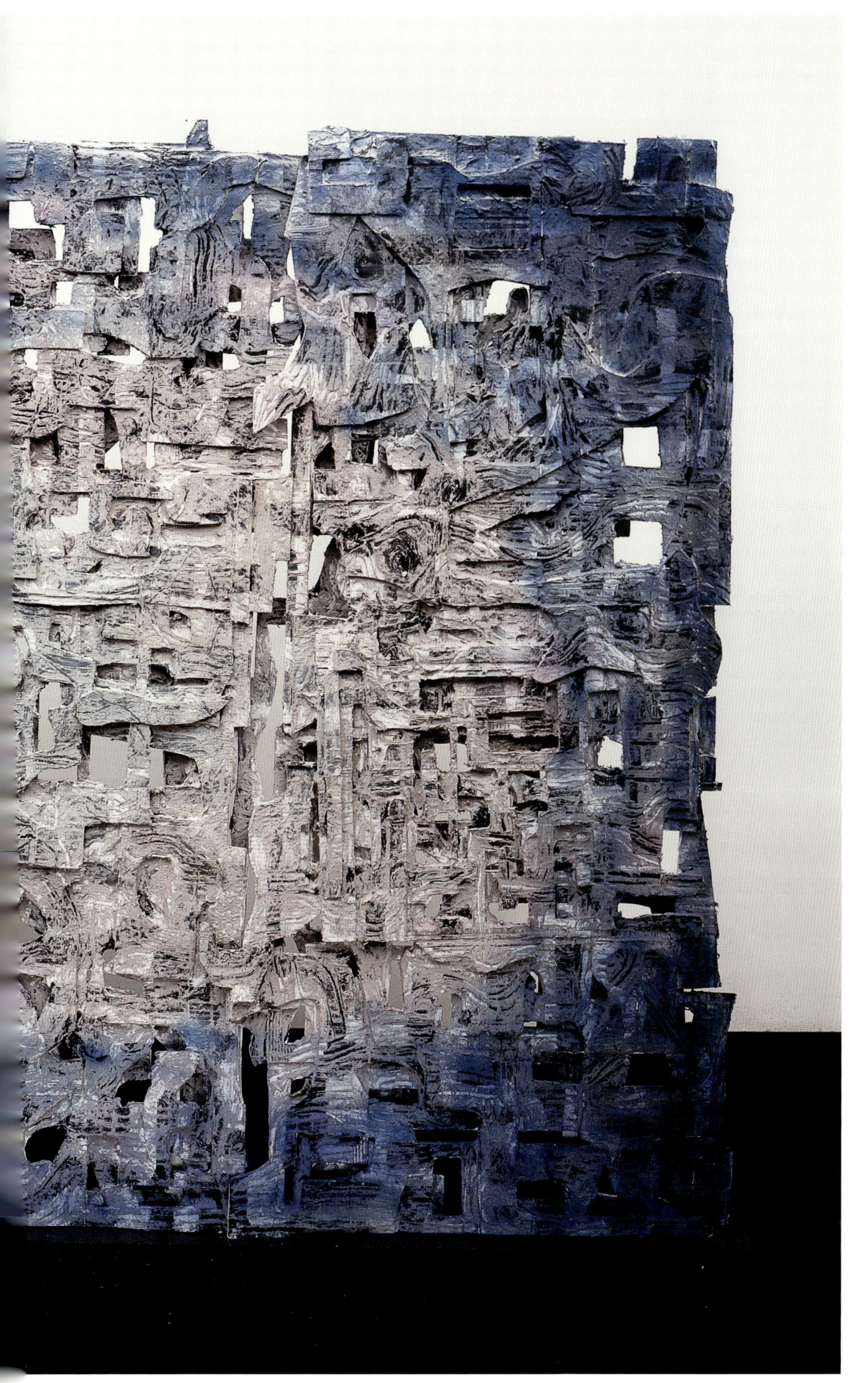

VIOLENCE

IB: Your father was interested in connections between media and violence. How does that same impulse to critique what is going on in the world around you seep into your own works?

JVDB: I rarely think about making a pointed critique through visual artwork. Art functions on the basis of symbolism; it's always one thing standing for something else, so its critical message is inherently suggestive rather than directive. The most it can become is agreeable to people as a symbol of a new meaning. If you try to inject a visual medium with a strong verbal intent it leads to a narrow interpretation. I don't know of many major social movements that have gained momentum on a narrow message. What art can do is give shape to a range of ideas and gather them towards a center. An art object becomes the wagon that people board to get to higher ground during a flood.

SVDB: I don't think of my work as a critique. With my work I am trying to understand what is happening in our time. I travel to get a sense of other communities and lives and bring them into the work in the hopes of getting closer to some idea of where we are as a civilization. I do feel my experience is very U. S.-centric at the moment, though, so I'd like to go further beyond this country in future projects.

IB: Is it important for artists to discuss the world around them? Is art a good place for activism?

SVDB: Definitively, yes and yes. Activism doesn't have to be heavy-handed in order to convey a message. I think it can be personal and intimate and still have a great impact. I like big statements and drama, but art does not have to operate on a massive or grossly political scale to be effective. In the case of my father's work, it can also be humorous or entertaining in its criticism.

JVDB: Yes, but it's very tricky to find the world. One moment when you sense seeing it, you can later realize you were looking through a small hole from underneath the dirt, seeing just a sliver of the sky. Remaining open to its ever-evolving profile while staying sensitive to details of its complexion demands an ongoing balance.

For example, you could think the world right now is all about high-speed communication and then see someone living in a van and realize that person lives in a world of bean oceans. There is no stable world as we imagine it, but the shifting idea of it leads to an unending pursuit ripe in potential. I want the world to be in my work, but as an inconspicuous lingerer at the heart of the problem. Then the work becomes more about the rise and fall of realization

Art plays an important role in activism when you consider it as one way to live. The world is constructed by different beliefs about value. Some people find money to have the utmost value and others regard meaning as the most important value. When you consider that the majority of people are primarily concerned with making money, you realize it's imperative there be some portion concerned with making meaning. The issue is not whether one is more right; it's more pressing to recognize how actions stemming from these pursuits of different values lead to drastically different visions of the world. Some would envision progress as an arrow shooting straight toward prosperity. Others would envision it as a choir emitting a circular sound that wraps around the world. Artists create a vision of the world where the mind is open and receptive to forces larger than our nature. If that did not occur we might fall victim to folly and strike ourselves with our own arrow.

IB: Johannes, can you describe bringing together a handmade, stone-age sensibility with hi-def pixels in your television sculpture?

JVDB: Pixels are the new building blocks of society. They are equivalent to the stones that built castles and erected ziggurats or temples, into which carvings about the gods were left to be deciphered. It's puzzling to think about the Internet and television as endless tablets scrolling into an unknown distance. Will their waves move into space and go beyond our gods to become the first records of our civilization that other life forms will encounter? Maybe Homer Simpson will surpass Homer of Greece. I think there is a great deal of subconscious anxiety created by seeing and processing all of this information but not being able to relate directly to it.

The piece in this show exaggerates the discrepancy between certain types of signals. It represents a fading signal of analogue television captured in the edifice of an enormous flat screen made of cardboard that looks like rock. Within this layering are encoded archetypes we all know: the black and white static of a television going infinitely backward and forward; the glow of a screen at night in a dark room putting us to sleep and causing dreams about being a dinosaur; the shallow engraving

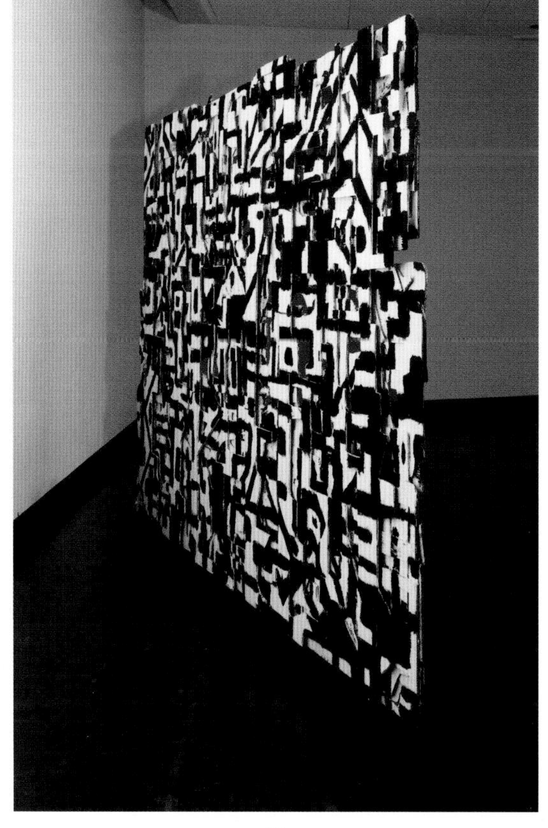

95

of messages in something hard, leaving traces of existence. These new and old archetypes show the emergence of the electronic screen as the new framework by which to comprehend life.

I worry we have over-empowered the cube, square, and rectangle so they store all of our records and keep us fixated. I read a text by a Native American mystic that said all of his people's power was lost when they were put in square houses, adding that everything in Native American culture was based on the circle because life moves in circular cycles. If you are persuaded by that sentiment, then we have been self-destructive in making ultimate squares in pixels, televisions, computers, and the urban design that thrives on their consumption. I'm not proposing to cease all squares but maybe to send out a global memo to remind our heads that we are also spheres.

IB: Sara, what inspired your work based in Detroit? What are some of the things you saw and photographed there?

SVDB: I traveled to Detroit in May 2009. At that time General Motors was nearing bankruptcy and the city in its fragility seemed to symbolize our nation's emotional state. It was once an important city that came to eminence during a time of rapid growth built upon human labor. Now it is contracting in size and fighting its abandonment. Detroit, like many American cities, is struggling to find a new existence in light of the decline of its industrial center and the loss of the infrastructure it provided. It is full of possibility—empty lots are becoming urban farms and abandoned buildings are becoming art and community centers. As a city, and as a social experiment, it speaks to the general quandary within our modern fragmented society. Will we recede into the nostalgia of past achievements and the simplicity of past lives or progress forward against adversity? Sometimes I feel we have leapt forward only to spend many years moving backward. Many small communities, like those trying to revitalize Detroit, are working toward great change and I hope the larger inertia of this nation will not prevent them. It is both inspiring and daunting to realize it all rests in us, and we in the end are responsible.

I consider this one large work composed of four panel-like images. The design of the structures with leaning panes of glass was inspired by the banks of broken factory windows in Detroit. Each structure within each of the four images is different in its configuration. I have tried to emphasize this shifting perspective by varying the lighting and camera position for each of the four panels. This is the first work where I have combined images I have taken on location, studio-based photographs, and found images. Formally, light and line run through many of the images. My hope is that through their scale, the four final prints achieve a feeling of a fragile architectural space that is held together at points by a delicate and precarious balance of elements.

The work moves through time from left to right across the four panels, and from back to front within each one. At the bottom rear in the first panel is Walker

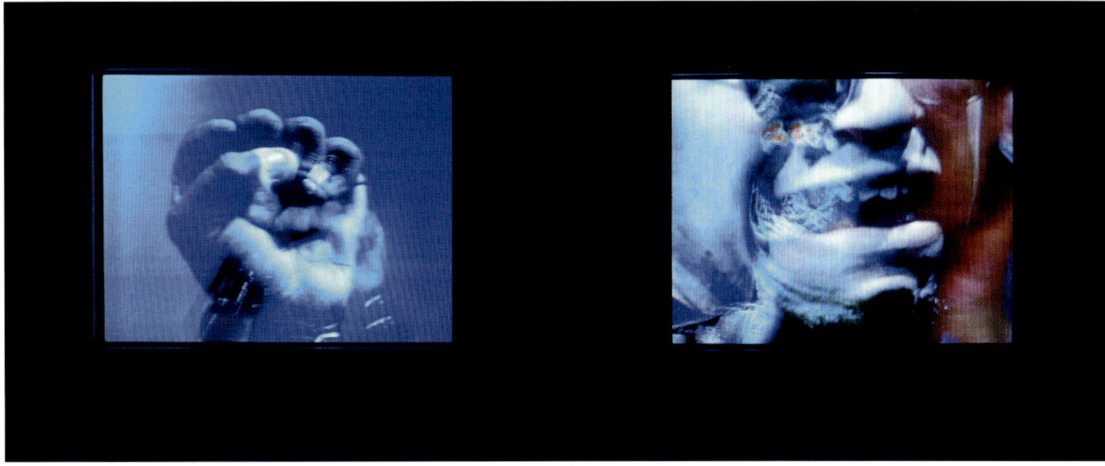

96

Evans's image of Belle Grove. At the mid-level is a Charles Moore image of a woman being hosed during a 1963 protest in Birmingham, her body obscured by the violent water. I saw the events of the civil rights movement as a precursor to the riots in Detroit. Since much of the African American population in Detroit migrated from the south, I thought the first panel should begin there. I was drawn to Moore's image because of its abstraction of the figure but I also felt it quietly represented an argument that has persisted with "concerned" photography: when to document tragedies and when to stop and help. At the front of the arrangement is an image I shot of an abandoned office building in Detroit, where the blinds have fallen askew.

Detroit feels like a city that is being forgotten almost as soon as it is being recognized. It has been frequently reported on in the news like many other places deeply affected by the economic downturn, but its decline has been occurring for many years, and only now do people seem to pay attention. This piece attempts to understand this moment in America and what led to this moment, not specifically the economy, but the state of the nation generally.

Violence captions

90 Stan VanDerBeek, *Untitled (from Breathdeath)*, 1963, ink on collage, 14 × 10 inches

91 Sara VanDerBeek, *A Composition for Detroit*, 2009, digital C-prints, left to right: 66 × 49 ¼ inches; 66 × 44 ¾ inches; 66 × 49 ¼ inches; 66 × 48 ¾ inches

92 Sara VanDerBeek, *A Composition for Detroit*, 2009 (details), digital C-prints

93 Stan VanDerBeek, *Panels for the Walls of the World (Fax Mural)*, 1970, telecopier transmission pages, 7 × 20 feet. Installation view, Walker Art Center, Minneapolis, 1970

94 Johannes VanDerBeek, *The Big Stone Flatscreen with Static*, 2010, cardboard, Celluclay, wood and paint, 89 ½ × 122 × 5 ½ inches

95 Johannes VanDerBeek, *The Big Stone Flatscreen with Static*, 2010, cardboard, Celluclay, wood and paint, 89 ½ × 122 × 5 ½ inches

96 Stan VanDerBeek, Stills from *Violence Sonata*, 1969, two channel video with sound. Originally broadcasted on WGBH-TV, Boston, alongside live studio performance, 53:54 minutes. Installation view, Guild and Greyshkul, New York, 2008

Fionn Meade

Johannes VanDerBeek

I

The television has been turned off. The signal has gone out. And with it much of the assurance that we might have found in collectively recalling its imagery, or gathering before its reflective light, or looking in expectation to its designated place in the living room or den. The domestic message of broadcast television has gone off air. Even its celebrated moments of historical optimism—a moonwalk, a wall come down, a tank turned away—seem far off and increasingly nostalgic, as does the methodic montage of television advertising with its car commercials, cleaning products, fast food and beer slogans. Not that the commodity glut has gone anywhere but the wireless age has replaced the "tube" era with multiple screens, multitasking, and a welter of audiovisual stimuli that requires and expects new levels of dispersed attention and immediate responsiveness.

Johannes VanDerBeek's *The Big Stone Flatscreen with Static* (2010) confronts the ubiquity of such screens and how they inherently contribute to our distraction even as it pays homage to the obsolescence of the analog television era. In the artist's comic yet elegiac vision, the flatscreen becomes a standing stone and cardboard takes on monumental status. Only as we step back from the roughhewn surface and imposing scale of the monolith does the glow of a television set become visible. As the oval outline of a television screen emerges from the intense blue-and-white, perforated pattern at the center of the sculpture's abstract composition, the viewer can zoom in or zone out. Coats of CelluClay slathered on VanDerBeek's jigsaw-like shapes give the standing wall an archaic patina, while the panel's back reveals a black-and-white pattern recalling the glitch and jitter of television static. Borrowing from both Op-Art strategies and early Abstract Expressionist mark-making, the wall typifies VanDerBeek's unpredictable style and freewheeling references.

Indeed, technological obsolescence and the repurposing of everyday, disposable materials represent bedrock themes within VanDerBeek's associative, high-energy practice. *Documentation of Body/Building* (2007), for example, a large-scale collage composed of black and white photographic images culled from vintage magazines, offers another version of the large screen patina or wall panel. Having sanded down the area in between images, but also some of the pictured faces, VanDerBeek underscores certain gestures and architectural details, working the surface into an agitated pitch as images rotate left and right, up and down, in a dizzying rotation that recalls the Constructivist photo-collages of Alexander Rodchenko even as it puts things resolutely in motion: a couple dances; a dour man clutches a steering wheel; a boy sprints in the snow; a

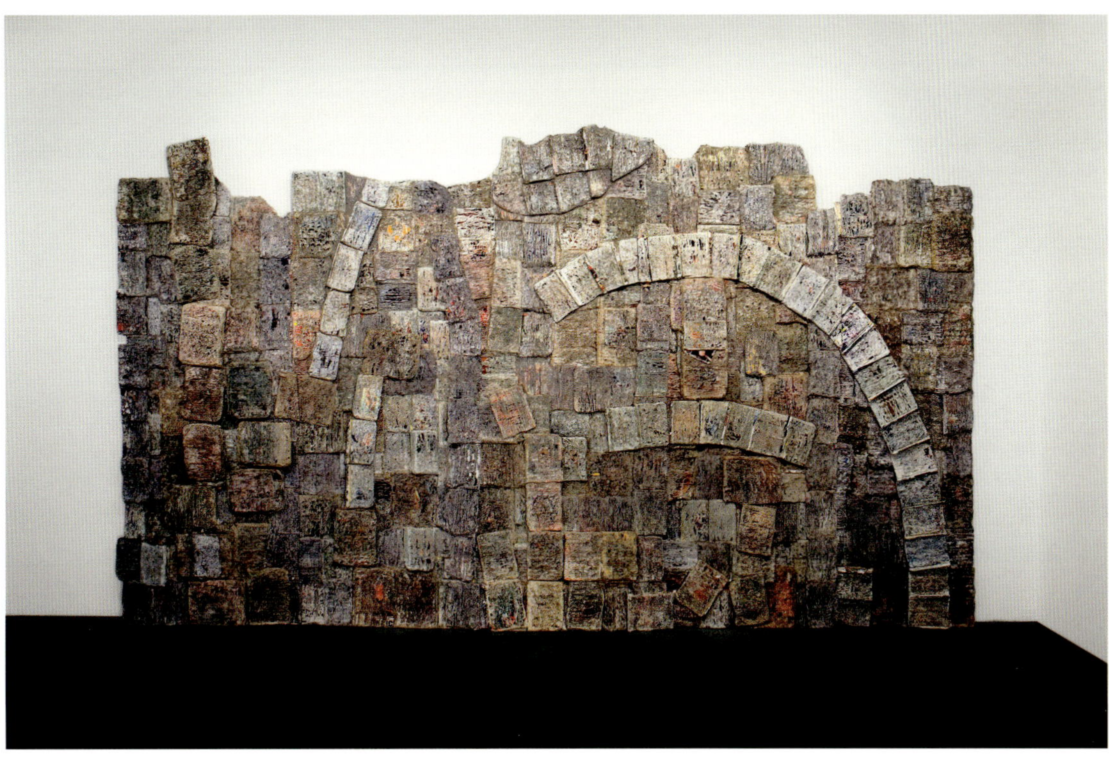

Johannes VanDerBeek, *Ruins*, 2007, *Life*, *Time*, and *National Geographic* magazines, wood, and glue, 9 ½ × 16 ½ feet

faceless young woman pauses above a chess game; an old woman peers down from an apartment window; a staircase unfolds; a man lies wounded behind barbed wire; a woman appears to float above a trampoline; telephones ring and get answered, and everywhere hands upon hands grasp, clutch, reach, hold, and choose. Gestural semblance gone haywire as the corporeal collapses into the architectural and vice versa.

The playful kinetic style of *Documentation of Body/Building* inescapably and unapologetically recalls the extensive collage work of the artist's father, Stan VanDerBeek, in his film animations of the late 1950s and early 60s. Vertiginous in impulse, Johannes' collage resonates with a particular passage from Stan VanDerBeek's 1966 essay "Re: Vision," a litany of impressions regarding what an innovative artist of his time should be concerned with: "simultaneous images and compression, abstractions, superimpositions, discontinuous information, social surrealism, episodic structure." While this partial list offers an acute assessment of the "screen culture" we inhabit today, it also elucidates many of Johannes VanDerBeek's own compositional tactics. However, just as his father committed his artistic career, in part, to exploring exponential image production and distribution through such strategies as computer-generated animation, searchable image databases, multi-channel projections and satellite broadcasts, so Johannes's early work has taken up precisely what comes after—after television, after the information age, after software, after dispersion, after images. Compressed and put to use as a readymade material, the circulated and recycled image becomes a primary source for associative connections and gestural affinities untethered from context or content—existing outside of illustrative time in VanDerBeek's anachronistic vision.

2

Splayed cans—cut open, welded together, and spray-painted—are erected into salutary totems, cartoonish figures, and precarious towers in a group of recent VanDerBeek sculptures. They bring to mind David Smith's *Tanktotem* series (1953-1960) in their thematic variation upon figurative form, recycled materials, and animistic leanings if not in their modest scale and lack of solemnity. Pared down, lightweight, and funny, the artist manages a mercurial pace in presenting a series of tactile, upright and witty rejoinders to the common view of the empty tin can as nothing more than detritus. From the voluptuous evocation of an archaic fertility figurine, *Venus*, to the Tatlinesque *John Beans Rising*, or the clustered profile of *A Family* (all 2010) the everyday can remains coarsely present in all of its performative turns, underscoring the artist's comfort with makeshift means. As with the earlier *Tin Can Jam* (2007), a candelabra-like structure that pops the top and pries open the middle of each component part, VanDerBeek pieces together immediately associative figures that seem to greet the viewer with a knowing nod, including the waggish pose of *Dog Horse* (2010), and the step it up humor of *Little Lift* (2010). Betraying a whimsical, on-the-move style, these sketch-like compositions revel in spontaneity. Provisional yet self-assured, they recall the notion of a "prior" technology that Claude Lévi-Strauss ascribed to the artist-as-bricoleur, one who works with "whatever is at hand" and allows for an approach that always "references some extraneous movement: a ball rebounding, a dog straying or a horse swerving from its direct course to avoid an obstacle." This willingness to change course lets the bricoleur accept how "it is always earlier ends which are called upon to play the means." Through VanDerBeek's unique embrace of "prior technology," material ends become gestural means in his highly mimetic practice.

Extending his totemic reach, a 2010 series of six kiosk-like sculptures affixes found aluminum display boxes atop black pedestals in a lineup of surreal figures. Painted intense acrylic tones of purple, yellow, red, orange, and blue, the boxes contain the most unlikely faces as a magazine page hovers within each, torn into the rudimentary outline of a face replete with eyes and mouths. Encircled with what appear to be halos of neon filament that have gone out, the faces give the impression of spirits summoned from an indeterminate past, re-animated specters from a discontinued circulation. Bent aluminum frames each jagged visage, painted in the same electric tone as the background, buzzing with a neon-like coloring that will never light up. *Smiling Lightning*, for instance, takes a magazine image of a nighttime lightning storm above an observatory and rips and tears out a bemused expression from the landscape, achieving the simplest of masks cut from an image of primeval wonder. Likewise, *Burning Face*, makes eyes of two archaic looking coins held up before a burning candle, and *Smoke Head*, pulls a face from a creepy

Johannes VanDerBeek, *Smiling Lightning*, 2010 (detail), wire, paint, paper, and steel, 65 ¾ × 21 ¾ × 12 inches

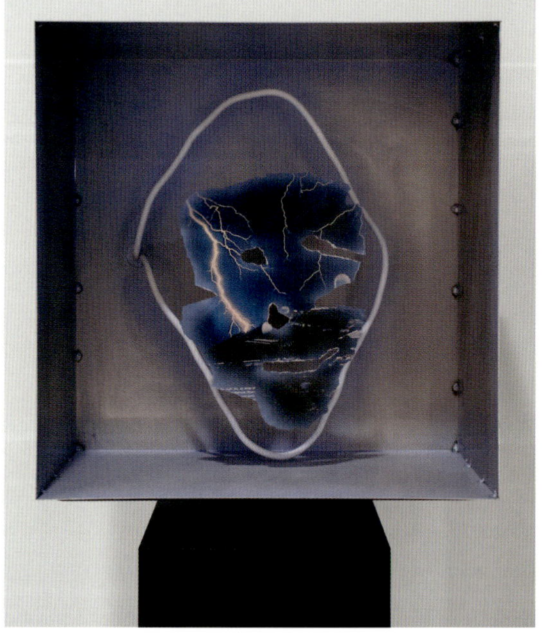

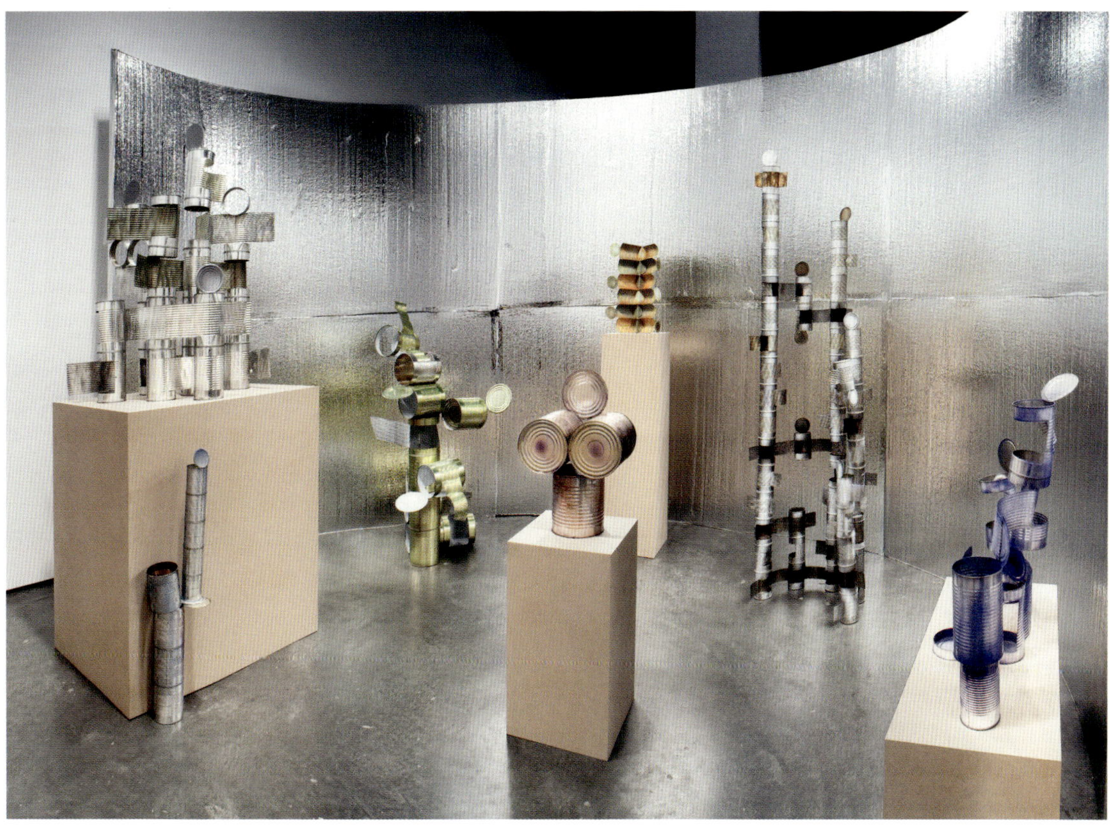

Installation view, *Johannes VanDerBeek: Another Time Man*, Zach Feuer Gallery, New York, 2010

vintage advertisement for paper lanterns depicting civil war heroes. Resulting in a clan of otherworldly masks, the upright effigies peer at the viewer as if from a burned out elsewhere. The light bulb will never be turned back on, and only the replica of its incandescence remains.

From the incendiary masks of the kiosk series to the standing aluminum mesh figures in the artist's most recent solo exhibition "Another Time Man," at Zach Feuer Gallery, New York, VanDerBeek deftly shifts from the totemic toward transparency and iridescent coloring, imbuing each of these mesh characters with the retinal impression of an afterimage. Blatant titles typecast the hollow figures as characters that have been blown in from a televisual realm. The tie-dye acrylic coating of *Hippie Ghost*, with its bracing stance, portrays a Jerry Garcia-like figure in a state of stoned surprise. Put back on its heels, the figure is emptied into an outline form that boasts a cliché headband, sunglasses, and a full beard; just exceeding mannequin scale, the counterculture personage appears to radiate with the dim glow of having left its image status behind for a tenuous three-dimensionality. Similarly, the standing-on-one-leg pose of *Indian Ghost* transposes an archetypal figure from television and film into a delusory, retreating materiality. Long spear in hand the warrior was propped stoically before the static side of *The Big Stone Flatscreen* at Feuer Gallery, while in the Tang exhibition it served as a projection surface for a Stan VanDerBeek slide piece. Along with *Woman Ghost*, a frontier-like figure with bustle and hat who peers at the viewer from around

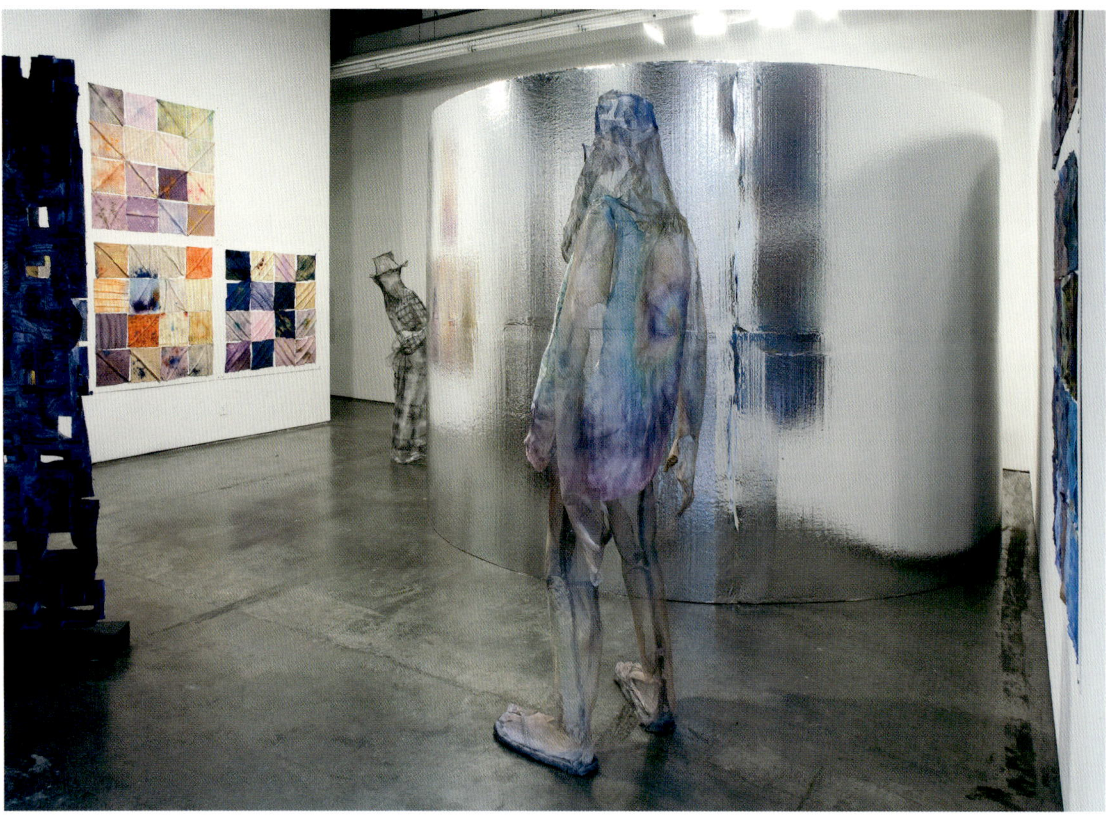

Installation view, *Johannes VanDerBeek: Another Time Man*, Zach Feuer Gallery, New York, 2010

a corner, VanDerBeek's mesh apparitions are brought into three-dimensional focus by still another variation upon the screen. Hovering on the wall behind the pioneer figure, for instance, are two abstract acrylic grids of pleated paper towel paintings adhered to masonite panels. Providing a pixel-like backdrop, *Towel Tablet 9* and *Towel Tablet 10* (2010) reveals a red grid upon stepping away, a doubling that echoes the composite nature of the serial composition. The readymade material is nearly pictorialized into the plane of painting, except that each square is more a component part than an autonomous composition, as referenced by their designation as numbered tablets. Related to the artist's longstanding use of magazine pages and newspapers, the paper towels are built up into mosaic-like panels that provide tension and counterbalance to VanDerBeek's totems and specters. Evincing a Richard Tuttle-like gift for ephemeral abstraction, the grids oscillate with an impression of refracted, prismatic light and emergent or faintly recalled geometry.

3

The treasures of time lie high, in urns, coins, and monuments, scarce below the roots of some vegetables. Time hath endless rarities, and shows of all varieties.

—Sir Thomas Browne, Hydriotaphia, or Urn Burial

Biers, sarcophagi, monuments, and ruins abound in Johannes VanDerBeek's ludic vision. Devoid of the melancholy often associated with entropy and fragmentation, however, the burial motifs that recur throughout his practice emerge instead from the unsettled recesses of gesture and mimetic storytelling, eliciting "shows of all varieties" in his modeling of the discarded, overlooked, and forsworn. The archeological look of *Ruins* (2007), for instance, constructs an architectural wall fragment reminiscent of ancient Middle Eastern architecture, but made completely out of magazine pages. Glued and compressed to mimic the contour and volume of stone blocks, the roughhewn paper aggregate was cut, gouged, and sanded down to a worn patina flecked with color—effectively erasing the mass-media connotations of the pages; in VanDerBeek's inversion of collage methods, images become accreted rather than aligned, the effaced surface of an indeterminate past. *Ruins (Culture Pants)* (2007) also from the artist's second solo exhibition at Zach Feuer Gallery, used the same worked-over surface to build a life-size bier upon which a pulped male figure lay with arms crossed, only his legs revealing collaged strips of imagery from such iconic magazines as Life, Time, and National Geographic. Laid out as if for interment or possible immolation, the figure further reveals VanDerBeek's fascination with burial and haunting while maintaining a sense of humor as evidenced by the title.

While smaller scale works from the same period, including *Untitled (God head)*, and *Untitled (Old Trashman)* (both 2007), maintain a more conventional relationship with collage—in both, VanDerBeek creates the contour of a facial profile by sanding down the outlined area of a built-up, layered collage—*Ruins* and *Ruins (Culture Pants)* step fully from relief methods into architectural and figurative scale. Departing as well from earlier tabletop works that depicted ruined cities composed of newspaper fragments, the man lying on the medieval-looking bier and the arched wall fragment mark a transition from collage to decisively sculptural concerns.

A more recent series continues to explore VanDerBeek's predilection for the funereal while complicating his formal vocabulary. With such highly suggestive titles as *A Rusty Square with Farm Markings* (2009) and *Devil Torso* (2010), the bent and crumpled surfaces of this series of sculptural wall hangings recall, in turn, crypt-like fragments, ancient sarcophagi, discarded heraldic shields, and abandoned machinery. Completely transformed from their material underpinning as layers of aluminum foil, dark pastel hues of magenta, sienna, and turquoise lend the surface of each piece in the series an aged, earthen patina—resulting in new relics from a bygone era. The two body-like outlines of *Former President* (2010), for example, clearly resemble sarcophagi, propped against the gallery wall like museum artifacts from ancient burial sites. Abstract scratches done with a ballpoint pen adorn the surface of each work in the series, occasionally approaching recognizable forms, only to recede into archaic-looking incisions that

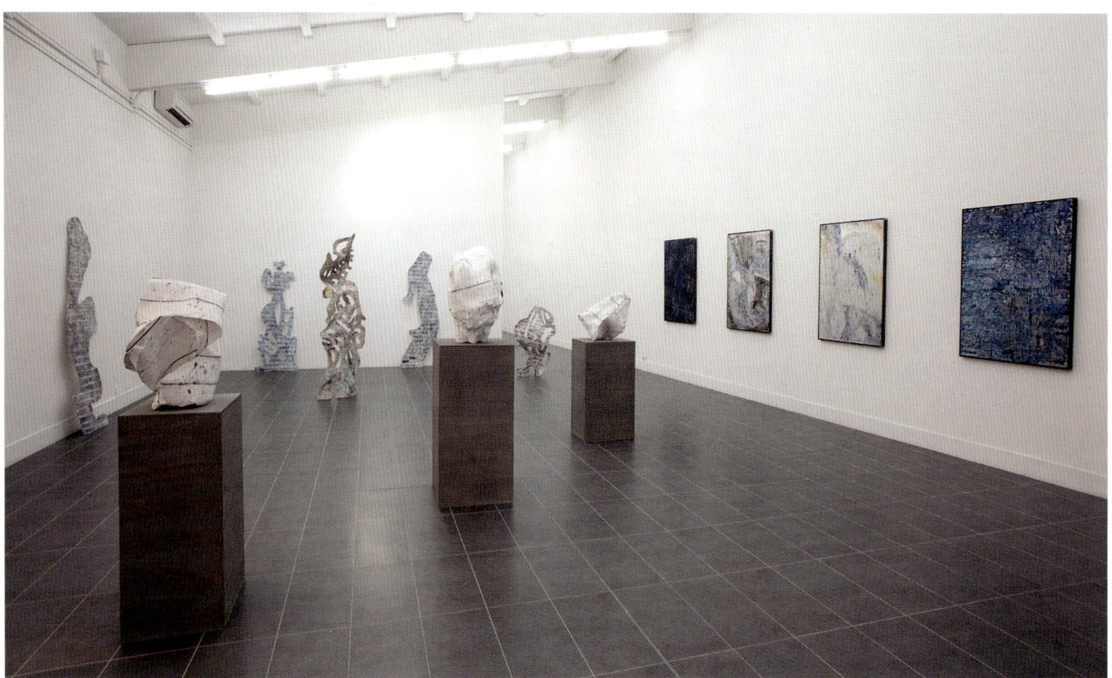

Installation view, *Johannes VanDerBeek, Thunder Ground Sky*, Brand New Gallery, Milan, 2011

opposite: Johannes VanDerBeek, *Sky Impression #2*, 2011, acrylic on foam, 49 × 34 inches

defeat deciphering. Similarly archaic and withholding, *It* (2009), hangs on the wall like a creased remnant from a fantastical industrial past where the imaginings of workers were recorded onto discarded sheets of assembly-line metal, while *The King* (2009) appears as bent and banged up as a shield used in repeated military campaigns.

However, the initially heavy appearance of these fragments gives way to an oneiric lightness. As with much of VanDerBeek's work, an atmosphere of death, aftermath, and visitation prevails, but always countered with outbursts of gestural mark-making and material ingenuity that exude boundless energy. The ballpoint incisions quiver, crisscross, and ultimately cancel any portentous reading, and the patina of burial encourages instead a view of death as everyday and immediate, as well as remote and effacing. If, as Walter Benjamin surmises, "Death is the sanction for everything the storyteller can tell," VanDerBeek's license is for an episodic style of narrative that proceeds by variation and comic gesture as well as by memorial and commemoration. Death becomes a variety show in his restless hands, finding seemingly inexhaustible forms of invocation.

Notes

1 Stan VanDerBeek, "Re: Vision," *American Scholar* 35, no. 2 (1966): 338-39.

2 Claude Lévi-Strauss, *The Savage Mind*, 1962, trans. John Weightman and Doreen Weightman (Chicago: University of Chicago Press, 1966): 19.

3 Ibid., 21.

4 Sir Thomas Browne, "Hydriotaphia (Urn Burial)," 1658, *Religio Medici, Urn Burial, Christian Morals, and Other Essays* (London: Walter Scott, 1886): 119.

5 Walter Benjamin, "The Storyteller," *Selected Writings*, vol. 3, 1935-38, ed. Howard Eiland and William Michael Jennings, trans. Howard Eiland (Cambridge, MA: Belknap Press, 2006): 150.

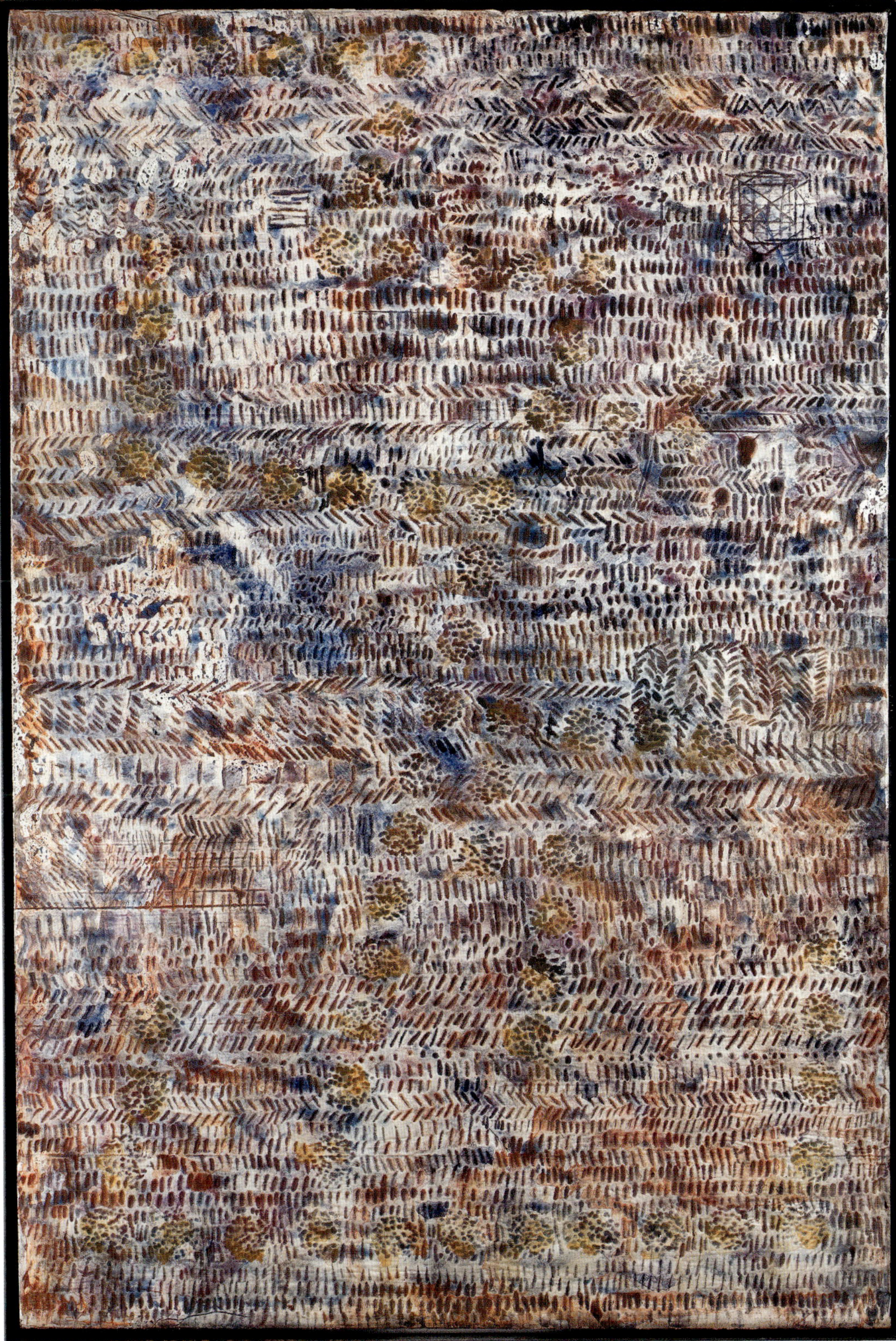

EYES

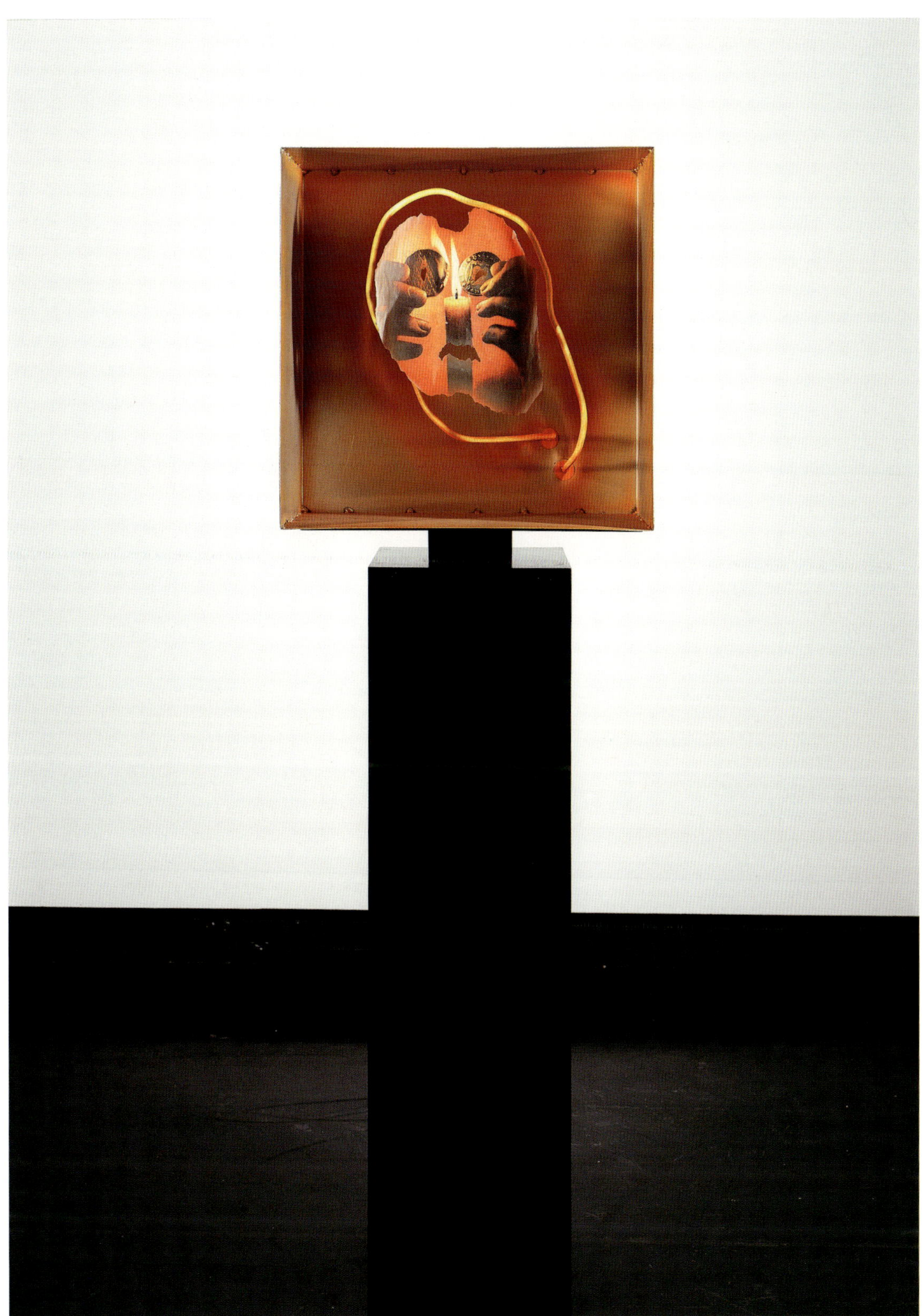

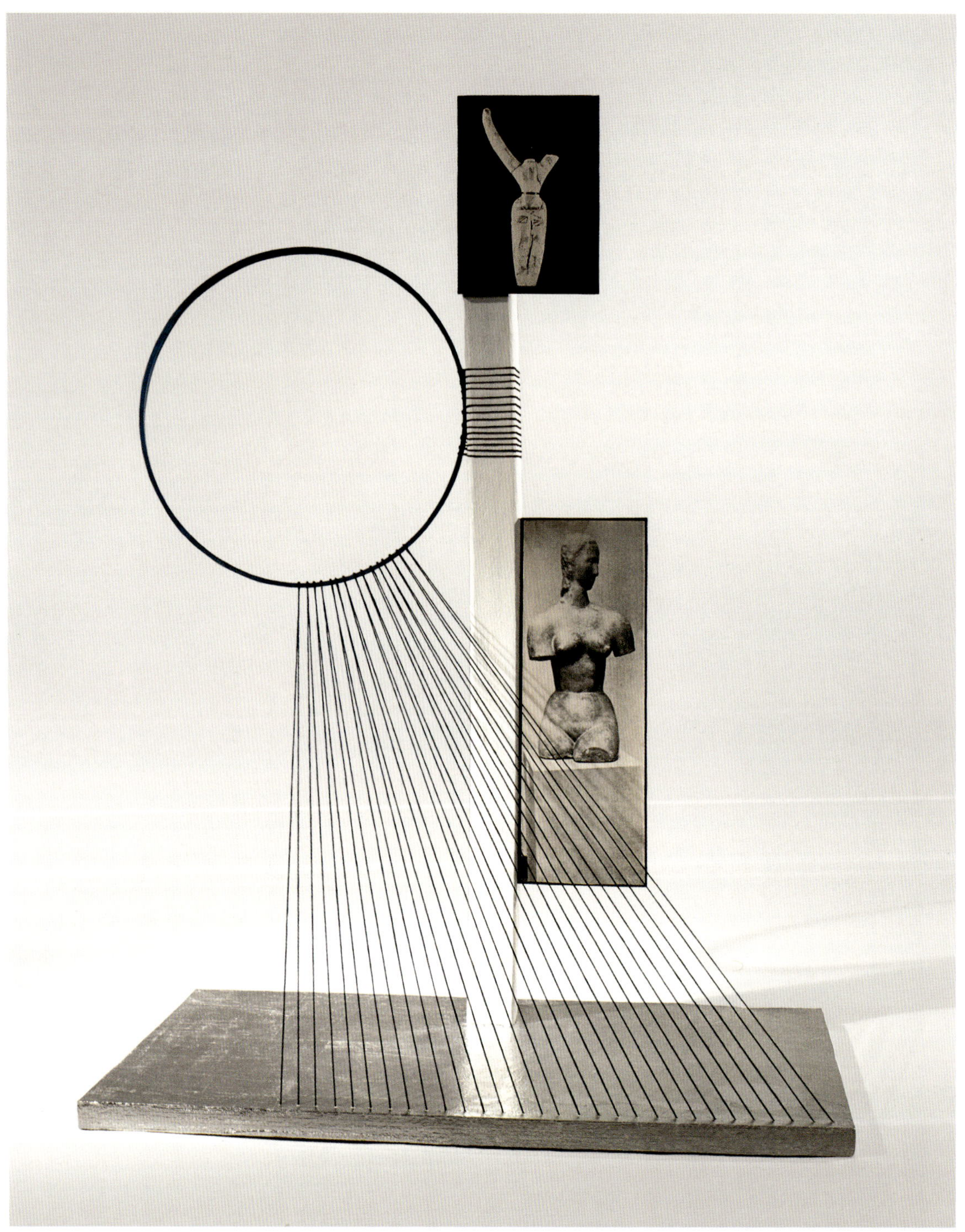

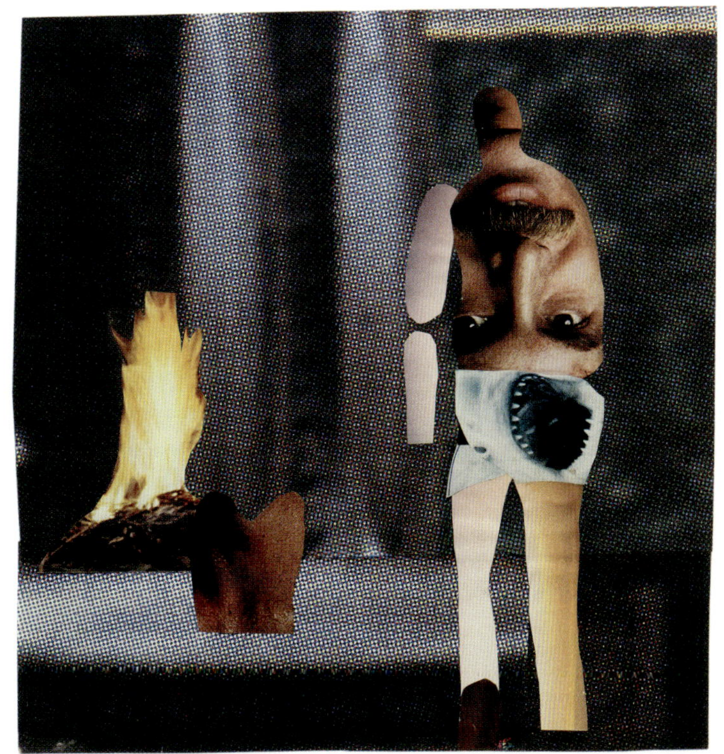

99

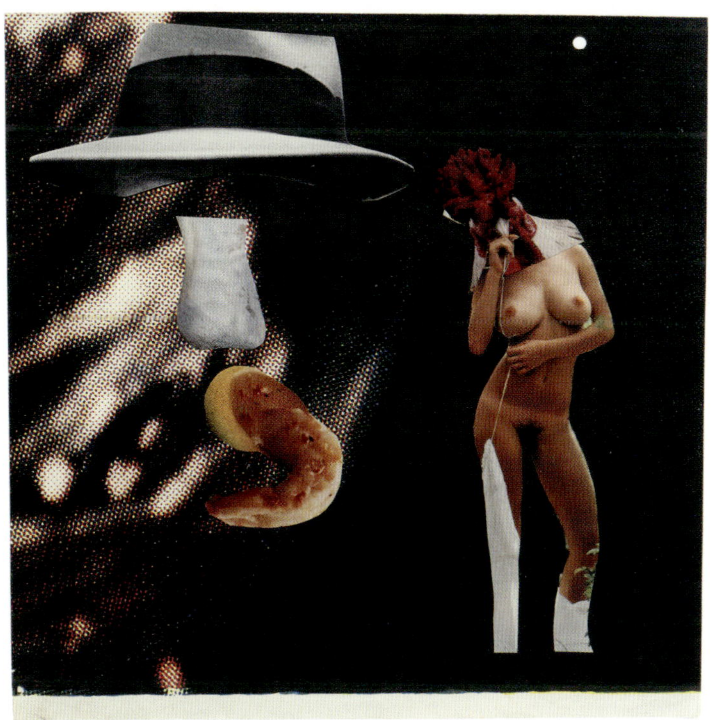

100

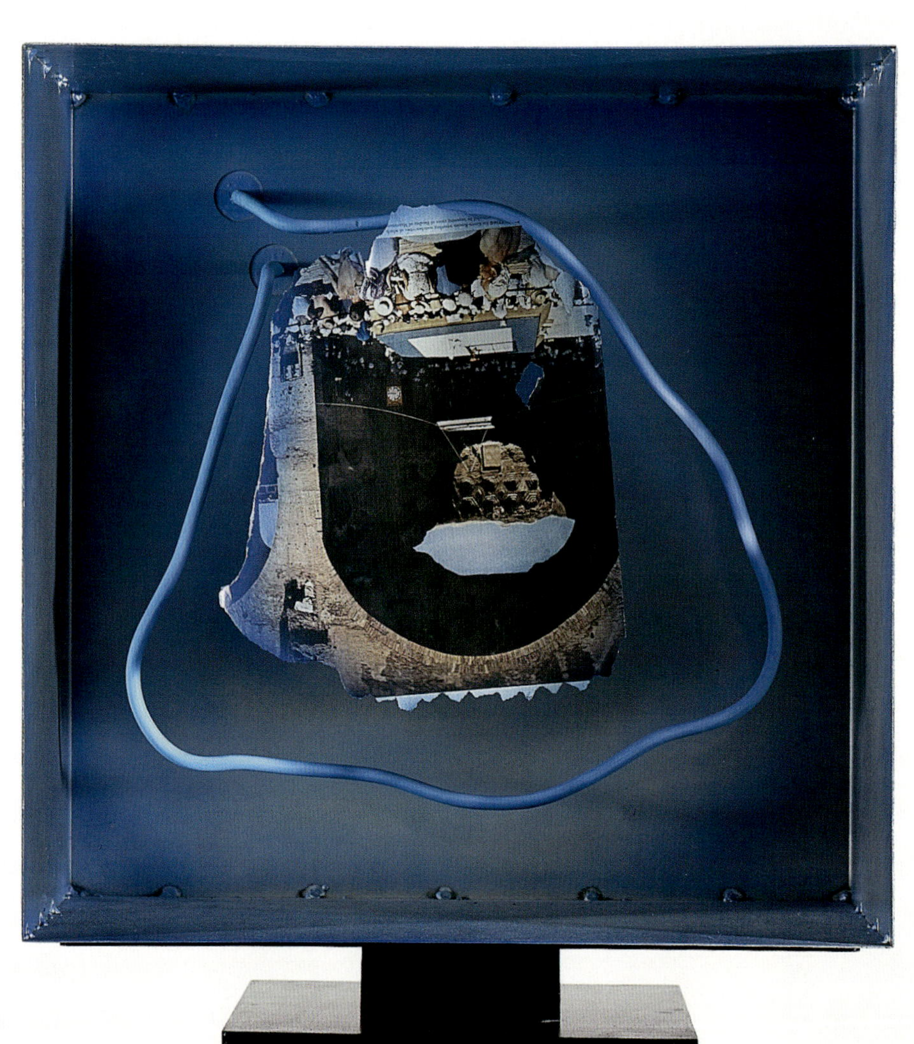

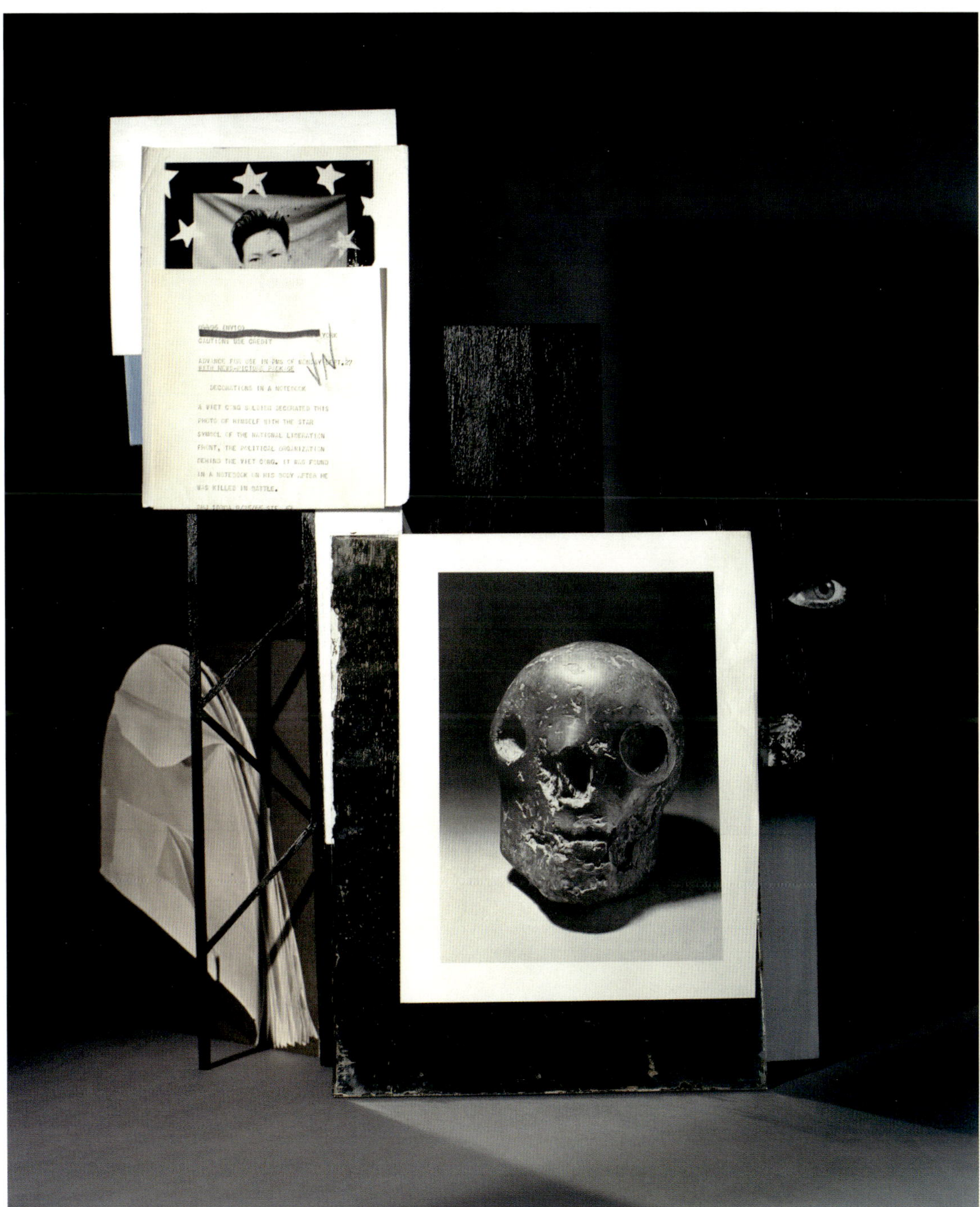

101 (opposite), 102

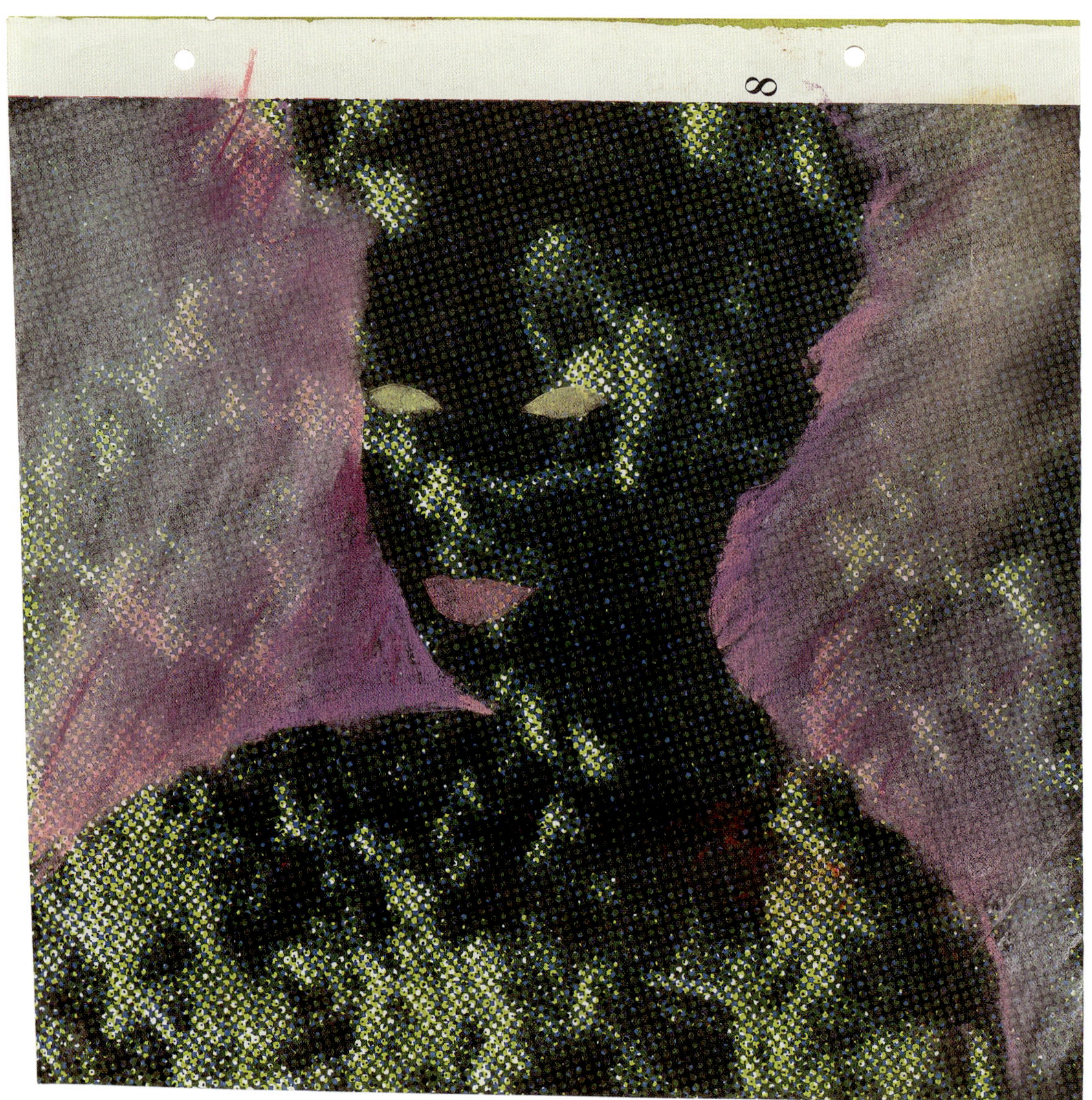

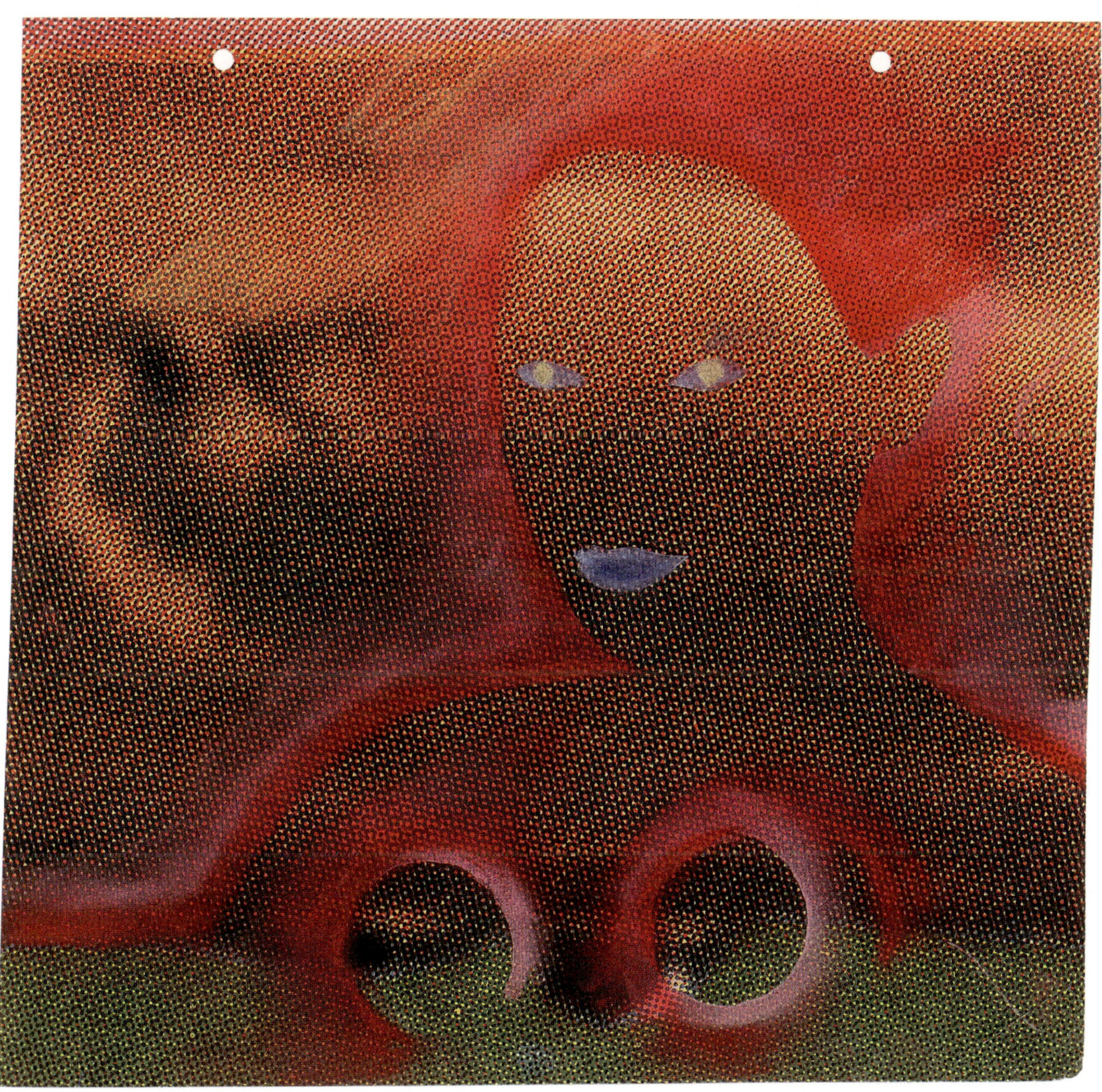

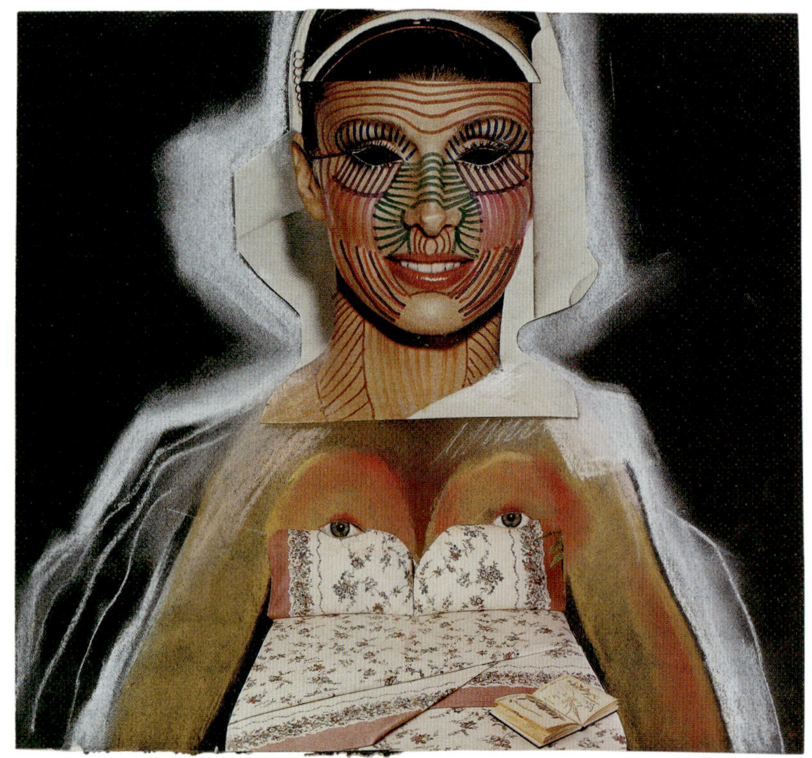

105

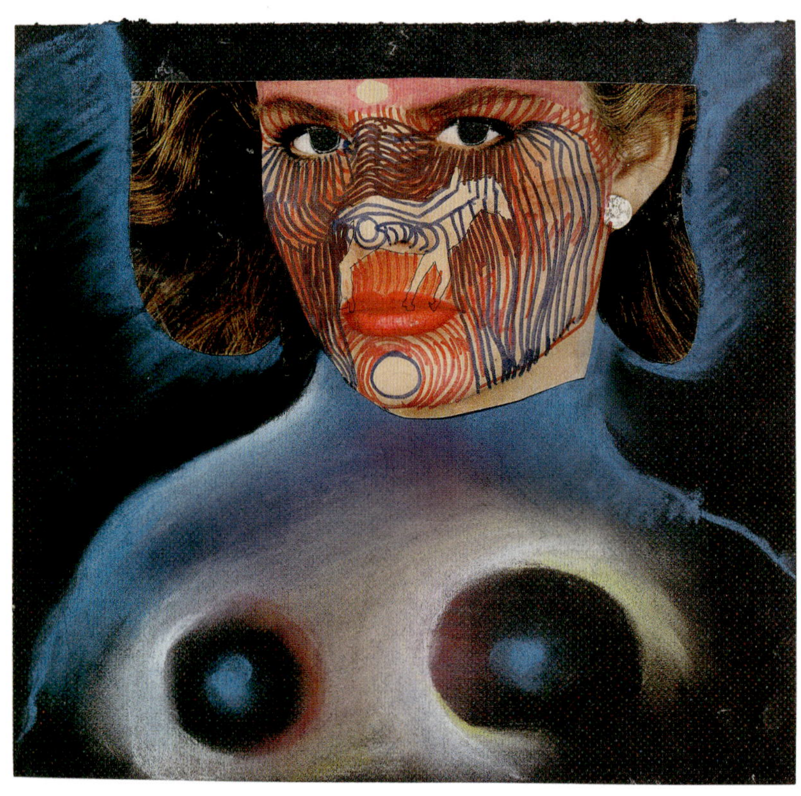

106

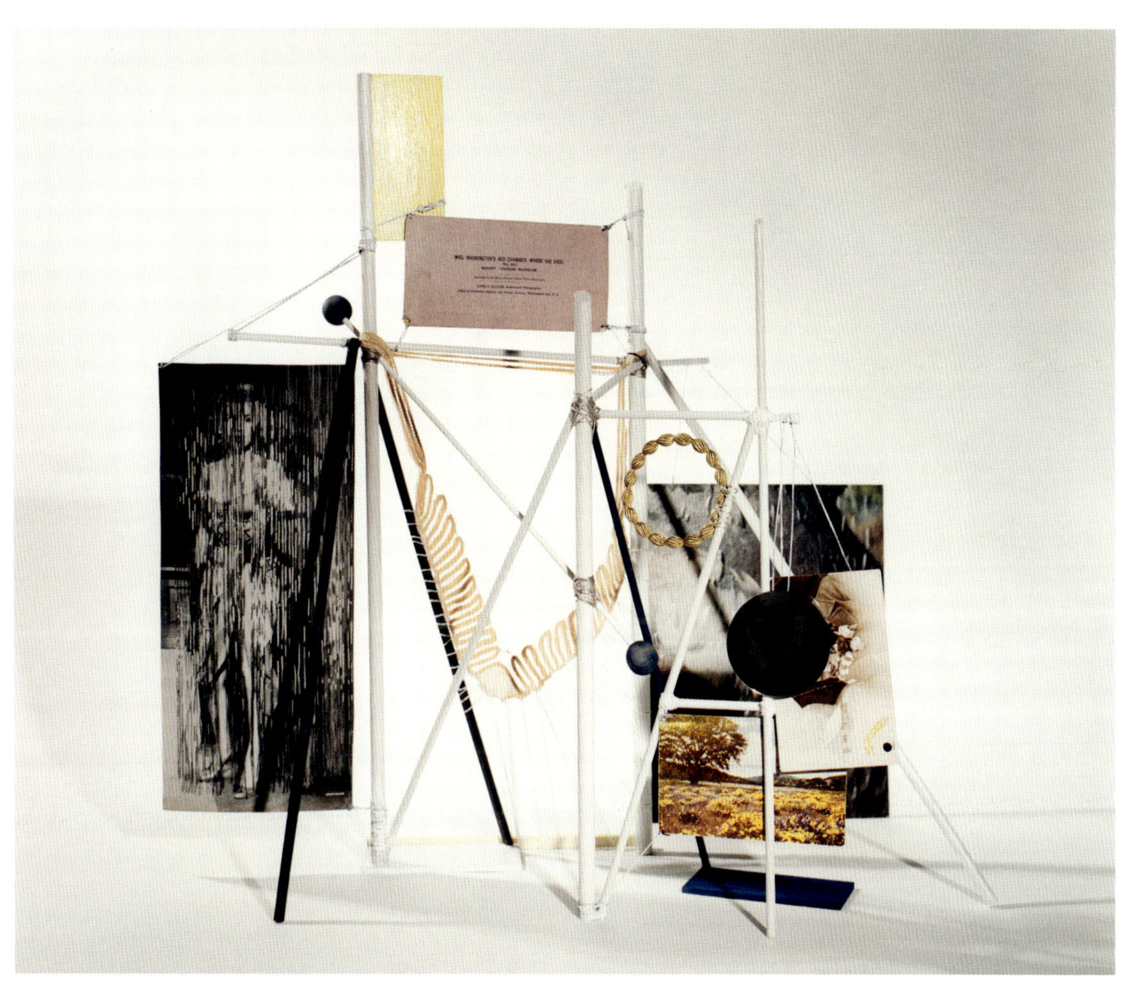

EYES

IB: What do eyes represent to you? Are they stand-ins for sight, for people, for yourselves?

JVDB: Eyes are a powerful source of nonverbal communication. I watched a program recently that suggested the whites of our eyes evolved in order to make prompts and directions more readable from a distance. It was actually about how dogs can read our eyes as cues of emotions and commands and that we share a unique bond with them because we can communicate so effectively. But if a dog can read our minds from the movement of a pupil, then human beings can tell a whole love story with just the wink of its lashes. The subtlety of the eyes' form in relation to the magnitude of their effect makes them magnetic focal points in an artwork. If they carry the weight of ageless signage then they can capture the arc of mankind. The presence and design of eyes in an artwork relies on their universality. Communicating this universal exchange is a powerful tool and makes them such an eternal symbol.

SVDB: The gaze of the subject in the images that make up these works directs the viewer's movement through the piece. The eyes present different perspectives and directions for the viewer to follow. The eye is vision, inner and outer.

IB: Are you surprised to find in your own works images similar to those in your dad's archive?

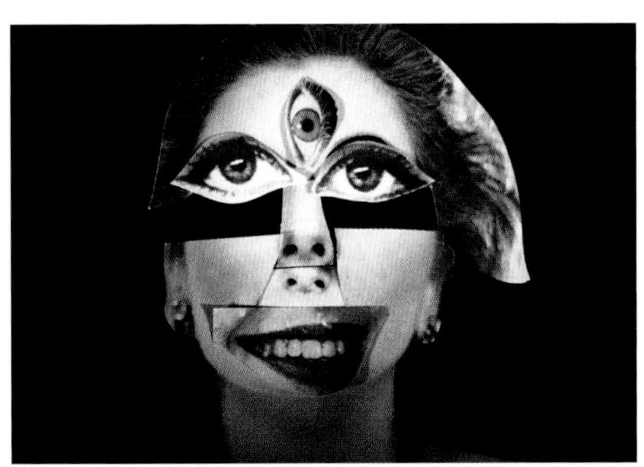

108

JVDB: Yes and no. At first it can be startling to see such strong similarities or even exact duplications. I flipped through his sketchbooks recently and saw ideas he had forty years ago that were identical to mine, though I had never seen them. It takes some time to understand how to handle that. An artist feels so much pressure about having a unique approach, so it becomes challenging to feel secure in your ways when you sense they stem so much from another person. In the case of my father, his ethos was so vivid I gather the dynamics of his mind left a far-reaching genetic imprint. I see reverberations of him in all of his children. I believe our genetic code has a mysterious way of carrying memories and experiences. When an idea occurs to me I have to recognize some of it's coming from my observation, but some also from an innate intuition that he is very much a part of. That's not to say my mother Louise does not have a sway on my behavior. In fact, I behave more like her than my father. She encouraged me to pursue art when she saw I so was inclined to draw. She was very loving and supportive in that way. I also think, because he died when I was so young, she thought it would comfort me to feel connected to him through making art. It was more normal in our family to be an artist, we were an inversion of the typical American family. To a certain extent our father was art; we learned about him by watching his films. I got to know his personality as I watched his imagery of things flying out of heads, and I took comfort that I came from some place in his head where there was so much going on. When I notice similarities I marvel at the being a part of a long spiritual chain strong with vision, but then I can also doubt how strong a link I am in that chain.

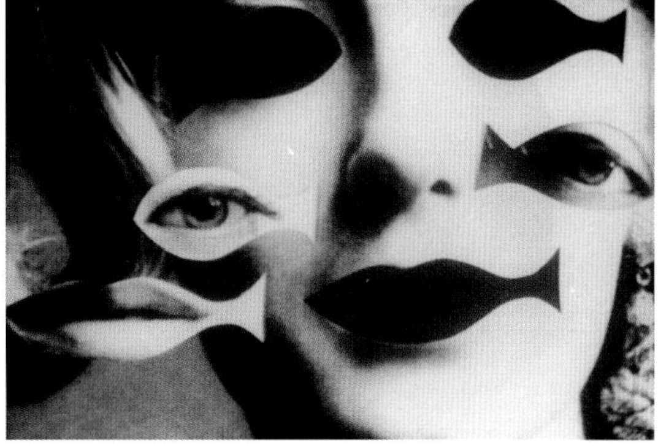

109

IB: Johannes, your three works this month combine magazine pages with found metal boxes and painted fluorescent light tubes. Can you talk about finding faces in the found imagery, and how you discovered the effect you could get from the painted wires?

JVDB: One part of my genetic conditioning is I can find a face in anything. I don't know if it's because I grew up watching his films, where faces appear out of every possible unexpected arrangement, or if he handed me the baton that tells you how to make a face out of a pair of coins and a candle. Finding a face in the right place is the real challenge. I hope for tension in the composition, where the face appears on the brink of falling apart. In this case I looked for images that represented light by various sources, such as candles, sky, or red elephants. I ripped them to accentuate their mask quality and then put them in the boxes as if they were relics. The painted tubes portray a similar fragility. The fleeting aspect of light is one quandary that drives representation. To capture it requires the help of some medium like a camera or paintbrush. I chose both in this instance because I wanted to layer various types of represented light. I imagined a time on the planet when neon was no longer available, and the pathos of having to make your own neon glow through homegrown methods. It's a half-goofy and half-sad subplot, but I think it shows the inherent impossibility of capturing light, and the perplexing feat of trying to do so.

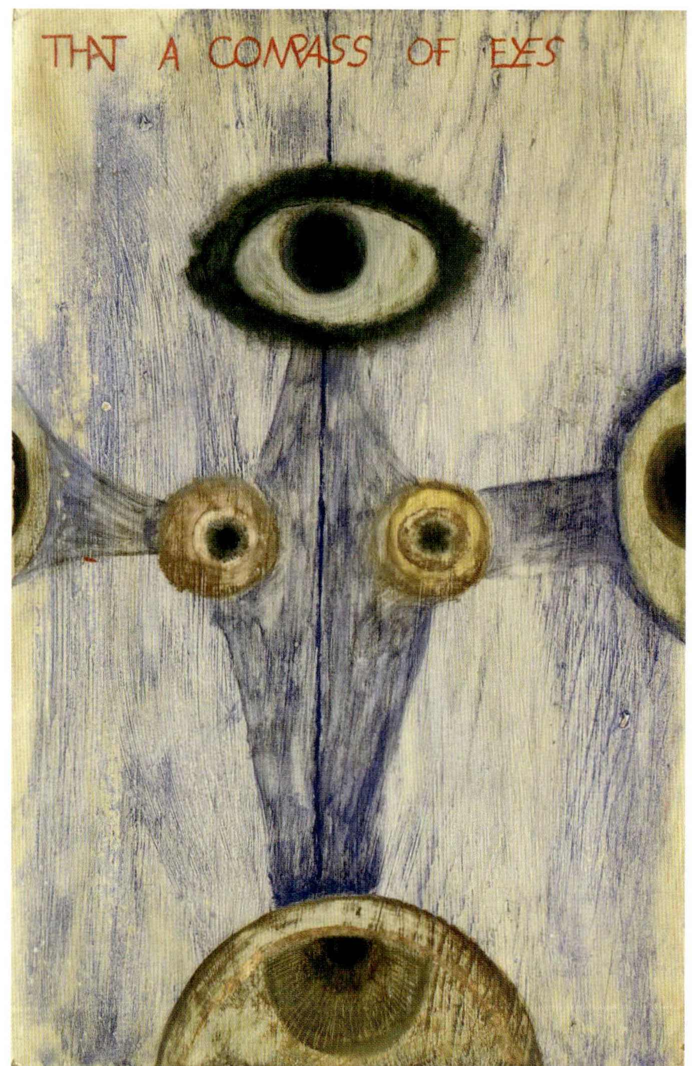

110

IB: Sara, *Decorations in a Notebook* has some potent and very legible imagery and objects. Can you talk about some of those things and what the combination says about war?

SVDB: While much of my work is centered in America, this piece actually feels a little less so due to the images of the Picasso sculpture and the Viet Cong soldier. The Vietnam War was still very much an American experience, but *Decorations in a Notebook* isn't about Vietnam per se; it's about the impermanence of life. When I found the image of Picasso's sculpture in a catalogue, I reveled in the deep eyes of the death's head and how effectively Picasso expressed the atrocities of warfare. Beyond the enormous stature of Picasso as a figure in art, he lived through both World Wars and is an almost talismanic figure for the dramatic changes of the last century. I used the Associated Press photograph of the Viet Cong soldier because of the Vietnam War's connection to both of the current wars in Afghanistan and Iraq. The caption crops the man's face so you can only see his eyes, and I associated his empty stare with the hollow sockets of Picasso's sculpture. Of course the skull brings to mind the traditions of memento mori, but I was also drawn to the dramatic lighting of Picasso's death's head, which parallels the way I constructed and lit my photograph. It's an image of an image of a soldier, of a sculpture, and, in a way, of an experience, in that I constructed and staged this assemblage. Through my combination of images and elements, these found images take on new meanings that reflect the larger continuum of our existence, in this work both distinctly American and, with its intimations of mortality, also about our larger human condition.

Eyes captions

97 Johannes VanDerBeek, *Burning Face*, 2009, wire, paint, paper, and steel, 65 3/4 × 21 1/2 × 12 1/2 inches
98 Sara VanDerBeek, *Eclipse 1*, 2008, digital C-print, 20 × 16 5/8 inches. Collection of The Frances Young Tang Teaching Museum and Art Gallery, Skidmore College
99 Stan VanDerBeek, *Untitled*, 1983, collage on billboard, 14 × 13 1/2 inches
100 Stan VanDerBeek, *Untitled*, 1983, collage on billboard, 12 3/4 × 12 1/8 inches
101 Johannes VanDerBeek, *Sky Mouth*, 2009 (detail), wire, paint, paper, and steel, 65 3/4 × 21 1/2 × 12 1/2 inches
102 Sara VanDerBeek, *Decorations in a Notebook*, 2006, digital C-print, 24 × 20 1/2 inches. Ann and Mel Schaffer Family Collection
103 Stan VanDerBeek, *Untitled*, 1983, pastel on billboard, 12 1/4 × 12 inches
104 Stan VanDerBeek, *Untitled*, 1983, pastel on billboard, 12 3/4 × 12 3/4 inches
105 Stan VanDerBeek, *Untitled*, 1983, pastel, marker, and collage on billboard, 12 × 12 1/2 inches
106 Stan VanDerBeek, *Untitled*, 1983, pastel, marker, and collage on billboard, 11 3/4 × 12 1/2 inches
107 Sara VanDerBeek, *Mrs. Washington's Bedroom*, 2006, digital C-print, 20 × 23 1/2 inches
108 Stan VanDerBeek, Still from *What Who How*, 1957, black and white film with sound, 8:00 minutes
109 Stan VanDerBeek, Still from *A La Mode*, 1957, black and white film with sound, 6:18 minutes
110 Stan VanDerBeek, *Untitled (That a Compass of Eyes)*, 1955–1957, paint and mixed media on wood, 11 × 7 1/4 inches

LANGUAGE

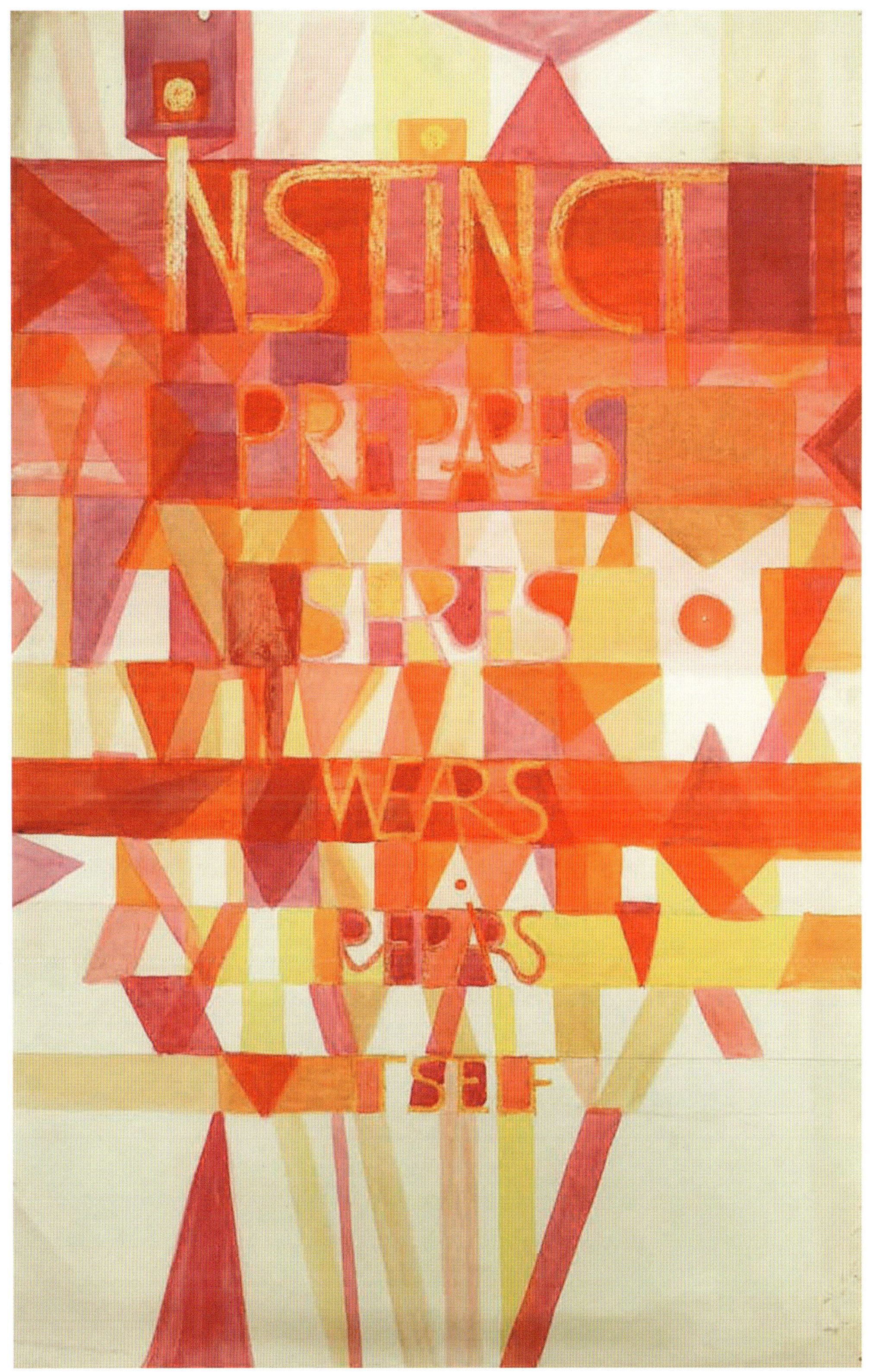
INSTINCT
WEARS

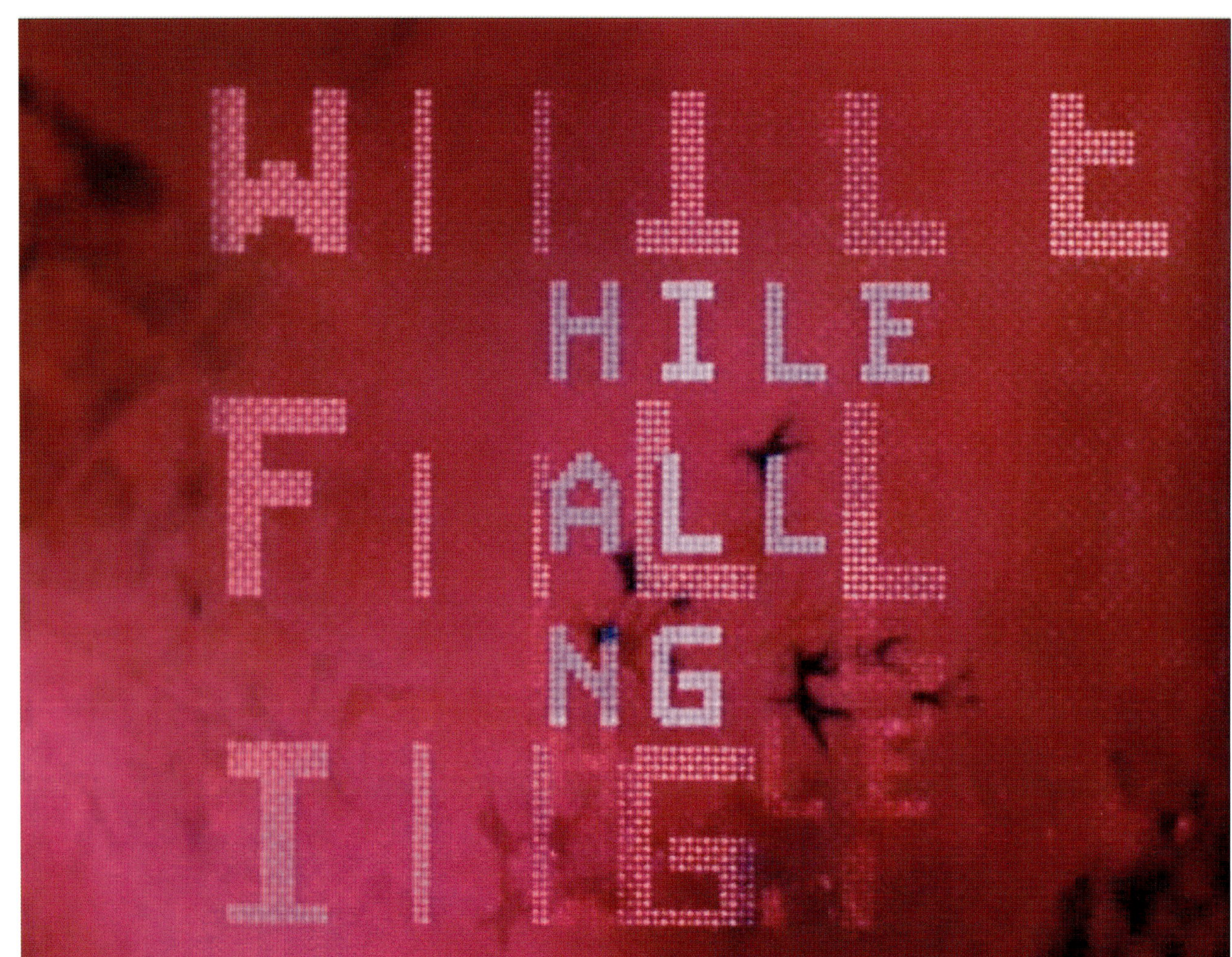
HILE
ALL
NG

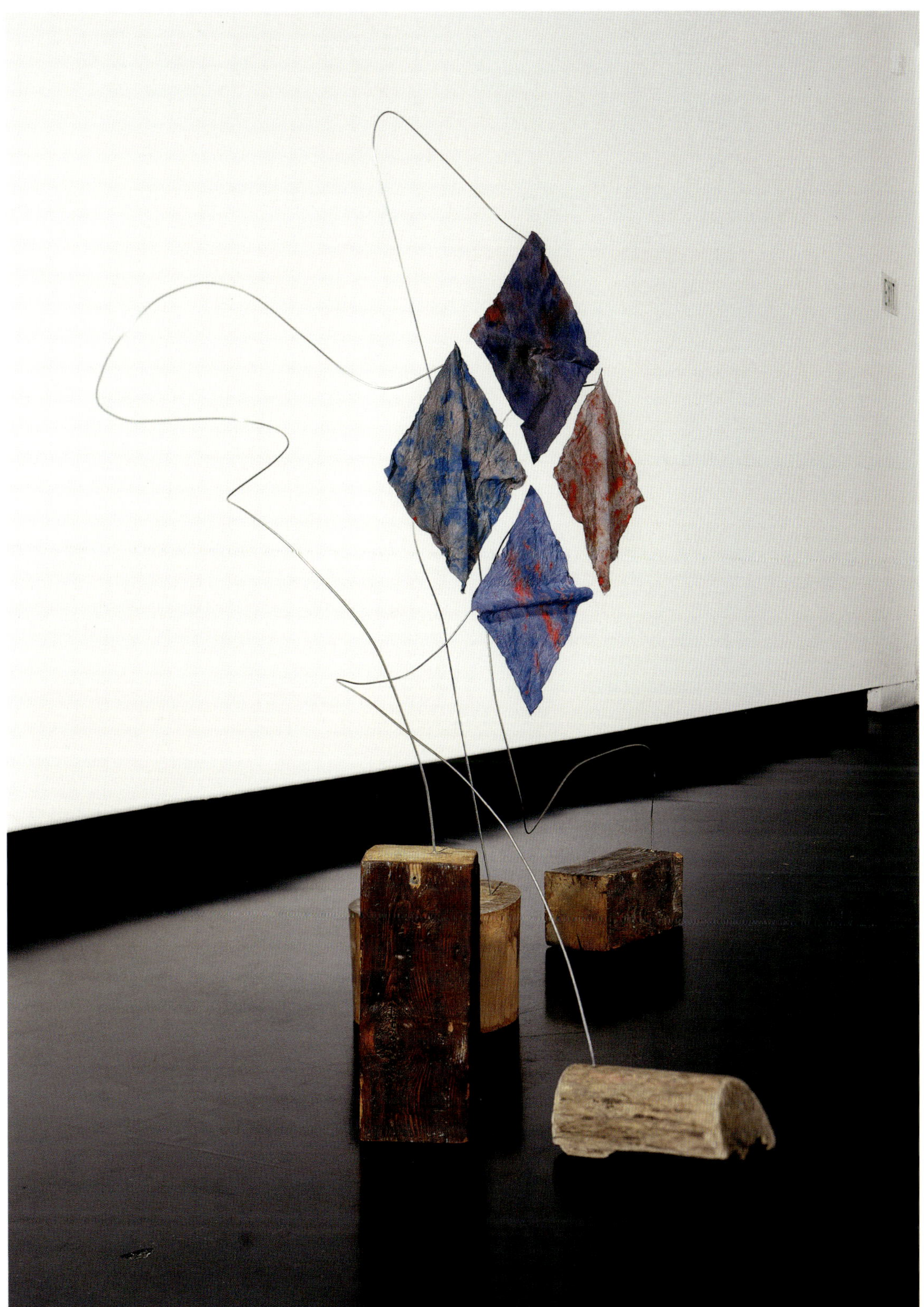

113, 114 (following)

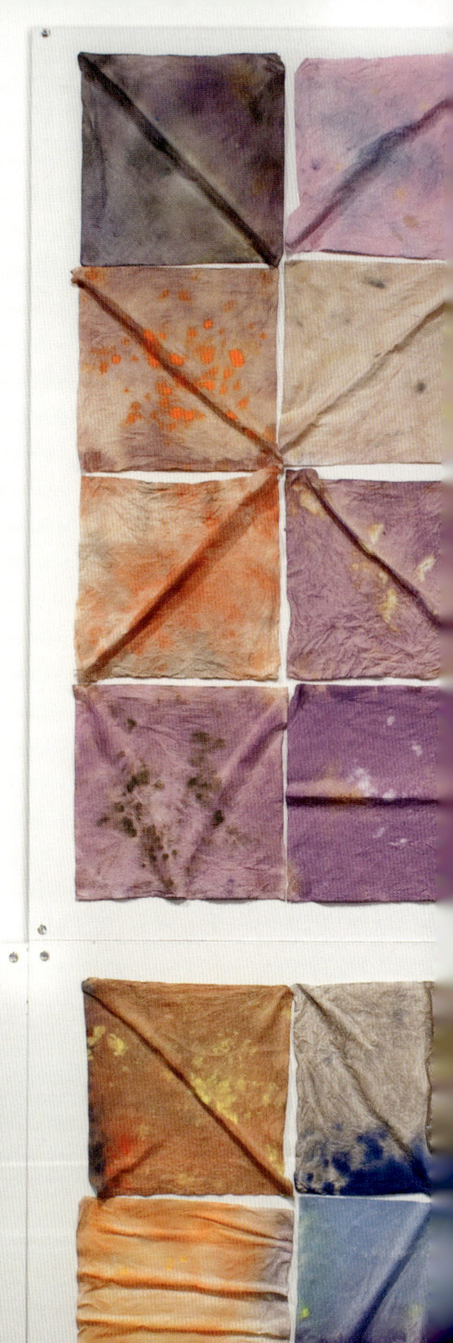
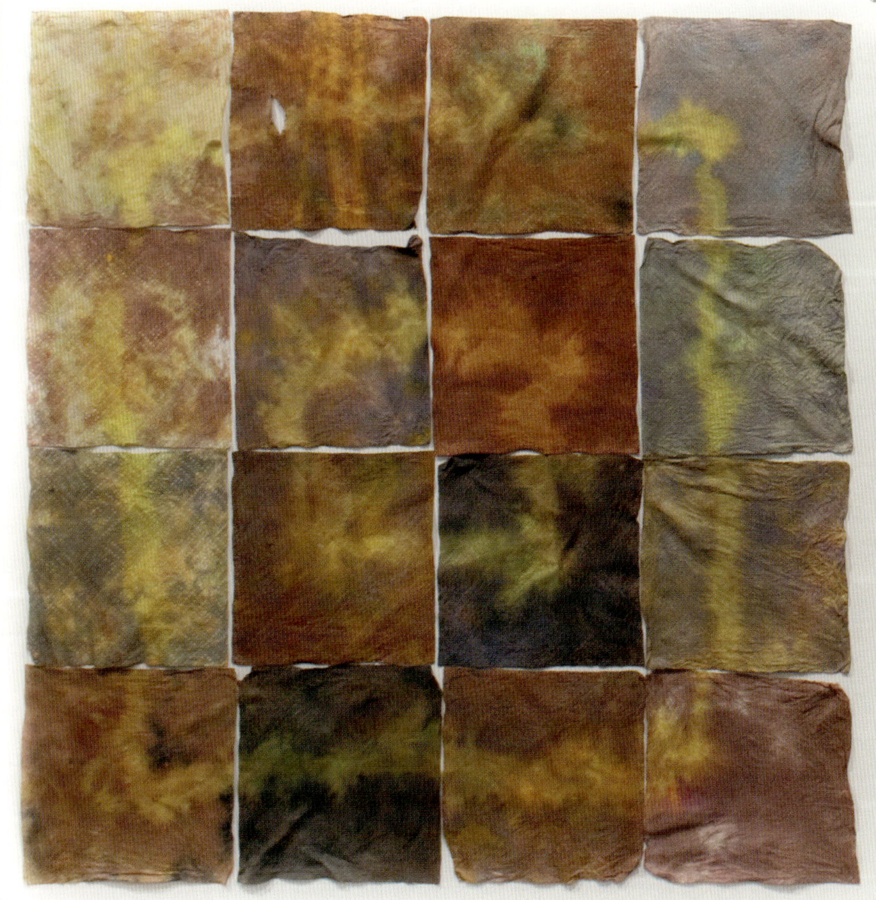
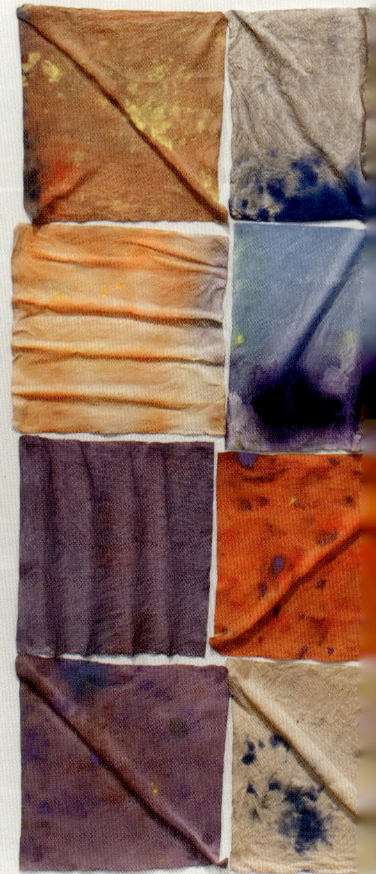

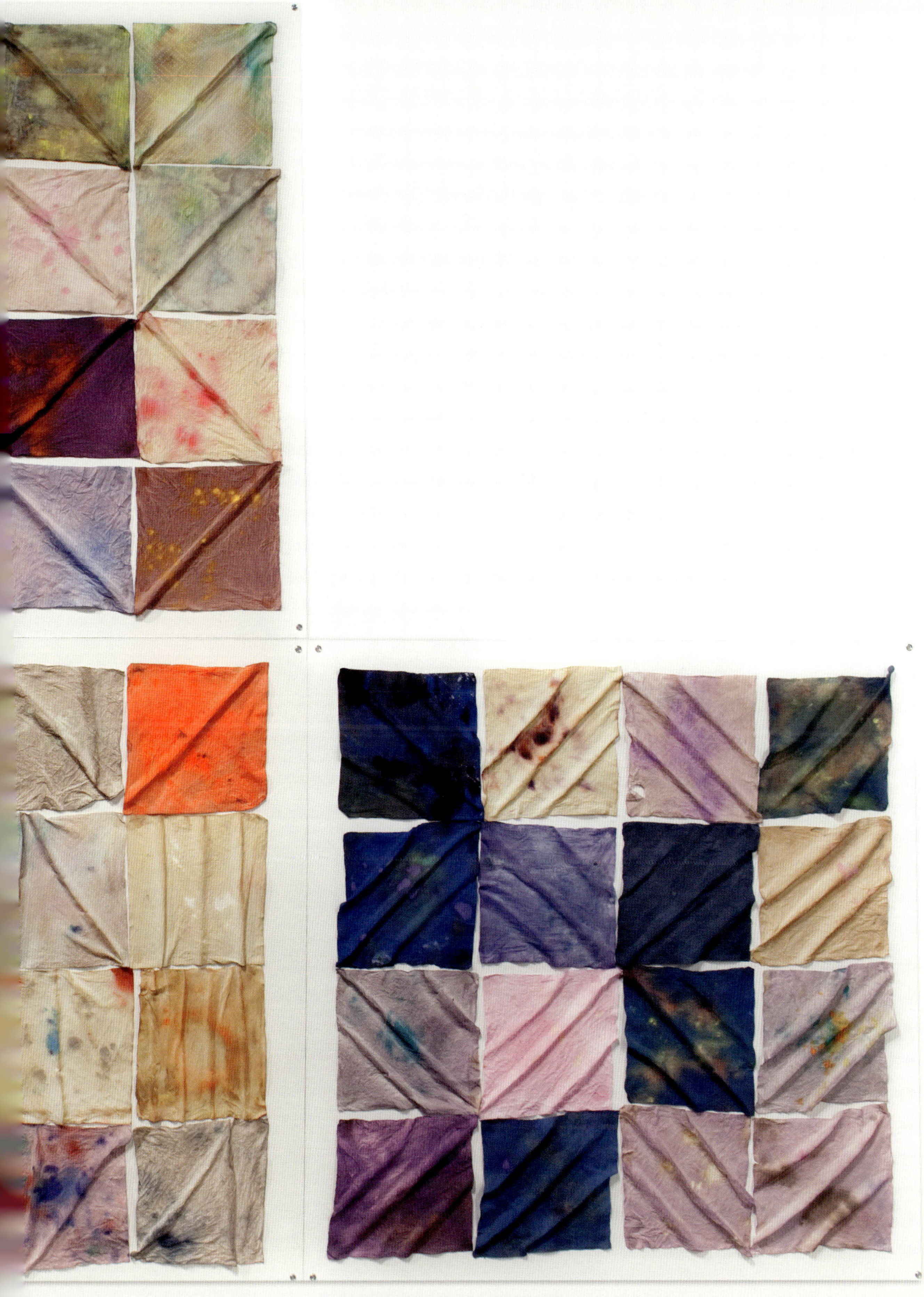

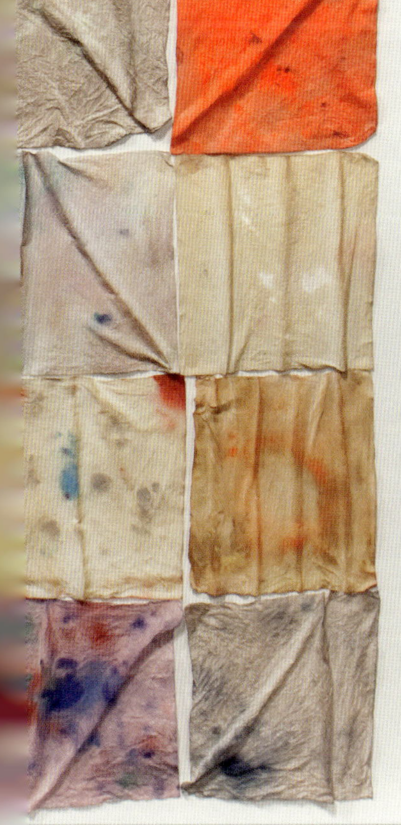

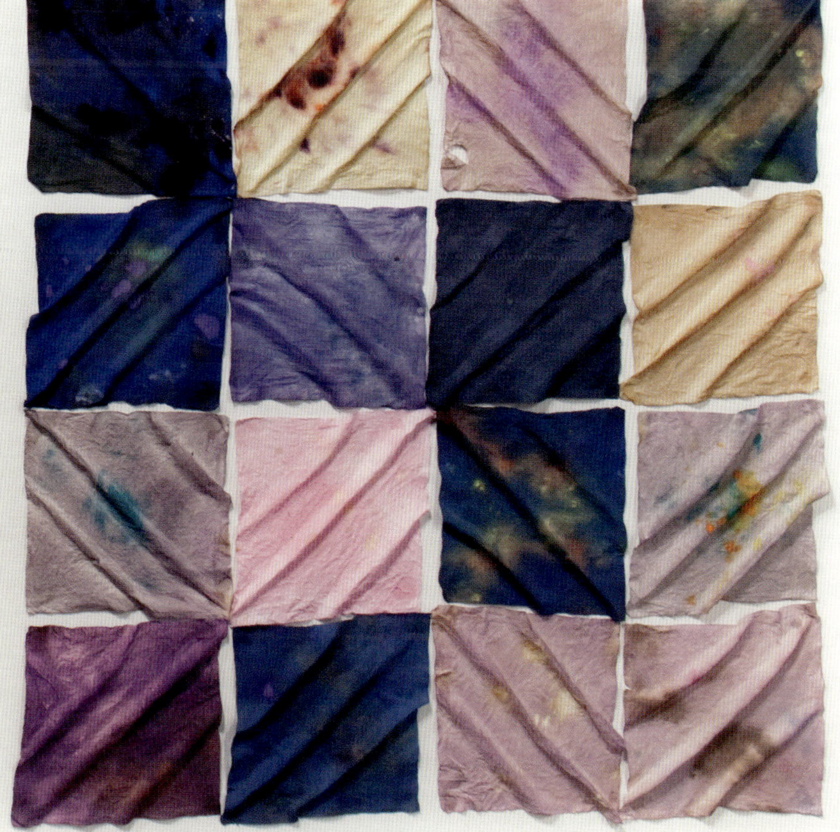

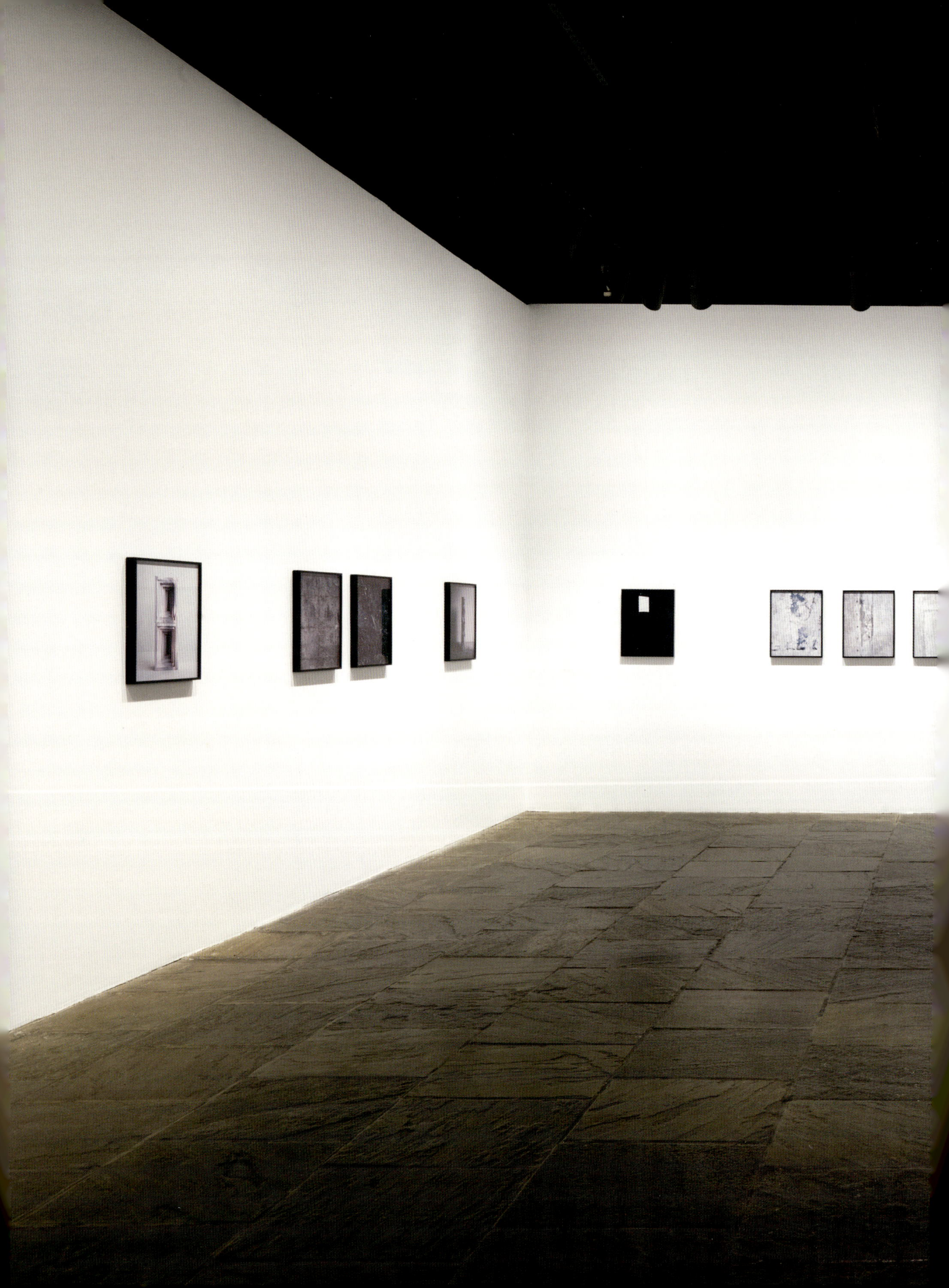

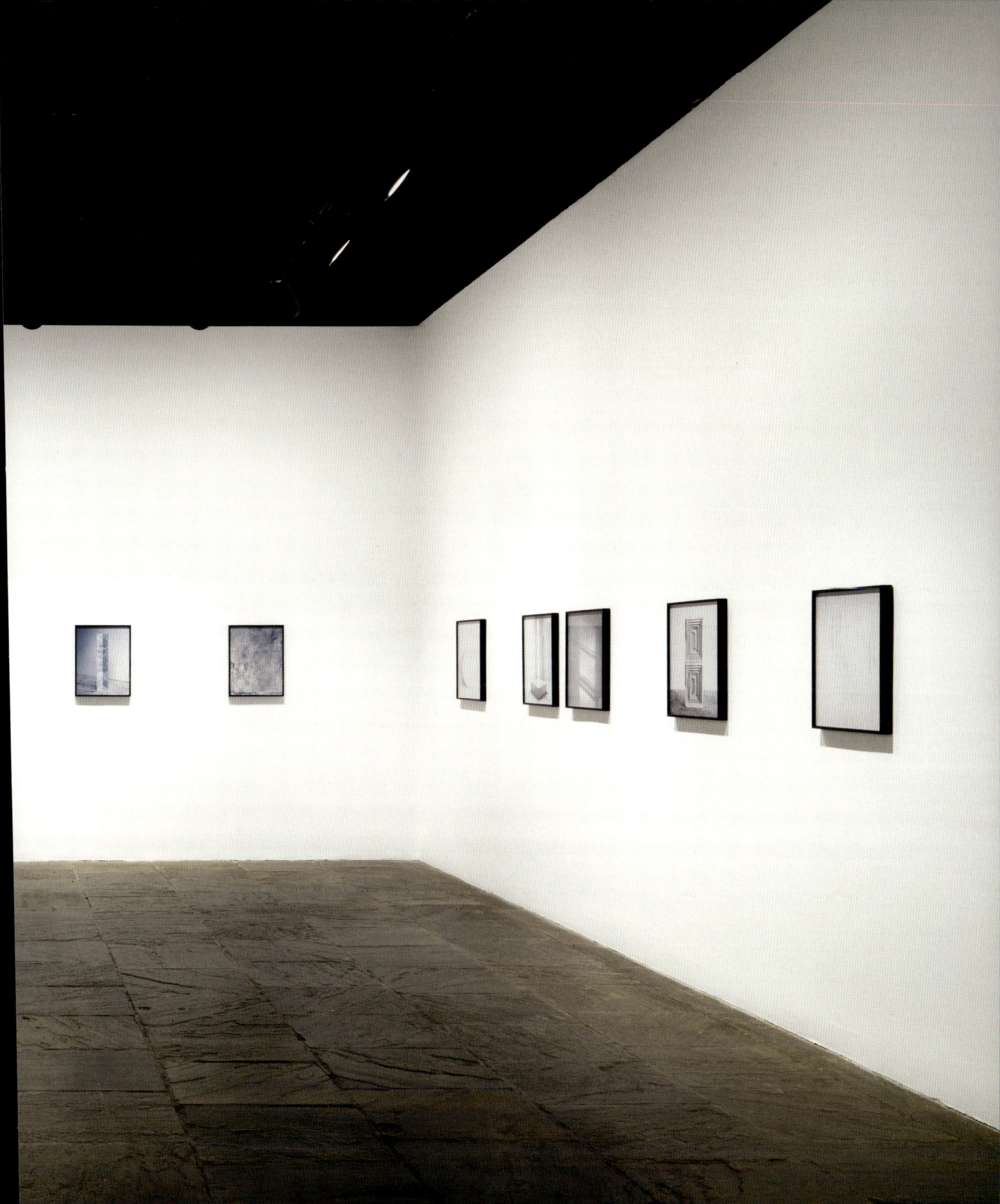

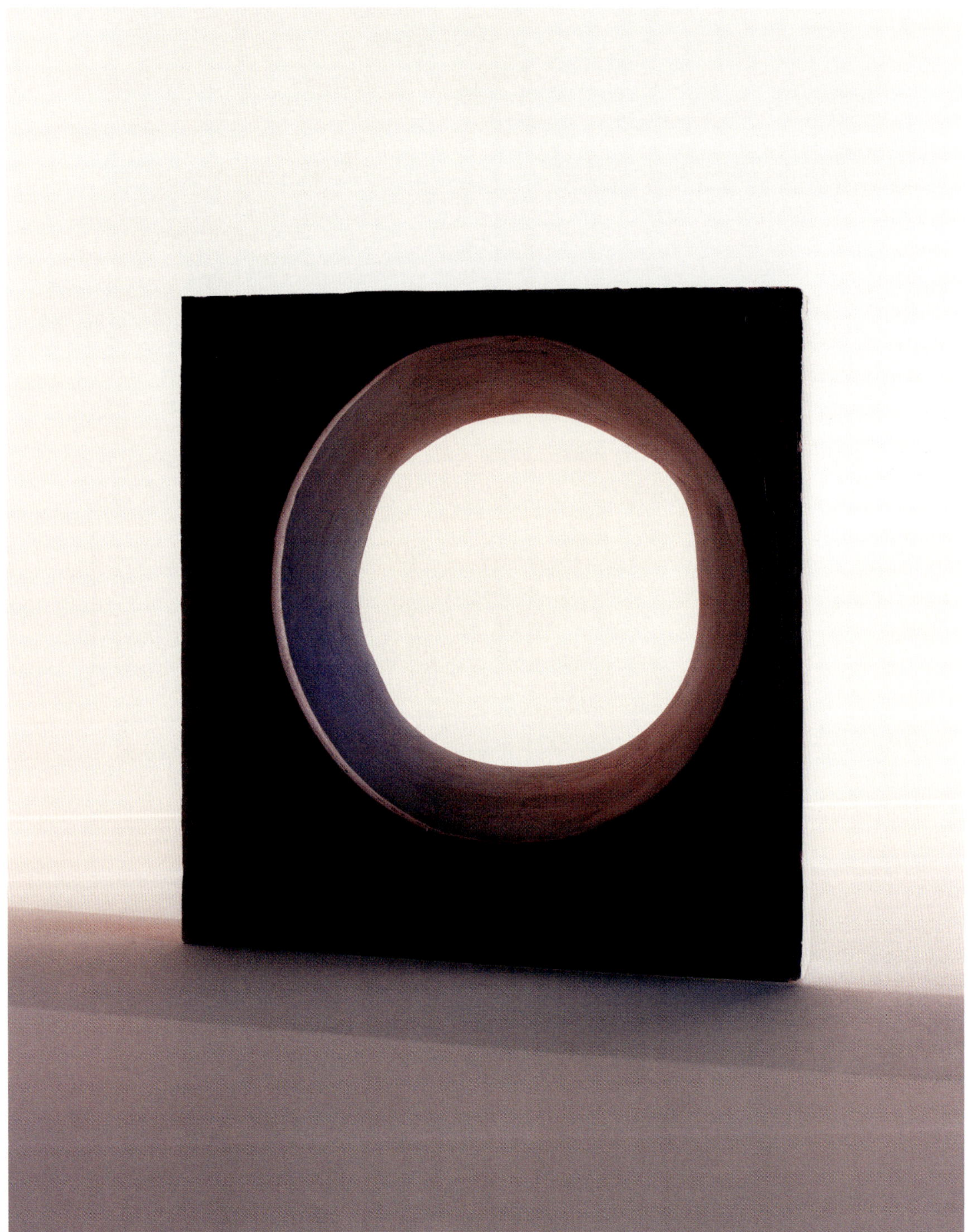

115 (previous), 116

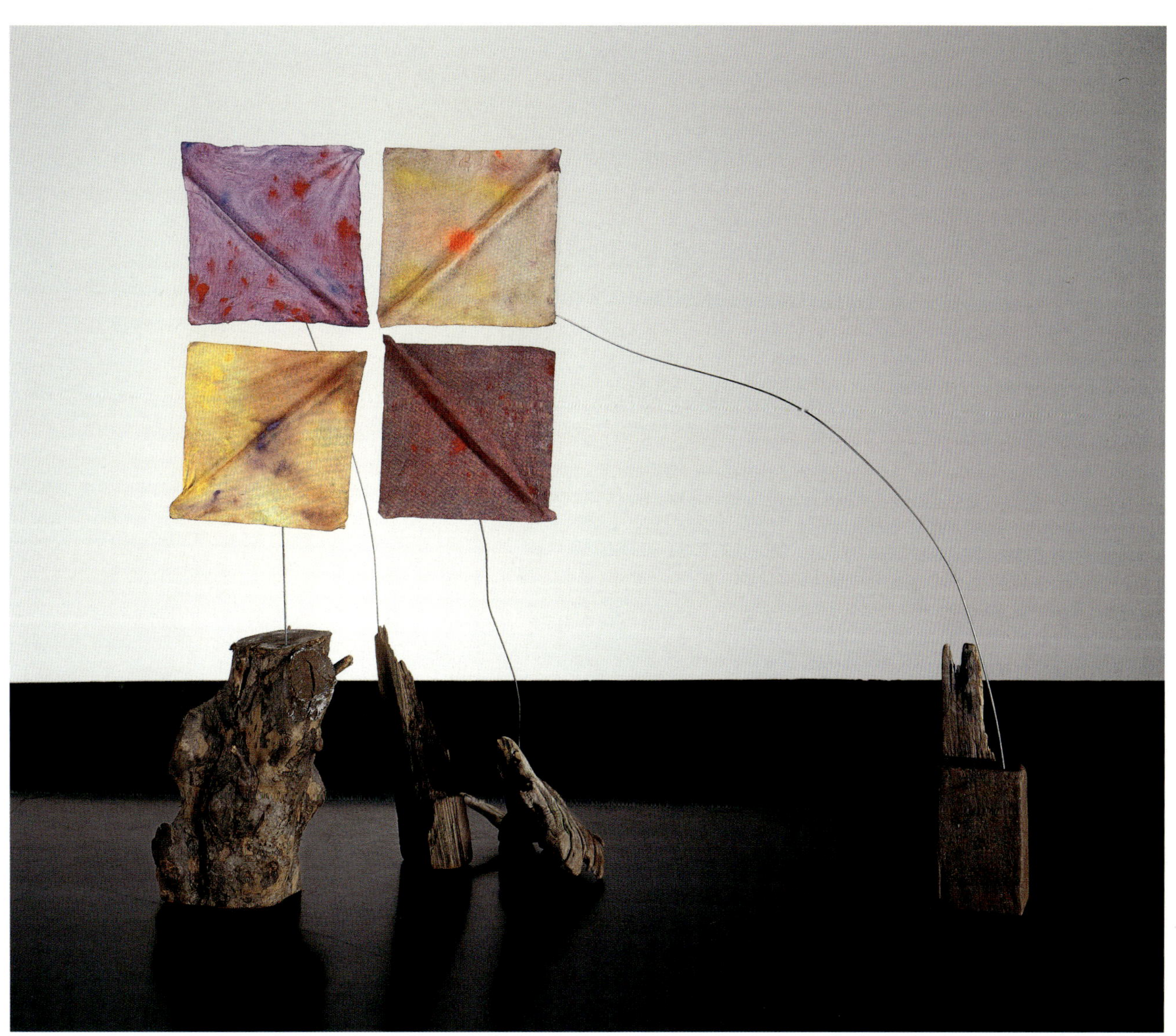

LANGUAGE

IB: Do you believe art is a language?

JVDB: Language does not always clearly say what it wants to say. Feathers. Never. Ever. Weather. These words bring shapes to mind. But are words just meant to rhyme or reason our thoughts through lines? Shapes, on the other hand, bring language to mind. "Read my lips: 'No new taxes.'" That is language that is a lie. Art is more like "Lip my Read…red my lip." That is a lie that makes a language. Would you rather say words that bring something to mind or make a thing that exists in actual time? Art can deflate words and dislodge them from their specific purpose. But when we look at something deflated, we have to use words to construct the proud porpoise.

My dad spoke of a "universal visual vocabulary" and in projects like Movie-Drome he pursued the creation of a visual data bank, where anyone in the world could access imagery beamed down from satellite. This was in the 1960s, when words became more charged than ever. He saw impending dangers in the fickle nature of words. He wrote once, "How does the world hang in the balance of a few nouns and verbs?" I believe language to be the most advanced form of abstract thought, and it has cannoned us way past the chimps and whales.

IB: Are you creating a symbolic language of your own with your artwork?

JVDB: I'm not sure yet. That may be clearer in the eyes of the viewer. I certainly don't feel I have refined a vocabulary up to this point. I'm looking for the right type of letters to use and feeling out what is the silhouette of their character.

IB: Sara, your work this month relates to a literary source. Can you describe the choice of that poem and how you used it to make this work?

SVDB: Many different experiences, events, and texts have informed this new body of work, but Walt Whitman's *Leaves of Grass* is the primary literary inspiration. His continued refinement and revision of his poetry throughout his life pushed me to consider how photography and my practice could become more open and operate in ways that evoke poetic phrasing, meter, and tone. I was also inspired to consider how through shifting contexts and combinations the work could create new meanings with each hanging. I see this hanging as part of an ongoing project that I hope to continue to add to and develop throughout my life to include many different interests, experiences and forms of image-making.

Here are two excerpts from Walt Whitman's introduction to *Leaves of Grass*. In my mind his words encourage awareness of the history that is in the present and of the meeting of the future and present that occurs in every new moment. His work also speaks of the impact of astute observation, and of the importance of retaining a level of purity in art's conveyance, the goal being to portray that which is seen simply and with little embellishment:

> *The greatest poet forms the consistence of what is to be from what has been and what is. . . . he says to the past, Rise and walk before me that I may realize you. He learns the lesson. . . . he places himself where the future becomes present.*
>
> *What I experience or portray shall go from my composition without a shred of my composition. You shall stand by my side and look in the mirror with me.*

In a sense his thinking contradicts photography, at least the way I work with it, as it mediates everything. Yet I saw this passage dealing more with a way of seeing. Whitman is very keen in his observations and they have opened me to see more. He represents all aspects of life in *Leaves of Grass*—dark moments

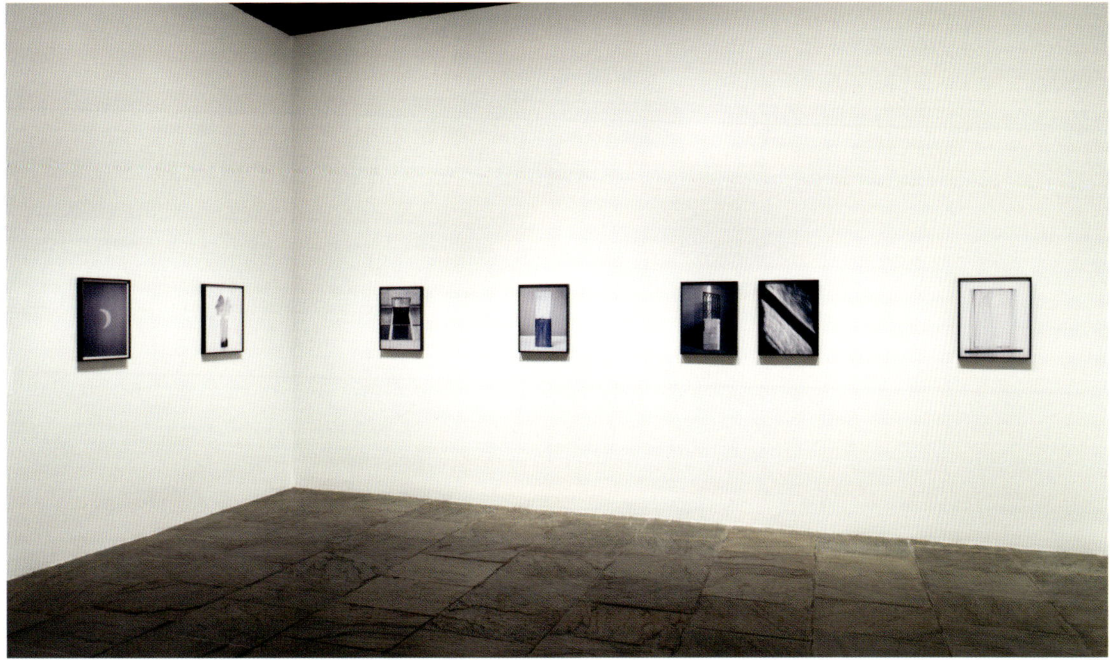

118

of brutality and violence as much as moments of beauty and light. I have tried to emulate this expansive inclusion of all aspects of our life experience through my image choices and in the creation of the sculptures. I distill and abstract the forms, but the cracking and darkness of some of the pieces imply at times a subtle violence, ruins, and emptiness.

Whitman experienced the Civil War and the change in our society that resulted with the abolition of slavery firsthand. He saw the great destruction and the new way of life that was to come out of the war. I believe the end of the Civil War marks the beginning of the modern era of America and that this modern nation was born of war. Photography was coming into prominence during this time, and, importantly, the medium moves from the studio to an in-the-field document, as Brady and others extensively documented the human and architectural casualties of the war. Photography's focus seems to shift to the impermanence of things, enacting the changing pace of existence in the modern age by capturing the forever fleeting experience of this new world. Loved ones had daguerreotypes made of themselves to share, considering the chance that it could become their last remnant or record of this individual. At this time, the photograph becomes entrenched in our cultural understanding as a significant object and, importantly, as a memorial. It could be a memorial to someone or something lost but also to a time, a moment that no longer exists. The melancholia and sadness inherent in the experience of seeing a photograph was propelled by photography's rise to prominence during the Civil War. I feel my interest in photographing ruins grows out of this history of the medium, especially its American practitioners.

IB: This work seems to signal a new way of making for you, and a new series of works. Would you talk about how this work may grow and change in the future?

SVDB: This body of work moves away from the simultaneity and collage-like aspects of my previous work to focus on singularity and an exploration of the single moment. Made with natural light in the studio, the images feel much closer to those taken out in the world. The light provides an element of chance and a lack of control, since the forms change with each movement in the light. I am currently working on some pieces shot in spaces that have a texture and history to them that bring another layer of reading to the image. I like that it is a real space, but I also like to photograph the space so it becomes somewhat abstracted, as in *Caryatid*, where the windows are blasted out and the light abstracts the room.

This new body of work at the Tang is also the basis for my exhibition *To Think of Time* at the Whitney, where I focused on three of Whitman's poems: *Song of Myself*, *The Sleepers*, and *To Think of Time*. Overall the loose narrative in these works for the Tang installation and *To Think of Time* address loss and change as framed in this larger sense of the moment. Ruins are significant

PoemField #4

OLD
OR OROR OR
POP POP POP
FOR FOR
FORM FORM FORM
FILM FILM
NO,1
POEMFIELD 4
FALLING WORDS
AS LEAVES
FALLING
SPEACH REACH
ON AND OFF
LIFE FORMS
WORDS
YES AND
YES AND NO
GONOGO
GOING
ON
GONE
ONE
ON
NO
GO
NO
GO
NO
GO
NO
OOOOOO GO NO GO

Poem field #5

fall
FALLING
ALL
FALLING
FOR FALLING
OR ALL FOR
FAR
FOR
FAR
MAN
FOR MANS KIND
FALL
MANS PLAN
WAITS
WAITING
WITS
WITNESS
MAN
FITS
WITNESS
WIT
INTO OTHER WIT
AS IF WIT KNOTS WIT
WHILE WAITING
OR
WHILE FALLING
FREE
FREE FALL

because they embody the physical manifestation of a state change and exist within a perpetual transition. They rest in two places: the structures that remain suggest the place or the person that once was, but they are also broken, crumbling, leaving this realm for that of memory and imagination. The foundations in the lower Ninth Ward, the images of which compose the majority of *The Sleepers* arrangement, exist as remnants but they also speak of the ghosts of the homes that they once were. I chose to focus on details and abstract compositions of the foundations because these are psychic spaces—places of dreams and the inner conscious now, and less places of the real world. They hold enough importance in the owner's memory to continue to tend to it though empty. They feel raw and bare, tremendously sad but hopeful too. It is a foundation that can be built on; it is scarred but resilient.

IB: Stan's works are two from the *Poemfield* series. What was this group of works?

SVDB: This was a series of films he made in the 1960s using early computer technology at Bell Labs. He worked with Ken Knowlton, a programmer who developed this mosaic style, called BEFLIX, of creating images with the computer. I think the language and image quality of these films is simple, succinct, and powerful. I particularly like *Poemfield #7* with its soundtrack by John Cage, its strong magentas, and its talk of peace during wartime.

IB: Johannes, you include painted paper towels hung on long thin wire that create a large "X" and "O" on opposite corners of the gallery. Do you consider these works drawings?

JVDB: I didn't think about them as drawings but they could be seen as an absurd three-dimensional rendering of how language can be formed. I knew we would exhibit the *Poemfields* series, which animates words into a complex flux of abstract patterns. When making these pieces, dad talked a lot about how our minds are less like railroad tracks and more like computers—that we process so many multiple thoughts at once that our minds rarely move in one direction. Formally, the *Poemfield* series addresses this by making a mosaic that constantly flickers into new shapes surrounding the words that emerge. I know they made these films with a very rudimentary computer program that utilized punch cards. Each card had a series of simple symbols like X's and O's to feed the computer the right information, which led me to think about an enlarged pixel being represented by a paper towel. I dipped the paper towel in paint, and as it dried I folded a little crease into it. It dried rigid, and then I suspended it in the air with thin metal wire attached to a piece of driftwood. The four driftwood pieces need to be positioned in an exact manner on the floor in order for the creases in the paper to match up and make a letter, in this case either "X" or "O." In the current of experience many words float by us. We pick and arrange them to make signals of thought. These signals are very precarious. In order for the right word to occur, the exact arrangement of signals needs to converge. When they do converge, they make meaning. My dad put it more simply in one of his *Poemfields*: "Meaning Moves."

Language captions

111 Stan VanDerBeek, *Untitled (Instinct Prepares Stares Wears Repairs Itself)*, 1950, paint on paper, 40 × 28 inches
112 Stan VanDerBeek, Still from *Poemfield #5*, 1967, color film with sound, 6:23 minutes
113 Johannes VanDerBeek, *O*, 2010, wood, wire, paper towel, and paint, 58 × 67 × 40 inches
114 Johannes VanDerBeek, *Towel Tablets*, 2010, paper towels and paint mounted to board, each, 48 × 48 inches
115 Installation view, *Sara VanDerBeek: To Think of Time*, Whitney Museum of American Art, New York, 2010
116 Sara VanDerBeek, *Departing Sun*, 2010, digital C-print, 20 × 15 ¾ inches
117 Johannes VanDerBeek, *X*, 2010, wood, wire, paper towel, and paint, 47 ½ × 56 ½ × 34 ¼ inches
118 Installation view, *Sara VanDerBeek: To Think of Time*, Whitney Museum of American Art, New York, 2010
119 Stan VanDerBeek, Typed text for *Poemfield #4* and *Poemfield #5*, c. 1966, ink on paper, 11 × 8 ½ inches

HOME

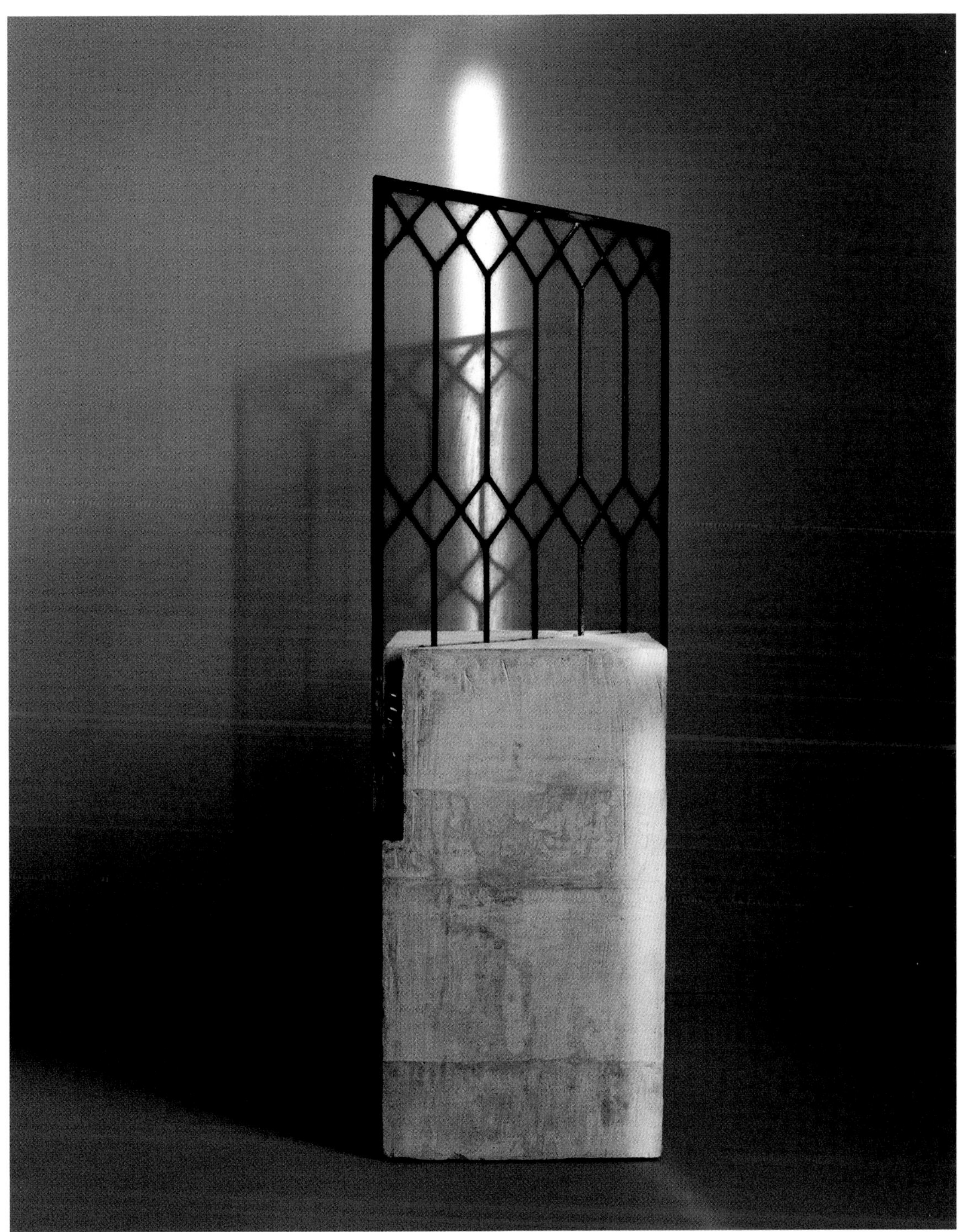

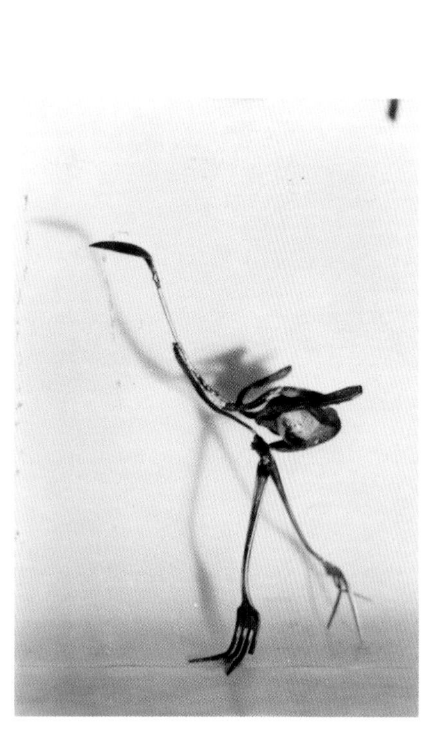

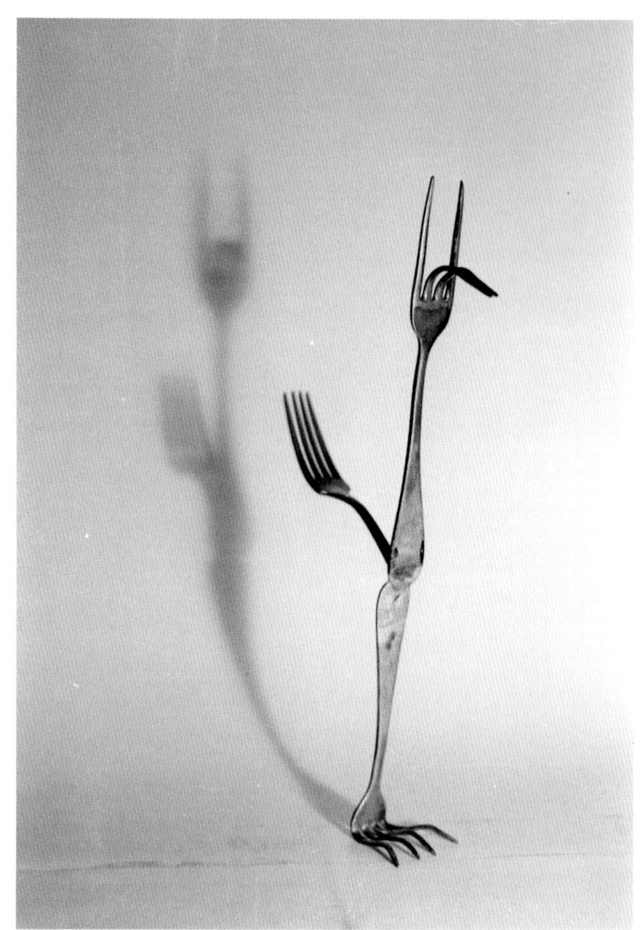

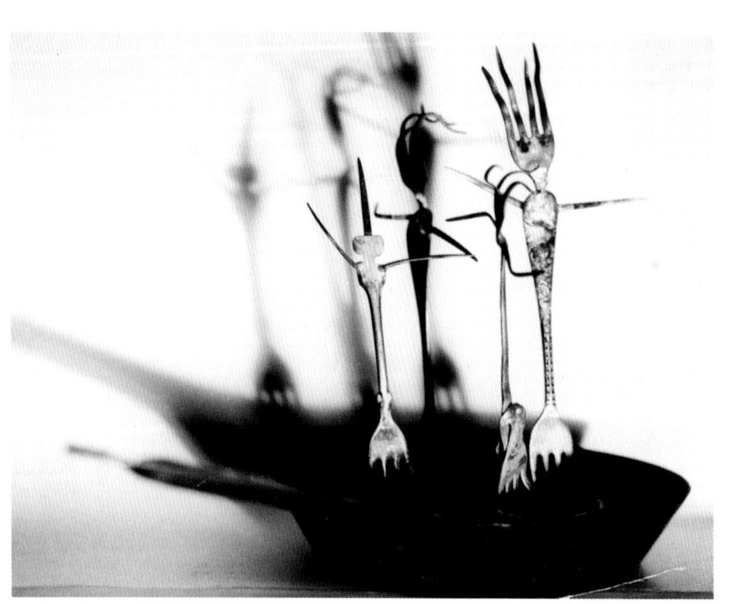

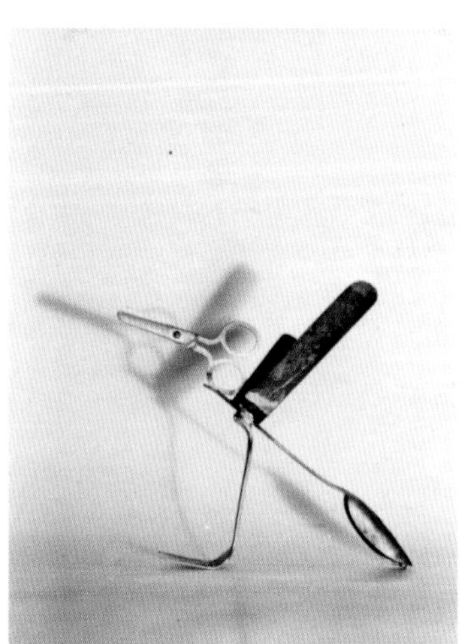

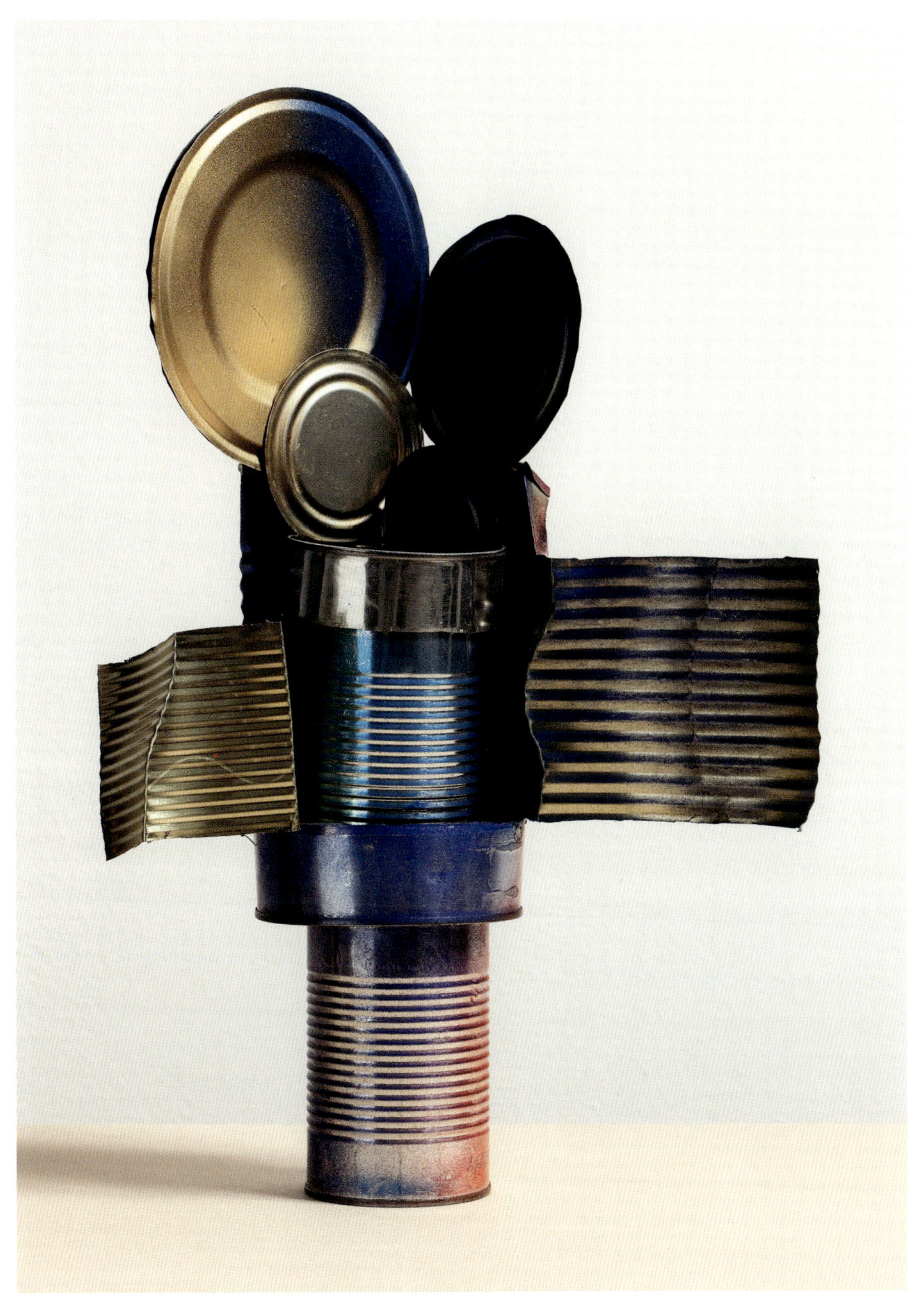

HOME

IB: Where did you find Stan's sculpture that forms the centerpiece of this last installation?

JVDB: My fiancée Anya, my older half-brother Max VanDerBeek from my dad's marriage with Johanna, his family, and I all took a trip to the Land, an artist commune in upstate New York started by several people from Black Mountain College. My dad resided at the Land for several years and worked on seminal projects there like the *Movie-Drome*. Max was showing us the structure he grew up in that our dad helped build in the sixties. It was a military-style bunker made out of metal arched compartments. He was amazed by how little it had changed since he was a kid—it still had the original stove, and even drawings he made with Johanna, still in perfect shape. It was a testament to the communal nature of the space because no one there ever owns his or her property—either that, or a testament to the laziness of the current owner. Either way, we benefited from the situation because we walked into a room and saw this little box my dad made with all these delicate metal structures inside. On the back, he had written in pencil, "To Johanna, Happy Birthday 1959." The owner gave it to us right away, and when this show came up it seemed more than appropriate to incorporate it.

IB: Johannes, when did you make the pattern houses, and how did you originally show them? Were you thinking about houses you knew, house types in architecture, or the idea of a home?

JVDB: I made them in 2005 as part of a window installation but never used them. They were made out of cardboard boxes, plaster, and burlap, with patterns based on Tudor houses. I've always thought Tudor-style houses make a hypnotic sequence when you drive past them quickly. At least that's how they appear in my dream. After I didn't use them I gave them to Anya as a gift, and they have been sitting on the top of our bookshelves ever since as little homes within our home.

IB: Sara, you have used parts of your family's home in your work at times. What are some of those objects? Why those things?

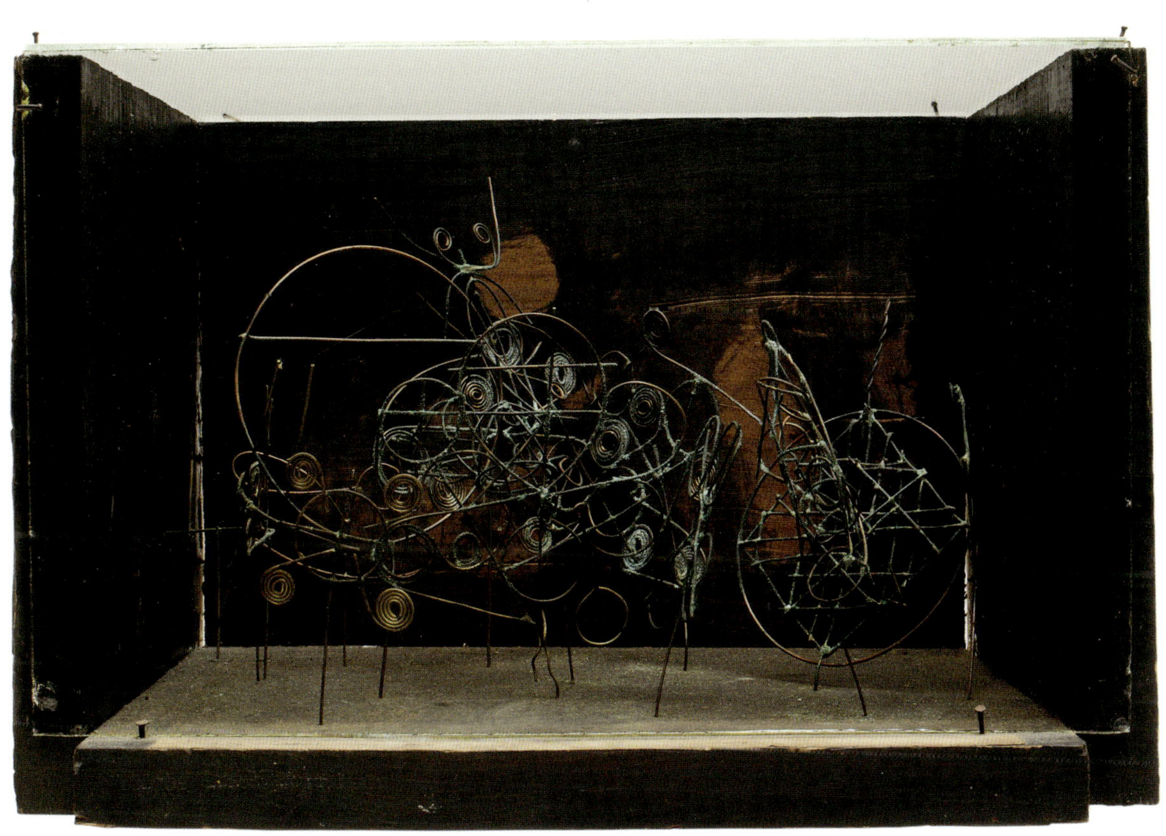

SVDB: The piece in this show uses aged wood from our home in Baltimore. I am currently using a lot of plaster, glass, wood, and metal for the sculptures. Most of the metal comes from found objects in Baltimore and New Orleans; the glass comes from Baltimore, New Orleans, and Detroit. All of these materials are building materials. The stains and remains of old paint on the wood or metal bring forward the tactile nature of memory and contribute a sense of discovery and chance to my practice.

Everything in this era of uncertainty is transitive. I equate the creation of the sculptures as an act representing this transitive state. The sculptures exist but are never shown, only seen in images, so they could almost be imaginary. Setting up these situations in which to document them constitutes a kind of performative act. My studio practice can at times feel like a performance, creating situations solely for the act of recording them. I hope that in photographing these sculptures, in using natural light, and in the composition, the printing, and the final installation, these images oscillate among many ways of reading.

IB: Your mother can no longer live on her own in your family home in Baltimore, and both of you have plans to get married next year. Can you reflect a bit on what home means to you these days?

SVDB: Loss can be gradual, as in the way we age, loss of youth, innocence, and idealism, but it can also be dramatic or sudden. This marks a time of great transition for us–we are founding the homes and relationships that will become the new centers of our families' lives, which is very exciting but I wish it wasn't my mother's sickness driving this time of change. Much of this change is standard, but given our father's death early in our lives, the house held a stronger power beyond its identity as our childhood home. It was a place he had been too. Now it is static, dream-like space built of collective memories, and while it still exists, the place we knew it to be has made that transfer from the physical realm to that of our imaginations.

JVDB: I will be the first to admit I had a very hard time selling the house in Baltimore, because it was the house my dad bought for my mom so they could raise a family. I grew up there and loved it. I knew buried in the wall of paint was some layer my dad had done, or that the rickety step was so because he only used one nail. I know my mom loved that house because she could still feel him in it. There were a lot of memories in the air, mixed with a little bit of mold from the basement we all dreaded going into. Funny enough, that basement bore a lot of fruit for this show. We kept finding more of his work stuck in the darkest corners, even up until the last day, when we found a trunk in the yard with a whole new series of collages in it. Now that it's finally gone, I'm slowly realizing that you have to reinforce those memories with the people that helped make them. Home is in the people that surround you. I have many great friends and family that are ever present in my consciousness.

IB: Can you talk a bit about looking back on the year of this exhibition and seeing all your work juxtaposed in these different combinations? What did you learn about your own work? Did you learn anything new about each other's work?

SVDB: I have learned so much from this show that it's hard to even begin to answer. Something that was incredibly significant to me was seeing Johannes make new works for almost every show and getting a very unique, intimate view of his practice. In his continual experimentation, Johannes is an inspiration—his questioning, his unique use of materials, and his distinct execution has made a deep impression upon me. It is always with great anticipation that I await to see his next work. But in this I also feel the resonance of our father's ongoing experiments and laugh and cry at the dance of these two kindred spirits separated if only by the great distance of existence. I felt I joined them in this dance and tried to move in ways that were not a waltz but more a folk round dance, weaving in and under arms. I felt welcomed into the revelry but it was also just as fun to sit and watch. In his whim and worry it is often in the furrowed brow of my brother that I see my father's vision of the future realized. As an internet-era child, attuned to the world and its attendant anxieties and subtleties, he is searching for a way to make dreams concrete, metal transparent, and ordinary objects transcendent. Tin can cathedrals and paper towel paintings are just two moments of transformation he has achieved that have profoundly impressed me.

Art is a means of connecting; like education, it is most successful when it is reciprocal. The artist learns as much from the audience as the student learns from the teacher and vice versa—the teacher learns from the student, the audience learns from the artist. I feel in creating this smaller circle of connection over the year, I have learned a great deal but it has also left an urge to learn more.

Seeing the many connections between all of our works has also led me to be more open to the idea of influence and bringing in other approaches into my work. The entire experience of creating and organizing the twelve different installations has pushed me to question myself and to look into new areas and ideas of what a practice, an artwork, and an exhibition can be.

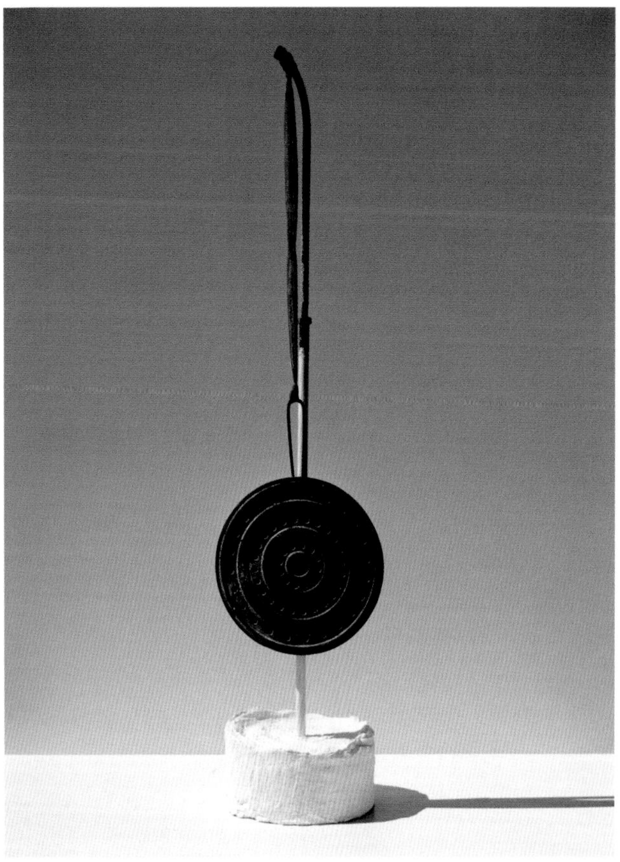

126

JVDB: It was a real wild ride. Appropriately so, since the premise of the show was my dad's idea for an Amazement Park that involved many moving parts and changing scenery. Along the way came some exhilarating moments, including making sculptures in the two days following my proposal to Anya. The monthly structure of the show posed an initial challenge because I had never produced work so frequently and constantly—I used to spend months on just one piece. I wanted to respond to the themes we determined for each show, which meant I had to make a new piece every three weeks and really change how I worked. From the beginning I saw it as a rare opportunity to get out of my habits and use it as a catalyst to loosen up.

I recognize it was also a special opportunity to think about my sister's and my dad's work from a new vantage point. We are a family, above all, but the exhibition enabled us to engage with one another as artists and grapple with the commonalities of our ideas and ideals. I wish he was around to be an active member, but his spirit was omnipresent. The exchange that ensued opened up

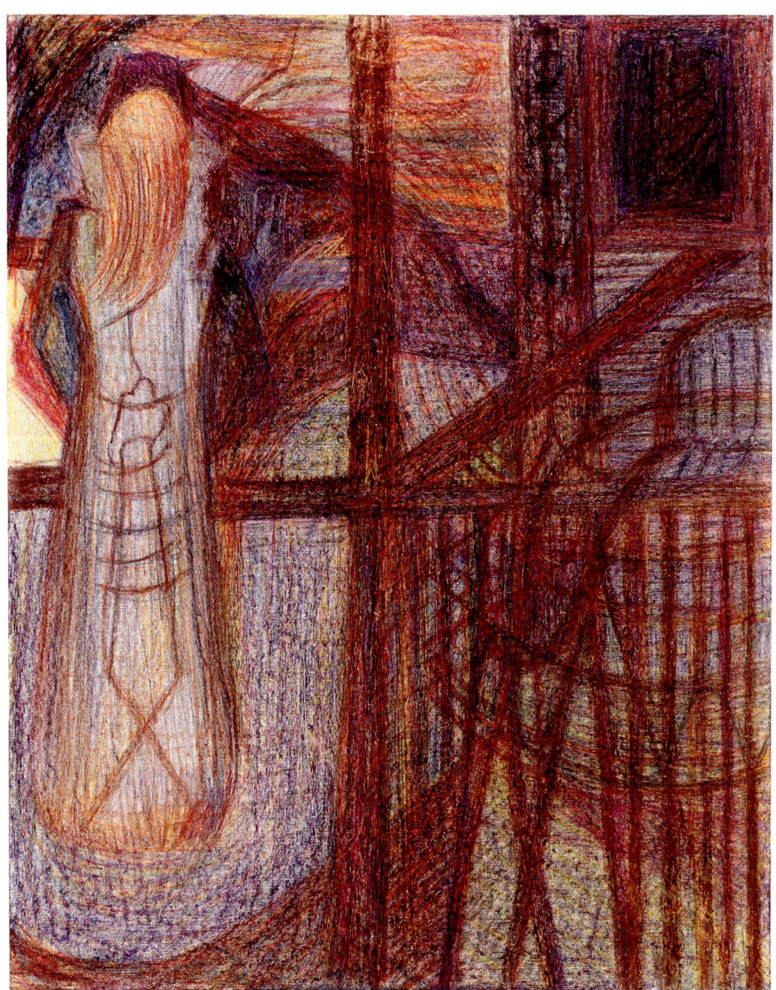

127

new ways of viewing their work, and in turn allowed me to develop my own interpretations. It presented an interesting challenge on a curatorial level to know what works would be exhibited, and then respond to them as an artist in a way not overly didactic or disparate. Some months proved more successful than others, obviously. When they were good, our commonalities resonated and our differences became exposed in a manner I found quite illuminating. During the show we called *Violence*, where we showed Dad's video *Violence Sonata* and Sara's *Composition for Detroit*, I got to hear Sara talk about her piece and realized she approaches her work a lot like a composer. Every element in her photographs functions like a single note, and as she pulls them together, they coalesce into a symphony of pictures. One element is no more important than the other but as an arrangement they gain more nuance than they would ever have individually. She is highly attuned to the way patterns form harmonies, or bursts in color lend excitement to the composition. I never sense a superfluous character or unwanted visitor in the space of her imagery. I greatly admire her precision in creating photos that take on as their subject the least precise facets of life such as memory and light. It gives her work a great deal of charge and makes for an elegant paradox. Our father was also a healthy paradox or was it a parrot and an ox, or a pair of docs? I think it may have been a paradise.

Home captions

120 Sara VanDerBeek, *Baltimore Window*, 2010, digital C-print, 20 × 16 inches
121 Stan VanDerBeek, Stills from *Looney Spoons*, 1959, black and white film with sound, 5:00 minutes
122 Johannes VanDerBeek, *A Family*, 2010, tin cans, acrylic paint, and epoxy, 17 ¼ × 12 × 7 ½ inches
123 Sara VanDerBeek, *Baltimore Arrival*, 2010, digital C-print, 20 × 16 inches
124 Sara VanDerBeek, *Baltimore Departure*, 2010, digital C-print, 20 × 15 inches
125 Stan VanDerBeek, *Birthday present for Johanna*, 1957, wire, wood, and glass, 7 ½ × 11 ½ × 8 ⅛ inches
126 Sara VanDerBeek, *Universe*, 2010, digital C-print, 20 × 14 ¾ inches
127 Johannes VanDerBeek, *Untitled*, 2009, crayon on paper, 23 × 18 ⅜ inches

Works in the Exhibition

Unless otherwise noted:
All works by Stan VanDerBeek, courtesy of The Estate of Stan VanDerBeek
All works by Sara VanDerBeek, courtesy of the artist and Metro Pictures
All works by Johannes VanDerBeek, courtesy of the artist and Zach Feuer Gallery
Dimensions listed in inches, h × w × d.

Means June 6–28, 2009

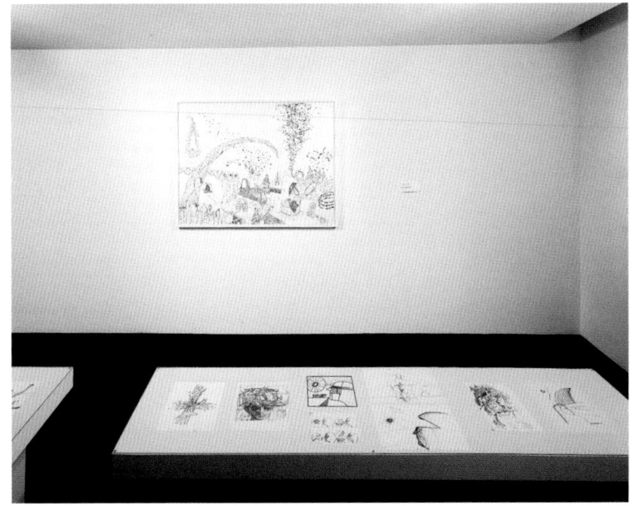

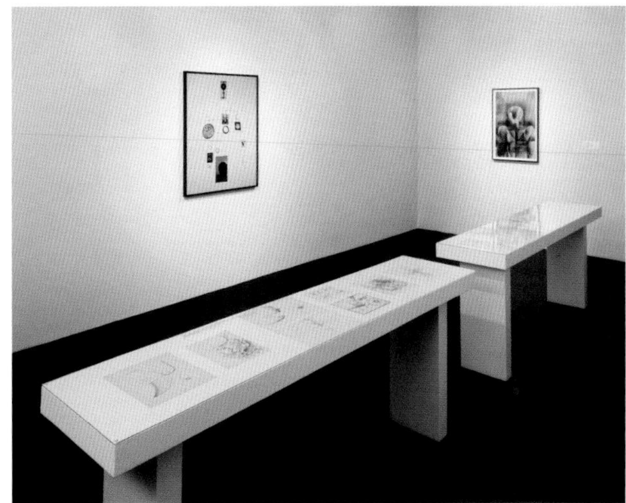

Stan VanDerBeek
Selection of drawings and sketches, 1955–1983
Graphite on paper
10 7/8 × 8 3/8 inches

Graphite on paper
10 7/8 × 8 3/8 inches

Graphite on paper
10 7/8 × 8 3/8 inches

Ink on paper
8 1/2 × 10 7/8 inches

Ink on paper
6 5/8 × 3 1/4 inches

Graphite on paper
6 1/4 × 5 1/4 inches

Ink on paper
8 1/4 × 11 1/4 inches

Ink on paper
8 1/4 × 11 1/4 inches

Ink on paper
10 1/4 × 7 inches

Ink on paper
10 3/8 × 7 7/8 inches

Ink on paper
10 3/8 × 8 inches

Ink on paper
7 1/4 × 7 1/4 inches

Ink on paper
5 7/8 × 6 3/4 inches

Ink on paper
8 1/4 × 11 1/4 inches

Ink on paper
8 1/4 × 11 1/4 inches

Ink on paper
11 × 8 1/2 inches

Untitled (rolling), 1955
Graphite and ink on paper
29 3/4 × 20 inches

Sara VanDerBeek
From the Means of Reproduction, 2007
Digital C-print
40 × 30 inches

Johannes VanDerBeek
Heads and Beams, 2004
Collage on paper
38 1/4 × 50 1/8 inches
Private Collection

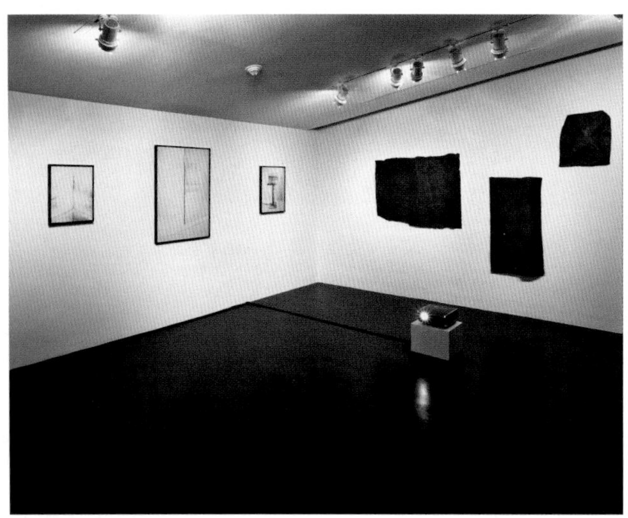

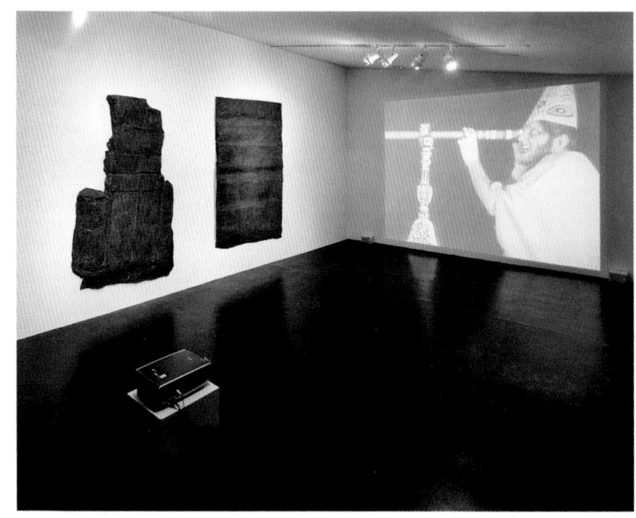

Stan VanDerBeek
Breathdeath, 1963
Black and white film with sound
14:33 minutes

Sara VanDerBeek
Belle Grove, 2009
Digital C-print
40 × 30 inches

Belle Grove, Second View, 2009
Digital C-print
24 × 20 inches

Mirror, Hollywood Boulevard, 2009
Digital C-print
20 × 15 ½ inches

Johannes VanDerBeek
Before After, 2009
Pastel and ink on aluminum foil
38 × 47 × 1 ½ inches

Door Column, 2009
Pastel and ink on aluminum foil
44 ¼ × 23 × 1 ⅞ inches

It, 2009
Pastel and ink on aluminum foil
75 × 42 × 3 inches

The King, 2009
Pastel and ink on aluminum foil
73 ½ × 49 × 2 ¼ inches

Turtle Boom Box Shield, 2009
Pastel and ink on aluminum foil
22 × 18 × 1 ¼ inches

Wheeeeels **August 1–30, 2009**

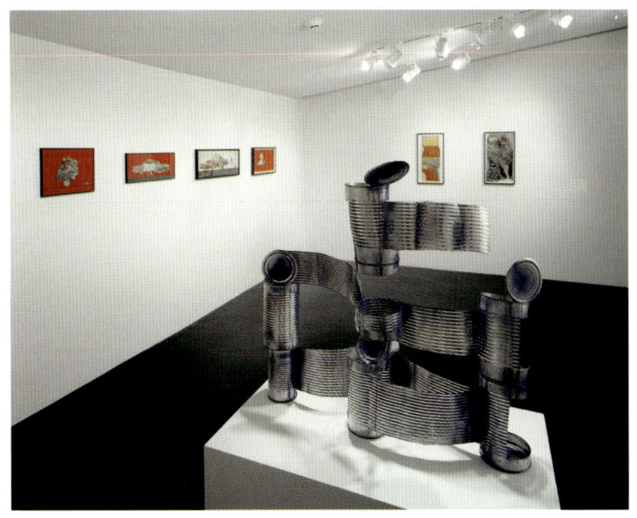

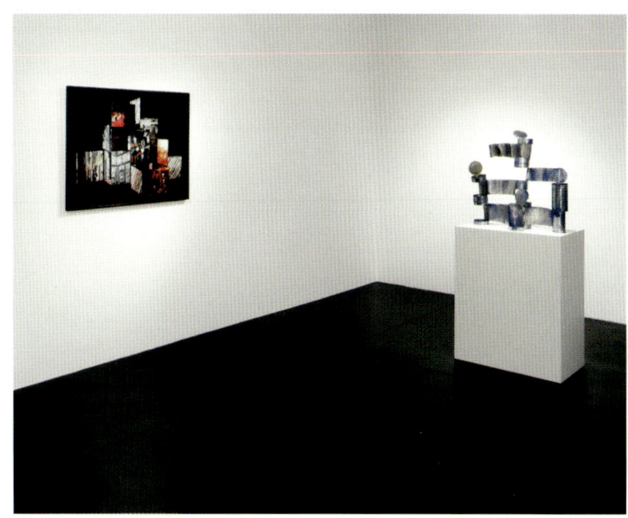

Stan VanDerBeek
Untitled (from Wheeeeels), 1959
Collage on paper
11 5/8 × 15 3/8 inches

Untitled (from Wheeeeels), 1959
Collage and ink on paper
8 3/4 × 21 7/8 inches

Untitled (from Wheeeeels), 1959
Collage and ink on paper
9 7/8 × 29 7/8 inches

Untitled (from Wheeeeels), 1959
Collage on paper
10 1/8 × 20 inches

Sara VanDerBeek
The Principle of Superimposition, 2007
Digital C-print
30 5/8 × 40 inches

Johannes VanDerBeek
Blue Cans, 2009
Tin cans, acrylic, and epoxy
26 1/4 × 27 1/4 × 13 1/2 inches

Crowded Face, 2009
Sanded magazine pages
22 1/2 × 12 1/2 inches

Wind and Words, 2009
Sanded magazine pages
23 5/8 × 9 7/8 inches

Superimposition **September 5–27, 2009**

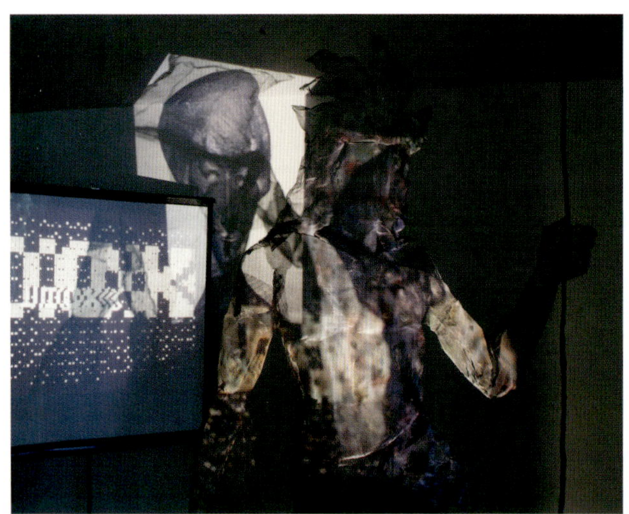

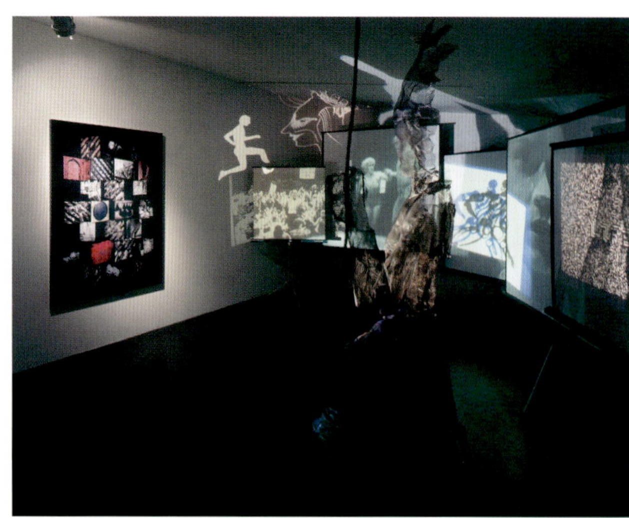

Stan VanDerBeek
Panels for the Walls of the World, 1967–2009 (approx. re-staging)
16 mm DVD transfers, 35 mm slides, overhead transparency projections
Installation dimensions variable

Sara VanDerBeek
The Principle of Superimposition II, 2008
Digital C-print
64 ½ × 44 ½ inches

Johannes VanDerBeek
Indian Ghost, 2009
Acrylic on aluminum mesh
85 ½ × 39 × 19 inches

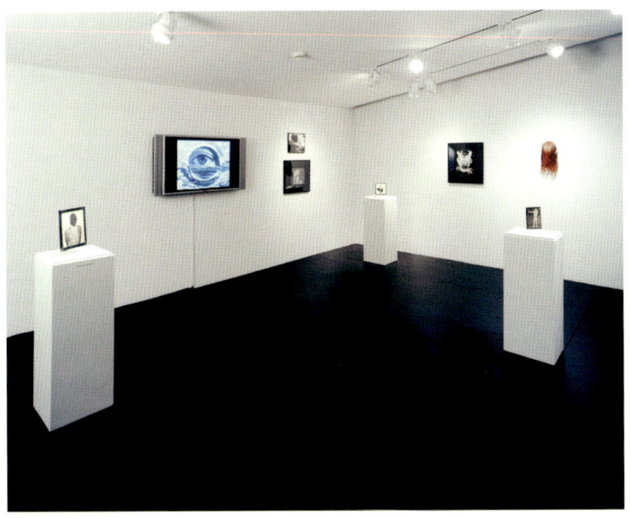

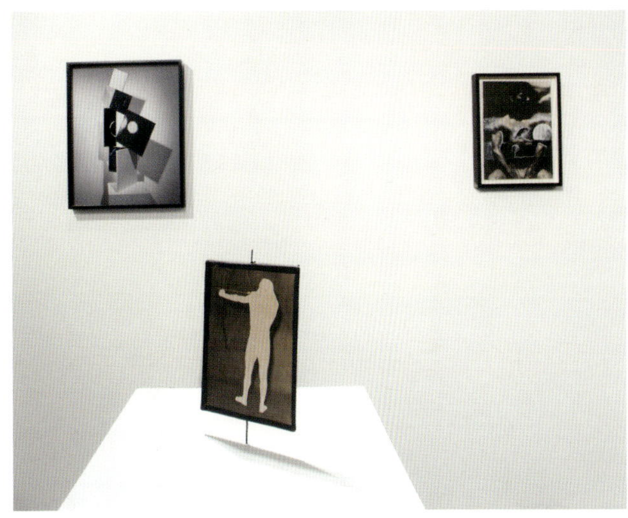

Stan VanDerBeek
Untitled (flip collage), 1958
Paper and tape on board, wire, and string
9 ¾ × 8 × ⅛ inches

Untitled (flip collage), 1958
Paper and tape on board, wire, and string
7 × 5 × ⅛ inches

Untitled (flip collage), 1958
Paper and tape on board, wire, and string
7 ¾ × 6 ¾ × ⅛ inches

Untitled (from See Saw Seams), 1964
Paint on found image
13 ¾ × 10 inches

Untitled (from See Saw Seams), 1964
Ink, paint, and paper on found image
13 ½ × 10 ¼ inches

Untitled (from See Saw Seams), 1964
Ink and paper on found image
10 ¼ × 13 ⅝ inches

Untitled (from See Saw Seams), 1964
Mixed media
9 ¼ × 11 ½ inches

See Saw Seams, 1965
Black and white film with sound
9:06 minutes

Sara VanDerBeek
Delaunay, 2008
Digital C-print
40 × 40 inches
The Carol and Arthur Goldberg Collection

Eclipse, 2008
Digital C-print
19 ⅜ × 15 ½ inches
Private Collection

Johannes VanDerBeek
The Battle of Waterloo, 2003
Wax and human hair
9 ½ × 8 × 6 inches
Collection of Ernesto Caivano, New York

Burning at the Stake, 2008
Foam, wax, and human hair
18 × 10 × 7 inches
Collection of Dennis Freedman, New York

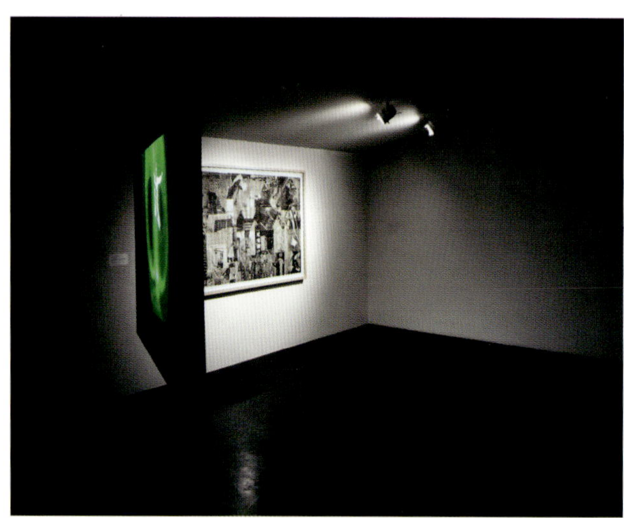

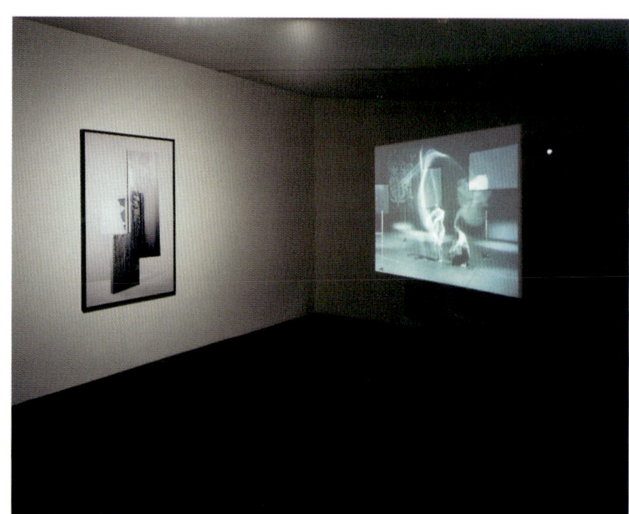

Stan VanDerBeek and Merce Cunningham Dance Company
Variations V, 1965
Film produced for German Television transferred to DVD
Music: John Cage
Film: Stan VanDerBeek
TV images: Nam June Paik
Dancers: Merce Cunningham Dance Company with Yvonne Rainer
49:23 minutes
Courtesy of The Estate of Stan VanDerBeek and Merce Cunningham Dance Company

Stan VanDerBeek and WGBH Studios
Video Variations, 1972
Video produced by WGBH and the Boston Symphony Orchestra transferred to DVD
6:48 minutes

Sara VanDerBeek
After, 2009
Digital C-print
60 × 40 3/8 inches

Johannes VanDerBeek
Documentation of Body/Building, 2007
Sanded magazine pages
61 7/8 × 43 3/4 inches
Private Collection

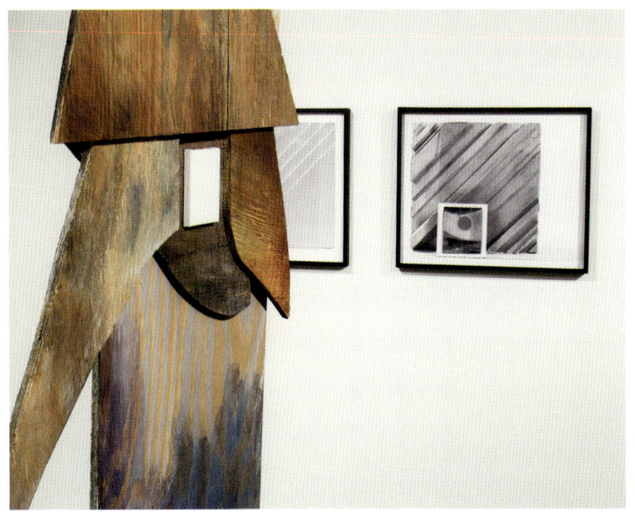

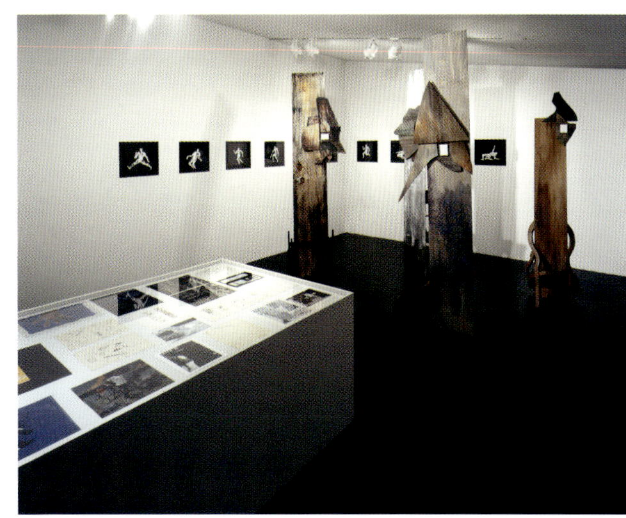

Stan VanDerBeek
Untitled (photograph of dancers at Black Mountain College), 1952–1954
Silver gelatin print
9 7/8 × 8 inches

Untitled (study for dwelling using modular forms), 1952–1954
Graphite on paper
8 1/2 × 11 inches

Untitled (architectural drawing), 1954
Graphite on paper
10 7/8 × 8 1/2 inches

Untitled (architectural drawing), 1954
Ink on paper
8 × 10 1/2 inches

Untitled (architectural drawing), 1954
Ink on paper
10 7/8 × 8 1/2 inches

Untitled (study for modular forms), c. 1955
Ink on paper
8 × 10 1/2 inches

Untitled (study for multi-panel painting), c. 1955
Ink on paper
11 × 8 1/2 inches

Untitled, c. 1955
Graphite on paper
10 7/8 × 8 1/2 inches

Untitled, c. 1955
Graphite on paper
10 7/8 × 8 1/2 inches

Untitled, c. 1955
Ink on paper
7 7/8 × 27 1/4 inches

Untitled, c. 1955
Ink and graphite on paper
11 × 8 3/8 inches

Untitled (from Mankinda), 1959
Paint on paper mounted on cardboard
10 works, each 14 × 17 inches

Untitled (from Mankinda), 1959
Paint on paper mounted on cardboard
10 7/8 × 8 1/2 inches

Untitled (study for Culture Intercom), 1963
Print
10 × 16 3/4 inches

Untitled (from See Saw Seams), 1964
Paint on acetate and paper
10 3/4 × 13 1/4 inches

Untitled (poster for One), 1965
Paint on paper mounted on cardboard
39 3/4 × 30 inches

Untitled (from Oh), 1968
Paint on acetate
10 ⅜ × 14 ⅛ inches

Untitled (study for early fax mural), 1969–1971
Ink on paper
8 ¼ × 11 inches

Sara VanDerBeek
Four Photographers, 2008
Digital C-prints
18 ½ × 20 ¾ inches
18 ½ × 22 ⅛ inches
18 ½ × 18 ½ inches
18 ½ × 22 ⅛ inches
18 ½ × 22 ⅛ inches
18 ½ × 20 ⅜ inches
Collection of Ken and Helen Rowe, London

Study for Four Photographers, 2008
Paint on silver gelatin print, image by Stan VanDerBeek
9 ⅞ × 8 inches

Study for Four Photographers, 2008
Paint on silver gelatin print
6 ¼ × 9 inches

Study for Four Photographers, 2008
Paint on silver gelatin print
9 ⅞ × 8 inches

Study for Four Photographers, 2008
Paint on silver gelatin print
9 ⅞ × 8 inches

Lines, 2009
Graphite and paint on printed image from *Look* magazine
13 ⅞ × 10 ¼ inches

Study for A Composition for Detroit, 2009
Graphite on printed page from *Life* magazine
Diptych, each 12 × 10 ¼ inches

Study for A Composition for Detroit, 2009
Paint on cover of *Life* magazine
11 ¼ × 10 ¼ inches

Study for A Composition for Detroit, 2009
Graphite on cover of *Life* magazine
10 ⅛ × 10 ⅜ inches

Study for White Series, 2009
Paint, graphite, and collage on printed pages from *The History of Photography* by Beaumont Newhall
Left: 11 ⅛ × 9 ½ inches
Right: 11 ⅛ × 9 ⅜ inches

Johannes VanDerBeek
Criminal Teen Moon Mask (around a small painting), 2009
Paint on wood, canvas, and chair
82 ½ × 19 ½ × 22 ¼ inches

Gypsy Hill Surgeon Chest (around a small painting), 2009
Paint on wood, canvas, and chair
96 ¼ × 24 ¾ × 27 ¼ inches

Hair Hut Horn Head (around a small painting), 2009
Paint on wood, canvas, and chair
96 × 25 ½ × 35 inches

Red Egypt Crow Jupiter (around a small painting), 2009
Paint on wood, canvas, and chair
95 ½ × 27 ¾ × 23 ½ inches

Time January 9–31, 2010

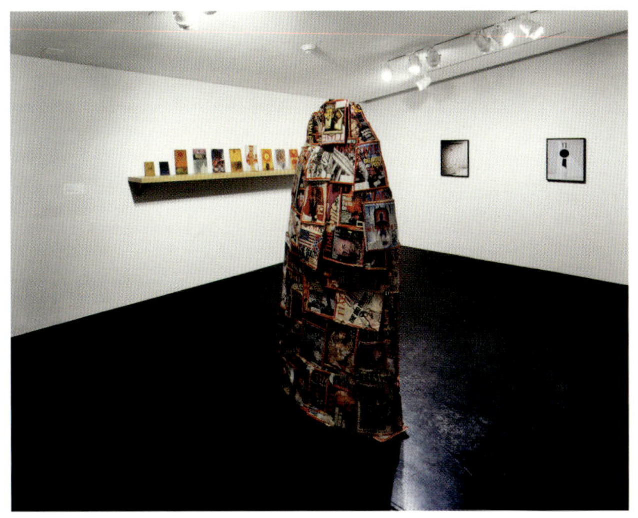

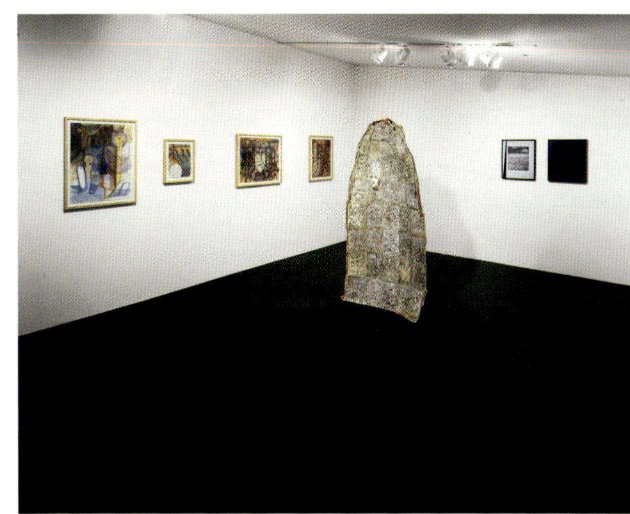

Stan VanDerBeek
All works *Untitled*, 1955–1957
Paint and mixed media on wood

5 ¾ × 4 ¼ × ¼ inches

5 ¾ × 4 ¼ × ¼ inches

10 ¾ × 5 ⅞ × ¼ inches

11 × 7 ¼ × ¼ inches

11 × 7 ¼ × ¼ inches

11 × 7 ¼ × ¼ inches

18 ¾ × 7 ¼ × ¼ inches

11 × 7 ¼ × ¼ inches

11 × 7 ¼ × ¼ inches

11 × 7 ¼ × ¼ inches

10 ¼ × 5 ¾ × 1 inches

5 ¾ × 4 × ¼ inches

5 ¾ × 4 × ¼ inches

Sara VanDerBeek
Black Mirror, 2009
Digital C-print
20 × 15 ¾ inches

Salome, 2009
Digital C-print
19 ¾ × 15 ¾ inches

One Hundred Years, 2009
Digital C-prints
2 parts, each 19 ¾ × 15 ¾ inches

Johannes VanDerBeek
It's Time!?, 2006
Time magazines, plaster, wood, and glue
73 × 38 ¼ × 11 ⅝ inches
Collection of Zach Feuer

All works *Untitled*, 2009
Crayon on paper

28 ½ × 22 ⅝ inches

14 × 11 inches

22 ⅝ × 28 ½ inches

23 × 18 ⅜ inches

Violence February 6–28, 2010

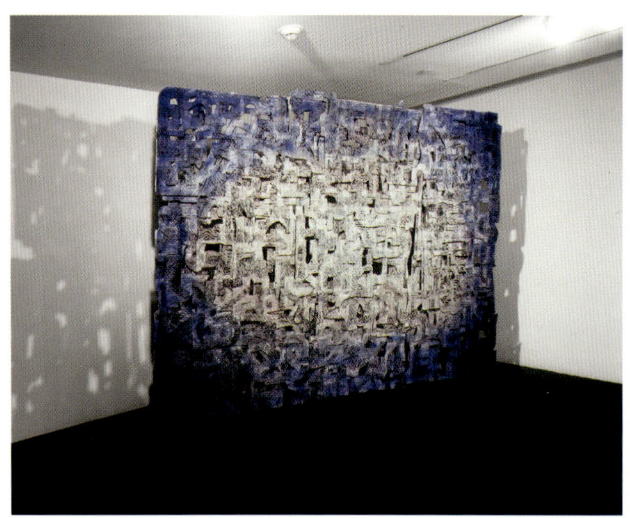

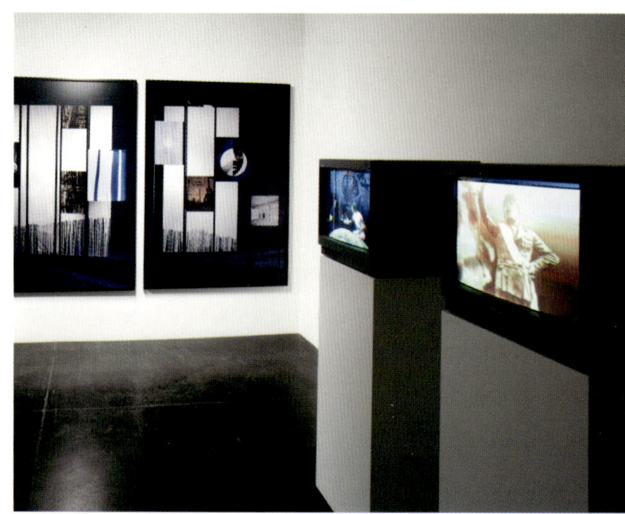

Stan VanDerBeek
Violence Sonata, 1969
Two channel video with sound
Originally broadcasted on WGBH-TV, Boston, alongside live studio performance
53:54 minutes

Sara VanDerBeek
A Composition for Detroit, 2009
Digital C-prints
66 × 49 ¼ inches
66 × 44 ¾ inches
66 × 49 ¼ inches
66 × 48 ¾ inches

Johannes VanDerBeek
The Big Stone Flatscreen with Static, 2010
Cardboard, Celluclay, wood, and paint
89 ½ × 122 × 5 ½ inches

Eyes March 6–28, 2010

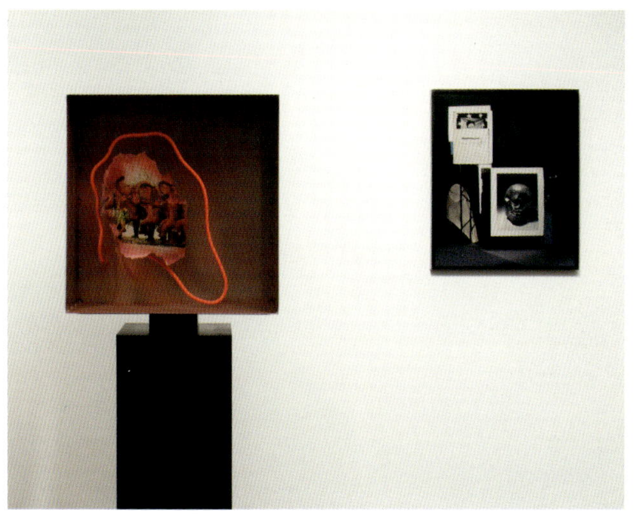

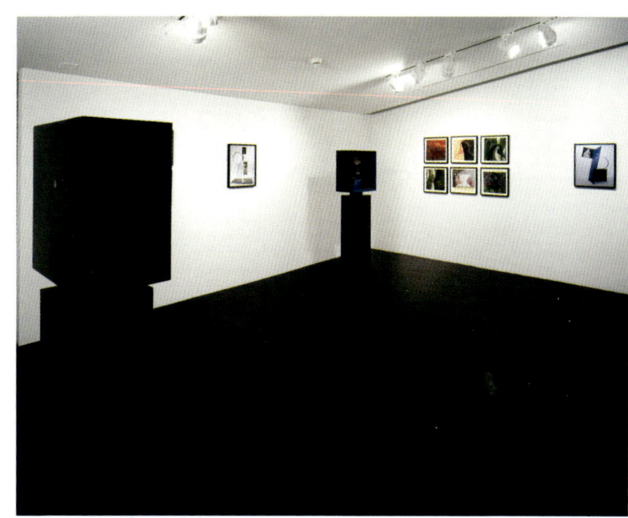

Stan VanDerBeek
All works *Untitled*, 1983

Collage on billboard
14 × 13 ½ inches

Collage on billboard
12 × 14 ¼ inches

Collage on billboard
12 ¼ × 15 ¾ inches

Pastel, marker, and collage on billboard
11 ¾ × 12 ½ inches

Pastel, marker, and collage on billboard
12 × 12 ½ inches

Pastel on billboard
12 ¾ × 12 ¾ inches

Pastel on billboard
12 ¾ × 12 ¾ inches

Pastel on billboard
12 ¾ × 12 ¾ inches

Pastel on billboard
12 × 12 ¼ inches

Pastel on billboard
12 ¼ × 13 inches

Pastel on billboard
12 ¼ × 12 inches

Sara VanDerBeek
Mrs. Washington's Bedroom, 2006
Digital C-print
20 × 23 ½ inches

Decorations in a Notebook, 2006
Digital C print
24 × 20 ½ inches
Ann and Mel Schaffer Family Collection

Eclipse 1, 2008
Digital C-print
20 × 16 ⅝ inches
Collection of The Frances Young Tang Teaching Museum and Art Gallery, Skidmore College

Eclipse 3, 2008
Digital C-print
20 ¾ × 16 ⅝ inches

Johannes VanDerBeek
Burning Face, 2009
Wire, paint, paper, and steel
65 ¾ × 21 ½ × 12 ½ inches

Elephant Skull, 2009
Wire, paint, paper, and steel
65 ¾ × 21 ½ × 12 ½ inches

Sky Mouth, 2009
Wire, paint, paper, and steel
65 ¾ × 21 ½ × 12 ½ inches

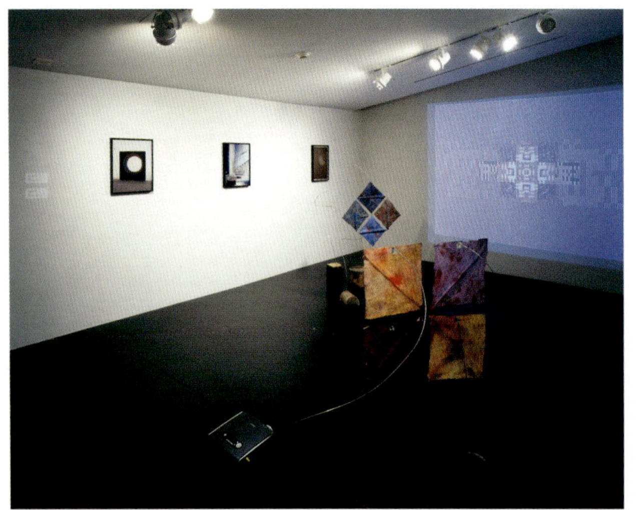

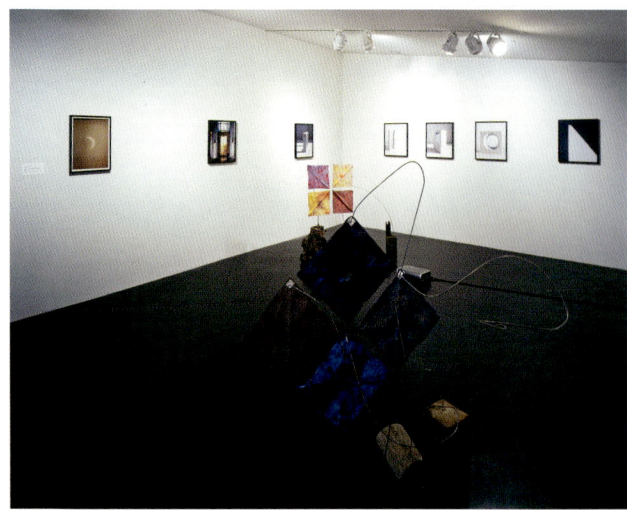

Stan VanDerBeek
Poemfield #5, 1967
Color film with sound
6:23 minutes

Poemfield #7, 1971
Color film with soundtrack by John Cage
5:38 minutes

Sara VanDerBeek
All Goes Onward and Outward, 2010
Digital C-prints
20 3/4 × 14 5/8 inches
20 3/4 × 16 5/8 inches
20 3/4 × 16 5/8 inches
20 3/4 × 16 5/8 inches
20 3/4 × 16 5/8 inches
20 3/4 × 16 5/8 inches
20 3/4 × 16 5/8 inches
20 3/4 × 16 5/8 inches
20 3/4 × 16 1/4 inches
20 3/4 × 14 5/8 inches

Johannes VanDerBeek
O, 2010
Wood, wire, paper towel, and paint
58 × 67 × 40 inches

X, 2010
Wood, wire, paper towel, and paint
47 1/2 × 56 1/2 × 34 1/4 inches

Home **April 26–May 2, 2010**

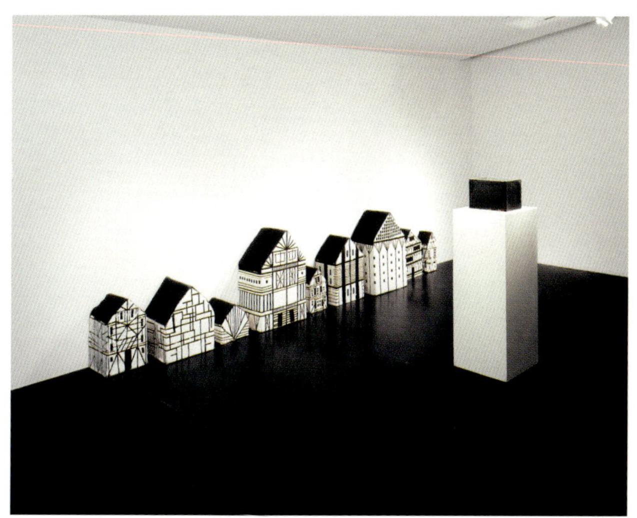

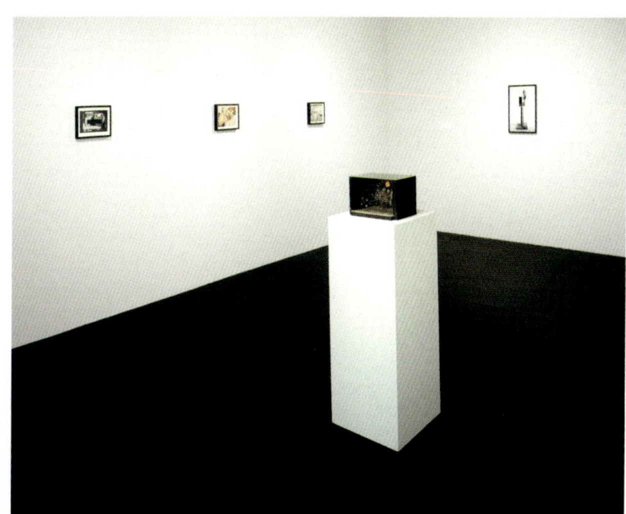

Stan VanDerBeek
Untitled (from A La Mode), 1955
Collage on paper
6 ¼ × 8 ⅜ inches

Untitled (from A La Mode), 1958
Ink on found photograph
7 × 8 ½ inches

Untitled (from A La Mode), 1958
Ink and paper on found photograph
6 ½ × 7 ¾ inches

Birthday present for Johanna, 1957
Wire, wood, and glass
7 ½ × 11 ½ × 8 ⅛ inches

Sara VanDerBeek
Paris, 2009
Digital C-print
19 ⅝ × 11 ⅝ inches

Johannes VanDerBeek
Pattern Houses, 2006–2010
Paint on burlap on cardboard
Installation dimensions variable

Contributors

Ian Berry is Associate Director and Susan Rabinowitz Malloy '45 Curator of The Frances Young Tang Teaching Museum and Art Gallery at Skidmore College. His curatorial projects at the Tang include *The Jewel Thief* (with Jessica Stockholder, 2010); *Twice Drawn* (with Jack Shear, 2006); *Living with Duchamp* (2003); and solo presentations of work by Nayland Blake, Kathy Butterly, Jim Hodges, Martin Kersels, Los Carpinteros, Amy Sillman, and Kara Walker. His recent publications include *Fred Tomaselli* (Prestel, 2009), *Tim Rollins and K.O.S.: A History* (MIT Press, 2009), and *Lives of the Hudson* (Prestel, 2010).

Anne Ellegood is Senior Curator at the Hammer Museum at the University of California, Los Angeles. Her recent exhibitions at the Hammer include solo presentations of work by Diana Al-Hadid, Keren Cytter, Mark Flores, and Friedrich Kunath, and the co-curated exhibition *All of this and nothing*. She has contributed to numerous publications, including *Artforum*, *Art Press*, *Vitamin 3-D: New Perspectives in Sculpture and Installation* (Phaidon, 2009), and *The Cinema Effect: Illusion, Reality, and the Moving Image* (Giles, 2008).

Fionn Meade is Curator at SculptureCenter in New York, where his recent exhibitions include *Knight's Move*, *Leopards in the Temple*, and *Time Again*. Other recent curatorial projects include *Nachleben*, co-organized with Lucy Raven at Goethe Institut, New York, and *Entr'acte* at Galerie Catherine Bastide, Brussels. His writing has appeared in numerous journals, including *Artforum*, *BOMB*, and *Parkett*, and in the recent catalogues *Elad Lassry* for Kunsthalle Zurich (JRP/Ringier, 2010) and *Mark Morrisroe* for the Fotomuseum Winterthur (JRP/Ringier, 2010).

Gloria Sutton is Assistant Professor of Contemporary Art and New Media at Northeastern University, Boston. Her curatorial projects include *How Many Billboards?* an outdoor exhibition at the MAK Center for Art and Architecture, Los Angeles and, as the Ahmanson Curatorial Fellow at the Los Angeles Museum of Contemporary Art, *MOCA Focus: Karl Haendel*. A founding member of rhizome.org, her writing on the history of media art is included in *Future Cinema: The Cinematic Imaginary after Film* (MIT Press, 2003) and *Mainframe Experimentalism: Early Digital Computing and the Experimental Arts* (forthcoming, UC Press).

Johannes VanDerBeek was born in Baltimore, Maryland in 1982, and received his BFA from Cooper Union School of Art and Science, New York in 2004. In 2003, he co-founded the artist-run gallery Guild & Greyshkul in New York with Anya Kielar and sister Sara VanDerBeek, which ran through 2009. His work was featured in solo exhibitions at Zach Feuer Gallery, New York (2007, 2010) and in group exhibitions at Portugal Arte 10 Biennial, Lisbon, Portugal (2010); MetroTech Center, Brooklyn, sponsored by the Public Art Fund (2009); and P.S.1 Contemporary Art Center, Long Island City (2006), among others.

Sara VanDerBeek was born in Baltimore, Maryland in 1976, and received her BFA from Cooper Union School of Art and Science, New York in 1998. After graduating, she worked as a commercial photographer in London before returning to New York in 2001. Two years later, she co-founded the artist-run gallery Guild & Greyshkul. Her work has been presented in solo exhibitions at the Whitney Museum of American Art, New York (2010); The Approach, London (2008); and D'Amelio Terras Gallery, New York (2006), and in group exhibitions at SculptureCenter, New York (2010); Solomon R. Guggenheim Museum, New York (2010); and Museum of Modern Art, New York (2009), among others.

Stan VanDerBeek was born in New York in 1927 and died in Baltimore, Maryland in 1984. He studied at Cooper Union School of Art and Science, New York and Black Mountain College, Asheville, North Carolina. In the 1960s and '70s, his work was included in the pioneering new media exhibitions *The Projected Image*, Institute of Contemporary Art, Boston (1968); *Cybernetic Serendipity*, Institute of Contemporary Art, London (1969); and *Software*, Jewish Museum, New York (1970). His work was included in the 1983 Whitney Biennial and was surveyed in the 2011 exhibition *Stan VanDerBeek: The Culture Intercom* at MIT List Visual Arts Center and Contemporary Arts Museum, Houston. For the last decade of his life he taught at University of Maryland, Baltimore County (1975–1984).

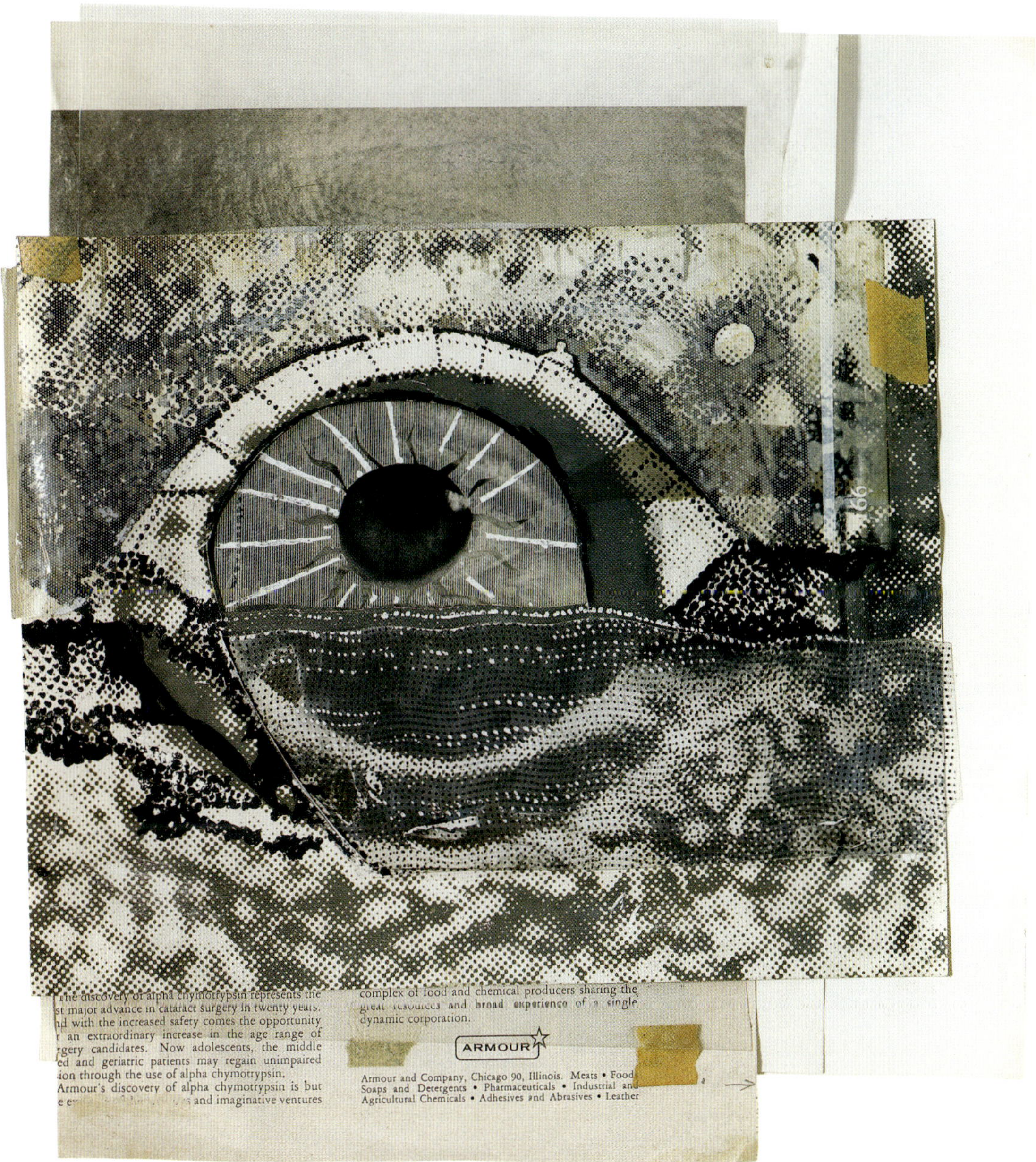

Stan VanDerBeek, *Untitled (from See Saw Seams)*, 1964, mixed media, 12 × 8 inches

Acknowledgments

Uncovering Stan VanDerBeek's archive box by box with Sara and Johannes was an eye opening experience like no other. Looking at collages and sketches for familiar and imagined structures and films revealed an artist whose spirit guided us through every step of our project. Thanks to Stan's first wife Johanna VanDerBeek for keeping these works for so many years and to Louise VanDerBeek, Johannes and Sara's mother, for her generosity and support.

This project began in conversations at Guild and Greyschul gallery. Thanks to all the artists who encouraged us along the way and especially to Chelsea Spengemann and Esme Watanabe who assisted us in so many ways.

Special thanks those that lent work to the exhibition. Thanks to Christopher D'Amelio, Trina Gordon, Miriam Grotte, and Lucien Terras at D'Amelio Terras Gallery; Grace Evans and Zach Feuer at Zach Feuer Gallery; Ernesto Caivano, Dennis Freedman, Carol and Arthur Goldberg, Frank and Patti Kolodny, Ken and Helen Rowe, Ann and Mel Schaffer, and especially to the artists.

This book is a whole exhibition in itself and we are fortunate to have excellent collaborators to help us make it. Thanks to designer Conny Purtill, photographer Arthur Evans, writers Anne Ellegood, Fionn Meade, and Gloria Sutton, and to Jay Rogoff and Ginny Kollak for editing advice. Thanks also to Michael Plunkett at Metro Pictures and Abigail Clark at Public Art Fund.

Thanks to the Tang Museum staff who worked together to make such a memorable show for the museum: Kristen Boyle, Ginger Ertz, Torrance Fish, Elizabeth Karp, Susi Kerr, Gayle King, Chris Kobuskie, Ryan Lynch, Patrick O'Rourke, Vickie Riley, Lori Robinson, Barbara Schrade, Kelly Ward, and John Weber. Thanks to our students and interns: Naomi Brown '12, Gregory Dellicarpini, Emily Devoe '10, Francesca Fanelli '09, Fran Gubler '10, Jessica Hass '10, Jordan Klein '10, Danika Lichtig, and to our installation crew: Samuel Coe, Jack Schaefer, and Shawn Snow.

Special thanks to Matthew Dipple and Anya Kielar for their ever-present support and critical suggestions at all stages of the project, and to curatorial assistant Megan Hyde who attended to all details of the project from start to finish. Most of all, my sincere thanks to Sara and Johannes for working along with me to create such an ambitious project. It was an experience driven by ideas, emotions, and invention that forced us to take risks and experiment in public. I am forever grateful and look forward to continuing our conversation about art and life into the future.

Ian Berry

opposite: Johannes VanDerBeek, *Hippie Ghost*, 2010 (detail), acrylic on aluminum mesh, 78 × 29 × 22 inches

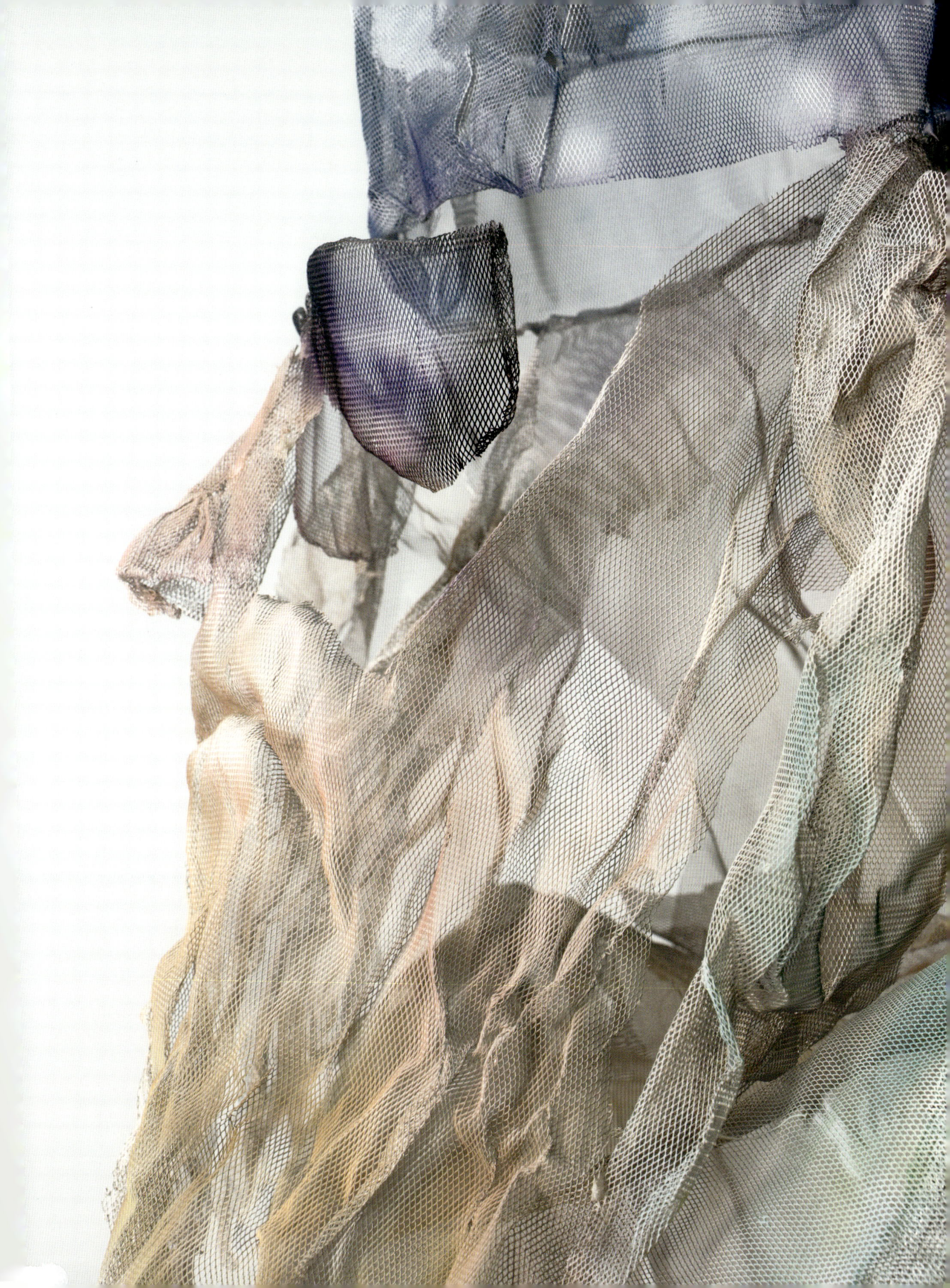

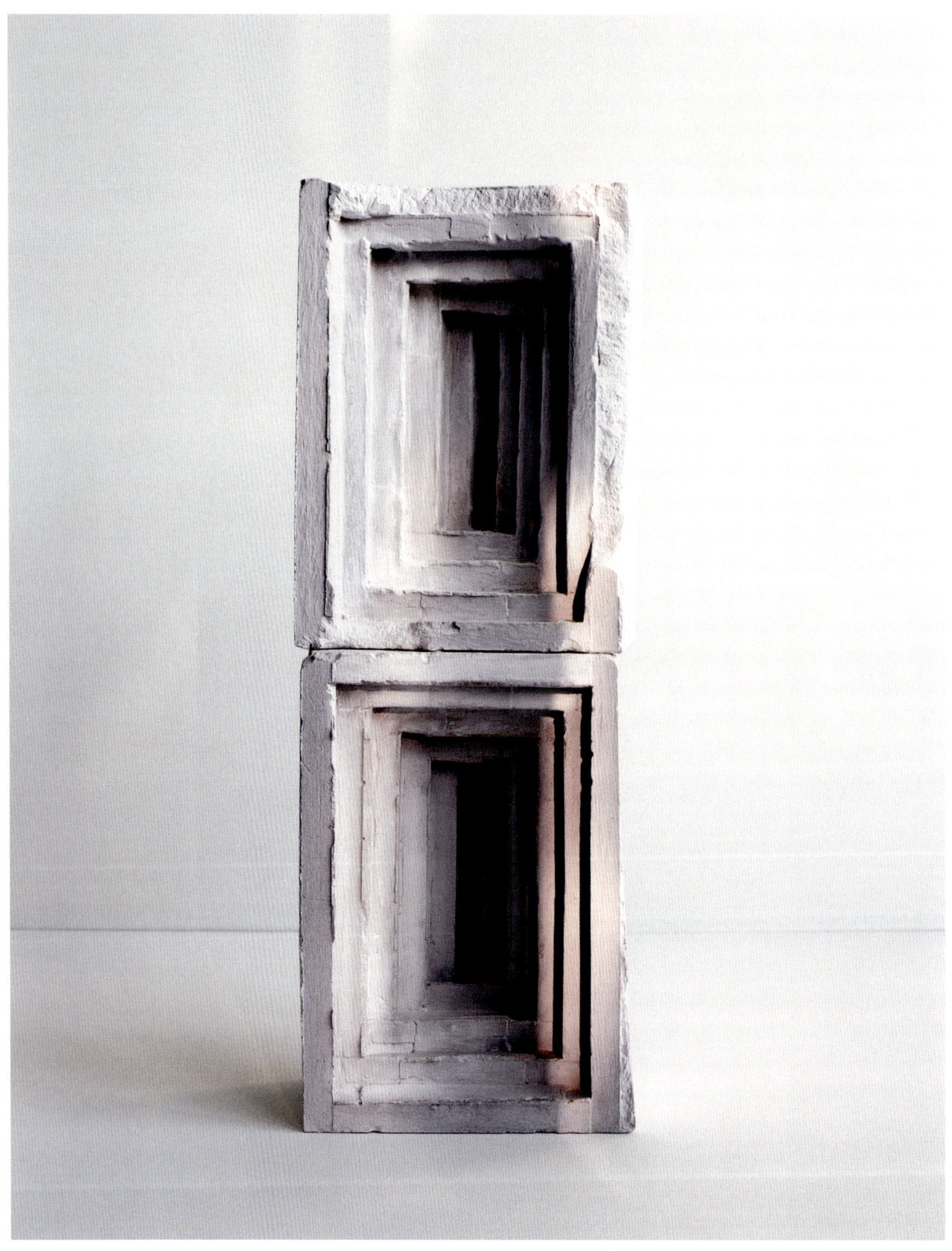

Sara VanDerBeek, *Temple*, 2010, digital C-print, 20 × 15 ¾ inches

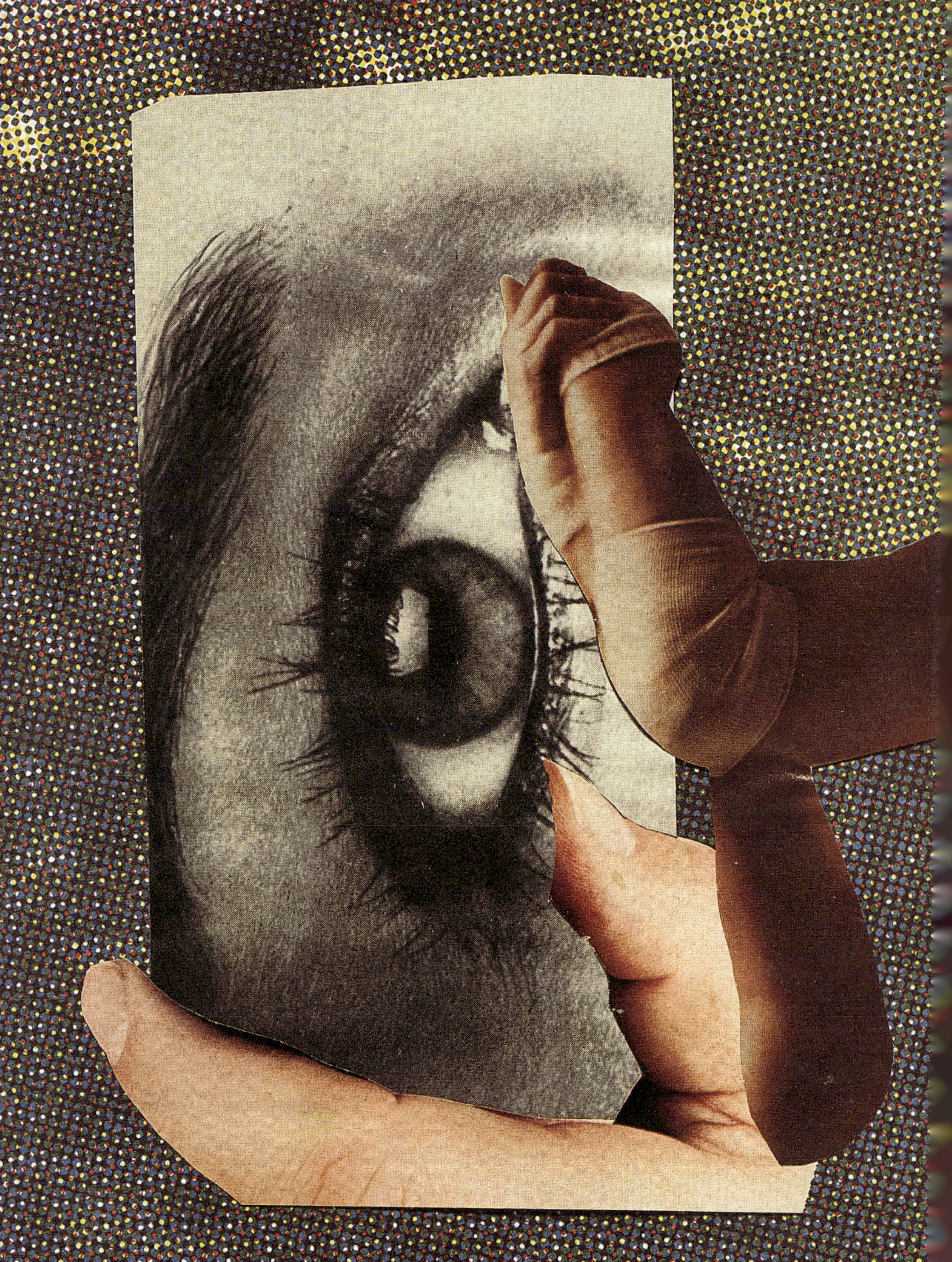